Deer

Law and Liabilities

Deer

Law and Liabilities
Second Edition

Charlie Parkes OBE *and John Thornley* OBE

Quiller

Copyright © 2008 Charlie Parkes OBE and John Thornley OBE

First Published in the UK in 2000
by Swan Hill Press
this edition published 2008
by Quiller, an imprint of Quiller Publishing Ltd

British Library Cataloguing in Publication Data
A catalogue record for this book
is available from the British Library

ISBN 978 1 84689 047 5

Typeset by Phoenix Typesetting, Auldgirth, Dumfriesshire
Printed in Malta by Gutenberg Press Ltd.

Quiller

An imprint of Quiller Publishing Ltd
Wykey House, Wykey, Shrewsbury, SY4 1JA
Tel: 01939 261616 Fax: 01939 261606
E-mail: info@quillerbooks.com
Website: www.countrybooksdirect.com

Dedication

Steven Beale & Ken MacArthur, B.E.M., F.B.D.S.
Without their friendship and encouragement this book would not
have been written.

Acknowledgements

Dr Tony Mitchell-Jones, Natural England;

Michael Smith, Scottish Landowners' Federation;

Graeme Taylor and Dick Youngson, Deer Commission for Scotland;

Bill Harriman, Head of Firearms, BASC;

Chris Probert and Fred Currie, Forestry Commission;

Mark Mason, Royal Ulster Constabulary;

Norma Chapman;

David Barnes, Lloyd-Barnes Solicitors, Ipswich;

Tony Slate and Paul Ramsbottom and Dick Udall, Derbyshire Constabulary;

Peter Lord, Solicitor, Derbyshire Constabulary;

Abby Turner, Data Protection Officer, Derbyshire Constabulary;

Stewart Scull, Game and Gamekeeping Officer, BASC;

Tom Bowler, DHSS Belfast;

John Milburne, DoE Belfast;

Barry Urton, HSE;

Mike Wellman, Cheshire Constabulary;

Christopher Borthen, *Stalking Magazine*;

Tom Brown, Northern Ireland Deer Society;

Chris Jackson, Countryside Alliance;

Ian Grindy, North West Water;

Dr Joachim Algermissen;

John Adams;

Keith Taylor;

Gerald Barry;

Richard Prior;

G.Kenneth Whitehead;

Sian Mosely, Derbyshire Constabulary;

Tony Chapman, Derbyshire Constabulary;

Adrian Evans, Derbyshire Constabulary;

LACOTS;

British Deer Farmers' Association;

National Game Dealers' Association;

British Wild Boar Association;

British Deer Society;

Charles Nodder, NGO;

Peter Watson, Deer Initiative;

Alan McCormick, BASC;

Mike Thornley, Forestry Commission;

Vanessa Charles, FSA

Eaton Hall · Chester

Since time immemorial deer have been treasured both as a source of food and as a sporting species. In more recent times they have also been recognised for their aesthetic value. They are our largest wild mammal and many people find pleasure in seeing them in the countryside. Their treatment by man has not always been humane and even today they are poached by ruthless gangs who have no respect for deer or the law.

Despite the pressures of poaching and our diminishing green belt, deer continue to increase and extend their range. In doing so, conflicts of interest have arisen. Their presence is not always welcome and although it can be beneficial to our natural environment, it can also be detrimental. Deer damage agricultural crops and can destroy young trees and thereby suppress woodland regeneration. In some areas they are a serious threat to road safety. Hence in many areas their numbers have to be controlled.

These issues increasingly focus on the legal implications of the welfare of deer, public safety and maintaining a balance with economic activities and environmental conservation. This book is devoted to explaining the law and liabilities involved and I am confident that its practical application will be a significant contribution to the welfare of deer and of immense value to all who have an interest in them.

THE DUKE OF WESTMINSTER OBE TD DL

Preface

by the

Executive Director of the Deer Initiative

Legislation affecting deer in the UK continues to be introduced and amended. The first revision of this book takes account of some important changes to the legislation affecting the management of deer and production of venison and provides a practical reference for landowners, occupiers, and deer managers alike.

Beginning with the status of deer in our countryside, it also covers their conservation throughout these islands. Regrettably, while deer are exceptional animals to observe, they are, when in large numbers, damaging to the environment and to many of man's interests.

The main part of the book is devoted to laws relating to the controls of deer and prevention from abuse. Included is dealing in venison, the use of firearms, trespass and poaching. The section on liabilities is a salutary reminder for all and stresses the need for risk assessment on which detailed guidance is given.

This is a welcome contribution to responsible deer management. It provides valuable reinforcement to the Best Practice Guidance produced by the Deer Commission for Scotland and the Deer Initiative for England and Wales. As such it fully supports the Deer Initiative aim 'to ensure the delivery of a sustainable, well managed wild deer population in England and Wales', and will help to ensure that the aim is accomplished with due regard to the law. I am confident it will be of equal use to those who operate in the remainder of the British Isles.

PETER WATSON

Contents

CHAPTER 1

Deer – Legal Status and Ownership

There are now over a million wild deer in the United Kingdom, apparently more than at the time of the Norman Conquest. Wild deer, especially our native red and roe deer, are an integral part of our natural and cultural heritage. They contribute significantly to the economic life of much of rural Scotland, especially in the more remote areas of the Highlands. Within an ever decreasing rural landscape the presence of deer adds a most appealing dimension to our way of life and view of the countryside. They are, after all, our largest wild land mammals and the opportunities for seeing them in their natural habitat are now greater than ever.

Historically, deer have been treasured as a rich source of food and a worthy sporting quarry. They have been hunted, originally for food, since the Stone Age. Royal deer hunts of the fifteenth century were full of pomp, ceremony and extravagance, underlining their status as the quarry of kings. However they have never been 'royal' animals, *regalia minora*.

During the Middle Ages a large number of deer parks were created. The deer were kept for hunting and as a ready supply of meat. It was not until the eighteenth century, however, that deer were seen as having an ornamental value on large country estates, some of which later imported different species from abroad. It was from some of these parks and estates that our non-indigenous species such as fallow and subsequently muntjac and Chinese water deer escaped and bred, eventually being recognised as 'wild'.

SPECIES AND DISTRIBUTION

Six species of deer now exist in the wild. They include our native red and roe deer together with the introduced fallow, sika, muntjac and Chinese water deer.[1] A herd of reindeer exists in the Cairngorms of Scotland, but these are privately owned and should not be classed as wild deer.

Since 1850 deer numbers and their distribution have increased substantially. It has been estimated that red deer numbers in Scotland doubled between 1963 and 1969. There are several explanations, but a major factor is the increase in suitable habitat, mainly forestry planting. This has, in some areas, both reduced the traditional red deer range and provided additional habitat for deer of all species. (The twentieth century saw an increase from 4 to 6 per cent in England alone of woodland cover.) In addition, with the extinction of the wolf, adult deer no longer have any natural predators.

Roe deer have substantially increased their range throughout England and the spread of muntjac following releases and escapes from many locations has been dramatic. Sika deer have also continued to spread, increasing concerns for the purity of the indigenous red deer, with which they can interbreed.

DEER SOCIETIES AND ASSOCIATED BODIES

There is now a wide range of organisations with interests in deer, some of which are elaborated upon below.[2]

The British Deer Society (B.D.S.)

The Society was formed in 1963 from a deer group within the Mammal Society, and has branches, each with its own council, covering the British Isles. The British Deer Society is a registered national charity with a charter to promote the welfare of deer. This is achieved by:

1. See chapter 7 for identification of each species.
2. See page 229 for address and contact details.

- technical advice to government, organisations and the public on deer management, legislation and conservation
- funding and practical support for research projects
- training novice stalkers and deer managers
- education to all age groups about the importance of deer in our environment

The Society is now based at Fordingbridge, Hampshire, and publishes the magazine *Deer* for its members.

The Northern Ireland Deer Society

The origins of the Society lie in the Ulster branch of the Irish Deer Society, which became an independent body separate from the British Deer Society in 1975. Its aims and objectives are compatible with those of the British Deer Society, which it may soon rejoin to become the Northern Ireland Branch.

The Deer Initiative

The Deer Initiative (DI) is a wide partnership comprising statutory agencies, nature conservation and animal welfare non-governmental organisations, Government, landowners and a range of other interests, who share a vision for a healthy and sustainable future for deer in England and Wales.

The Partnership was brought together in 1995 and the current approach to delivery through the DI Ltd/Partnership was put in place in 2004. In drawing together this strategy, DI has undertaken a review of current approaches and operations to ensure that it remains fit for purpose in achieving its aim.

The DI:

- Advises government (central and regional) and our partners on the national and regional policy, support and priorities required for the sustainable management of wild deer.
- Acts as a central focal point for improved communications on all matters relating to wild deer for the Partnership, landowners, land managers and the public.
- Promotes public safety on the roads in relation to wild deer.

The work of the partnership at a local level is delivered through a network of deer liaison officers and advisors who respond to national and regional issues co-ordinating partner and landowner efforts.

The Deer Initiative's aims, context for action and objectives are detailed on page 23.

The Deer Commission for Scotland (D.C.S.)

Formerly known as the Red Deer Commission this statutory body was established in 1959. It has powers to promote the sustainable management of deer, including advising deer managers on the conservation and control of deer and authorising action outside the general framework of the close seasons to protect against deer damage to agriculture and forestry. The DCS is to merge with Scottish Natural Heritage (see chapter 3).

The British Association for Shooting and Conservation (B.A.S.C.)

Formerly the Wildfowlers Association of Great Britain and Ireland (WAGBI), BASC is Britain's largest country shooting organisation and employs over one hundred staff to provide a wide range of support for those who enjoy shooting sports. Of particular note is the assistance available in respect of legal representation and access to expert witnesses for court cases relating to firearms. BASC has nearly 15,000 active stalking members and is a representative body for deer stalkers and deer managers. In addition to operating a very active assessment centre for Wild Deer Management Qualifications Ltd, BASC delivers training on a diverse range of subjects, including sporting rifle, dogs for deer, ammunition reloading and wild boar familiarisation and is taking a leading role in setting standards and qualifications.

The Deer Management Department can call upon three dedicated full time members of staff and have developed several very popular deer stalking schemes which provide access to stalking opportunity for its members or the chance to stalk a species of deer that they would not normally encounter. The insurance provided through membership is very comprehensive and covers all recreational shooting and conservation activities, including angling, and is valid throughout Europe. By filling in a short form this cover can be extended free of charge for anyone involved in attending road traffic accidents involving wildlife.

BASC is involved in developing best practice guidance for the management of deer in Great Britain and for the management of wild boar in England.

See Chapter 7 re Stalking Competency Qualifications.

The National Gamekeepers' Organisation

The NGO was formed in 1997 by a small group of gamekeepers who felt that their profession was inadequately represented. Today it has over 12,000 gamekeeper and supporter members. The NGO's motto is 'Keeping the Balance' and it campaigns via the media and through lobbying to increase understanding of gamekeeping, its needs and its benefits. A separate NGO Charitable Trust assists with the education of gamekeepers and helps children to understand the role of gamekeepers in today's countryside.

Many NGO members are involved in the management of sustainable deer populations. The organisation has implemented game meat hygiene training and plays an active role in consultation on deer and other wildlife issues.

The Countryside Alliance

In 1997 the British Field Sports Society, the Countryside Movement and the Countryside Business Group merged to form the Countryside Alliance. One of its aims is to promote, protect and preserve traditional country sports and related activities. Regional and county branches of the Alliance are governed by committees and most have a stalking representative for their area. Deer management in the West Country, where red deer were hunted with hounds, is strongly supported by the Alliance, which strives to protect the interests of those involved and the welfare of the deer in its opposition to the ban on hunting.

The U.K. Association of Professional Deer Managers (U.K. A.P.D.M.)

Formed in 1998 to protect the interests of those engaged in deer management as a profession, the Association's aims are:

- to enhance the standards and maintain the integrity of the deer-stalking profession
- to gain and maintain the confidence of landowners and their agents
- to gain and maintain the confidence of client stalkers

The Association has the full support of the British Deer Society. Its members are subject to a code of practice which should ensure integrity and a high standard of deer management.

The British Deer Farmers' Association

In addition to our wild deer there is a considerable number of captive deer in deer farms, parks or private estates. Deer farming has increased in recent years as venison has become a popular meat, particularly following the BSE crisis in beef cattle. The British Deer Farmers' Association, which also covers Northern Ireland, was formed in 1978 to further the interests of deer farmers. It is a nationally accepted body representing deer farming to government departments and the public and private sectors. One of its objectives is to maintain and improve the welfare of deer on enclosed land.

The National Game Dealers' Association (N.G.D.A.)

The N.G.D.A. was founded in 1979 with the primary object of safeguarding and promoting the general commercial interests of members, encouraging best practice throughout the industry and promoting the consumption of all types of game and venison. Membership is open to all licensed U.K. game dealers and processors and to retail licensed game dealers.

The St. Hubert Club of Great Britain

The St. Hubert Club of Great Britain was founded in 1953 to create fraternity amongst sportsmen all over the world. Its aim is the conservation and pursuit in a sportsmanlike manner of all types of game.

The St. Hubert Club is primarily concerned with the training of its member stalkers, and was the first organisation in the United Kingdom to plan and operate a formal programme of training, both in theory and in practice. In addition to its stalker training the St. Hubert Club also provides a congenial meeting ground for the exchange of members' views and experiences. The idea, so profoundly united with nature, wildlife, and sport, helps in creating friendship among people who understand and appreciate the opportunities presented through sport. The Club is actively concerned with the conservation and management of deer.

LEGISLATION

Deer, whether they be wild or captive, have always created conflicts of interest in terms of both their management and their potential as sporting species. Where such conflicts exist, the law has an important role in safeguarding their welfare. Complaints often arise from over-population causing crop and environmental damage. A fine balance therefore exists between deer numbers and the need to protect the natural heritage. Stalking, whether professionally as a means of control or for sport, is strictly regulated by the firearms legislation which is elaborated upon in chapter 6.

History

Through the ages, various provisions have been made by Act of Parliament for the protection of deer with grave penalties for those who broke the law. The Normans did much to develop the forest laws that applied to large tracts of countryside to ensure that there were sufficient deer to be hunted by the nobility and to provide for the royal table. Many of the older statutes were repealed by the Larceny Act, 1861. This Act, which was replaced by the Theft Act, 1968, created specific offences of taking deer from both forests and deer parks together with offences of illegal possession of carcases or poaching equipment. The legislation only covered unauthorised taking and did not protect deer from being treated like vermin – being killed indiscriminately, regardless of breeding season, using totally inadequate firearms.

Now, at the turn of the twenty-first century, extensive legislation exists to protect deer of all species, wild and captive, safeguarding their welfare in matters relating to humane methods of killing, poaching and the provision of close seasons to preserve the species. However, variations exist between the law in England and Wales, Scotland and Northern Ireland.

The legislation on which this book is based is not exhaustive and loopholes exist. It will also be appreciated that matters affecting deer, and those who manage them, are diverse. Consequently a wide cross-section of legislation, outside that specifically relating to deer, is involved.

Main Acts relating to deer

The principal legislation providing protection for deer is as follows. In England and Wales it is the Deer Act, 1991, which provides protection for deer of any species and includes the carcase of any deer or any part thereof. Venison is defined separately.[3]

The Deer (Scotland) Act, 1996, provides protection for deer as specified, i.e. fallow, red, roe, sika and any other species of deer specified by order of the Secretary of State. It includes the hybrids of those species (currently red and sika) and, where appropriate, the carcase of any deer or any part of it.[4] The legislation for Scotland, where deer contribute significantly to the rural economy, has over the years sought to bring about a more purposeful move towards deer management via the powers of the Deer Commission.

In Northern Ireland the protection for deer is provided in Part III of the Wildlife (Northern Ireland) Order, 1985. The Order relates to any deer with the exception of offences relating to close seasons in respect of fallow, red, sika or any hybrids of these species. The sale and purchase of venison is regulated under Article 23.[5]

OWNERSHIP AND RIGHTS TO TAKE WILD DEER

Wild deer that are free to roam from one person's land to another belong to no one; they are ownerless. They are wild animals, *ferae naturae*, and therefore are known as *res nullius*, things without an owner.[6]

Ownership of the land which wild deer may occupy does not carry with it any rights of ownership of the deer whilst they remain wild. However, the Common Law has always conveyed to the landowner certain rights in respect of the use of the land and things found upon it. Consequently deer found dead on the land, caught accidentally in fences or killed in some other way become the property of the landowner, subject to any legal agreement in which the rights may have passed to another – e.g. in a sporting lease.

It is suggested that the ownership of cast antlers is also vested in the owner of the land on which they fall and that someone removing them without authority may be liable if the matter were disputed. Similarly, the ownership of deer killed in road accidents passes to the owner of the land upon which the collision has occurred. This will

---

3. See chapters 2 and 5.
4. See chapter 3.
5. See chapter 2.
6. The Case of Swans 1592 -Co.Rep.15b at 17b.

Who owns cast antlers?

normally be the adjacent landowner rather than the highway authority. However, the driver has no claim on the landowner in cases involving wild deer regardless of whose land they were on immediately prior to the collision. The driver has no legal right to retain the deer carcase.

The spread and increase of wild deer in the U.K. have led to serious national concern not only for road safety but also for the conservation and welfare of the species involved. The problem is not merely restricted to a few counties with high densities of deer. Accidents involving deer pose a significant risk of human injury and damage to vehicles and is closely correlated to the size of the species concerned. Reliable statistics for the U.K. relating to accidents involving deer are not available; road traffic legislation does not require the mandatory reporting of such accidents to the police unless someone other than the driver involved is injured.[7] Research for the Highways Agency, however, suggests there are 30,000–50,000 road accidents involving deer annually in the U.K., and that up to 400 people are injured and 10 killed as a result.

Considerable research has been undertaken into methods designed to prevent deer-related accidents. Whilst some have had a measure of success, only full-height deer fencing has been found to significantly reduce accidents. Civil litigation may in the future be pioneered in areas of new development in which the highway authority has not adequately safeguarded road users from the dangers caused by deer.

7. The Road Traffic Act, 1988, requires road accidents involving horses, asses, mules, cattle, pigs, sheep, goats and dogs to be reported to the police in certain circumstances.

A number of issues have arisen from dealing with deer casualties, including response schemes, legal requirements for firearms,[8] humane methods of dispatch,[9] dealing with the public and disposal of carcases. A code of practice is being developed by B.A.S.C.

Theft

Originally wild deer were not regarded as property at Common Law or under the Larceny Acts and therefore they could not be stolen in any circumstances whilst they remained wild. However, the Theft Act, 1968, now recognises them as 'property' and defines the circumstances in which they may be stolen.

Section 1(1) of this Act provides:

> A person is guilty of theft if he dishonestly appropriates property belonging to another with the intention of permanently depriving the other of it; 'thief' and 'steal' shall be construed accordingly.

Section 4(4) provides:

> Wild creatures, tamed or untamed, shall be regarded as property; but a person cannot steal a wild creature not tamed nor ordinarily kept in captivity, or the carcase of any such creature, unless either it has been reduced into possession by or on behalf of another person and possession of it has not since been lost or abandoned, or another person is in the course of reducing it into possession.

As a general rule with regard to wild deer, theft will only be committed if they are taken after they have passed into someone's possession or constructive possession, e.g. where deer have been shot or captured for some reason in circumstances where they are confined in an area where they have no means of escape. There will be situations in which it will be clear that the deer are 'property belonging to another' and where they have been 'reduced into possession or are in the process of being reduced'. The most obvious are deer that have been shot and are in the process of being taken off the hill *en route* to the larder or venison dealer. A person taking a carcase without authority in this situation, say from an argocat or trailer, will commit theft if the intention is to permanently deprive the owner of it.

Wild deer caught-up, kept in deer farms or held in securely fenced parks for whatever reason are reduced into possession and therefore

8. See chapter 6.
9. See chapter 7.

clearly capable of being stolen. However, if they escape it may be said that 'possession has been lost or abandoned', in which case a subsequent unauthorised taking will be poaching rather than theft. As discussed later in respect of 'captive' deer, it is unlikely that possession would be abandoned in circumstances where the deer are not wild or were clearly identifiable as such.

The overall effect of this legislation is that deer, whilst in their wild state – free to roam where they please – cannot be stolen. It would make no difference if the deer were caught-up and ear tagged then released back into the wild or indeed if they were tended during the winter months by supplementing their feeding. A similar situation exists with the tagging of reared or caught-up pheasants that are then released into the wild and fed by a gamekeeper. Deer can, of course, be poached and the laws described in chapter 9 provide protection, not only for the deer, but also for the landowner's rights described earlier.

The Theft Act does not apply in Scotland although the Common Law offence of theft in Scotland imposes similar criteria.

Sporting rights

Traditionally the rights of owners of land have included the exclusive right to kill and take wild animals on their land,[10] subject of course, to the laws that protect those animals and any legal agreement to the contrary e.g. where the sporting rights to the deer have been let. These rights are known in law as 'incorporeal hereditaments' and may be extended to an occupier or anyone else by licence. It should be noted that where the rights to take deer have been reserved by the landowner, or have been let to a third party, the occupier will have a right to take deer only if acting on their authority.

Agricultural tenants do not normally acquire the sporting rights to their holdings automatically by virtue of their agricultural lease and often the sporting rights will have been reserved by the landlord. If they are not then the rights do transfer with the possession of the land to the new tenant.[11] This is not the case in Scotland where the right is considered as personal to the owner of the land.[12]

In England and Wales an occupier or tenant who suffers serious crop damage by marauding deer can take action outside the close season but this does not convey any independent rights to kill the deer over and above that of the owner. In this situation deer of the same species causing the damage could only be shot by the occupier or

10. Blades v. Higgs 1865. 11 H.L.Cas.621.
11. Pochin v. Smith 1887 52 J.P.4; Anderson v. Vicary 1900.
12. Saunders v. Pitfield 1888. 58 L.T.108.

tenant if they had a legal right to kill the deer – i.e. they hold the sporting rights themselves or have the authority of the landowner or person with the sporting rights to the deer. In Scotland the tenant has an absolute right to protect crops by killing deer.[13]

Are deer game?

Deer should not be classed as game or described as such. Historically the Game Acts never included deer within such a definition and when the intention has been to include deer within legislation affecting game they have been specifically referred to. In Scotland it has been conceded by the Crown that 'game' in the Game (Scotland) Act 1832, does not include deer and the court has held that the inclusion of deer was not a tenable construction of 'game' when the history of the 1832 Act was examined.[14]

The fact that in certain circumstances i.e. on unenclosed land,[15] a licence to kill game is required to take deer can be misleading. The Game Licences Act, 1860, which makes this provision, does not include deer within the definition of game but lists them separately together with woodcock, snipe and rabbits.

In England and Wales deer were not seen as a traditional sporting species to the same extent as in the Highlands. Sporting rights and leases mainly relating to game would rarely specify deer and it was common for deer to be excluded in the wording of deeds. However this was challenged in 1987 by the Inglewood Investment Company who owned the sporting rights to 1,000 acres of Cannock Chase in Staffordshire. The company sought a declaration that the Forestry Commission was not entitled to kill deer on the estate. A deed of 1921 was referred to which reserved the rights to 'all game' and it was contested this included deer. The case was eventually decided in the Court of Appeal. Dismissing the company's appeal, Lord Justice Dillon sitting with Lords Justices Butler-Sloss and Staughton said the word 'deer' was 'conspicuous by its absence' in terms of the deed which reserved sporting rights to Lord Hatherton over 'all game, woodcock, snipe and other fowl, hares, rabbits and fish'. Lord Justice Dillon said that in legislation when deer were meant to be included they were expressly mentioned and when they were not specified they were taken to be excluded. He rejected the company's argument that deer should be included because they were animals fit for food and usually sported after.

13. See chapter 4.
14. Ferguson v. Macphail 1987 SCCR 52.
15. See chapter 7. (A Game Licence is no longer required in England and Wales to take deer on unenclosed land).

It is advisable therefore that sporting rights to take deer should be specific in terminology and actually refer to deer. Use of the word 'game' is not accurate or sufficient. Deer are not game as described earlier and such reference may lead to uncertainty and dispute as to whether deer were ever intended to be included in the rights. We would go even further and suggest that the document should include the species or simply specify 'any deer'. Such rights should be in a written form of licence and signed. These should be detailed and accurate in respect of the area of land over which the right exists and ideally incorporate a map. Provisions as to licence fee and periods of notice can also be included, together with the right to take away deer once they have been killed. It is desirable that such licences be drafted by a lawyer familiar with the subject.

The management of deer and statutory rights

In addition to those who possess the right to take deer by virtue of land ownership or sporting rights, legislation exists in Scotland to ensure that owners of land take appropriate action to control deer numbers. In cases where they do not the Deer Commission is given certain rights within the Deer (Scotland) Act, 1996, to kill deer over and above the rights of the owner.[16] However, no opposing legislation exists anywhere in the country to protect a species from culling to the point of extinction. There are no legally binding management controls and consequently landowners, if so minded, are entitled to exterminate every deer on their land provided they comply with the existing law governing seasons and permitted methods of taking. This is not the case in other parts of Europe where regional controls can be enforced in terms of the maximum number of deer culled.

This is clearly a most unsatisfactory situation in terms of both the future welfare of our wild deer and their effective management, on which many other species of flora and fauna depend.

Aims of the Deer Initiative

The stated aim of DI is to ensure the delivery of a sustainable and well-managed wild deer population in England and Wales.

It achieves this both through the direct efforts of partners themselves and through focused and co-ordinated activity and projects run through the partnership's executive arm – Deer Initiative Ltd. Throughout its activities the DI adopts a humane, responsible and

16. See chapter 3.

sensitive approach to the management of wild deer. It seeks to be the leading authority on all matters relating to deer management, works by building consensus and is open and transparent in all its dealings within the partnership and with the public.

Context for action

All species of deer, except Chinese water deer are increasing in numbers and expanding their ranges in England and Wales. Fallow, roe and muntjac deer are now widespread, while red and sika are locally abundant. It is now believed that deer of at least one species are present in nearly every 10 kilometre square of Great Britain. This expansion has been encouraged by changes in land use, particularly the expansion of forestry that has increased suitable habitat for foraging and shelter. Researchers believe that there is currently no reason why the trend in increasing deer numbers and range expansion should not continue.

Virtually all woodlands in Britain have evolved in the presence of deer. Deer are an important part of woodland ecosystems and can, depending on their density, increase or decrease the variety of habitat within them. In the past, populations would have been kept in balance through natural predation, food supply, disease and climatic effects.

However, there is a wealth of evidence that indicates that growing numbers are causing adverse effects upon the natural systems that support them, leading to declines in the conservation status, or in extremis loss, of some of our most precious woodland habitats.

Following the 'Earth Summit' in Rio de Janeiro in 1992, the UK government committed itself to the sustainable management of forests that provide a wide range of benefits to society. This commitment was detailed in the publication of Sustainable Forestry, The UK-Programme Sustainable Development, the UK-Strategy8 and Biodiversity, the UK Action Plan. On a European scale, the Helsinki Resolutions and the Natura 2000 programme each make commitments to the sustainable management of forests. More recently a Strategy for England's Trees, Woods and Forests was launched by DEFRA (June 2007). The sustainable management and development of our current and future woodland resource therefore will rely upon continued and active management of deer populations.

The negative impacts upon habitat are likely to be exaggerated in the short-term through increased development pressures across the rural and urban landscape. These range from the new home building programme to the growth of 'horse-culture' in the urban fringe to possible intensification of agriculture for improved food and fuel security (e.g. biofuels). In the medium to long-term the effects of climate change are likely to become more obvious and conservation planning has already begun on the most effective ways to adapt to possible new scenarios. Adopting both landscape-scale and ecosystem-services approaches will be essential in ensuring flexible responses to the coming period of substantial uncertainty. The DI has been at the forefront of working at a landscape-scale and is developing an ecosystem-services approach to the range of issues that impact deer management.

The growth in the number of deer, in conjunction with the growth in road traffic means that there are an increasing number of road traffic accidents involving deer. It is estimated that there may be around 80,000 deer-related road traffic accidents a year with a growing number of human fatalities. In addition to this tragic loss of life, these incidents also cause immeasurable suffering to both people and deer.

Like all wild animals, deer are subject to a range of naturally occurring diseases and incidence of infection increases with higher populations. Transmission of infection and parasites between species is also a higher risk. Increased incidence of zoonotic disease transfer between deer and livestock is being reported as well as increasing reports of Lyme disease in people (transmitted by the deer tick).

Deer also impact on the tree, agricultural and horticultural crops adjacent to the woodland and also, in suburban and urban areas, may visit and damage gardens. That said, deer also provide a range of direct economic benefits from recreational, sporting and associated industries including the embryonic, though growing, wild venison market.

Despite these growing conflicts, people wish to see deer in the wild – and are thrilled when they do so. In many areas where deer are considered by ecologists and foresters to be a pest, the general public are not aware that they pose a threat to woodlands and there is considerable work to be done in order to raise levels of understanding. There is a growing need to engage a wider public in a debate on possible futures.

The overarching outcome/vision of the Deer Initiative is the achievement and maintenance of a sustainable and healthy population of deer in England and Wales.

The DI aim is to ensure the delivery of the above and in so doing:

- Contribute to the conservation and sustainable management of woodlands and other habitats; in particular, the achievement of favourable conservation status of protected areas such as Sites of Special Scientific Interest
- Halt the growth of, and subsequently reduce, the number and seriousness of deer-vehicle collisions on our roads

25

- Build the capability to react effectively to contain and control emerging zoonoses relating to deer

The DI plans to achieve these outcomes by focusing upon five strategic activities/objectives:

1 Managing deer: to continue to manage populations at a landscape scale through partnership working.
2 Developing the evidence base: to review, collect and, where necessary, commission research and evidence-gathering on population dynamics, management methodologies and other fields as required.
3 Building capacity: to ensure that best-practice knowledge and skills are utilised across the sector, through the development and encouragement of accredited training and professional support for all those with deer management remits and interests.
4 Informing and communicating with policy-makers, decision-takers and the general public: to ensure that high quality, evidence-based information is available and effectively disseminated to all those with both a direct and indirect impact upon the issues related to deer management; to engage the wider public in developing understanding of the issues, the challenges and possible solutions.
5 Building and maintaining an effective delivery partnership: to ensure the most efficient, sustainable and cost-effective delivery of the outcome.

Capture and handling

Many of the traditional methods of capturing deer, the origins of which go back thousands of years, involve catching them alive, usually as a prelude to their slaughter for food and clothing. Pits, snares, spear traps and many other devices, now illegal, have been used to kill or immobilise deer. Methods over the years have changed although, as described in chapter 10, immense cruelty is still involved in modern-day poaching.

The use of pits is no longer considered safe or effective, although netting is still an important technique of physical capture, particularly for small and medium-sized deer. The use of drugs to immobilise large animals such as deer is long established and derives from the use of curare-like substances obtained from the bark of trees in the Amazon basin. Considerable research during the twentieth century has been undertaken and has led to the development of new weapon systems and drugs. Effective and relatively safe drugs that can be delivered in a variety of ways now enable deer to be temporarily immobilised. However the use of drugs is not a technique that can easily be applied to wild deer, especially in woodland. It is therefore more appropriate for use in zoo, park and farm situations.

The capture and handling of wild deer is now controlled by legislation. This provides, under appropriate licence, for their capture and handling in circumstances which would otherwise be illegal due to the method used or time of year. Such circumstances include removing deer from one area to another, or taking deer alive for scientific or educational purposes.[17] In England this is controlled by licence issued by Natural England and for Wales by the Countryside Council for Wales. In Scotland advice should be sought from the Deer Commission. In Northern Ireland licences are issued by the Department of the Environment.

Applicants for such licences are required to specify full details of their aims and purpose in taking deer alive, together with the species, number and sex. The method of capture and the applicant's experience in handling deer or other large animals must also be stated. Where the use of stupefying drugs or muscle-relaxing agents are intended, their use should be justified. The type of drug and dosage for each species together with the weapon to be used must be given.

Careful consideration is given to such applications and licences are issued only if all conditions are satisfied and the purpose justified. Where licences are granted they are subject to whatever conditions are considered appropriate for the particular circumstances. For example they may include carrying and producing a copy of the licence to a police officer on demand, guidelines on the safe and humane handling of live deer to be followed, close supervision of equipment used to take or transport deer, the fact that deer should be immobilised for as short a period as possible and kept under supervision until fully recovered, and the submission of a report after the operation to the issuing authority.

Under the firearms regulations[18] Home Office authority must be obtained before using dartguns and blowpipes. There are also statutory constraints on the possession, supply and administration of certain drugs; questions about possession and supply should be directed to the Home Office Drugs Branch. Queries concerning the administration of such drugs should be directed to Department for Environment, Food & Rural Affairs Animal Health Division.[19]

17. See chapter 2.
18. See chapter 6.
19. See page 231 for contact details.

Hunting with hounds

Following the Hunting Act the traditional hunting of wild deer with hounds is now restricted to Ireland. The use of hounds is not permitted in Scotland but there are some exemptions in England and Wales allowing the use of hounds to flush deer to guns.

Historically some hunts used a captive or 'carted' stag or hind being released from a trailer and then hunted purely for sport, often to be recaptured at the end of the hunt and placed back in the cart. Hunting wild deer with a pack of hounds is still practised in Northern Ireland but is subject to the conditions of a licence issued under section 26 of the Wildlife Act 1976.

CAPTIVE DEER

Throughout the ages deer have been exploited and domesticated. Archaeological evidence exists from China and Europe to suggest that they may have been partially domesticated many centuries before the Romans and Greeks confined their deer to walled or fenced areas. Many of the deer were kept for the purpose of providing venison and so the idea of deer farming was born many years ago.

Theft

Deer that are tamed or in captivity are deemed under the Theft Act, 1968, as being property capable of being stolen and therefore anyone taking them without authority or permission would commit a theft, as defined earlier. Deer rustling is not common, perhaps because the fencing is more secure than that used for other livestock. Where deer are taken from the wild without authority the offence is poaching rather than stealing.[20]

In circumstances where deer are suspected of being stolen, proof of ownership would be required, but difficulties arise in the identification of unmarked deer. Deer kept in deer farms should be conspicuously marked so that they can be identified. This is normally done by an ear tag linking the deer to the owner. Photographs may prove useful, particularly if a beast has a distinguishing feature, which is more likely with the male of the species through antler identification but may not always be conclusive.

Some years ago an interesting case arose in Derbyshire in which a

20. See chapter 9.

captive red deer stag was taken during the night from within a securely fenced area in the park of a stately home. It was quickly noticed the following morning that the beast was missing. A subsequent search of the area revealed half the carcase hidden away in the undergrowth.

Observations were mounted by the police and park warden on two consecutive nights but to no avail. The carcase was therefore removed. On the third night a van was seen in the vicinity by the warden. It looked suspicious and he alerted the police. It was later stopped some miles from the park and searched. To the officer's surprise, venison was found in the rear together with a hacksaw.

When interviewed the driver said the meat had been purchased as dog meat from an unknown man in a lay-by near a local market town. As for the cutting equipment, this had only been used for cutting metal. Forensic scientists were able to prove that within the teeth of the saw were fragments of bone. Needless to say the magistrates did not believe the man's story and they convicted him of handling stolen property since it could not be proved he was involved in the original theft. Nowadays, forensic scientists could put the case beyond doubt by the analysis of DNA samples linking the venison left behind with that found in the van.

If captive or tame deer have escaped they remain the property of the owner, unless the owner has abandoned rights to them, and anyone taking them without authority would be stealing them. However if the taker believed them to be wild, it would be difficult to secure a conviction unless it was shown the person knew they were tame or from captive stock. Clearly if the deer were easily identifiable as belonging to captive or tame stock such a defence would be weakened. Irrespective of the taker's culpability in these circumstances and provided identification could be satisfactorily made, title in the carcase would remain with the original owner.

Deer of a species not generally accepted as being 'wild' in this country should be readily identifiable as belonging to someone. For example if an elk appeared whilst you were waiting in your high seat you would have difficulty in proving you considered the beast to be wild and ownerless. Clearly it would be reasonable to assume this was someone's property and any taking of the animal would be theft. If shot, a more appropriate charge may be criminal damage.

Reindeer in Scotland

The reindeer in the Cairngorms and Glenlivet in Scotland pose an interesting case. Incidents have occurred in the past in which their status has had to be considered. Some view them as wild, others as

An elk in this country would not be considered wild and ownerless.

captive or tame. The herd, approximately 130 strong, is privately owned and was established in 1952. Over fifty beasts are free ranging in an area of 6,000 to 7,000 acres on the northern slopes of the Cairngorms. They are a tourist attraction and a support scheme exists in which individual reindeer can be 'adopted'. The animals are domesticated and tame. Under the supervision of a guide the tourist can walk amongst the herd, stroking and feeding them. Some of the animals are tagged and between the months of April and September they are all herded into a 1,000-acre enclosure. We would suggest in the circumstances the animals should not be treated as wild, *ferae naturae*, but in the same way as other livestock on the open hill, i.e. as property belonging to someone. Hence they could be stolen or damaged. Should this issue be disputed it would be for the courts ultimately to decide on the merits of a particular case whether the deer were wild or the property of someone.

The liabilities of keeping deer

The keeping of animals brings with it responsibilities, not only in terms of the criminal law but also in terms of civil liability. In civil law a distinction is made between two classes of animals – those which belong to a dangerous species and those which do not.

The Animals Act, 1971 (England and Wales) and the Animals (Scotland) Act, 1987, both deal with civil liability involving injury or damage caused by animals. It will be noted that there are some differences between the two Acts. However, generally speaking owners of animals that are either regarded as a dangerous species or known to

Reindeer

have dangerous tendencies are liable should they damage property or injure someone.

The Animals Act, 1971

Section 2(1) says that where any damage (which includes death of or injury to any person including disease or impairment of mental condition) is caused by an animal which belongs to a dangerous species the keeper of the animal is liable for the damage. A dangerous species is defined as one 'which is not commonly domesticated in the British Islands and whose fully grown animals . . . are likely unless restricted to cause severe damage'.

The Act does not specify which species fall within this category. The majority of these animals are of a type more likely to be kept in zoos or safari parks. Many species will clearly fall into the class of 'dangerous', e.g. lions or tigers, but both camels and elephants have been held to be dangerous.[21]

There are no species of deer specified in the Dangerous Wild Animals Act, 1976,[22] which makes provision for licensing control in the interests of public safety and nuisance. However the Act will apply

21. McQuaker v. Goddard 1940 1KB.687. and Filburn v. People's Palace and Aquarium Co. Ltd. 1890 25QBD.258. respectively.
22. Wild boar, however, are included.

to deer of any species if the circumstances fall within the criteria
detailed in section 1(2) below:

> Where damage (or injury) is caused by an animal which does not
> belong to a dangerous species a keeper of the animal is liable if:
>
> (a) the damage is of a kind which the animal, unless restrained, was
>   likely to cause or which, if caused by the animal, was likely to be
>   severe; and
>
> (b) the likelihood of the damage or of its being severe was due to char-
>   acteristics of the animal which are not normally found in animals
>   of the same species or are not normally so found except at partic-
>   ular times or in particular circumstances; and
>
> (c) those characteristics were known to that keeper or were at any time
>   known to a person who at that time had charge of the animal . . .

A 'keeper' of an animal is defined as someone who owns the animal
or has it in their possession.

The Animals (Scotland) Act, 1987

> A person is liable for any damage or injury caused by an animal if:
>
> (a) at the time of the injury or damage complained of, he was a keeper
>   of the animal;
>
> (b) the animal belongs to a species whose members generally are by
>   virtue of their physical attributes or habits likely (unless controlled
>   or restrained) to injure severely or kill persons or animals, or
>   damage property to a material extent; and
>
> (c) the injury or damage complained of is directly referable to such
>   physical attributes or habits.

It follows therefore that as owner or person in charge of an animal
you may be liable if someone is injured or damage is caused if it can
be shown that you had knowledge of a certain animal's unnaturally
harmful tendencies and that no action had been taken to prevent such
an occurrence. This would apply to captive deer, particularly roe
bucks for example that are potentially dangerous at certain times of
the year and red deer during the rut.

There have been many cases taken to court, some of which have
set precedents, but there is an important Common Law principle
which the courts are willing to apply in such cases, involving the
ordinary duty of care as set out in the case of Fardon v. Harcourt-
Rivington 1932 as:

Quite apart from the liability imposed upon the owners of animals or the person having control of them by reason of knowledge of their propensities, there is the ordinary duty of a person to take care either that his animal or chattel is not put to such a use as is likely to injure his neighbour – the ordinary duty to take care.

Exceptions to liability exist under both Acts and cover situations where it can be shown that the injury or damage caused is due to the fault of the person suffering it, or that they had voluntarily accepted the risk thereof or that at the time they were trespassing.

As is so often said in legal matters, the courts will make judgements on the merits of a particular case and will take account of judgements and cases stated.

CRUELTY

Legislation exists to protect deer from acts of cruelty, whether they be wild or captive. However, the law is much stronger in respect of the latter. The circumstances in which offences of cruelty to wild deer may be committed in England, Wales and Scotland are covered in chapter 7.

Captive deer kept for the production of food, skin or antlers fall within the definition of 'livestock' and animal welfare legislation exists to protect them from being caused unnecessary pain and distress. All domestic and captive deer are additionally protected against acts of cruelty under the Protection of Animals Act, 1911 (England and Wales), Animal Welfare Act 2006, the Protection of Animals (Scotland) Act, 1912, and the Welfare of Animals Act (Northern Ireland) 1972.

The Agriculture (Miscellaneous Provisions) Act, 1968 and Welfare of Animals Act (Northern Ireland) 1972 says in Part I, section 1:

> Any person who causes unnecessary pain or unnecessary distress to any livestock [this includes deer as defined earlier] situated on agricultural land and under his control or permits such livestock to suffer any pain or distress of which he knows or may reasonably be expected to know commits an offence.

The term 'agricultural land' is defined as land used for agriculture within the meaning given by the Agriculture Act, 1947. This gives a wide interpretation which includes livestock breeding and keeping, grazing and meadow land and the use of land for woodlands where that is ancillary to the farming of land for other agricultural purposes.

Regulations made under section 2 of the above Act include the Welfare of Livestock (Prohibited Operations) Regulations, 1982, as amended.[23] These regulations covering England, Wales and Scotland prohibit certain operations on animals situated on agricultural land, in particular (Paragraph (xii)) the removal of any part of the antlers before the velvet is frayed and the greater part of it has been shed. The regulations do not apply to any act lawfully done under the Animals (Scientific Procedures) Act, 1986,[24] to the rendering of first aid in cases of emergency, or to the performance of operations by a veterinary surgeon for the proper treatment of disease or injury.

In Northern Ireland the Welfare of Animals Act (section 14) prohibits any operation which is performed without due care and humanity or which involves interference with the sensitive tissues or bone structure without the use of anaesthetic. Exemptions permit minor operations by veterinary surgeons, tail docking and castration.

The Animal Welfare Act 2006 [England and Wales] contains provisions relating to the harm, promotion of welfare, licensing and registration of activities involving 'protected animals'. The Act provides for the issue of codes of practice.

In this Act 'animal' means a vertebrate other than man and an animal is a 'protected animal' for the purposes of this Act if:

(a) it is of a kind which is commonly domesticated in the British Islands,

(b) it is under the control of man whether on a permanent or temporary basis, or

(d) it is not living in a wild state.

Unnecessary suffering

(1) In relation to a protected animal, a person commits an offence if his act, or a failure of to act, causes an animal to suffer, or he knew,

---

23. Welfare of Livestock (Prohibited Operations) (Amendment) Regulations, 1987. SI 1987/114.
24. This Act provides for a system of licensing control of experimental and other scientific work carried out on living animals.

or ought reasonably to have known, that the act, or failure to act, would have that effect or be likely to do so and the suffering is unnecessary.

An example would be a failure to feed captive deer or treat injuries.

The offence also extends to persons having responsibility for protected animals who permitted such acts or failures by other persons. This would include the owner of a business being responsible for the acts or failures of his employees.

Nothing in this section applies to the destruction of an animal in an appropriate and humane manner.

Duty of person responsible for animal to ensure welfare

A person commits an offence if he does not take reasonable steps to ensure that the needs of an animal for which he is responsible are met to the extent required by good practice.

For the purposes of this Act, an animal's needs shall be taken to include: its need for a suitable environment and diet; to be able to exhibit normal behaviour patterns; any need it has to be housed with, or apart from, other animals; or to be protected from pain, suffering, injury and disease.

The Protection of Animals Act, 1911, the Protection of Animals (Scotland) Act, 1912 (these acts may be cited together) and the Welfare of Animals Act (Northern Ireland) 1972 state:

Section 1(1)

Ill-treatment:

(a) It is an offence to cruelly beat, kick, ill-treat, over-ride, over-drive, torture, infuriate or terrify any animal, or to cause the animal any unnecessary suffering by wantonly or unreasonably doing or omitting to do any act.

Persons who cause, permit or procure such acts also commit the offence.

Transportation

(b) It is an offence to cause an animal unnecessary suffering by the manner in which it is conveyed or carried.[25]

Fighting and baiting

(c) It is an offence to cause, procure or assist at the fighting or baiting of any animal or to keep or use premises for the purpose.

25. Additional offences may be committed under the Transport of Animals (General Order) 1973.

Poison and drugs

(d) It is an offence to administer any poisonous or injurious drug or substance to any animal.

Operations

(e) It is an offence to subject any animal to an operation which is performed without due care and humanity.[26]

Dehorning (Northern Ireland only)

It is an offence to use rubber bands or any other form of constriction for the purpose of dehorning any animal.

Abandonment

A cruelty offence is also committed under the Acts as follows:

If a person having charge or control of any animal abandons it, permanently or not, without reasonable cause or excuse, in circumstances likely to cause the animal unnecessary suffering.

The Protection of Animals Acts, 1911 and 1912 were amended by the Abandonment of Animals Act, 1960, to include this provision, which is also contained in the Act relating to Northern Ireland.

It has been held that it is impossible to say whether an animal has been abandoned without considering the length of time that it had been left. The question of the owner's intention on leaving the animal is of some relevance. Where an owner has made or attempted to make arrangements for the animal's welfare, he could not be said to have abandoned it.[27]

Explanatory notes and exemptions

The 1911 Act was a consolidating Act and amalgamated previous legislation. The phraseology relating to cruelty can be seen as unnecessarily confusing and the terms overlapping, and this has been commented upon by the High Court. In referring to the policy underlying the legislation one judge commented that it was high time the law was expressed in clear, intelligible modern language.[28]

An owner shall be deemed to have permitted cruelty by failing to exercise reasonable care and supervision in respect of the protection of the animal. The words describing the acts of cruelty create separate offences.

26. See page 21 Animals (Scientific Procedures) Act, 1986.
27. Hunt v. Duckering 1993. TLR 23.3.93.
28. Isted v. CPS 1998. 162 JP 513.

The expression 'animal' means any domestic or captive animal. 'Domestic animal' includes farm animals, as defined in the Act, together with dogs, cats or fowl, or any other animal whatever the species which is tame or which has been or is being sufficiently tamed to serve some purpose for the use of man.

'Captive animal' means any species of animal, bird, fish or reptile which is in captivity or confinement or which is maimed, pinioned or subjected to any appliance or contrivance for the purpose of hindering or preventing its escape.

The legislation in Northern Ireland refers to *any* animal, which would include those that are wild.[29]

Section 1(3)b states that nothing in section 1 shall apply to the coursing or hunting of any captive animal subject to certain conditions. This is elaborated upon in chapter 7.

The courts have decided that the mere infliction of pain for a necessary purpose is not cruelty but that unnecessary and unreasonable abuse of an animal is an offence of cruelty.[30] It is for the courts to decide on the circumstances of individual cases.

29. As to when a wild animal in England, Wales and Scotland may be deemed captive see chapter 7.
30. Ford v. Wiley 1889.

CHAPTER 2

Conservation and Protection in England, Wales and Northern Ireland

In the nineteenth century the legislators' attention was directed mainly at the preservation of game, normally defined as game birds and hares. Deer have never been defined as game but have often been included in the game laws. For example the wording in the Game Licences Act 1860, 'game or any deer', clearly differentiates between game and deer. [This Act was repealed in 2007.]

Whereas the game laws have remained almost unchanged between 1831and 2007, deer legislation was created in 1963 and 1980. The 1963 Act dealt with close seasons, unlawful methods and crop damage. Its failure to address poaching was resolved by the 1980 Act which; made deer poaching a criminal offence; controlled the sale of venison; gave the police powers to enforce the 1963 and 1980 Acts and the courts powers to confiscate deer, weapons, equipment and vehicles. Unlike other poaching legislation and the fisheries law in particular, there was, and remains, no power of arrest by landowners or occupiers.

The Deer Act 1991 consolidated the two Acts and several amendments contained in various other Acts. It also made some minor wording changes to the deer legislation. This Act was further amended in 2007 by The Regulatory Reform (Deer)(England and Wales) Order 2007 and The Regulatory Reform (Game) Order 2007.

In this Act deer means deer of any species, any hybrid of different species of deer, and includes the carcases or any part thereof. The Act makes some exceptions for farmed deer.

POACHING

Section 1(1) of the Act states:

> It is an offence, without the consent of the occupier, owner or other lawful authority, to enter any land in search or pursuit of any deer with the intention of taking, killing or injuring it.

Section 1(2) states:

> It is an offence, without the consent of the occupier, owner or other lawful authority, while on any land, to:
>
> (a) Intentionally take, kill or injure any deer or attempt to do so.
>
> (b) Search for or pursue any deer with any such intent, or
>
> (c) Remove the carcase of any deer.

But under section 1(3), the person will not be guilty under (1) or (2) above if:

> (a) he believed he would have had the owner's or occupier's consent, if he/she had known of the circumstances, or
>
> (b) he believed he had a lawful authority.

These offences are discussed in greater detail in chapter 9.

CLOSE SEASON

Under section 2(1) it is an offence for anyone to take or intentionally kill any deer listed in Schedule 1 during the close season. It is also an offence under section 5 to attempt to commit the offence.

CLOSE SEASONS   All dates inclusive

Chinese Water Deer	
Buck	1 April to 31 October
Doe	1 April to 31 October

Fallow Deer	
Buck	1 May to 31 July
Doe	1 April to 31 October

Red Deer	
Stags	1 May to 31 July
Hinds	1 April to 31 October

Red/Sika Deer Hybrids	
Stags	1 May to 31 July
Hinds	1 April to 31 October

Roe Deer	
Buck	1 November to 31 March
Doe	1 April to 31 October

Sika Deer	
Stags	1 May to 31 July
Hinds	1 April to 31 October

Muntjac

There is no statutory closed season for this species. It is recommended that when culling female muntjac immature or heavily pregnant does are selected to avoid leaving dependent young.

There are several exceptions which allow the taking of deer in the close season. Under section 2(3), the close seasons do not apply to the killing of conspicuously marked farmed deer enclosed within a deer-proof barrier where deer are kept, by way of business, for breeding, meat or other foodstuffs, skins or other by-products. The killing must be done by the farmer, or his/her servant or agent.

Conspicuously marked farm deer.

Taking deer at night

Under section 3 it is an offence to take or intentionally kill deer of any species at night (i.e. between one hour after sunset to one hour before sunrise). It is also an offence under section 5 to attempt to commit the offence.

Exceptions to close seasons and night close times

Prevention of suffering

Under section 6(2) it is not an offence under sections 2 or 3 relating to close seasons and night close times to kill or take a deer to prevent its suffering if injured or diseased. Section 6 (2A) was added in 2007 to include the taking or killing of a deer that the person reasonably believes:

a.   has been deprived in any way (other than by unlawful killing by that person) of a female deer on which it was dependent; or
b.   is about to be deprived, by death from disease or a lawful taking or killing, of a female deer on which it is dependent.

In such circumstances a trap or net, normally prohibited by section 4(1)(a) (b), may also be used.

Humane dispatch

Section 6 (4) was extensively modified in 2007. The restrictions on firearms for humane despatch were replaced with 'any reasonable means'.

6 (4) A person shall not be guilty of an offence under section 4(1) or (2) (using prohibited methods or firearms) when using any reasonable means for the purpose of killing any deer if he reasonably believes that the deer has been so seriously injured, otherwise than by his unlawful act, or is in such condition, that to kill it is an act of mercy.

A typical example would be a stalker or keeper called out to deal with a road casualty. The exception is not applicable to the person who commits any unlawful act which results in the deer being injured.[31]

'Any reasonable means' means any method of killing a deer that can reasonably be expected to result in rapid loss of consciousness and death and which is appropriate in all the circumstances (including in particular what the deer is doing, its size, its distance from the closest position safely attainable by the person attempting to kill the deer and its position in relation to vegetative cover).

Prevention of damage

Section 6(1) Deer can also be killed during the close season and at night under section 98 of the Agriculture Act 1947 to prevent damage. This exception would require the issue of a specific order from DEFRA. See further exceptions for occupiers and authorised persons on page 45.

Scientific purposes

Section 8 provides for the issue of licences by Natural England or the Countryside Council for Wales to remove deer from one area to another or to take deer alive for scientific or educational purposes, thereby exempting the holder from sections 2 to 4.[32]

31. The use of firearms and other methods are discussed in chapters 6 and 7.
32. See chapter 1.

UNLAWFUL WEAPONS

The poacher's arsenal is a mixture of modern and medieval technology, ranging from infrared sights, light-intensifying devices, four-wheel-drive vehicles and sophisticated firearms to the crossbow, snare and hunting dog.

Traps, snares, poison and nets

Under section 4(1)(a) it is an offence to set in position any trap, snare, poisoned or stupefying bait so placed as to be calculated to injure any deer coming into contact. Under section 4(1)(b) it is an offence to use any trap, snare, poisoned or stupefying bait or any net to kill or take any deer.

Firearms, bows and arrows, and drugs

Under section 4(2)(a), it is an offence to use any of the following to take, kill or injure any deer:

- a rifle less than a .240 or with a muzzle energy less than 2,305 joules (1,700 ft/lb)
- a rifle bullet other than soft or hollow nosed
- an air weapon
- a smooth-bore gun or cartridge for such

In 2007 Section 6 (6) was added permitting a rifle not less than .220 inches and a muzzle energy of not less than 1,356 joules (1,000 foot pounds) for muntjac and Chinese water deer. Ammunition is a soft-nosed or hollow-nosed bullet weighing not less than 3.24 grammes (50 grains).

The Act now permits the use of any reasonable means for the humane dispatch of deer. This could include the use of any shotgun or rifle of any calibre with any ammunition. However the Act retains a specific exemption for a smooth-bore gun used as a slaughtering instrument if it is not less than 12 bore, has a barrel less than 24 inches and is loaded with AAA shot or larger. This kind of weapon was traditionally carried by hunts to dispatch a deer at bay. With the introduction of the Hunting Act it is difficult to envisage a good reason for such a weapon which requires a firearms certificate due to the short barrel.

Under section 4(2)(b)(c), it is an offence to use any of the following to take, kill or injure any deer:

- an arrow, spear or similar missile
- missiles, whether discharged from a firearm or otherwise, containing a poison, stupefying drug or muscle relaxant

The Wildlife and Countryside Act 1981 prohibits the use of a bow or crossbow to kill or take any animal.

Motor vehicles

The Act was amended in 2007 to allow deer to be shot from a vehicle providing it was stationary and with the engine switched off. This minimises the risk of injury due to a misplaced shot by shooting from an unstable or moving platform.

Under section 4(4), it is an offence to discharge a firearm or project any missile at any deer from a powered vehicle (e.g. car, boat, aircraft, helicopter or hovercraft) when the vehicle is moving or the engine is running or to use such a vehicle to drive deer.

It is also an offence under section 5 to attempt to commit these offences.

Under section 4(4), it is an offence to discharge a firearm or project any missile at any deer from a powered vehicle (e.g. car, boat, aircraft, helicopter or hovercraft) or to use such a vehicle to drive deer. It is also an offence under section 5 to attempt to commit these offences. Under section 4(5) such actions are not illegal, however, if carried out by, or with the written authority of, the occupier of any 'enclosed land where deer are usually kept, and in relation to deer on that land'.

As far as we are aware, there is no case law to guide us in relation to the interpretation of the section. The Deer Act does not define the wording. However in the Deer (Scotland) Act 1996, 'enclosed' means 'enclosed by stock-proof fence or other barrier'. It does not define 'enclosed land where deer are usually kept'. Jemmison v. Priddle 1971 gave a ruling on 'enclosed land' in relation to an exemption within the Game Licensing Act, 1860. For the purposes of this Act this was taken to mean land enclosed by normal agricultural hedges as opposed to moorland where no enclosures existed.[33]

Historically similar wording can be traced back to the Larceny Act, 1861 (now replaced by the Theft Act, 1968). Section 13 related to offences of taking deer in 'any inclosed land where deer shall be usually kept'. The purpose of the section would appear to be to protect what were viewed then as 'wild deer' in large parks or forests

33. See chapter 7.

that were walled or fenced. The Common Law provided protection for other deer that were considered 'tame'. Section 15 of the Act made it an offence unlawfully and wilfully to destroy any part of any fence on land where 'deer are usually kept'. This tends to suggest that the areas were deer-proof and the deer therein captive.

In our opinion the wording 'inclosed land where deer are usually kept' implies the land is used for such a purpose and would warrant deer-proof boundaries.

Attempts to commit offences and possession of equipment

It is an offence under section 5 to attempt to commit any offence under sections 2–4. It is also an offence to possess for the purpose of committing an offence under section 2 or 4:

   i. An article prohibited under sections 4(1)(b), 4(2)(b) or (c) above, or
   ii. Any firearms or ammunition

EXCEPTIONS FOR OCCUPIERS AND AUTHORISED PERSONS

Under section 7(4) an authorised person is:

- the occupier of the land on which the action is taken
- a resident member of the occupier's household authorised in writing by the occupier
- a person in the occupier's service (e.g. an employee) authorised in writing by the occupier
- a person having the right to take or kill the deer or a person authorised in writing by him (e.g. a shooting tenant, gamekeeper and guests)

Crop damage

If deer are causing serious damage, under section 7(1)(2) and subject to the conditions laid down in section 7(3), an authorised person may:

- take or kill the deer by shooting during the close season on cultivated land, pasture or enclosed woodland
- use a smooth-bore gun to kill the deer on any such land, at any time, if it is not less than a 12 bore and is loaded with AAA shot or a single non-spherical bullet, not less than 22.68 grammes (350 grains), commonly known as a rifled slug

However, the authorised person must be able to show that:

- there was reason to believe that deer of the same species were causing, or had caused damage to crops, vegetables, fruit, growing timber or any other form of property on the land
- it was likely that further serious damage would be caused
- the action was necessary to prevent it

This exemption provides a loophole in that some farmers plant crops close to woods or land containing deer with the intention of attracting them through an open gate or broken-down fence onto the land.

Where an authorised person takes action against marauding deer to protect crops etc., the killing must take place on the land where the damage is occurring, and not the land where the deer come from.[34] Chapter 4 deals with crop damage in more detail.

EXCEPTIONS PERMITTED UNDER LICENCE

Moving and releasing deer

Under section 8 Natural England or the Countryside Council for Wales can issue a licence which exempts an individual from offences relating to specific acts under section 2, 3 and 4 (close season, night and prohibited methods). The purposes of such a licence are to remove deer from one area to another or to take deer alive for scientific or educational purposes. The licence may permit the use of

(a)   any net, trap, stupefying drug or muscle-relaxing agent of a type authorised by the licence; or

34. See the case of Traill v. Buckingham in chapter 4.

(b)   any missile carrying or containing such stupefying drug or muscle-relaxing agent and discharging any such missile by any means authorised by the licence.

Culling in close season

Under section 8 (3A-3C) a licence may be granted in relation to any land to take or cull deer in the close season for the purpose of:

(a)   preserving public health or public safety, or
(b)   conserving the natural heritage.

In granting the licence it must be satisfied that:

(a)   preserving public health or public safety – there is a serious risk of the specified deer putting public health or public safety at risk;
(b)   conserving the natural heritage – there is a serious risk of the specified deer causing deterioration of the natural heritage;
(c)   In both cases there is no satisfactory alternative to taking and killing the deer of the species and description to which the application relates during the close season.
(d)   the applicant has a right of entry to the land for the purpose of taking or killing deer under the licence; and
(e)   if the licence is to relate to red, roe or fallow deer, the taking or killing to be authorised by the licence will not compromise the ability of that species to maintain the population of deer in question on a long-term basis within its natural range in the numbers which exist after the taking or killing has taken place.

Night shooting

Under section 8 3D-3F Natural England or the Countryside Council for Wales can grant a licence permitting the control of deer at night.

A licence may be granted for the purpose of:

(a)   preserving public health or public safety,
(b)   conserving the natural heritage (natural heritage means flora and fauna, geological or physiographical features or natural beauty and amenity of the countryside); or
(c)   preventing serious damage to property.

The licensor must be satisfied that:

(a) preserving public health or public safety – there is a serious risk of deer putting public health or public safety at risk;

(b) conserving the natural heritage – there is a serious risk of deer causing deterioration of the natural heritage (natural heritage means flora and fauna, geological or physiographical features or natural beauty and amenity of the countryside);

(c) preventing serious damage to property – property on the land has been seriously damaged in the year preceding the licence application;

(d) there is no satisfactory alternative to taking and killing the deer at night;

(e) the applicant has a right of entry to the land for the purpose of taking or killing deer under the licence; and

(f) if the licence is to relate to red, roe or fallow deer, the taking or killing to be authorised by the licence will not compromise the ability of that species to maintain the population of deer in question on a long-term basis within its natural range in the numbers which exist after the taking or killing has taken place.

The licence will state:

(a) the purpose for which it is granted;

(b) the land to which it relates;

(c) the species and descriptions of deer to which it relates;

(d) the method by which the licensee may take or kill deer; and

(e) the period, not exceeding two years, for which it is valid.

A licence may also be subject to conditions and failure to comply with the licence is an offence.

Releasing deer

Under section 14(1) of the Wildlife and Countryside Act, it is illegal to release or allow to escape into the wild any animal which:

(a) is of a kind which is not ordinarily resident in and is not a regular visitor to Great Britain in a wild state; or

(b) is included in Part 1 of Schedule 9 [includes sika and muntjac].

ENFORCEMENT

Enforcement by authorised person

For the purpose of enforcement, an authorised person is the owner or occupier of land or someone authorised by them or having the right to take or kill deer on that land. If such an authorised person reasonably suspects that someone is or has been committing offences under section 1(1)(2) (poaching) they may require the person to give their full name and address and quit the land forthwith. There are no powers of arrest and no guarantee that any name given is genuine. At best such action may only scare the poacher off the land but your objective may be achieved. There is little chance of a prosecution unless the police are involved, who may use their general powers of arrest under the Police and Criminal Evidence Act.

Failure to comply with such a request is an offence, but only a police officer has the power of arrest or the means of obtaining the name or address if it is refused. The owner or occupier or their employee may treat the suspected person as a trespasser and eject them from the land using reasonable force.

If a police officer stops a vehicle containing a carcase the officer will not know if the deer is wild or from a deer park or farm. In such cases the officer could initially treat the situation as one of theft until the ownership or otherwise of the deer is established. Where deer are considered to be captive, tamed or domestic (e.g. farmed deer or deer enclosed in a deer park), they may be classed as property; in which case the offence of theft under the Theft Act, 1968 may be committed and a citizen's arrest made.[35]

Enforcement by the police

Under section 12, the police are given additional powers of enforcement. A police officer who reasonably suspects that someone is or has been committing any offence under the Act may enter any land (but not a dwelling house), and, if he or she suspects that evidence may be found, may without warrant:

- stop and search the suspect
- search or examine any vehicle, animal, weapon or other thing
- arrest the suspect under the Police and Criminal Evidence Act 1984 general arrest conditions
- seize and detain anything that is evidence or liable to be confiscated by the court

35. See chapter 9 p.210.

- sell deer or venison and retain the proceeds until the case is decided at court

Forfeitures and disqualification

On conviction the court may order the confiscation of:

- deer or venison in respect of the offence or found in the person's possession
- any vehicle, animal, weapon or other thing used to commit the offence, or which was capable of being used to take, kill or injure deer and was found in their possession

For offences under sections 1 and 10 the court may cancel his/her firearm or shotgun certificate.

PROTECTION AND CONSERVATION IN NORTHERN IRELAND

Deer protection in Northern Ireland is covered by Part III of the Wildlife (Northern Ireland) Order, 1985, which is substantially similar to the Deer Act, 1991. The hunting of deer with hounds is permitted under conditions of a licence.

Except where otherwise provided, 'deer' means deer of any species and their hybrids, and includes those on enclosed land where deer not in the wild state are usually kept. The Order makes some exceptions for farmed deer.

Close season

Under Article 19(1) it is an offence for anyone to take or intentionally kill any deer listed in Schedule 10 during the close season (i.e.

red, fallow or sika). Hybrids of these species are included in the Schedule. It is also an offence under Article 5 to attempt to commit the offence.

CLOSE SEASONS

Red Deer	All dates inclusive
Stags	1 May to 31 July
Hinds	1 March to 31 October
Fallow Deer	
Buck	1 May to 31 July
Doe	1 March to 31 October
Sika Deer	
Stags	1 May to 31 July
Hinds	1 March to 31 October

There are certain exceptions, which are explained below.

Taking deer at night

Under Article 19(2) it is an offence to take or intentionally kill any deer at night (i.e. between one hour after sunset to one hour before sunrise).

Firearms

Under Article 19(3)(a) and Schedule 11 it is an offence to use any of the following to take, kill or injure deer:

- a rifle less than a .236 or with a muzzle energy less than 2,305 joules (1,700 ft/lb)
- A rifle bullet other than a bullet not less than 100 grains (6.48 grammes) or an expanding bullet designed to deform in a predictable manner and thereby increase its effective diameter upon entering tissue
- any air weapon
- any smooth-bore gun or cartridge for such
- any weapon which discharges a missile by gas propellant
- any form of handgun other than a slaughtering instrument[36]

Under Article 19(3) it is an offence for any person to discharge a firearm or project any missile from a mechanically propelled vehicle

36. Article 2(2) Firearms (Northern Ireland) Order, 1981.

at deer (this does not apply to anything done by, or with the written authority of, the occupier of enclosed land where deer not in the wild state are usually kept, in relation to deer on that land).

Removing, transporting and marking deer

Under Article 19(4) it is an offence for any person to –

(a)   take and remove any live deer;

(b)   mark, or attach any tag, ring, collar or other device to any live deer; or

(c)   use aircraft to transport live deer (except inside the aircraft).

Exceptions

Article 20(2) specifies that nothing in Article 19 shall make unlawful:

- anything done by a vet when treating deer; or
- in relation to 19(1) close seasons; 3(b) shooting from a vehicle; or (4)(a)(b) taking or marking live deer, anything done by, or under the direction of, a person certified by the Department of Agriculture who keeps and breeds deer by way of business, in the course of business; or
- any act done to protect a person immediately endangered by deer on enclosed land where deer not in a wild state are usually kept, if the act is reasonable in the circumstances.

Another exception involves crop protection (see chapter 4 for more detail), and Article 20(7)(b) permits the use of any shotgun and ammunition for the dispatch of a deer which had been so seriously injured, otherwise than by the unlawful act of the dispatcher, or was in such a condition that to kill it was an act of mercy. A typical example would be a stalker or keeper called out to deal with a road casualty. The exception is not applicable to the person who commits any unlawful act which results in the deer being injured.

Poaching

Article 22(1) states it is an offence, without the consent of the occupier, owner or other lawful authority, to enter any land in search or pursuit of any deer with the intention of taking, killing or injuring it. Under Article 22(2), it is also an offence, without the consent of the occupier, owner or other lawful authority, while on any land, to:

- Intentionally take, kill or injure any deer,
- Search for or pursue any deer with any such intent, or
- Remove the carcase of any deer.

But under Article 22(3), the person will not be guilty under (1) or (2) above if:

- he reasonably believed he would have had the owner's or occupier's consent, if he/she had known of the circumstances, or
- he has other lawful authority to do it.

These offences are discussed in greater detail in chapter 9.

Unlawful weapons

Article 12 prohibits the use of self-locking snares, bows, crossbows, arrows, spears and sound recordings to kill or take any wild animal including deer.

Red, fallow and sika deer are also included in Schedule 6 of the Order which further prohibits the use of:

- traps and snares
- drugs and poison
- automatic or semi-automatic firearms
- a metal bar, hammer or similar
- a device for illuminating a target or night-sighting device
- an artificial light, mirror or dazzling device
- gas or smoke

In addition the use of a mechanically propelled vehicle in immediate pursuit of such deer for the purpose of driving, killing or taking them is an offence.

Movement and release of deer

Article 21 allows for licences to be granted by the Department of Environment for scientific and educational purposes or for removing deer from one area to another.

Article 15 prohibits the release or escape into the wild of any animal which:

- is of a kind not ordinarily resident in and is not a regular visitor to Northern Ireland in a wild state or
- is included in Part 1 of Schedule 9

The release of red, fallow or sika requires a licence from the Department of Environment and the release of other species would be illegal.

Enforcement and penalties

Enforcement by authorised person
For the purpose of enforcement, an authorised person is the owner or occupier of land or someone authorised by him or having the right to take or kill deer on that land. Under Article 22(5) if such an authorised person reasonably suspects that someone is or has been committing offences under Article 22(1)(2) (poaching) he may require the person to give his full name and address and quit the land forthwith. There are no powers of arrest and no guarantees that any name given is genuine. At best such action may only scare the poacher off the land but your objective may be achieved. Failure to comply with such a request is an offence.

Enforcement by the police
Under Article 25, the police are given additional powers of enforcement. A police officer who reasonably suspects that someone is or has been committing any deer-related offence under Part III of the Order may enter any land (but not a dwelling house), and, if he suspects that evidence may be found, may without warrant:

- stop and search the suspect
- search or examine any vehicle, animal, weapon or other thing
- arrest the suspect using general arrest powers under Article 26 of the Police and Criminal Evidence Act
- a constable may enter any land other than a dwelling house
- seize and detain anything that is evidence or liable to be forfeited by the court; deer and venison must be produced to a court which may order it to be sold, destroyed or liberated

A search warrant can be granted in respect of offences under Articles 19 and 23.

Forfeitures and disqualification
Under Article 27(7) on conviction the court:

- shall order the confiscation of deer or venison in respect of which the offence was committed; and

- may confiscate any vehicle, animal, weapon or other thing used to commit the offence.

For offences under Articles 1, 10, 11 and 13(3)(c) the court may also disqualify a person from holding a game dealer's licence and cancel his/her firearm or shotgun certificate.

CHAPTER 3

Conservation and Protection in Scotland

The legislation covering the protection of deer in Scotland is the Deer (Scotland) Act 1996 and a number of Orders made under previous Acts:

- the Deer (Firearms etc.) (Scotland) Order 1985
- the Deer (Close Seasons) (Scotland) Order 1984
- the Licensing of Venison Dealer (Application Procedures etc.) (Scotland) Order 1984
- the Licensing of Venison Dealer (Prescribed Forms etc.) (Scotland) Order 1984

The Act is divided into four parts:

- Part I: The Deer Commission for Scotland
- Part II: Conservation, control and sustainable management of deer
- Part III: Offences in relation to deer
- Part IV: Dealing in venison and enforcement

The species in Scotland are red, fallow, sika, roe and red/sika hybrids, which may explain the conditional definition of deer in the Act: 'deer' means fallow, red, roe and sika and any other species specified by the Secretary of State, and includes any hybrid of those species and, where appropriate, 'the carcase of any deer or any part of it'. In our view the last phrase appears to cater for venison dealing and poaching.

The Deer Commission has formulated a strategy for wild deer including guidance to minimise the spread of sika deer because of their ability to cause considerable damage to woodland and hybridise with the native red deer. DCS recognises that sika are established across many parts of mainland Scotland and are likely to continue to spread. Where there is local agreement, their spread and damage they cause will be minimised through active management, particularly through the control of pioneering stags. Although sika deer are covered by the legislation, they are an alien species living in the wild, and further releases or movements are banned. Any attempt to introduce muntjac is also prohibited. Under section 14(1) of the Wildlife and Countryside Act, it is illegal to release or allow to escape into the wild any animal which

(a)   is of a kind which is not ordinarily resident in and is not a regular visitor to Great Britain in a wild state; or

(b)   is included in Part 1 of schedule 9 [includes sika and muntjac].

The basis of the legislation is that deer may only be taken or killed by shooting in the daytime during the open season. Obviously, such strict criteria would cause many problems for farmers and occupiers of land, so the law allows for culling in specified circumstances.

PART I: THE DEER COMMISSION FOR SCOTLAND

The Deer (Scotland) Act 1996 consolidated the provisions from the Deer (Scotland) Act 1959 which established the Red Deer Commission. The change of title in 1996 to the Deer Commission for Scotland was accompanied by a change of remit to include: the sustainable management of deer; damage to the natural heritage, agriculture or woodlands; deer welfare; and deer which are causing a danger to the public. The remit was also extended to include fallow, roe and sika.

The Deer Commission for Scotland undertakes a wide range of activities throughout Scotland in relation to deer management. It has regulatory functions including Deer Control Agreements, particularly in relation to biodiversity issues, authorisations to cull deer at night and out of season, and the collecting of data on the number of deer killed and processed by game dealers. It also publishes Best Practice guidance and other guidelines designed to improve standards of deer management; consults and advises widely on deer management issues; promotes and actively participates in the operation of Deer Management Groups; undertakes and commissions research; conducts deer counts; assists in training; collaborates with other agencies on deer related and wider policy issues; and advises the Scottish Government on all deer matters in Scotland.

Land below the 450-metre contour is in great demand for a number of uses, especially forestry; and in order that all interests are protected, deer control carries a high priority. In this respect it is vitally important to balance numbers with available winter range. Deer managers have a responsibility to minimise the risk of deer damage and cannot expect farmers and crofters to overwinter their deer; consequently the law makes provision for agricultural occupiers to protect their crops. The annual culls of red deer in 1996–7 and 1997–8 were 61,482 and 61,627 respectively.

The Commission needs information to carry out its functions. Under section 40 it can require occupiers to provide returns of the numbers of deer killed on their ground. Occupiers include tenants or sub-tenants, whether in actual occupation of the land or not. Failing to supply the information is an offence.

Farmed deer

Under section 43, apart from the exceptions below, the Act does not apply to farmed deer, which are deer of any species kept as livestock on agricultural land and enclosed in a deer-proof barrier. The exceptions are:

- killing otherwise than by shooting when slaughtered in the field
- the use of a firearm which is not approved
- venison dealing

PART II: CONSERVATION, CONTROL AND SUSTAINABLE MANAGEMENT OF DEER

Close seasons

Under section 5 and the Deer (Close Seasons) (Scotland) Order, 1984, no person shall take or wilfully kill or injure specified deer in the following close seasons:

Species	male	female
Red deer, sika deer and red/sika hybrids	21 October–30 June	16 February–20 October
Fallow deer	1 May–31 July	16 February–20 October
Roe deer	21 October–31 March	1 April–20 October

Section 5(5) stipulates that it is an offence to take, wilfully kill or injure deer during the close season unless certain exceptions apply. This includes attempts and preparatory acts to kill deer. The Deer Commission has powers to adjust the close seasons in certain locations to meet seasonal conditions.

These dates were fixed for both welfare and sporting purposes but, in the case of red deer particularly, mainly on animal welfare grounds. Stags are usually well run after their exertions during the rutting season towards the end of October. And hinds are heavily pregnant by spring and have dependent calves at foot after mid-June.

It should be noted that the Deer Commission is not a policing authority and the decision to prosecute remains with the police and procurator fiscal.

Under section 5(6), the Deer Commission can authorise the owner, occupier or a person nominated in writing by either of them, to take or kill and sell or otherwise dispose of deer during the close season where they are satisfied that:

(a)   the taking or killing is necessary
   (i)   to prevent serious damage to unenclosed woodland or the natural heritage generally, or
   (ii) in the interests of public safety; and
(b)   no other reasonable means of control are adequate in the circumstances.

Natural heritage includes fauna and flora, geological or physiological features and the natural beauty and amenity of the countryside.[37]

The Commission may also authorise the taking of deer for scientific purposes.

37. See chapter 4 for more on crop protection.

Control agreements

Competing with livestock for food.

Section 7(1)(a) states:

> Where deer on any land have caused, are causing or are likely to cause:
>
> (i) damage to woodland, to agricultural production including crops or foodstuffs, or directly or indirectly to the natural heritage generally; or
>
> (ii) injury to livestock (includes farmed deer) by serious overgrazing of pastures, competing with livestock for supplementary feed; or otherwise; or
>
> (iii) have become a danger or potential danger to public safety; the Commission can consider measures to reduce the numbers of deer in an area which may include taking or removal of deer from an area. This might include sites of particular economic or conservation value or sites where public safety is at risk such as roads.

For the purpose of this section natural heritage includes any alteration or enhancement of the natural heritage which is taking place, or is proposed to take place, either naturally or as a result of change of use determined by the owner or occupier of the land.

Following evidence showing habitats on designated areas are in poor condition and after consultation with interested parties including owners and further baseline habitat surveys the Joint Agencies (DCS, Forestry Commission Scotland, Scottish Government Rural Payments Inspectorate Department and Scottish Natural Heritage) may draw up a control agreement for the specified area. The agreement will contain the measures to be taken; the number, species, sex and class of deer to be killed, taken or removed; the measures to be taken by owners and occupiers; and time limits.

The Commission is now using voluntary control agreements. It is targeting and agreeing with Deer Management Groups owners and other agencies balanced deer populations and target culls, especially of females. Many deer management groups have created deer management plans involving estate staff and owners in thinking carefully about population structures, distribution and impact.

These can be as relevant to deer management groups without designated sites present as to those with.

In some cases landowners may be offered financial assistance from the joint agencies to carry out management measures required to return the habitats to favourable condition or in the case of public safety sites to negate any further risk.

A control agreement may be made in anticipation of future damage, injury or danger, but a control scheme (see below) may only be made where deer have caused, or are causing, serious damage or injury or are and remain a danger to the public, necessitating action.

Control schemes

Under sections 8 and 9 where the Commission cannot secure a control agreement or the agreement is not being carried out they *shall* make a control scheme to prevent serious damage, injury or danger. Such schemes cannot be invoked in the case of altering or enhancing the natural heritage.

A control scheme specifies the measures to be taken by individual owners and occupiers, but they cannot require the erection of a deer-proof fence. If the owner or occupier does not implement the measures the Commission can take the required action and sell the deer taken. In practice this would be the most likely outcome after the failure of a voluntary section 7 control agreement or the failure to reach a voluntary agreement. Any expenses incurred by the Commission in excess of the proceeds from the sale of the deer are recoverable from the occupier or owner. Aggrieved owners and occupiers may appeal to the Scottish Land Court to vary the amount to be recovered. The Commission may, in a particular case, waive their right to such expenses.

Under section 13, a person who refuses or wilfully fails to comply with a requirement of a control scheme or who wilfully obstructs a person acting under an authorisation issued under Part II commits an offence.

Emergency measures

If the Commission considers that the powers outlined above are inadequate to deal with serious damage, injury or danger it can, under section 10, implement emergency measures. These can include a written request to the person with the rights to take deer on that land to undertake the killing of deer forthwith. If the person is unable or unwilling to comply with the request then the Commission can authorise another person to take the deer. Where the deer constitute a danger or potential danger to the public and shooting such deer may constitute a danger to the public other methods can be approved. Such situations could include deer near airports, railway lines, school playgrounds and parks.

Section 15 allows persons authorised in writing by the Commission to enter land at any reasonable times to exercise functions under section 10. Under other circumstances the power to enter land is permitted following the service of a notice on the owner and occupier.

Game licence

Under Section 38 persons authorised or required by the Commission to kill deer under the Deer Act do not require a game licence.

Other provisions

Persons authorised or required by the Commission to kill deer do not require a game licence (section 38).

Under section 39, without prejudice to sections 8(8), 9, 10(10) and 12(1) the Commission shall have no power to dispose of deer taken under its authority.

PART III: UNLAWFUL TAKING AND KILLING[38]

The basis of the legislation is that deer may only be taken or killed by shooting with the appropriate firearm, in the daytime, during the open season. It therefore prohibits the use of traps, snares, nets, dogs and other methods.

Under section 17 it is an offence:

(i)   Without legal right or permission to take, wilfully kill or injure deer on any land [take means taking deer alive].
(ii) To remove the carcase of any deer from any land without legal right or permission from someone having such legal right.
(iii) To wilfully kill or injure any deer otherwise than by shooting [shooting means with the prescribed firearm and ammunition].

38. Poaching offences are discussed in greater detail in chapter 9.

There is a view based on the game laws that where deer are legitimately shot on land where authority exists, but fall dead over the boundary, they can be recovered. Whilst this may provide a 'legal right' in (ii) (under the Deer Act 1996) above there remains the issues of trespass and ownership of the carcase at civil law.[39]

Night shooting

Under section 18 it is an offence to wilfully kill or injure deer at night. Night is the period between the end of the first hour after sunset to the commencement of the last hour before sunrise. The Commission may authorise persons to take deer at night under the terms of their Code of Practice,[40] notwithstanding anything contained in an agreement between the occupier and the owner of agricultural land or woodland. Those authorised to control deer at night must be registered as fit and competent with DCS.

Use of vehicles

Section 19, to drive deer by vehicle, on any land, for the purpose of taking or killing them, requires written authorisation from the Deer Commission for Scotland.

DCS may authorise a land owner or any person nominated in writing by the owner, to use a vehicle (excluding aircraft or hovercraft) to move deer for culling associated with management.

Any person issued with an authorisation to move deer with a vehicle must comply with a 'Code of Practice', prepared and published by the Deer Commission for Scotland in pursuance of Section 37(5)(b) of the Deer (Scotland) Act 1996.

'Vehicle' does not include aircraft or hovercraft. See the Code of Practice on use of vehicles for driving deer on page 69.

Section 20, it is an offence:

- to shoot at deer from a moving vehicle or aircraft
- to use an aircraft for transporting live deer other than in the interior of the aircraft unless done by or under the supervision of a veterinary surgeon or practitioner

The Commission has produced best practice guidance to provide information and guidance on the potential uses of helicopters to assist

39. See chapter 7.
40. See pages 72–75.

in deer management activities and safeguarding welfare when heli-copters are used in the presence of deer.

Helicopters provide a means to support and co-ordinate operations involving culling with teams of rifles, including:

- Assessing culling areas.
- Determining the location, number, and sex of deer on the ground.
- Locating suitable groups of deer to be targeted.
- Fast and efficient deployment of rifles.
- Co-ordinating teams on the ground.
- Co-ordinating communications between ground teams and any base station.
- Monitoring the welfare of deer targeted by any operation.
- Monitoring surrounding area for members of the public who may be moving toward the culling area and relay details and instructions to relevant teams.
- When required, locating and observing wounded and/or orphaned animals and directing the rifle team.
- Fast and efficient retrieval of carcases.

It is legal for:

Anyone to use a helicopter to move deer where they do not have the intention to take, or wilfully kill, or injure the deer. For example, deer can be moved in order to count them, clear them from an area where they are causing damage or pose a threat to safety. Any person holding the legal right to take deer may use a helicopter to move deer with the intention to take only, provided they do not cause unneces-sary suffering. Section 41(2) of the Act.

It is illegal to:

Use a helicopter to move deer with the intention of killing them. Section 19(1) of the Act.

However the Deer Commission for Scotland may under certain specific conditions drive deer with the intention to kill. Section 14 of the Act.

Firearms and ammunition

Under section 21, the Secretary of State can specify in an Order the classes of firearms, ammunition, sights and other equipment for the lawful killing of deer. Persons who fail to comply with the Orders commit an offence. The current Order is The Deer (Firearms etc.) (Scotland) Order, 1985.[41]

41. See the firearms chart on page 116 and chapter 6.

Under section 21(5) it is an offence wilfully to injure a deer with any firearm or ammunition.

Section 22
If two or more persons act together to do any act which is an offence under sections 17 to 21 then, according to section 22, each person commits the offence.

Illegal possession of deer

Under section 23 an offence is committed by a person who is in possession of a deer, firearms or ammunition in circumstances which infer that:

1. he obtained the deer by committing an offence under sections 5 or 17 to 22; or
2. he had used the firearm or ammunition for the purpose of committing an offence under sections 5 or 17 to 22; or
3. he knew that:
   (i) an offence under sections 5 or 17 to 22 had been committed in relation to the deer; or
   (ii) the firearm or ammunition had been used for committing an offence under sections 5 or 17 to 22.

The evidence of one witness is sufficient to charge and convict.

It is a defence to section 23 if the accused can show that no such offence had been committed, or that he had no reason to believe such an offence had been committed.

A person who acts in good faith in connection with the prevention or detection of crime or investigation or treatment of disease does not commit the offence.

Exemptions for certain acts

Prevention of suffering
Under section 25 an offence is not committed in respect of any act done for the purpose of preventing suffering by an injured or diseased deer or by any deer calf, fawn or kid deprived, or about to be deprived, of its mother.

A typical example of this exemption would be a stalker or keeper called out to deal with a road casualty. It applies to any person who will undertake the necessary action and in these exceptional circumstances the suffering animal may be dispatched by some means other than shooting with a prescribed firearm.[42] See DCS Best Practice guidance on humane dispatch.

Crop protection in the close season[43]

Under section 26 it is lawful for a person to take or kill, and sell or dispose of any deer found in the close season on:

(a)   arable land, improved permanent pasture (other than moorland) and land which has been regenerated so as to be able to make a significant contribution to the productivity of a holding which forms part of that agricultural land; or

(b)   enclosed woodland.

where the occupier has reasonable grounds for believing that serious damage will be caused to crops, pasture or human or animal food-stuffs on that agricultural land or to that woodland if the deer are not taken or killed.

The action can be taken by the occupier or the following if they are authorised in writing by the occupier:

- the owner in person
- the owner's employees
- the occupier's employees
- any person normally resident on the land
- any other fit and competent person approved in writing by the Commission

and in relation to enclosed land (other than moorland) i.e. arable land, improved permanent pasture and land which has been regenerated which is part of a common grazing, the subsection also applies to a person who for the purposes of the subsection is both duly authorised in writing by the grazings committee (provided the grazings committee have such reasonable ground as is mentioned in that subsection) and approved as is mentioned in paragraph (d).

It is conceivable that a particular nominee might be competent to kill deer on the occupier's land if he lawfully held the required firearm for the purpose, but might be considered unfit or unsuitable for the purpose by the Commission – for example, a novice deer manager without appropriate experience of culling deer.

Woodland in this context means not just commercial forestry plan-

---

42. See chapter 7 for more on humane dispatches.
43. See chapter 4 for more on crop protection.

tations but any land on which trees are grown, any such trees and also the vegetation amongst the trees on that land. A woodland is enclosed if it is surrounded by stock-proof, but not necessarily deer-proof, fencing or other barriers.

Serious damage is not defined and is a difficult area. For the purpose of section 26 the applicant should be able to satisfy themselves that damage is occurring or likely to occur to their land specified under paragraph (a) or (b).

Guidance is available on habitat impact assessment and DCS authorisations in the DCS Best Practice Guides.

Nothing contained in an agreement between an occupier and the owner of the land shall prohibit the above lawfully conducted control. However if the landowner or owner of the sporting rights believes that no damage is occurring or likely to occur they can challenge the actions or intentions of the tenant in court (section 26(3)).

Deer may be taken during the close season for reasons other than crop damage but only if such activities are authorised in writing by the Commission.

Use of shotguns

Generally the use of shotguns is neither permitted nor recommended. However the Orders made under the Act do permit the persons listed on page 66 to use specified shotguns and ammunition for crop control as defined in section 26.

The shotgun must be not less than 12 gauge loaded with:

- for shooting any deer, a single rifled non-spherical slug weighing not less than 380 grains (24.62 grams); or a cartridge loaded with SSG or larger
- for roe deer, a cartridge loaded with AAA or larger

PART IV: DEALING IN VENISON AND ENFORCEMENT[44]

Search and seizure

Under section 27,

- a police constable may seize any deer liable to be forfeited on conviction of an offence under the Act

44. See chapter 5 for more on venison dealers and game meat handling.

- a sheriff or justice of the peace may grant a search warrant to the police, if satisfied there is reasonable suspicion that an offence under Part III or sections 36(1) or (4) has been committed and evidence of it is to be found on any premises or in any vehicle
- the police authorised by such a warrant, in addition to searching the premises etc., may also search every person found therein or whom they reasonably suspect of having recently left or to be about to enter, and seize any article they have reasonable grounds to believe is evidence relating to the offence
- in cases of urgency the police, having reasonable suspicion that an offence under Part III or sections 36(1) or (4) has been committed, may stop and search without a warrant any vehicle where they believe evidence may be found

Arrest

Under section 28 a police officer may arrest any person found committing an offence under Part III of the Act.

Cancellation of firearm certificates

Section 31(2) states that on conviction for an offence under sections 17–23 the court may cancel any firearm or shotgun certificate.

Cancellation of venison dealer certificate

Under section 31(5), on conviction for an offence under Part III or section 36 the court may disqualify a person from holding or obtaining a venison dealer's certificate.

Disposal of deer

Under section 32, where a deer is seized under the Act and is liable to forfeiture, it may be sold and the net profits will then be liable to forfeiture.

CODES OF PRACTICE

The latest versions of the following codes of practice and other best practice guides are available from the Deer Commission for Scotland and can be downloaded at www.dcs.gov.uk

The use of vehicles

Code of Practice on the Use of Vehicles
for the Purposes of Deer Management

Prepared and published by the Deer Commission for Scotland in pursuance of Section 37(5)(b) of the Deer (Scotland) Act, 1996. Further guidance on driving deer with vehicles is available from The Deer Commission for Scotland or at www.dcs.gov.uk.

Any person issued with an authorisation to drive deer by vehicle is obliged to comply with this Code of Practice. Failure to do so can result in an authorisation being withdrawn.

1. INTRODUCTION

The Deer (Scotland) Act 1996 restricts the driving of deer by vehicle, on any land, for the purposes of taking or killing them to those people with written authorisation from the Deer Commission for Scotland.

The Commission may authorise the owner of any land which deer are on, or any person nominated in writing by such an owner, to use any vehicle in circumstances where it may be necessary to drive and take alive or kill deer, during the hours of daylight, for the purposes of deer management. The Commission will require to be satisfied that this method of culling is necessary, that no other method would be appropriate under the circumstances and, that the person authorised is fit and competent for the purpose.

Authorisations are subject to such conditions as may be specified, including the precise area where such work is to be carried out. The Commission will determine when authorisations will be issued for each sex and species of deer and determine the period of their validity.

Firearms safety and the humane dispatch and welfare of deer are paramount in the issue of authorisations for driving deer by vehicle and must be the overriding consideration of operators.

For the purposes of this Code 'deer management' does not include driving deer in the course of any sporting activity; and 'vehicle' does not include any aircraft or hovercraft.

2. COMPLIANCE WITH THE FOLLOWING CONDITIONS IS OBLIGATORY

Authorisations issued by the Commission for the driving of deer by vehicle contain the following obligatory conditions and will only be valid if these conditions are adhered to:

2.1   For the killing of RED, SIKA, RED/SIKA CROSSES AND FALLOW DEER, a rifle using ammunition of not less than 6.48 grams (100 grain) soft-nosed bullets, with a muzzle velocity of not less than 746.76 metres (2,450 feet) per second and a muzzle energy of not less than 2,373joules (1,750 foot/pounds), must be used.

2.2 For the killing of ROE DEER, a rifle using ammunition of not less than 3.24 grams (50 grain) soft-nosed bullets, with a muzzle velocity of not less than 746.76 metres (2,450 feet) per second and a muzzle energy of not less than 1,356 joules (1,000 foot/pounds), must be used.

2.3 A shotgun may not be used unless specifically authorised by the Commission and in such circumstances the bore and type of ammunition to be used will be specified in the Authorisation.

2.4 Authorisations must be returned to the Commission within 7 days of the date of expiry and include all details of the number, species and sex of deer killed.

3. SITUATIONS UNDER WHICH AUTHORISATIONS MAY BE GRANTED

3.1 Agricultural Areas: To drive deer which are coming on to crops to an area with a safe backdrop for killing, away from human habitation and domestic stock, where they can be clearly seen and killed.

3.2 Woodland Areas: To drive deer which are in woodlands or areas which are being replanted or regenerated to areas with a safe backdrop where they can be clearly seen and killed.

3.3 Natural Heritage: To drive deer, for the purposes of management and control in sensitive areas of natural heritage value, to areas with a safe backdrop where they can be clearly seen and killed.

3.4 Open Range: To drive deer, for the purposes of deer management and population control, to areas with a safe backdrop where they can he clearly seen and killed.

3.5 Deer in Public Places: To drive deer away from areas of potential threat to public safety to adjacent areas where they may be safely removed or killed.

4. PRINCIPLES AND METHODS

4.1 The local Deer Management Group and other directly affected neighbours should he advised of the proposals.

4.2 A main consideration in driving deer to places where they can be conveniently or more safely shot is to do this with minimum stress to the animals.

4.3 Operators should be familiar with the terrain, behaviour pattern and likely direction of movement of the deer and work must he planned to coincide with their natural daily movement pattern. Care should be taken not to drive deer over unduly rough or difficult terrain where the risk of injury may be high.

4.4 Vehicle operators should remain at reasonable distances from deer being driven to avoid panic and prevent family groups being split up. Deer should not be driven at excessive speeds or over long distances.

4.5 If fences have to be negotiated, sections must be temporarily dropped or gates left open.

4.6 Shooting should only be carried out in areas where there are suitable backstops and care must be taken when shooting one deer not to injure others. Shooting from an elevated position such as a high platform or trailer can enhance the efficiency of the operation. Shooting must not take place from within vehicles.

4.7 Operators should, where possible, refrain from driving groups of female deer during periods of late pregnancy. If it must be done it should be with the minimum stress to the animals.

4.8 Where possible only small groups of deer should be driven to areas where they can he killed and all orphaned calves must be shot during the operation or immediately after the event. The repeated driving of deer on successive days often results in lower levels of success.

4.9 Operators should ensure that deer are standing still and clear of a group at the time of shooting. A heart/lung shot (up to 100 metres for roe and up to 200 metres for larger deer) is recommended. Shooting in excess of these distances should not be attempted. Where the use of a shotgun has been authorised by the Commission, shooting should not exceed a distance of 25 metres for all species.

4.10 Only vehicles that are suitable for the terrain should be used.

4.11 Operators should observe all safety precautions relating to the use of vehicles, firearms and deer welfare.

4.12 Where possible, any person likely to be in the vicinity of the operation should be notified and requested to keep clear of the area.

4.13 General precautions in the interest of public safety on the discharge of firearms include warning neighbouring occupiers, the police and shooting away from roads, houses, gardens and livestock.

Code Of Practice For Shooting Deer At Night

Prepared and published by the Deer Commission for Scotland in pursuance of Section 37(5)(a) of the Deer (Scotland) Act 1996. Further guidance on shooting deer at night is available from The Deer Commission for Scotland or at www.dcs.gov.uk.

Any person issued with a night shooting authorisation is obliged to comply with this Code of Practice. Failure to do so can result in an authorisation being withdrawn.

1. INTRODUCTION

The Deer (Scotland) Act 1996 restricts the shooting of deer at night to those people with written authorisation from the Deer Commission for Scotland. The statutory definition is the period between the expiration of the first hour after sunset and the commencement of the last hour before sunrise.

The Commission may authorise an occupier of agricultural land or of woodland or any person nominated in writing by such an occupier, to shoot at night, any species of deer for the purpose of crop protection if such a person is considered fit and competent. The Commission must also be satisfied that night shooting is necessary to prevent serious damage and that no other method of control, which might reasonably be adopted, would be adequate. Authorisations are subject to such conditions as may be specified, including the precise area to be covered and the Commission will determine the period of its validity.

If requested by the owner of the land, an occupier is obliged to supply, as soon as practicable after being requested to do so by the owner, information as to the numbers of deer of each species killed under such authorisations within the period of 12 months immediately preceding the date of request.

Firearms safety, the humane dispatch and welfare of deer are paramount in the issue of night shooting Authorisations and must be the overriding considerations of operators.

2. COMPLIANCE WITH THE FOLLOWING CONDITIONS IS OBLIGATORY

Night shooting Authorisations issued by the Commission contain the following obligatory conditions and will only be valid if these conditions are adhered to:

(1)   The local police must always be informed prior to night shooting being carried out.

(2)   For the killing of RED, SIKA, RED/SIKA CROSSES AND FALLOW DEER, a rifle of a calibre capable of firing ammunition of not less than 8.42 grams (130 grain) soft-nosed bullets, with a muzzle velocity of not less than 746.76 metres (2,450 feet) per second and a muzzle energy of not less than 3,051 joules (2,250 foot/pounds), must be used.

(3)   For the killing of ROE DEER a rifle of a calibre capable of firing ammunition of not less than 6.48 grams (100 grain) soft-nosed bullets, with a muzzle velocity of not less than 746.76 metres (2,450 feet) per second and a muzzle energy of not less than 2,373 joules (1,750 foot/pounds), must be used.

(4)   Where the use of a shotgun is authorised by the Deer Commission the bore and type of ammunition to be used will be specified in the Authorisation.

(5)   Authorisations must be returned to the Commission within 7 days of the date of expiry and include all details of the number and sex of deer killed.

3. RECOMMENDED OPERATING TEAM AND EQUIPMENT

For health and safety and animal welfare reasons the Commission recommends a minimum number of 2 operators when shooting at night.

However, the ideal crew for night operations should be: driver, light-operator and marksman. The duties of each person are:

Driver	To position the vehicle on instructions of the light-operator and to confirm the location of fallen animals.
Light-operator	To locate and select the most suitable targets and keep count of kills.
Marksman	To discharge the shot.

Whilst two people can operate successfully, a third makes the operation safer and more efficient. Where a vehicle is not used, an independent light-operator is essential.

Telescopic Sights	Should be not less than 4 x 36. The use of light-intensifying, heat sensitive or other special sighting devices is prohibited under Section 5 of The Deer (Firearms etc.) (Scotland) Order 1985.
Binoculars	7 or 8 x 50.
Spotlights	Operated from the vehicle battery, should be at least 250,000 candle power.
Hand-lights	12 volt 55 watt halogen bulb operated from a rechargeable power pack. Hand torches for carcase recovery are helpful.
Dogs	The use of a trained dog for carcase recovery is recommended, particularly in woodland.

4. GUIDANCE AND GOOD PRACTICE

Before night shooting takes place operators must make themselves thoroughly familiar with the location where shooting is to be carried out and, where possible, neighbouring occupiers should be informed. Shooting should only be carried out in areas where there are suitable backstops. Particular attention must be paid to human habitation, roads, railways, footpaths and livestock.

Deer must be fully visible and clear of obstructions such as tree branches or foliage before a shot is attempted. The recommended distance is under 1OOm and the target area is the shoulder. Head or neck shots should not be attempted.

The provisions of Section 20(1)(a) of the Deer (Scotland) Act 1996 make it illegal to shoot deer from a moving vehicle. A vehicle bonnet or a roof hatch can, however, provide a platform for marksmen to gain accurate shots. Modern swivel type bipods can be advantageous. Shots should never be taken by stretching across the driver or passenger or across the roof of a vehicle because of the risk of someone emerging from the opposite door or simply walking unseen in front of the rifle. The use of an externally mounted shooting rail can enhance the efficiency of night shooting. Communication between the marksman and cab crew is essential and no person should step outside the vehicle unless given the all clear by the marksman.

In circumstances where it is unsafe to discharge a high velocity rifle, the Commission may authorise the use of a shotgun but will stipulate the bore and type of ammunition to be used.

All normal safety precautions relating to the use of firearms must be strictly observed.

Spotlighting is particularly effective for dealing with small groups of deer. Larger groups should be avoided as survivors may quickly associate danger with a bright light.

A first aid kit should always be carried and portable communication equipment is recommended. Details of location and expected time of return should be given to a third party.

CHAPTER 4

Crop Protection

Whilst deer stalking is important economically and socially, the regulation of deer numbers is now considered essential for many environmental reasons, including successful forestry and the welfare of the deer themselves. There will always be potential conflict where deer encroach on cultivated lands and need to be culled to protect crops.

Whilst the law can be an ass at times the legislators often have good reason for prohibiting certain activities, especially when they involve firearms with the potential for either a risk to public safety or unnecessary suffering to animals – the use of shotguns against deer, particularly roe, was once commonplace in some areas.

The economic implications of an expanding roe deer population was not realised in the early days – there was little protection for newly planted trees and deer-control policies were in their infancy. Deer management was often very crude. Roe were treated as vermin, just like the fox, and were dealt with in a similar manner, being driven to waiting guns and indiscriminately shot, often with shotguns. On many estates the fox and deer drives kept the roe in check, but the dreadful statistics told their own stories: a 20 per cent rate of kills to cartridges was considered above average. As a consequence many deer were left to die a painfully slow death. A few stalkers and deer managers, knowing the value of humane and selective culling, did much to educate those responsible to the more professional use of the rifle.

The change was incorporated into the legislation which now governs the choice of weapon to shoot deer: in England and Wales Schedule 2 of the Deer Act, 1991; in Northern Ireland the Wildlife (Northern Ireland) Order, 1985; and in Scotland the Deer (Firearms etc.) (Scotland) Order, 1985. The fundamental difference is that in England, Wales and Northern Ireland it is the calibre of the rifle that is the main criterion, while in Scotland it is the ammunition only – it is lawful to use any rifle capable of firing such ammunition. This is why the 22 centrefire, provided the energy requirements are met, is permitted against roe in Scotland but not in England.[45]

This situation is not ideal, especially for the stalker operating on both sides of the border.

ENGLAND AND WALES

The Deer Act, 1991, provides for the taking of deer in certain situations during the close season for the purposes of crop protection. It also allows for the conditional use of shotguns at any time.

Section 7(1) allows an authorised person (see below) to shoot deer out of season on cultivated land, pasture or enclosed woodland provided that the conditions in section 7(3) apply. These are:

(a)   Deer of the **same species** are causing or had caused damage to crops, vegetables, fruit, growing timber or any other form of property on the land;

(b)   It is likely that further serious damage would be caused; and

(c)   Action was necessary to prevent it.

Although the Act does not define the meaning of crops, the scope appears to be very wide. This exception specifies crops, fruit and vegetables, but it may be possible to justify a case to include pasture especially when used for grazing. The term 'growing timber' implies any form of woodland or forestry, be it wild, managed or commercial. Areas of waste land or set-aside are unlikely to be classed as crops but it could be argued that they come under the term 'or any other form of property on the land'.

In most circumstances it is expected that a rifle meeting the require-

---

45. See chapter 6 for more on firearms.

ments for deer control would be used. However there are further exceptions for authorised persons to use smooth-bore guns (shotguns) at any time of year.

Under section 7(2) an authorised person can also control any deer, on any land, at any time with a shotgun which is not less than a 12-bore and is loaded with either AAA shot or a single non-spherical bullet, not less than 350 grains (i.e. a rifled slug). A Firearm Certificate is required for the slug ammunition but not AAA. The authorised person must be able to show that the conditions under section 7(3) above apply.

An authorised person is:

(a) the occupier of land on which the action is taken;
(b) a resident member of the occupier's household authorised in writing by the occupier;
(c) a person in the occupier's service [e.g. an employee] authorised in writing by the occupier; or
(d) a person having the right to take or kill the deer on the land on which the action is taken or any person acting with the written authority of a person having that right [e.g. the shooting tenant or person authorised by him].

Where an authorised person takes action against marauding deer to protect his crops etc., the killing must take place on the land where the damage is occurring, not the land where the deer come from.

In the case of Traill v. Buckingham 1972, damage was being caused to crops on Buckingham's land. It was believed that the deer responsible were to be found in a wood adjoining his, but occupied by Traill. The wood had previously belonged to Buckingham's father, who sold it but retained the right to shoot deer and other animals in the wood. During the close season Buckingham entered the wood and shot a red hind. Although found not guilty of killing out of season at the magistrate's court, the Queen's Bench Division decided otherwise, on the basis that although he had the shooting rights in the wood, under the Deer Act, 1963, he was only entitled to deal with marauding deer on land where the damage was caused and not on adjoining land.

In this case the retention of shooting rights in the contract by Buckingham did not make him an occupier of his neighbour's wood or a person with the written authority of the occupier, who would be entitled to kill deer in the wood causing damage to the trees.

Sale of venison out of season

Sale out of season is allowed provided the deer are lawfully killed.

SCOTLAND

The situation in Scotland is significantly different. The Deer Commission is empowered by the Deer (Scotland) Act, 1996, to advise landowners and occupiers on the conservation of land and the natural heritage. In severe cases the Deer Commission can require action to be taken and employ its own staff to carry out control measures.[46]

Under the Deer (Scotland) Act, 1996, it is lawful for a person to take or kill, and sell or dispose of, any deer found on:

1. arable land, improved permanent pasture (other than moorland) and land which has been regenerated so as to be able to make a significant contribution to the productivity of a holding which forms part of that agricultural land; or
2. enclosed woodland

where the occupier has reasonable ground for believing that serious damage will be caused to crops, pasture or human or animal food-stuffs on that agricultural land, or to that woodland, if the deer are not killed.

The action can be taken by the occupier or the following, authorised in writing by the occupier:

- the owner in person
- the owner's employees

46. See chapter 3.

- the occupier's employees
- any person normally resident on the land
- any other competent person approved in writing by the Deer Commission

As we saw in chapter 3, it is conceivable that a particular nominee might be competent to kill deer on the occupier's land if he lawfully held the required firearm for the purpose, but he might be considered unfit or unsuitable for the purpose by the Commission – for example, a novice deer manager without appropriate experience of culling deer.

Woodland in this context means not just commercial forestry plantations but any land on which trees are grown, any such trees and also the vegetation amongst the trees on that land. A woodland is enclosed if it is surrounded by stock-proof, but not necessarily deer-proof, fencing or other barriers.

Serious damage is difficult to define but a Best Practice Guide-Definition & Methodologies for Assessment is now available from the Deer Commission. It can be qualified in turnip fields, developing corn fields and silage fields but damage to permanent grassland is more difficult to assess. Damage to woodlands at different stages of woodland growth is quantifiable, e.g. browsing of leading shoots and bark stripping. Along with Scottish Natural Heritage the Commission is investigating methods for assessing damage to habitats and the significance of damage. In some communities browsing is beneficial in allowing species diversity.

Nothing contained in an agreement between an occupier and the owner of the land shall prohibit the above lawfully conducted control. However if the landowner or owner of the sporting rights believes that no damage is occurring or likely to occur they can challenge the actions or intentions of the tenant in court (section 26(3)).

Deer may be taken during the close season for reasons other than crop damage but only if such activities are authorised in writing by the Commission.

The Act does not cater for the use of shotguns but the Deer (Firearms etc.) Order, 1985, permits the persons listed above to use specified shotguns and ammunition for crop control as stated above. The shotgun must be not less than 12 gauge loaded with:

- for shooting any deer, a single rifled non-spherical slug not less than 380 grains or a cartridge loaded with SSG or larger
- for roe deer, a cartridge loaded with AAA or larger

Sale out of season

Sale out of season is allowed provided the deer are lawfully killed.

NORTHERN IRELAND

Article 20(6) allows a person to kill or injure deer in the close season by shooting deer on cultivated land, enclosed pasture, enclosed woodland or garden grounds but that person must be able to satisfy a court:

(a)   that he is an authorised person; and
(b)   that he had reasonable grounds for believing that deer of the same species were causing, or had caused, serious damage to crops, pasture, vegetables, fruit, growing timber or any other form of property on that land, pasture, woodland or those grounds; and
(c)   that there was likelihood of further damage and that such damage was likely to be serious; and
(d)   that his action was necessary to prevent further damage.

An authorised person is:

- the occupier of the land on which the action is taken
- a resident member of his household authorised in writing by the occupier
- a person in his service (e.g. an employee) authorised in writing by the occupier
- any person having the right to take or kill the deer or a person authorised in writing by him (e.g. the shooting tenant, his gamekeeper and invited guns)

Under article 20(7), if deer are causing damage within the conditions specified in Article 20(6)(a) to (d) above an authorised person may use a smooth-bore gun to kill the deer on any such land, at any time, if it is not less than a 12-bore and is loaded with AAA shot or a single non-spherical bullet, not less than 22.68 grammes (350 grains), commonly known as a rifled slug.

Sale out of season

The requirements are the same as for England and Wales.

COMPENSATION

Domestic livestock are capable of trespass and it is possible to make a claim against the owner for the damage they cause under the Animals Act, 1971, or Animals (Scotland) Act, 1971. The position with wild animals is different, since they have no owner to make claims against.

Historically the tenant farmer on a sporting estate could only stand and watch as his master's quarry ravaged his crops. In 1880 the Ground Game Act eased the situation by granting tenants the right to take hares and rabbits – a right which could not be taken from or even signed away by the tenant in a contract.

The Deer (Scotland) Act, 1996, introduced a similar provision regarding deer. Under section 26(3) an occupier effectively has a concurrent right to take or kill deer for crop protection purposes in the circumstances described earlier. The section states that nothing contained in any agreement between an occupier of agricultural land (not moorland) or enclosed woodland and the owner shall prohibit the occupier from taking or killing deer to prevent serious crop damage. This provision would not prevent the occupier from also claiming compensation, but in practical terms it does give him lawful authority to protect his livelihood.

In England and Wales the law does not confer on the occupier the rights to take deer in this situation unless by agreement with the landowner or the person holding the sporting rights to the deer. In circumstances where the tenant of an agricultural holding suffers crop damage from deer and is restricted from culling them – i.e. the rights are vested in the owner or someone else and no written permission exists – a claim for compensation can be made under the Agricultural Holdings Act, 1986, or in Scotland the Agricultural Holdings (Scotland) Act, 1991.

To claim compensation, a tenant must give his landlord written notice within one month of the damage becoming evident and give him the opportunity to make an inspection of a growing crop before it is harvested or, if damaged after harvest, before it is removed from the land. A written notice of the claim is then sent to the landlord within one month after the expiry of the year in respect of which the claim is made. For the purposes of such a claim, a year normally ends on 29 September or another date agreed with the landlord. Where the shooting rights are held by a third person (e.g. a shooting tenant or syndicate), the landlord is entitled to be indemnified by the third party against such claims, which may be settled by arbitration under the Act.

RESTRICTION ON USE OF LEAD SHOT

The Environmental Protection (Restriction on Use of Lead Shot) (England) Regulations, 1999, [amended in 2002] and the Environmental Protection (Restriction on Use of Lead Shot) (Wales) Regulations 2002.

The Regulations seek to prevent the poisoning of wildfowl by ingestion of lead shot through feeding. Consequently the use of lead shot is now prohibited over land where waterfowl feed and over certain Sites of Special Scientific Interest (SSSIs) listed in the Regulations.

Although this will not impact on the use of a stalker's rifle (section 1 firearms) it will apply to the use of shotguns where permitted for crop protection on any area where shot is likely to fall on or over the foreshore or any of the listed SSSIs in England and Wales.

In Scotland the use of lead shot anywhere over a wetland is prohibited including pest control and clay pigeon shooting.

Prohibition on use of cartridges containing lead shot

England and Wales

> No person shall use lead shot for the purpose of shooting with a shotgun
> (a)   on or over any area below high-water mark of ordinary spring tides;
> (b)   on or over any site of special scientific interest included in Schedule 1 to these Regulations; or
> (c)   any wild bird included in Schedule 2 to these Regulations [as amended] i.e. any species of duck or goose, coot and moorhen

Scotland

The Environmental Protection (Restriction on Use of Lead Shot) (Scotland) (No. 2) Regulations 2004

No person shall use lead shot for the purpose of shooting with a shotgun on or over wetlands.

A wetland is defined under the Ramsar Convention as areas of marsh, fen, peatland or water whether natural or artificial, permanent or temporary, with water that is static or flowing, fresh, brackish or salt, including areas of marine water the depth of which at low tide does not exceed six metres.

The Regulations grant powers to police officers and other persons 'authorised' by the Secretary of State.

Several scenarios spring to mind:

- A police officer may investigate a case where a shotgun has been used under the exemption for crop protection. If the area in question is on or adjacent to the foreshore or a listed SSSI enquiries may be made in respect of the type of shot used.
- A police officer inspecting a game dealer's premises might come across deer carcases containing shot and ask questions about the shooter.
- A warrant could be obtained to enter and examine premises if access is refused, for example an estate larder. An investigation could be quite wide and extend, for example to the examination of purchase records.

CHAPTER 5

Food Safety and Dealing in Venison

This chapter covers the requirements of the Deer Acts, relevant legislation and guidance concerning food hygiene, animal by-products and food waste together with guidance issued by the Food Standards Agency (FSA).

HYGIENE AND HANDLING OF VENISON

Development of Legislation and Guidance

In 2004, the European Parliament passed legislation designed to improve food safety. The following regulations are relevant across the EU; Regulation (EC) No 178/2002, Regulation (EC) No 852/2004, Regulation (EC) No 853/2004 and have been implemented in England, Wales, Scotland and Northern Ireland by the following:

Food Hygiene (England) Regulations 2006
Food Hygiene (Scotland) Regulations 2006

Food Hygiene (Wales) Regulations 2006
Food Hygiene (Northern Ireland) Regulations 2006

The Regulations apply to all types of food including venison, game and any other wildlife carcase entering the food chain. Wild deer and feral wild boar are classified as large wild game and therefore come within the scope of the Regulations. However a distinction is made in the Regulations between wild and farmed deer.

The Food Standards Agency, following consultation with interested bodies have produced a draft entitled 'The Wild Game Guide (2008)'. Much of the following information is produced from this guide. The guide itself provides a number of practical scenarios relevant to deer stalking and the supply of wild deer carcases which readers may find useful.

There is a separate Food Standards Agency guide to the food hygiene and other Regulations for the meat industry (2007). This guide is relevant to those who buy in wild deer that are shot by others and produce meat from it.

Legislation in respect of food standards is complex and no doubt will be subject to change in the future. Deer stalkers are advised therefore to refer, not only to the Regulations themselves, but any current updates or amendments to the Wild Game Guide. In addition, professional advice may be sought from a number of sources including your Local Authority Environmental Health Department.

Scope of the EC Regulations :

Regulation (EC) number 178/2002 lays down the general principles and requirements of food law and procedures in matters of food safety, including traceability of food, feed and food producing animals.

Regulation (EC) number 852/2004, also known as H1 provides general hygiene rules applying to all food businesses.

Regulation (EC) number 853/2004 also known as H2 provides additional hygiene rules applying to businesses producing food of animal origin. Section IV of annex III of this Regulation covers wild game supplied to and processed in approved game handling establishments (AGHEs).

The Regulatory Reform (Game) Order, 2007, amended the Game Act 1831, Deer Act 1991 and the Game Licences Act 1860. They removed the restriction in England and Wales on dealing in venison during the closed season by allowing anyone to sell venison all year round, provided the deer was lawfully killed. Hitherto, the sale of venison to the public was restricted to licensed game dealers only. Also removed is the requirement to keep records under Section 11 of The Deer Act 1991 relating to the sale and purchase of venison. However, records will have to be kept to the level specified in EC Regulation 178/2002, commensurate with the size and nature of your activities as referred to later.

The game licence and venison dealing legislation remains unchanged in Scotland.

LEGAL REQUIREMENTS

There will be circumstances where as a deer stalker handling deer carcases you may have to satisfy certain requirements and qualifications to comply with the law. There will also be situations where you will need to become registered as a food business operator (FBO). However, a number of legal exemptions apply dependent upon the scale of activities and to whom the venison is supplied.

You may find the following brief statements helpful prior to gaining a more in depth knowledge of the subject :

- Everyone must exercise 'due diligence' when involved in handling deer carcases intended for human consumption
- AGHE means an Approved Game Meat Establishment
- FBO means a Food Business Operator
- You do not have to be a 'trained hunter' if the venison is for your own consumption or you supply only small quantities of deer to final consumers
- Trained Hunter presence and subsequent declaration is required in cases where deer carcases are sent to AGHEs
- AGHEs should refuse to accept any deer carcase without an accompanying trained hunter declaration
- If a trained hunter is unexpectedly absent and no declaration made the head and viscera must accompany the carcase to the AGHE suitably labelled
- 'Large Wild Game' includes Deer and Wild Boar
- Deer should be bled and gralloched (stomach and intestines removed) as soon as possible after shooting
- If you supply AGHEs from your larder you are required to register as a food business operator [FBO] with the local authority
- Special provisions exist in relation to wild boar carcases the meat from which may enter the food chain
- European law on food safety is now in force

- Wild deer are, in most circumstances, exempt from the animal by-products legislation
- If you skin and prepare meat from a carcase for regular supply to others you are required to register as a food business with your local authority.

DEFINITION OF WILD GAME

The requirements applicable to food businesses supplying game for human consumption are dependent upon whether the game dealt with is considered to be wild or farmed. Regulation EC number 853/2004 annex I defines wild game as – wild ungulates and lago-morphs, as well as other land mammals that are hunted for human consumption and are considered to be wild under the applicable law in the member state concerned, including mammals living in enclosed territory under conditions of freedom similar to those of wild game. Wild ungulates are hooved animals – mainly deer in the UK but also wild boar.

The definition states that animals, in this case deer, living in an enclosure does not prevent them from being classified as being wild. The decision as to whether an animal is wild or farmed should be determined with reference to the conditions and the circumstances in which deer live. Each operation should be judged on its own merits and the following issues should be considered.

- There should be sufficient room for the herd to roam naturally.
- The herd should be self-maintaining. Numbers should be kept up through natural reproduction from animals within the herd. (If culled deer are replaced with deer brought in from outside, then the herd would not be considered as living in conditions of freedom similar to those of wild game.)

Method of taking from the wild

Wild deer must have been killed by hunting, if it is to be supplied for human consumption. If a deer is killed in a road accident the carcase cannot be legally transferred into the food chain.

Private consumption and the 'hunter exemption'

If you only shoot a small quantity of deer for your own private consumption which includes selling to private individuals, then you are not affected by the EC Food Hygiene legislation, as you would not be classed as a food business. What constitutes a 'small quantity' is to be 'self-defining'. Consultations with interested parties in the past have failed to produce agreement on placing any figure on an upper limit. Clearly if this exemption were to be abused by an undertaking of a more organised set of activities perhaps involving considerable numbers of deer, you may be deemed to be running a food business and therefore the Regulations would apply.

The EC Food Hygiene Regulations allow for private domestic consumption to include the occasional supply to others, of food you have prepared at home. This is known as the 'hunter exemption'. The majority of recreational stalkers and many professional stalkers will fall into the category of shooting what may be viewed as a small quantity, and selling the carcases in the fur to private individuals (final consumers), butchers, restaurants etc.

In these circumstances they need not register as a food business but are responsible for supplying safe food under general food law. However, if you are operating a larder and supply only a small amount to an AGHE in addition to private individuals then you will need to register as a food business (FBO) with the local authority. Rules on traceability may be interpreted by your local authority as a need for your premises and/or vehicles to be registered so that action can be quickly taken in the event of a food incident.

If you process a deer carcase by skinning and preparing the meat prior to supply, then you are required to register as a food business because you are supplying prepared wild game meat. This applies even if the quantity is small. Premises will have to comply with the relevant requirements for their structure and hygienic operation (Regulation 852/2004). Requirements for Hazard Analysis and Critical Control Points (HACCP) and managing food risk and traceability will also apply.

The EC Food Hygiene Regulations allow pubs, restaurants and the like, to purchase such carcases, or venison from stalkers in small quantities. However they are advised to check with the local authority as to any amendments to their FBO registration. They will also need to meet the traceability requirements of Regulation 178/2002 and comply with the provisions of Regulation 852/2004. They are also likely to require a separate processing area for initial carcase preparation, e.g. skinning and evisceration.

PRIMARY PRODUCERS AND THE PRIMARY PRODUCER EXEMPTION

The EU food hygiene regulations regard shooting wild game – 'hunting' – for human consumption as a primary production activity.

So an individual who shoots game alone, a hunting party and an estate which organises shooting are all primary producers.

Primary products in the wild game sector are the products of hunting – i.e. in-fur and in-feather game that has undergone no more than any necessary preparation that is part of normal hunting practice. This does not have to be done 'in the field', but can be done in game larders.

PRIMARY PRODUCERS SUPPLYING AGHEs

Any primary producer supplying an approved game handling establishment (AGHE) must:

- ensure a trained person is present and completes relevant documentation;

[NB An AGHE is entitled to refuse to accept carcases where the bona fide involvement of a trained person (as set out in Regulation 853/2004) cannot be established, though there is provision in the Regulations where a trained person is unexpectedly unavailable.]

- be registered with the Local Authority under the registration of food businesses requirement;
- comply with the food business operator's responsibilities, including both the general hygiene provisions for primary production in Regulation 852/2004 and the specific provisions for the initial handling of large/small wild game in Regulation 853/2004 when it is subsequently supplied to an AGHE;
- meet the traceability requirements of Regulation 178/2002.

PRIMARY PRODUCER EXEMPTION

When primary producers are not supplying AGHEs, there is an exemption from the above rules when supply is in small quantities. However, this is only when in-fur/in-feather carcases are supplied direct to the final consumer and/or to local retailers directly supplying the final consumer.

In the UK these terms are currently being interpreted as follows:

- Small quantities are now regarded as self-defining because demand for in-fur/in-feather carcases from final consumers and local retailers is limited.
- Local is within the supplying establishment's own county plus the greater of either the neighbouring county or counties or 50 km/30

miles from the boundary of the supplying establishment's county.

- Direct supply to the final consumer is not restricted by what is local. An individual or an estate can supply final consumers who order from them via the internet/mail order as well as those who collect themselves.

Declaration by trained hunters

A numbered declaration must be attached by the 'trained person' to each deer carcase stating that following an examination the animal has been found to be free of any abnormal characteristics, abnormal behaviour or environmental contamination. If there is evidence of abnormalities, but the carcase is still being submitted to the AGHE, then the abnormalities should be indicated by the trained person. The declaration form or tag, can be used for this purpose and the information recorded. The declaration statement should be struck out. In all cases the date, time and place of killing should be indicated. (See specimen form reproduced later.)

QUALIFICATIONS AND TRAINING FOR TRAINED HUNTER STATUS

TRAINING OF HUNTERS IN HEALTH AND HYGIENE

The Regulations require that persons who hunt wild game with a view to placing it on the market for human consumption must have sufficient knowledge of the pathology of wild game, and of the production and handling of wild game and wild game meat after hunting, to undertake an initial examination of wild game on the spot.

It is however enough if at least one person of a hunting team has the knowledge referred to above.

The trained person could also be the gamekeeper or the game manager if he or she is part of the hunting team or located in the immediate vicinity of where hunting is taking place. In the latter case, the hunter must present the wild game to the gamekeeper or game manager and inform them of any abnormal behaviour observed before killing.

Training must be provided to the satisfaction of the competent authority [FSA in the UK] to enable hunters to become trained persons. The Food Standards Agency recommends that all hunters undertake training. It should cover at least the following subjects:

(a)   the normal anatomy, physiology and behaviour of wild game;

(b)   abnormal behaviour and pathological changes in wild game due to diseases, environmental contamination or other factors which may affect human health after consumption;

(c)   the hygiene rules and proper techniques for the handling, transportation, evisceration, etc. of wild game animals after killing; and

(d)   legislation and administrative provisions on the animal and public health and hygiene conditions governing the placing on the market of wild game.

The competent authority should encourage hunters' organisations to provide such training – as can be seen below.

Hunter and industry-based training and assessment

If you are an experienced gamekeeper and/or a member of the National Gamekeepers' Organisation (NGO) with experience then you can attend one of the courses being run by the NGO. These courses will introduce you to the requirements of Regulation 853/2004 and will provide you with practical solutions to help meet the needs of the new legislation. At the end of the training you will undergo an end-of-course assessment and, providing you achieve the required mark, you will be issued with an NGO certificate to prove your competence.

If you are based in Scotland you should contact the Scottish Gamekeepers Association or the British Association for Shooting and Conservation.

Vocationally Related Qualification (VRQ) Wild Game Meat Hygiene training and assessment

This newly developed, nationally recognised qualification has been developed by Lantra (the Sector Skills Council) to support the needs of the new legislation. It is currently being offered via a number of different training organisations around the UK including BASC and many land-based training providers and agricultural colleges. The training offered by these organisations introduces you to the needs of the new legislation and prepares you for your VRQ assessment. The assessment is based on a multiple-choice question paper. It is a modular assessment and leads to a certificate in Wild Game Meat Hygiene endorsed as large game, small game or both, according to the papers taken. Certification is offered via one of two national awarding bodies, Lantra Awards or the Royal Society for the Promotion of Health (RSPH).

Deer management training and assessment

Those who wish to start deer-stalking are likely to undertake the DSC Level 1 Certificate. From December 2005 the requirements of Regulation 853/2004 became an integral part of the DSC Level 1, so the certificate will provide proof of the knowledge required.

Management of food risks

Management of food risk in the wild game industry begins with the individual hunter. He/she should always be on the lookout for abnormal behaviour before killing and the scope for environmental contamination as well as any abnormalities found after killing.

The trained person needs sufficient knowledge and skill to identify abnormal characteristics that may indicate that the meat presents a health risk.

Where there is a requirement for a trained person to be present, it is still the responsibility of individual hunters to report abnormal behaviour before killing or suspected environmental contamination to the trained person. Individual 'untrained' hunters supplying direct to local retailers or to final consumers under the primary producer exemption or the hunter exemption, need to be particularly vigilant if they are not able to draw on the expertise of a trained person. Where wild game carcases are being supplied to approved game handling establishments (AGHEs) or where certain retail exemptions are being claimed there is a specific requirement for a trained person. If the trained person is unexpectedly unavailable, carcases can still be sent to the AGHE but, in the case of large wild game, certain viscera that a trained person would remove must now accompany it (see below for details).

TRANSPORT OF CARCASES

You should prevent avoidable contamination and deterioration of carcases during transport. Vehicles should be kept clean and where necessary disinfected after use. This will go some way to demonstrate 'due diligence' under food safety legislation. You should ensure the cold chain is maintained and chilling should start within a reasonable time frame to achieve a temperature through the meat of no more than 7 C.

Active chilling in the game larder, and the use of refrigerated vehicles to transport game from the larder to the approved game handling establishment, will be necessary to manage food risks.

However, the regulation provides for: 'where climatic conditions so permit, active chilling is not necessary'. In the UK active chilling is likely to be necessary except for the very coldest times of the year and where storage and delivery times are short.

Active chilling should begin in the game larder if some time is likely to elapse before shot game reaches the game-handling establishment. You should take care not to 'heap' carcases on top of one another at any time, particularly during transport.

If delivering to an AGHE is only occasional (as opposed to supplying to a private individual/final consumer – referred to earlier under the hunter exemption) it is unlikely that the local authority would want to register you or your vehicle formally. Remember you may only supply to an AGHE if the carcase is accompanied by the 'trained hunter' declaration. Where carcases are transported to AGHEs on a more regular basis and the journey prolonged refrigerated transport will be required together with registration with the local authority.

It is accepted that dogs are often used in deer stalking activities and ponies used in Scotland to transport shot deer off the hill. However, care should be taken to guard against contamination from other animals or pests. The latter point being relevant where deer are shot in isolated areas and not immediately removed.

Deer or wild boar carcases must not be frozen before skinning. Transport operators should check that game is chilled (and not frozen) when collected from the primary producer and when delivered to the AGHE.

DEER LARDERS

Deer larders especially if equipped with a chiller enable carcases to be stored in compliance with food safety legislation and guidance by preventing contamination and maintaining the cold chain.

Larders generally used to store deer carcases in the fur including necessary carcase preparation as part of normal stalking practice are governed by the EU regulations. This is classed as a primary production activity. It should be noted if you operate a larder and supply some of the carcases to an AGHE you are required to register with the Local Authority as a Food Business Operator [FBO].

The use of your game larder for:
- any necessary carcase preparation that is part of normal hunting practice (because it is often preferable to do this at the game larder rather than in the field); and/or
- storage of in-fur or in-feather game...

is permitted by the EU regulations under 'storage and handling of primary products at the place of production' and 'facilities used in connection with primary production'.

Where approved game handling establishments (AGHEs) are being supplied and initial evisceration and removal of head and lower legs, etc. of deer is carried out at the game larder rather than in the field, the trained person needs to be present at the game larder. This also applies in the retail-to-retail exemption (see retail exemptions).

If a deer is shot and a trained person is unable to do the examination, it can only be sent to an AGHE in exceptional circumstances. For example, a trained person was unavailable due to something unforeseen. In such cases the head and viscera (except for the stomach and intestines) must be sent with the body (suitably labelled if already removed) to the operator of the approved game handling establishment (AGHE), so that a full post-mortem inspection can be carried out by the official veterinarian

If you carry out plucking, skinning or further preparation of game meat these processes go beyond primary production. The EU food hygiene regulations require these processes to be carried out in approved game handling establishments (AGHEs) unless:

- the person doing the plucking/skinning or further preparation was a member of the hunting party (see hunter exemption); or
- the operator of the game larder qualifies for retail exemptions.

If you operate a deer/game larder you should :

- make sure the larder has sufficient capacity to cater hygienically for your maximum production;
- make sure game is protected against contamination, including from animals and pests;
- keep the larder clean and, where necessary after cleaning, disinfect it in an appropriate manner;
- use clean or potable water to prevent contamination;
- prevent the introduction and spread of contagious diseases

transmissible to humans through food and report the suspicion of such diseases to the competent authority;

- ensure people handling game and game meat are in good health and undergo training in health risks;
- store and handle waste and hazardous substances so as to prevent contamination;
- ensure the cold chain is maintained.
- Chillers should be of an appropriate size, structure and layout in line with the operational requirements of the business. Please consult your local Environmental Health Officer before commissioning the installation of a chiller.
- Do not keep skin-on and skinned carcases in close proximity inside the chiller. You should ensure carcases are effectively separated to avoid contamination even if skinned carcases are wrapped in protective food safe material.

Even if you are exempt from Regulation 852/2004 (by supplying game for private domestic consumption or under the primary producer's exemption) the installation of a deer larder equipped with chiller together with adherence to the above recommendations will significantly reduce food risk. This will also indicate 'due diligence' within the meaning of the Food Safety Act 1990.

Deer stalkers/managers should always ensure they are operating in line with the latest guidance. Best practice guides are now available on the internet from the Deer Initiative and Deer Commission for Scotland covering hygiene, gralloch, larders, carcase handling, butchering, inspection, health, parasites and diseases.

The Wild Game Guide is also available from the FSA but it will be the local authority inspectors who will enforce the legislation, guidance and good practice.

NOTIFIABLE DISEASES

Any notifiable disease must be immediately reported to the Police, DEFRA Divisional Veterinary Officer (in Scotland the Scottish Office Agriculture, Environment and Fisheries Department), the Animal Health Inspector and, in the case of Anthrax, the Consultant in Communicable Disease Control (formerly the Medical Officer for Environmental Health).

The following diseases are notifiable:

Deer	Wild boar
Bluetongue	Foot and Mouth Disease
Warble Fly	Classical Swine Fever
Bovine Tuberculosis	African Swine Fever
Foot and Mouth Disease	Swine Vesicular Disease
Epizootic Haemorrhagic Virus	Anthrax
Anthrax	

The Food Standards Agency has introduced voluntary Trichinella testing of feral wild boar as part of its monitoring scheme for Trichinella in the UK. Regulation (EC) 854/2004 requires Member States to carry out Trichinella testing on all animals susceptible to Trichinellosis. The Agency is seeking to have GB recognised as Trichinella free, and thus to be exempted from the requirement to test all slaughtered pigs. However, even if this action is successful, it will be necessary to carry out surveillance for Trichinella in feral wild boar in order to demonstrate continuing country freedom. To enable feral wild boar to be tested the Agency will rely on voluntary testing by hunters. This will involve hunters carrying out Trichinella sampling of feral wild boar that has been shot and sending the sample to an appropriate laboratory for testing. All expenses associated with the taking of samples will be paid for by the Agency. This means that the sampling kit, the cost of posting the sample together with the cost of the testing will be paid for by the Agency.

If you wish to take part in the scheme please telephone 0207 276 8377 or alternatively send an e-mail to WildGameGuidance@food-standards.gsi.gov.uk

DISPOSAL OF GRALLOCH AND ANIMAL BY-PRODUCTS

The process of producing venison from healthy wild deer culled in the open countryside involves a number of processes from which by-products result. Historically some confusion has existed over the legal requirements and what is best practice in relation to the disposal of by-products and food waste arising from the culling of wild deer. The following legislation is relevant :

The Animal By-Products Regulations, 2005 (ABPR)
The Waste Framework Directive, 2001, adopted in 2003
Regulation (EC) No. 852/2002

The Animal By-Product Regulations prohibit the routine or adhoc burying or burning of animal carcases. However the carcases of all wild animals are exempt from the scope of the regulations with two exceptions :

- those suspected of being infected with a disease communicable to humans or animals
- deer whose bodies or parts of bodies are used to produce game trophies.

Carcases or parts of carcases suspected of carrying disease as referred to above must be disposed of in accordance with the appropriate regulations.

It is contended that deer shot in the U.K. are shot primarily for their venison as part of deer management plans. Consequently where a deer is processed in line with FSA guidance as venison for human consumption the retention of a trophy head should not bring the carcase or the head within the scope of the ABPR.

Currently the ABP Regulations are only applied to approved premises, i.e. Approved Game Handling Establishments (AGHEs). Farmed deer are covered by the regulations which do not define wild deer. Proposed amendments in the future may bring wild deer into the scope of the regulations in circumstances where they are sold to AGHEs or venison is privately produced by individual trained hunters. At the present time in situations where a considerable number of wild deer by-products are derived, with the exception of gralloch, incineration on site or removal by licensed carrier is recommended.

Wild deer viscera

Deer must be delivered as soon as possible after initial examination accompanied by whatever appropriate parts are required which should be identifiable to the relevant carcase. Provided a trained person's declaration is submitted with the deer carcase, the body need not be accompanied by the head and viscera. In the event of the carcase being submitted without a trained person's declaration (due to the trained person being unexpectedly unavailable), then the head and the heart, lungs and liver, but not the stomach and intestines, must accompany the body.

In respect of feral wild boar, a species susceptible to Trichinosis, the head [except tusks] and diaphragm must accompany the body, even if a trained person is submitting the carcase. The official veterinarian at the AGHE will conduct the Trichinella testing. See notifiable diseases on page 96.

Disposal of the gralloch

The disposal of the gralloch of a deer at the point of shot or nearby is thought to be currently acceptable practice unless of course public access or other unique circumstances dictate it to be more appropriate to remove it from the site e.g. disease is suspected following examination. Disposal of gralloch by leaving in the open at the site of shooting or nearby is increasingly seen as being environmentally beneficial in terms of recycling and feed for carrion and other omnivores.

The Environment Agency [EA] has a mechanism for exempting low-risk activities akin to much of the deer management situations in the U.K. and it is hoped that the current practice of gralloch being left at the point of shot or nearby will be confirmed as an exempt activity and the disposal of other general by-products by way of properly constructed burial pits be approved.

Food waste

The Waste Framework Directive outlines the conditions in which the disposal of waste should take place. Dependent on its category it may have to be subjected to burning, burial, bio-treatment or rendering.

The EC Regulation no 852-2004, Chapter VI, details the following provisions -

1. Food waste, non-edible by-products and other refuse are to be removed from rooms where food is present as quickly as possible, so as to avoid their accumulation.
2. Food waste, non-edible by-products and other refuse are to be deposited in closable containers, unless food business operators can

demonstrate to the competent authority that other types of containers or evacuation systems used are appropriate. These containers are to be of an appropriate construction, kept in sound condition, be easy to clean and, where necessary, to disinfect.

3. Adequate provision is to be made for the storage and disposal of food waste, non-edible by-products and other refuse. Refuse stores are to be designed and managed in such a way as to enable them to be kept clean and, where necessary, free of animals and pests.

4. All waste is to be eliminated in a hygienic and environmentally friendly way in accordance with Community legislation applicable to that effect, and is not to constitute a direct or indirect source of contamination.

CONTROLS ON VENISON DEALING

The laws applying to game dealing originated in the Game Act 1831. The Game Act 1970 introduced some amendments but the legislation did not cater for today's society or markets. The situation was resolved in England and Wales following a government review resulting in a Regulatory Reform Order in 2007 amending the Deer Act 1991 and the relevant Game Acts.

Previously the Game Act 1831 required dealers in game and venison to be licensed in England. Section 13 of the Game Licences Act 1860 extends the provisions to Wales and Scotland. Northern Ireland is covered by the Game Preservation Act (Northern Ireland) 1928, the Wildlife (Northern Ireland) Order 1985 and Miscellaneous Transferred Excise Duties Act (Northern Ireland) 1972. There were several loopholes in respect of game but the subsequent deer legislation included amendments on venison dealing which make the situation clearer.

In England and Wales the sale of venison to the public was restricted to licensed game dealers only. The 2007 Order removes the requirement to hold a local authority licence and an excise licence in order to deal in game or venison. The restrictions on dealing in game birds and venison during the close season are also removed. Game and venison can now be sold all year round provided that the animal in question was lawfully killed.

In Scotland licensed game dealers may only trade in game and persons wishing to trade in venison are subject to an additional licensing procedure under the Deer (Scotland) Act 1996.

Transactions between English and Scottish dealers may be made across the border, provided that they are recorded on the prescribed forms and that both parties are licensed in their own countries. In

Northern Ireland there is no restriction on lawfully imported venison other than recording the transactions.

Farmed deer and live sales

Generally the Deer Acts only apply to farmed deer in certain circumstances, for example killing out of season, method of killing and sale of carcases. Such matters are covered in chapters 2 and 3. Sales of live deer are not governed by the Acts but carcases and venison from any source, wild or farm, are subject to controls.

Sale and purchase: England and Wales

Venison

The Deer Act 1991 does not control the sale of live deer, only venison and carcases which are defined by Section 16. Farmed venison is governed by the controls on sale.

The term deer means any species and includes the carcase or any part of it: venison includes imported meat and means the carcase, or any edible part of the carcase, which has not been canned or cooked.

Section 10(3)(4) Deer Act 1991

It is also an offence for anyone to sell, possess for sale, purchase, offer to purchase or receive venison from any deer which he knows or believes has been illegally taken or killed under any preceding provisions of the Deer Act (close season or unlawful methods). Sell includes barter and exchange.

Forfeiture Section 13 Deer Act 1991

On conviction for any offence under the Act the court may order the forfeiture of any deer or venison found in the person's possession together with any vehicle, animal, weapon or other thing used to commit the offence.

In addition, if the offence is under sections 1 (poaching) or 10 (venison dealing) the court may cancel any firearm or shotgun certificate held by him.

Scotland

The Deer Scotland Act 1996 relates only to those species of deer defined in an Order made by the Secretary of State. But the sections of the Act controlling the sale of venison include all species and farmed venison. Venison is defined by section 33(7) as the carcase or any edible part of the carcase of a deer, and 'deer' means deer of any species, whether or not deer within the meaning of section 45 of this Act, and includes farmed venison.

Anyone wishing to trade in wild or farmed venison is required to be licensed under the Deer (Scotland) Act 1996. The Deer Commission also has a statutory role in the regulation and inspection of venison dealers. Such a body does not exist south of the border.

The licensing authority in Scotland is an Island or District Council and may grant a licence, valid for three years, to anyone it considers fit to deal in venison, under the Licensing of Venison Dealers (Application Procedures etc.) (Scotland) Order 1984.

The application can be made by an individual or by his agent involved in the day to day running of the business, perhaps the manager of one of his premises. Full names and addresses of the applicants are required. If the applicant is a company, details of the registered office, directors, partners, etc. are also needed. In both cases, the address of any premises used for handling the venison within the area of the authority must be included, together with any other information which may be additionally required by the authority.

Copies of an application for grant or renewal are sent to the local chief constable, fire authority and the Deer Commission. The authority may then make inquiries as to the suitability of the applicant and may take the results into account when considering the application; but where they intend to do so, the applicant must be notified and given the opportunity to reply.

The authority may refuse an application, but must give reasons for so doing. If a licence is granted or renewed, it may be subject to reasonable conditions which may include the inspection of venison.

Where a licence is not granted or renewed, the applicant may lodge an appeal to the Sheriff within 28 days. A person dealing only in venison does not require an excise licence. Issuing councils must supply details of licence holders to the Deer Commission, chief constable and fire authority.

Records

Section 34 of the Act requires the keeping of records and the Licensing of Venison Dealers (Prescribed Forms etc.) (Scotland) Order 1984 prescribes the format of records to be kept which must be in a book. This appears to prohibit the use of loose sheets which may be altered and replaced but the Deer Commission accepts computerised systems.

The dealer must enter in his record book forthwith full particulars of all his purchases and receipts of venison. Forthwith is not defined in the Act but the dictionary says 'immediately, at once, right away'

Where venison is purchased or received from another dealer, or from a dealer in England only the following details need to be recorded:

- That the venison was received,
- Name and address of the other dealer,
- The date purchased/received,
- The species of deer, provided it is possible to identify it,
- The number of carcases and sex of the venison – see page 106 on sexing of carcases.

All imports of venison from other countries need to be fully documented.

A police officer or a person authorised in writing by the Secretary of State or the Deer Commission, may inspect the records.

The dealer shall produce for inspection:
- the record book,
- any invoices and other documents which relate to the records,
- all venison in his possession or under his control, or
- venison on premises, or in vehicles under his control
- and allow copies or extracts from the record book or documents to be made.

The book must be retained for three years from the last entry and other documents for three years from the date of the entry relating to them.

Offences

Section 36 of the Deer (Scotland) Act 1996 contains a number of offences in relation to venison dealing:

Section 36 (1)
It is an offence to sell, offer for sale, possess or transport for the purpose of sale at any premises, any venison unless:

1. he is a licensed venison dealer, or
2. in possession or transporting for the purpose of selling to such a dealer (e.g. a stalker or landowner), or
3. has purchased the venison from a licensed dealer e.g. butcher.

A police officer could obtain a search warrant to enter unlicensed premises.

Unlike English legislation, canned and cooked venison come within the Scottish definition, but (3) above permits the hotelier to serve venison if purchased from a venison dealer.

It would also appear that any unlicensed person, a butcher or supermarket, for example, may sell or possess any venison if purchased from a licensed venison dealer. Frozen and processed venison purchased from a licensed dealer can also be sold in unlicensed shops.

Section 36 (4)
It is an offence to sell, offer for sale, possess for sale, transport for sale, purchase or receive, any carcase which one knows or has reason to believe was unlawfully killed.

Section 36(5)
Any licensed venison dealer failing to keep records or making false entries commits an offence.

Section 36(6)
Anyone obstructing the inspection of such records commits an offence.

Disqualified from holding a licence

Section 34(5)
Anyone convicted of an offence under Part III (illegal taking of deer) or section 36 (venison dealing offences) may be disqualified by the court from holding, or obtaining a venison dealer's licence.

NORTHERN IRELAND

A game dealer's licence is issued by the Department of Health and Social Services which administers the Miscellaneous Transferred Excise Duties Act (Northern Ireland) 1972. Applicants must first obtain a Certificate of Good Character from a Magistrates Court. This legislation also extends the definition of game to include deer for game dealing purposes.

The Game Preservation Act (Northern Ireland) 1928 Section 3 and 3A require dealers to keep a register of transactions in the proscribed form to be kept for three years, together with invoices and other documentation. This aspect is the responsibility of the

Department of Environment. Hygiene is the responsibility of the Department of Agriculture.

The main offences relating to dealing in venison are found in the Wildlife (Northern Ireland) Order 1985 but there are numerous other offences relating to game dealers in the Miscellaneous Transferred Excise Duties Act.

The term venison includes imported meat and means the carcase, or any edible part of the carcase, but not canned or cooked venison.

Article 23 (1)
It is an offence for anyone other than a licensed game dealer to sell, offer or expose for sale or possess for sale any venison during the prohibited period. The prohibited period only relates to venison from a species protected by a close season (i.e. red, fallow, and sika) and begins ten days after the start of the relevant close season. Therefore a stalker may only sell, or possess for sale, such venison during the open season and the first ten days of the relevant close season. Licensed dealers may possess and sell during the prohibited period.

Article 23 (1)
It is an offence for anyone other than a licensed dealer to sell, offer or expose for sale venison at any time unless the sale is to a licensed dealer. The stalker wishing to sell venison direct to friends or to a restaurant must be licensed as a dealer, even in the open season.

Article 23 (2)
It is also an offence for anyone to sell, possess for sale, purchase, offer to purchase or receive venison from any deer which he knows or believes has been illegally taken or killed under the Order e.g. close season or unlawful methods.

DETECTING MALPRACTICE AND POACHING

Anyone purchasing, processing or selling venison should establish the origin of the carcases offered to him as failure to do so may render him liable. Turning a blind eye to the following may prove expensive:

- Failure to record full and accurate records
- Buying carcases with dog marks
- Buying carcases with shotgun wounds
- Buying carcases shot with unlawful weapons – especially .22 rimfire and crossbow
- Buying out of season – a dealer ought to be able to sex a deer in

carcase form and should be aware of the close season for male and female of the species.

Sexing carcases

This is relatively straightforward if presented with the whole animal. However a headless and gralloched beast is more difficult and may require internal examination. In some cases the mere weight, or lack of it, can be indicator. The pelvic conformation is reliable in the skeleton but not in the hanging carcase, although the internal shape and size of the pelvic canal may give a guide. If the posterior abdominal muscles are intact [i.e. if the linea alba has simply been split without trimming muscle around the udder or scrotum] then the inguinal canals give a good guide, since the male will have cremaster muscle and probably remnants of tunica vaginalis and cord through the ring, which is larger than in the female. If this tissue has been trimmed, there are differences between the male and female blood vessels arising from the aorta, since the spermatic arteries are far smaller than the corresponding uterine arteries and the internal pudendal artery in the male is far larger than in the female. However clean the carcase, it should always be possible to detect the sites of attachments of the broad ligament of the uterus and of the ovarian ligaments and finally, the root of the penis is usually left in place as it courses over the posterior rim of the pubis.

Sale out of season

The Deer Act 1991 exempts the killing of deer out of season by occupiers of land (to prevent crop damage) and deer farmers. But prior to the 2007 Regulatory Order, there was no provision for deer legally killed out of season to be sold by the occupier, stalker or deer farmer to a licensed dealer. The Order has simplified the situation in that provided the deer have been lawfully killed out of season the carcases can be sold.

Records and traceability

In recent years there has been a significant growth in UK supermarket sales of game meat and their overriding concerns are hygiene, traceability, animal welfare and consumer confidence. Increasingly supermarkets are managing the production from estate to store, including feed and use of drugs, to ensure traceability and quality. Such control is difficult with wild game and venison but supermarkets do insist on standards in the processing of game once it reaches approved game handling establishments (AGHEs)the licensed game dealer. The National Game Dealers Association (NGDA) has been keen to portray venison as a high quality product but is concerned about the threats to consumer and market confidence posed by poached deer. The sale or purchase of poached deer is a criminal offence.

Accurate dealer records and local authority health inspections are seen as the way ahead but the support of NGDA members, the police and the courts is vital.

The BASC and BDS campaigns against poaching continue to raise awareness of the cruelty, hygiene and commercial issues involved with deer poaching and theft.

Licensed dealers should keep records that identify the seller of a deer carcase. Accurate records ensure traceability and should identify poachers and their venison. In practice records are often incomplete through ignorance or intention and have received little police or local authority attention in the past. Local Authority Environmental Health Officers have their own powers to inspect premises involved in food preparation.

There seems little doubt that a rigorous system of carcase identification would help to identify illegally killed deer and consequently tackle this activity more effectively. However existing legislation and guidance provides exemptions for small quantities of deer being supplied to final consumers and it is in this area that traceability may be lost. Whilst extensive powers for the police and food safety authorities exist the problem has historically been with a lack of enforcement and stricter controls are called for to combat illegally taken deer.

Section 11 Deer Act 1991 was repealed by the 2007 regulatory order removing the requirement for licensed dealers to keep records under the Deer Act in England and Wales. However records are now required to be kept under the provisions of EC Regulations.

Traceability is about identifying suppliers and customers and uses the principle of 'one step back and one step forward' so that food can be traced along the supply chain.

Regulation 178/2002 applies to all food business operators including primary producers, even those that benefit from exemptions, and covers the whole food and feed chain.

FBOs are required to have in place systems and procedures that allow for traceability information to be made available to competent authorities on demand. Copies of invoices and your game book (or similar) may be sufficient. Such records are likely to include the location and date deer were shot.

The key information to be recorded is the name and address of the supplier/customer, the date and the nature of the products. Final consumers do not have to be individually identified. However, it may be useful to record how much game you supply direct to final consumers.

Trained persons who supply carcases to an AGHE are required to complete a Large Wild Game Declaration giving details of date, location, species, sex and weight and their own qualification, identification and contact details.

SPECIMEN FORMS

A. SUGGESTED FORMAT FOR LARGE WILD GAME DECLARATION

FRONT

LARGE WILD GAME DECLARATION		
Tag Number:	Species:	ROE FALLOW RED
Date/Time of Kill: ..../.............		MUNTJAC SIKA CHINESE
Location/Estate:..............................		OTHER...............................
Sex: M F Weight: .... (KGs)		

BACK

I declare in accordance with EU Regulation 853/2004 that no abnormal behaviour was observed before killing and there is no indication of environmental contamination. I have inspected the head, pluck and viscera without observing abnormalities*.

Notes:..

Trained person qualification:...........................Contact details ....

Name:.. ....

Signature:................................. ....

*The Trained Person should check for 'EAT NOT' ear tags - indicating Large Animal Immobilon has been administered. If these are present, the entire carcase is unfit for human consumption and should not be submitted. Further information is available on the RCVS web-site at http://www.rcvs.org.uk

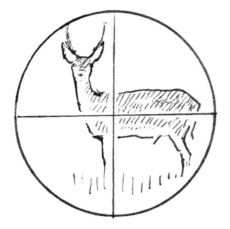

CHAPTER 6

The Use of Firearms for Deer

Deer have no natural predators in this country and therefore their numbers must be regulated and kept in balance with the environment. The most effective and humane way for this to be done is by the proper and careful use of firearms. Whether it is done by the professional or recreational stalker matters not: one standard of proficiency applies. The safety of the public, domestic animals and the humane killing of deer are the main considerations of deer management involving the use of firearms.

Historically, deer have been shot with all types of weapons. Many of these have been unsuitable and much unnecessary suffering has been caused. Many deer, particularly roe, were shot with shotguns during what were known as 'deer drives'. Through education and best practice, this has now ceased and the use of shotguns or other unsuitable weapons would now be illegal in these circumstances.[47]

The high-velocity rifle has emerged over the years as the most effective firearm for use against deer. When used with a telescopic sight, calibrated to the point of aim (zeroed), it can be devastatingly

---

47. See chapters 2 and 3 for the circumstances in which shotguns can be used.

accurate over a considerable distance. Provided the bullet is correctly placed, deer can be shot humanely with little damage to the venison.

LEGISLATION

The legislation governing firearms and their use has to strike a balance of protecting the public against their misuse on the one hand, and allowing legitimate users to own and have easy access to rifles on the other. Ignorance and misunderstanding abound on the subject of the ownership and use of firearms. The two terrible but isolated tragedies arising from their misuse in recent years have highlighted the problems of achieving the right balance between restriction and access for legitimate use.

There has been a raft of gun control laws from 1509 onwards, but the first modern Firearms Act was introduced in 1920, prior to which there was little effective control on their possession. Subsequent legislation has introduced provisions to control the use of certain firearms in the interest of public safety. This is reflected in the control of the more powerful weapons, the restrictions on young persons, and the provisions against the use of firearms in the commission of crime. In recent years the number of certificate holders has virtually halved from 256,000 in 1968 to 133,000 in 1997. Despite the tight controls, which often penalise the legitimate stalker, the criminal use of unlicensed firearms continues. Rifles, apart from those chambered for low-powered .22 inch rimfire ammunition feature very little in criminal offences.[48]

Current legislation is complex, with a number of Acts that generate new provisions and amendments to the original Act. The danger here is that those who manage deer, either professionally or as a sport, are likely to fall foul of the law due to the confusion created by its complexity. Nevertheless, of course, ignorance of the law is no excuse.

The Firearms Act, 1968 (which applies to England, Wales and Scotland) is the main statute governing the possession, control and use of firearms. The Firearms Rules, 1989, prescribed the form of firearm and shotgun certificates and detailed the conditions under which firearm certificates are held. These rules were replaced by the Firearms Rules, 1998.

The Firearms (Amendment) Act, 1988, substantially amended the main statute, bringing stricter controls particularly in relation to the ownership of shotguns, which were redefined by the Act. The

48. T. A. Warlow, *Science and Justice* 1996 36(1) 55–58.

provisions of the European Weapons Directive were absorbed into U.K. legislation in 1992. The main changes were additions to the list of prohibited weapons, restrictions on use by people under 18 years, controls on sale and purchase in countries within the European Union and the introduction of the European Firearms Pass (E.F.P.).

The Firearms (Amendment) Act, 1997, was speedily introduced following an urgent review of firearm controls in which the Government took cognisance of Lord Cullen's Report of the Public Inquiry into the Shootings at Dunblane Primary School. The Act introduced tighter controls, which included a general prohibition on handguns. In addition, deer stalkers were affected by the prohibition of expanding ammunition.

Northern Ireland has its own separate legislation and the main provisions affecting stalkers are contained within the Firearms (Northern Ireland) Order, 1981. This legislation is similar in parts to that contained within the Firearms Act, 1968. Where there are differences which may affect the stalker these are elaborated upon within the text.

The Firearms (Amendment) Act, 1988, section 22(1) provided for the establishment of the Firearms Consultative Committee an independent body to keep under review the working of the Firearm Acts. However this has now been disbanded.

Of particular note to deer stalkers were the supportive views of the F.C.C., expressed to the government in respect of expanding ammunition and the use of pistols for the humane dispatch of animals. In its ninth report for example, it recommended:

> In the light of the general ban on handguns, the Government should consider whether the ban on expanding ammunition serves any useful purpose and, if not, its repeal.

The subject of the use of both expanding ammunition and handguns by those involved with the management of deer is dealt with in detail later.

The requirement for a firearm certificate

The legislation creates different controls and licensing requirements for certain types of firearm and ammunition defined by the Firearms Acts, 1968 to 1997. Three main classes of firearm exist:

- firearms (section 1)
- shotguns (section 2)
- prohibited weapons (section 5)

Some weapons are defined as 'firearms' but may not need to be licensed – e.g. air weapons that are not declared specially dangerous, or firearms regarded as antiques. But all firearms that can be legally used for deer require a valid firearm certificate. Shotguns can be used in specified circumstances, and a valid shotgun certificate is required. Firearm certificate applications and the exemptions that apply are detailed later in the chapter.

What is a firearm?

The use of firearms against deer is strictly regulated by deer legislation, which lays down both permitted and prohibited weapons and ammunition, and these are elaborated upon later. For the purposes of firearm legislation, a 'firearm' is defined as follows (section 57(1) Firearms Act, 1968, and Article 2(2) Firearms (Northern Ireland) Order, 1981):

> A lethal-barrelled weapon of any description from which any shot, bullet or other missile can be discharged and includes:
>
> (a)   any prohibited weapon (whether lethal or not); and
> (b)   any component part of such a lethal or prohibited weapon; and
> (c)   any accessory to any such weapons designed or adapted to diminish the noise or flash caused by firing the weapon.

In addition to this definition case law provides further guidance in cases which have been disputed.

A **'lethal-barrelled'** weapon is one capable of causing injury from which death may result. It follows that the majority of weapons are going to fall into this class, including air weapons. A signal pistol has been held to be a firearm although it was never designed to injure or kill.[49] The description 'barrelled' requires the weapon to have some form of cylinder or tube from which a projectile can be discharged. Hence a crossbow is not classed as a firearm.[50]

A firearm can be **'discharged'** by any means, including gunpowder, gas, spring and air pressure. It is not essential that the weapon is capable of firing ammunition. If it can be quickly and readily converted to enable firing then it may be classed as a 'firearm' for the purposes of the Acts.[51] See also section 1(1)(b) Firearms Act,

---

49. Read v. Donovan (1947) KB826.
50. Restrictions on sale and use of crossbows by juveniles are set out in the Crossbows Act, 1987. See chapter 9 for a discussion of their use in poaching.
51. Cafferata v. Wilson (1936) All E.R. 149.

1982; the test is that no special skill is required on the part of the person doing the conversion, and that ordinary tools for home D.I.Y. work can be used.

The term **'prohibited weapon'** is defined under section 5(1), Firearms Act, 1968, as amended[52] as:

(1) Any firearm so designed or adapted that two or more missiles can be successfully discharged without repeated pressure on the trigger.

(2) Any self-loading or pump-action rifled gun other than .22 rim-fire.

(3) Any firearm which either has a barrel less than 30cm or is less than 60cm overall, other than an air weapon, a muzzle-loading gun or a firearm designed as signalling apparatus.

(4) Any self-loading or pump-action smooth-bore gun (not an air weapon or .22 rim-fire) with either barrel less than 24 inches or overall length less than 40 inches.

(5) Any smooth-bore revolver gun (not 9mm rim-fire or a muzzle-loading gun).

(6) Any rocket launcher or mortar.

(7) Any firearm which is disguised as another object e.g. walking stick (unless regarded as an antique).

The term **'component part'** relates only to the parts of a firearm that are pressure bearing from the force of the explosion like the barrel, bolt or action. Items such as telescopic sights, which are normally regarded as accessories, may be referred to as component parts but because they are not essential to the firing of the weapon their possession, purchase or sale are not restricted and do not require to be entered on a firearm certificate.[53] However, any device designed to diminish the noise or flash of a weapon, such as a sound moderator (silencer), is required to be included on a firearm certificate whether it is fitted to a weapon or held separately. Certificates are not required for sound moderators for shotguns or air weapons.

'Ammunition' includes ammunition for any firearm as well as grenades, bombs etc., whether capable of use with a firearm or not. It is generally accepted to include four components: projectile, charge, primer and case.

The definition of **'prohibited ammunition'** will be of interest to stalkers as, following the introduction of the Firearms (Amendment)

---

52. Firearms Act, 1988, Amendment Regulations, 1992, and Firearms (Amendment) Act, 1997.
53. Watson v. Herman (1952) 2 All E.R. 70.

Act, 1997, this now includes a general prohibition on expanding ammunition and missiles. However, its use against deer is obligatory, and it is catered for within the exemptions as elaborated upon later.

Under section 5(1) as amended, prohibited ammunition is defined as:

- any cartridge or bullet designed to explode[54] on or immediately before impact
- any ammunition containing any noxious liquid, gas or other thing
- if capable of use with a firearm any grenade, bomb, rocket or shell designed to explode
- any ammunition which incorporates a missile designed or adapted to expand on impact (expanding ammunition)

PERMITTED FIREARMS AND AMMUNITION FOR DEER

It is essential for those who shoot deer to be familiar with the Deer Acts applicable to the countries in which they intend to shoot. The Acts stipulate not only the firearms and ammunition that are permitted for use against deer, but also those that are prohibited.

---

54. This refers to a form of explosive charge within the projectile as opposed to expanding-type bullets.

Some fundamental differences exist between the Acts in the specification of rifles and ammunition. In England and Wales it will be noted that it is the *calibre* of the weapon and its *muzzle energy* that are the main criteria for lawful use. In Scotland the criteria relate to the *ammunition, muzzle energy* and *velocity*. It would therefore be legal to use any rifle capable of firing that ammunition with the required power. In Northern Ireland it is a combination of both rifle calibre, ammunition and muzzle energy. The result is that certain weapons may be legal on one side of the border but not the other, which is by no means ideal for the stalker who shoots in both England and Scotland; for example .22 centre-fire cartridges (minimum .222 Remington but not the Hornet) can only be used in Scotland, and then only for roe. In England and Wales .22 centre fire can now be used for muntjac and Chinese water deer but not roe.

The following chart, which consolidates the provisions, is provided for ease of reference. The circumstances in which shotguns may be used are shown and these should be read in conjunction with chapter 4 on crop damage.

Firearms permitted for killing deer in England, Wales, Northern Ireland and Scotland

ENGLAND AND WALES	
Rifles and ammunition:	Calibre of not less than .240 in or muzzle energy of not less than 1,700 ft/lb
	Bullet must be soft-nosed or hollow-nosed
	Muntjac and Chinese water deer only. Calibre not less than .220 inches and a muzzle energy of not less than 1,356 joules (1,000 foot pounds). Bullet must be soft-nosed or hollow-nosed weighing not less than 3.24 grammes (50 grains)
Shotgun:	Not less than 12-bore. A shotgun may be used only by the occupier and certain others, who must be able to prove serious damage (see Deer Act, 1991, section 7)
Shotgun ammunition:	Rifled slug of not less than 22.68 g (350 grains) or AAA shot
Prohibitions:	Any air gun, air rifle or air pistol

NORTHERN IRELAND

Rifles:	Calibre of not less than .236 in (6 mm)
Rifle ammunition:	Muzzle energy of not less than 1,700 ft/lb (2,305 joules)
	Bullet of not less than 6.48 g (100 grains)
	Expanding bullets designed to deform in predictable manner
Shotguns:	Not less than 12-bore. A shotgun may be used only by the occupier and certain others, who must be able to prove serious damage (see Wildlife (Northern Ireland) Order, 1985, section 20)
Shotgun ammunition:	Rifled slug of not less than 22.68 g (350 grains) or AAA shot
Prohibitions:	Any air gun, air rifle, air pistol or gas-propelled weapon; any pistol, revolver or handgun other than slaughtering instrument

SCOTLAND

Rifle ammunition:	**Roe deer:**	Bullets of not less than 50 grains AND Muzzle velocity of not less than 2,450 ft per sec. AND Muzzle energy of not less than 1,000 ft/lb
	All deer:	Bullets of not less than 100 grains AND Muzzle velocity of not less than 2,450 ft per sec. AND Muzzle energy of not less than 1,750 ft/lb
	Expanding bullets designed to deform in predictable manner	
Shotguns:	Not less than 12-bore. A shotgun may be used only by the occupier and certain others, who must be able to prove serious damage (see Deer (Firearms etc.) (Scotland) Order, 1985, No. 1168)	
Shotgun ammunition:	**All deer:**	Rifled slug of not less than 380 grains or shot not smaller than SSG
	Roe deer:	Shot not smaller than AAA
Prohibitions:	Any sight specially designed for night shooting	

Calibre

As the development of firearms evolved, a classification was introduced according to the size of the bore of the gun barrel – the nominal diameter of the bore measured across the lands, expressed in decimal points of an inch for British and American guns, and millimetres for Continental guns. The measurement became known as the *calibre* of the weapon.

Muzzle energy

Muzzle energy is calculated from the formula:

$$\frac{\text{bullet weight} \times (\text{muzzle velocity})^2}{\text{acceleration of gravity } (450,400)}$$

For example a 150-grain bullet with a muzzle velocity of 2,800 ft per sec. (.270 Winchester) would have a calculated muzzle energy of:

$$\frac{150 \times 2,800 \times 2,800}{450,400} = 2,611 \text{ ft lb}$$

If there is any doubt as to whether a particular combination of rifle and bullet meets the required ballistic performance as given above, then advice should be sought from a reputable firearms dealer or the manufacturer. Alternatively the Deer Commission for Scotland and the B.A.S.C. Deer Officer can be consulted. A chart of ballistic performance of most popular calibres is available from the Deer Commission.[55]

Expanding ammunition

Section 10 of the Firearms (Amendment) Act, 1997, creates a number of exemptions in respect of the use of expanding ammunition. Its possession, purchase or acquisition must be authorised by a firearm certificate or visitor's firearm permit, which should contain a condition restricting the expanding ammunition to use in connection with any one or more of the following activities:

- the lawful shooting of deer
- the shooting of vermin or, in the course of carrying on activities in connection with the management of any estate, other wildlife

55. See page 229 for contact details.

- the humane killing of animals
- the shooting of animals for the protection of other animals or humans

We must stress that this exemption applies only to the requirement of authority under section 5, and that a firearm certificate under section 1 is still required and must contain the condition referred to above. The exemption not only caters for the ammunition's use in deer shooting but also for its use in activities *connected with* deer shooting. Without strict legal guidance or a court ruling, the words 'in connection with' are open to different interpretations by different licensing authorities. It is clear from the debate that took place during the preparation of the legislation that it was the government's intention to ensure that the use of expanding ammunition catered for the preparatory stages that may have to be followed to ensure that deer are shot humanely. As Baroness Blatch stated, 'That includes allowing the certificate holder to zero or adjust the gun sights as well as general testing and practice.'

It is our opinion that any action that is directly related to these activities falls within the exemption, including practising with expanding ammunition at inanimate objects. It should be appreciated that for deer to be shot humanely, accuracy and knowledge of the vital killing areas are essential. This is only possible by ensuring not only that the user is proficient but also that the equipment and ammunition are capable of producing the required ballistic performance. It follows therefore that both practice and the testing of both equipment and ammunition, of the exact type to be used on live deer, is essential.

Stalkers should not be restricted as to how often they practise or what quantities of ammunition they use to achieve accuracy. It should also be appreciated that some individuals will require more practice than others. A check of accuracy may be necessary on a regular basis or as a result of a miss or knock to the sights.

Training and education in stalking competence, which requires the participant to use a rifle and expanding ammunition, should also be seen as preparatory to the humane shooting of deer. However it is not a prerequisite for the grant of a firearm certificate.

Difficulties arise in the interpretation of the exemption when considering whether any type of rifle competition shooting could be classed as being 'in connection with' the lawful shooting of deer. Regional branches of the British Deer Society regularly hold such competitions, and B.A.S.C. considers that they are run in connection with the lawful shooting of deer as they are designed to enhance marksmanship and thus encourage humane shooting.

Generally, competition shooting *per se* would not fall within the criteria. However, there may be situations where the winning of a competition may be shown as ancillary to the test of stalking marksmanship and therefore one may argue this could then be seen as being in connection with the lawful shooting of deer. If it were put to the test, a court would have to decide on the basis of the merits of the individual case, using the natural sense and common use of the words.

The exemption also provides that expanding ammunition may be used for 'the shooting of vermin or, in the course of carrying on activities in connection with the management of any estate, other wildlife'. If you intend to use your rifle in these circumstances your certificate must include this condition, otherwise such use will be unlawful. The shooting of non-target species and wild boar are elaborated upon in chapter 7.

If you are in any doubt as to whether or not your use of expanding ammunition falls within the legal exemption, remember that it is your responsibility to ensure that you comply with the conditions of your certificate; we would therefore advise you to consult the firearms licensing department responsible for issuing your certificate. Alternatively you may contact the Firearms Department at the B.A.S.C. for advice.[56]

Exemptions to prevent suffering

Each of the Acts relating to deer make exceptions for dealing with injured or diseased deer in circumstances where the use of firearms would otherwise be illegal. In Scotland this is extended to cover the prevention of suffering of dependent offspring.

England and Wales – Deer Act, 1991, section 6(4) and (4A)
Section 6(4) was replaced in 2007 bringing it in line with the law in Scotland. A person shall not be guilty of an offence under Section 4(1) or (2) by reason of the use of any reasonable means for the purpose of killing any deer if he reasonably believes that the deer has been so seriously injured, otherwise than by his unlawful act, or is in such a condition, that to kill it is an act of mercy.

'Any reasonable means' means any method of killing a deer that can reasonably be expected to result in rapid loss of consciousness and death and which is appropriate in the circumstances (including in particular what the deer is doing, its size, its distance from the closest position safely attainable by the person attempting to kill the deer and its position in relation to vegetative cover).

56. See page 229 for contact details.

Consequently any firearm can be used in these circumstances. However stalkers should note that the use of any section 1 firearm still requires the appropriate condition relating to humane dispatch on the firearm certificate.

Handguns are not included as prohibited weapons and, provided the appropriate firearm certificate is held, could legitimately be used in these circumstances.

Northern Ireland (The Wildlife (Northern Ireland) Order, 1985)
A person shall not be guilty of an offence under article 19(3)(a) (prohibited firearms and ammunition) by reason of the killing of any deer by using any smooth-bore gun, if he shows that the deer had been so seriously injured, otherwise than by his unlawful act, or was in such a condition, that to kill it was an act of mercy.

Schedule 11 of the Act specifically prohibits the use of handguns.

Scotland (The Deer (Firearms etc.) (Scotland) Order, 1985)
A person shall not be guilty of an offence against this Act or any order made under it in respect of any act done for the purpose of preventing suffering by an injured or diseased deer; or a deer calf, fawn or kid deprived, or about to be deprived, of its mother.

The effect of this exemption in relation to the use of firearms, is that any firearm of any description can be used in the circumstances of a mercy killing without contravening the law relating to deer.

The use of handguns for dispatching wounded deer

It will be noted that the use of handguns for the mercy killing of deer is not prohibited by the Deer Acts in England and Wales or Scotland. In addition, an exemption exists under section 3 of the Firearms (Amendment) Act, 1997, in circumstances where an appropriate firearm certificate is held and it is subject to a condition that it is only for use in connection with the humane killing of animals. This has been held to include the humane dispatch of wounded or injured deer.[57] In applying for such a certificate you are required to demonstrate that you have a good reason for possessing a handgun for this purpose and chief constables must consider cases on their individual merits. In the case of Hughes v. The Chief Constable of South Wales, 1998, the appeal was dismissed on the basis that the court was not satisfied that the appellant's reason for retention of a .38 Smith & Wesson six-shot revolver was for the humane destruction of animals.

57. Goodman & Newton v. The Chief Constable of Derbyshire 1998.

Association of Chief Police Officer guidance is that the preferred option is a .32 single-shot pistol.

Carrying a handgun in addition to a rifle, for the sole purpose of dispatching a wounded beast, is frowned upon by many experienced stalkers. The late John Hodgkiss, with whom we regularly exchanged legal views, summed up our thoughts in a letter on the subject:

> The question of applications for firearm certificates for pistols for destroying deer which have been wounded during the course of stalking continues to arise. Allow me, please, to be categoric about this. Whilst even the most experienced and conscientious stalker will, alas, sooner or later fail to kill a deer outright, such a situation should occur only as an extreme exception. Even then, with proper fieldcraft – and, ideally, the use of a trained dog – the animal will always be tracked down and dispatched (with rifle or, if needs be, the customary *coup de grace*). There is NO case for the use of handguns (of any calibre).
>
> In this country deer are big game and should be regarded as such, and frankly, any person who cannot attain the standards implied in the previous paragraph should not go out after deer. Any applicant must make sure as humanly as possible that he kills cleanly with the first shot or only stalks in the company of a competent stalker or ceases to stalk until he is able to do so on his own, proficiently, responsibly and safely. In any case, handguns of all types are far from easy to handle accurately and reliably even after considerable practice, and their use would be even more precarious in the case of a wounded deer which may be struggling or in an awkward position.[58]

Whilst many people view the handgun as being an unnecessary appendage when stalking there are situations where its use is appropriate and 'good reason' should not be difficult to establish. Many deer managers and rangers are regularly called out, often by the police, to deal with casualties. In this situation, where the beast is under some control, the use of a handgun is justified. The issue of a certificate for such use should additionally cater for the dispatching of wounded deer trapped in fences or disabled by farm machinery etc.[59]

---

58. Letter to the authors, dated 20 September 1990, from the late John Hodgkiss, past Vice-president of the British Deer Society and the Chairman of the Federation of Deer Management Societies.
59. Liabilities in respect of the humane dispatch of deer are covered in chapter 7.

There are situations where the use of handguns is appropriate. However the use of a shotgun for this purpose is now common practice.

FIREARM CERTIFICATES

All firearms that are permitted for use against deer fall within the scope of section 1 of the Firearms Act, 1968, and if you wish to acquire, possess or use such weapons a firearm certificate is required. The exception is the conditional use of shotguns, for which a shotgun certificate is required.[60]

The term 'possession' should be viewed in its widest possible sense. It includes not only physical possession but also 'constructive' possession – e.g. where the firearm is in a house or vehicle under the control of a person who is aware of its presence.[61] One aspect of possession was considered in Hall v. Cotton and Treadwell (1986).[62] Here the learned judge said:

> Cases of momentary delivery of a shotgun to another person in for example, a temporary emergency, or for the purpose of inspection, could hardly be said to have involved either a transfer by the deliveror or the taking of possession by the deliveree; equally, a spouse or servant temporarily entrusted with the custody of a shotgun by its owner would in normal circumstances be regarded as the owner's agent; there would thus be no transfer by the latter, nor acceptance of any more than the barest custody by the former . . .

60. See the chart on pages 115–116 and chapter 4 on crop damage.
61. Sullivan v. Earl of Caithness (1976) 1 All E.R.
62. 83 Cr. App. R 257.

This tends to mitigate against the excesses of a strict interpretation of 'possession'.

Exemptions

There are numerous exemptions to the requirement for firearm certificates both in terms of types of weapons and circumstances of use. The following have been selected as being of relevance to stalkers and deer managers.

The 'estate rifle'

The Firearms (Amendment) Act, 1988, made provision for the use of what is commonly and erroneously referred to as the 'estate rifle'. Section 16 states that a rifle may be borrowed, by a person aged 17 or over, from the occupier of private premies (which includes land) and used on those premises in the presence of the occupier or his employee providing the latter holds the appropriate firearm certificate, but the rifle and ammunition can only be used in accordance with the conditions of that certificate. Ammunition may also be purchased or acquired under this exemption. In practice, this is normally acquired direct from the owner of the rifle, and in these circumstances the transaction would not need to be entered on the certificate. Any remaining surplus ammunition should remain with the certificate holder. It must be stressed that where a rifle is used in the presence of the employee, the employee himself must possess a certificate covering his use of it.

The term 'occupier' is not defined in this context by the Act, and in the absence of a legal ruling, it is open to interpretation. Occupation of land must be broad in nature and enforceable through the courts, it is generally accepted that it would include a person who holds the sporting rights to deer.

This exemption is of particular benefit to visitors from abroad or those who wish to stalk occasionally without the need or expense of purchasing a rifle and obtaining a certificate.

Carrying a firearm for the certificate holder
A person may carry, but not use, a firearm or ammunition belonging to another person without the need for a firearm certificate, provided it is for the certificate holder's use and under his instruction and for a sporting purpose only.[63] This is normally interpreted as applying to gun bearers, loaders etc.

Crown servants
Crown servants are allowed to possess, purchase or acquire firearms and ammunition in connection with their business or occupation. As Crown servants, the Forestry Commission rangers who use firearms in their work are covered by the Crown exemption. However, any personal firearms that they may hold must be covered by a firearm certificate.

Shotguns
A shotgun certificate is not required where a person borrows a shotgun from the occupier of private premises, provided it is used on those premises and in his presence.

Restrictions on young persons

Children under fourteen cannot possess section 1 firearms or ammunition. It is an offence to make a gift of or lend a firearm to a child, or to part with possession to a child unless he is carrying it for, and under the instruction of, the owner who is the holder of an appropriate certificate and using it for sporting purposes.

Young people between the ages of fourteen and seventeen are not permitted to purchase or hire any firearms or ammunition. However provided they hold a valid firearm certificate they may possess and use section 1 firearms and ammunition in accordance with the terms of the certificate. They can only acquire such weapons by gift or loan where both parties possess firearm certificates authorising the transaction.

63. Shooting rats is not a sporting purpose – Morton v. Chaney (1960) 3 All E.R. 632.

Different regulations apply in Northern Ireland. The Firearms (Northern Ireland) Order, 1981, article 26, states:

(1)   Except as provided by paragraphs (3) and (4) anyone under 18 years of age who purchases, acquires or has in their possession a firearm or ammunition, shall be guilty of an offence.

(2)   A person who sells or transfers a firearm or ammunition to any person prohibited by this article from possessing such firearm or ammunition, shall be guilty of an offence.

(3)   It is *not* an offence for any person to have in their possession a firearm or ammunition if –

(a)   they show that under the Order they are entitled to possess without holding a firearm certificate

(b)   they show that they are entitled to possess by virtue of article 15 (they possess firearm or shotgun certificates granted in Great Britain).

(4)   It is *not* an offence for a person age 16 years or above to –

(a)   have a firearm or ammunition for sporting purposes where he is in the company and under supervision of another person not under 18 years of age, who holds a firearm certificate for the firearm and ammunition; or

(b)   purchase, acquire or possess a shotgun, or any other firearm not exceeding .22 calibre, and ammunition therefore for the purpose of destroying or controlling animals and birds on either agricultural land occupied by him or on which he works and also resides.

Application for the grant of a certificate

If you wish to acquire, possess or use any firearm or ammunition to which section 1 of the Act applies, unless one of the exemptions applies you must first obtain a firearm certificate from the chief officer of police for the area in which you reside. A certificate will be granted if the chief officer is satisfied that the applicant has good reason for requiring the weapon and that there is no danger to public safety or the peace. Discretion to grant or refuse an application rests with that chief officer, in whom is vested the responsibility to ensure that a certificate is not granted to a person of intemperate habits or unsound mind, or who for any reason is unfitted to be entrusted with a firearm.

There is a right of appeal to the Crown or Sheriff Court against a refusal to grant or renew a certificate and or the revocation of a certificate.[64] If you are dissatisfied with the decision we recommend that you seek early advice from a solicitor well versed in such matters. Alternatively if you are a member of the B.A.S.C. you should contact their Firearms Department. Notice of appeals must be made within twenty-one days of receipt of the chief officer's notice of decision, unless leave has been sought to appeal out of time.

Certificates are issued in the form of a folding booklet and specify either the number of firearms possessed or the number which may be acquired, or both. There is no limit on the number of firearms that can be held but a good reason must be demonstrated in respect of each weapon. It is usual for deer stalkers to possess more than one calibre of weapon and good reason can be made out on the basis of the species of deer to be shot or the nature of the stalking terrain. For example a smaller calibre may be requested for roe, and the stutzen-type rifle for woodland. Stated on the certificate will be the amount of ammunition which may be possessed at any one time and the amount which may be purchased. Subsequent purchases of firearms or ammunition over the initial number authorised must only take place following a variation of the certificate.

Conditions

The Firearms Rules, 1998, impose the following statutory conditions on certificate holders:

- The holder must, on receipt of the certificate, sign it in ink
- Firearms and ammunition must be kept in a secure place
- Any theft, loss, destruction or deactivation of a firearm must be reported to the police
- Any change of permanent address must be notified to the police

Additional conditions may be imposed by the chief officer at his discretion. These may relate to where the firearms are to be kept, or restrict where and under what circumstances they may be used. The chief officer may at any time vary such conditions and can require the production of the certificate within twenty-one days for this purpose. A certificate may be revoked if it is not produced, and there is no appeal in these circumstances.

---

64. There is no right of appeal against a chief officer's decision not to vary the conditions – R. v. Cambridge Court, Ex Parte Buckland (1968).

Completion of the form

Application forms (form 101) are obtainable from police stations. The same form is used for the grant, renewal and variation of a certificate. Once issued the certificate will last for a period of five years; prior to expiry it will be necessary to apply for renewal. The form makes provision for you to request a shotgun certificate to run coterminously with the firearm certificate. The shotgun certificate will expire on the same day as the firearm certificate. If both applications are dealt with at the same time the fee payable for the grant or renewal of the shotgun certificate will normally be less.

The form is generally self-explanatory and is split into sections, A–F, to cater for varying applications. Explanatory notes are included on the reverse side of the form and cover most of the common queries raised. If difficulty is experienced in completion of any part of the form we recommend that you contact your local licensing department or firearms licensing officer. If you are a B.A.S.C. member you can also contact the B.A.S.C. Firearms Department.

Previous convictions
You are required in law to reveal whether or not you have been convicted of any offence. You are not entitled to withhold such information, which includes motoring offences and convictions outside Great Britain. Convictions that are classed as 'spent' under the Rehabilitation of Offenders Act, 1974, are also required to be declared. Both a conditional discharge and an absolute discharge, but not a caution, count as convictions for this purpose. (On renewal or variation, details need only be given of convictions since the existing certificate was issued.)

Choice of weapon
Where a firearm is to be purchased or acquired it is not necessary for the make and identification number of the weapon to be stated on the form, as this is unlikely to be known at the time of application. Such details would be required to be endorsed on the certificate by the seller or giver, who will first check that the certificate authorises you to possess that type of weapon. It is not unusual for stalkers to be uncertain when choosing a calibre. There is considerable choice and much debate on the virtues of the calibres permitted for use against deer. If you are unsure and wish to press ahead with your application your licensing department may accept an application requesting authorisation to possess a rifle between certain calibres – e.g. .243–.308 – rather than restricting your choice. However you should clarify this at the time as not all licensing departments permit

this, some require you state a specific calibre. Such details would subsequently be entered on the certificate at the time of purchase or acquisition (table 1 on the back of the certificate).

Ammunition

The amount of ammunition you ask to purchase and possess needs to be appropriate to your intended use of the weapon. Applications are judged on an individual basis and chief officers are asked to be flexible and pay due regard to the needs of the applicant.

You should ensure that you have catered for the amount you may need to use on zeroing and practice, particularly if a new firearm or telescopic sight has been purchased. By comparison the amount used on actually shooting deer is usually quite small. The quantity you request to possess at any one time should be considerably greater than the amount to be purchased, in order to allow for an operating surplus.

If you load your own ammunition you will need to take account of the quantities you may wish to load at any one time. You will also need to include a separate quantity for expanding bullets (or missiles) which are now classed as ammunition in their own right and count towards the allocation on the certificate. The application form requests the inclusion of expanding ammunition and expanding missiles. Some licensing departments have recognised the distinction between expanding bullets/missiles and loaded cartridges and have set two levels of authority on certificates where requested. It is usually more economical to purchase expanding bullets in large quantities which are often packaged in minimum lots of 100. It should be appreciated therefore that the quantity of loaded cartridges by comparison will be much lower.

Section 35 of the Violent Crime Reduction Act 2006 restricts the sale and purchase of a cap-type primer designed for use in metallic ammunition for a firearm. It is an offence for a person to sell a primer to which this section applies, or an empty cartridge case incorporating such a primer, unless authorised. Persons authorised include: registered firearms dealers; holders of relevant firearms certificates or persons authorised by them to purchase the primers on their behalf. Certificates must be produced at the time of purchase.

The Control of Explosives Regulations, 1991 (C.O.E.R.) provide exemptions for private use of up to 5 kg of smokeless powder (U.N. 0160 & 0161) used for the reloading of rifle ammunition. The storage of over 5 kg of these smokeless powders require licensing with the local authority under the Explosives Act, 1875. The acquisition of primers is subject to an exemption order, but they are included in the total amount of explosive allowed to be kept without licence (the explosive content of a typical cartridge primer is approximately .8 grain).

C.O.E.R. permits the keeping of small-arms ammunition/primers (cartridges made-up in assembled form) of up to 15 kg. This allows for all normal quantities of cartridges required by stalkers to be stored. In calculating the amount of ammunition you may keep, it is the net weight of powder and primer components that is used rather than the total weight of the cartridges.

The amount of non-expanding bullets/missiles you may keep is not restricted and these items do not require to be shown on your firearm application form.

Reason for requiring the firearm and place of intended use
In stating the reason for the use of a firearm stalkers should give careful consideration to both the species to be shot and the place they wish to stalk. The terms 'deer stalking', 'the lawful shooting of deer' and 'deer control' or 'culling' all adequately describe the intended purpose, provided they take account of the Deer Acts with regard to permitted firearms and ammunition. No further description of the intended use should normally be necessary. However there are weapons for which you may need to be specific in stating your intended quarry – e.g. .22 centre-fire for roe deer in Scotland. You should remember to state that you will require to zero the rifle in addition to the sporting purpose stated.

The Deer [Regulatory Reform] [England and Wales] Order 2007 made provision for the shooting of smaller species of deer [muntjac and Chinese water deer] with .22 centrefire rifles. Following consultation with ACPO a policy recommendation was made for a period of no more than five years that it would not be in the public interest

to seek to prosecute persons for shooting the above species of deer where they have an existing lawful possession of a firearm that would meet the requirements of the legislation but do not have a condition on their firearms certificate to take deer. At renewal or variation a decision would then be made as to the certificate holder's good reason to shoot the above species of deer.

If you wish to take the opportunity to shoot species other than deer, such as wild goats or foxes, you should enter these on the form, otherwise you will not be authorised for such use of the weapon. The situation with feral wild boar is dealt with in chapter 7.

The majority of certificates for stalking rifles will have territorial restrictions, particularly for a first-time applicant who may find a condition restricting him to one approved area. Generally, whilst the certificate will detail the place of use requested on the initial application, it should provide for the holder to shoot elsewhere on condition that permission with that class of firearm has been given by the person who owns the shooting rights or from whom they may be leased or otherwise obtained. The effect of this condition quite rightly puts the responsibility on the *user* of the firearm to make his own judgement on where it is safe to shoot deer at a particular place. In the right circumstances even a garden may be safe and in the wrong circumstances the open hill may be equally unsafe. It should be stressed that if a firearm is used recklessly or without due regard to suitable backstops then nowhere in the country is safe.

In providing details of the place you intend to use the weapon, or have been invited to shoot, you should bear in mind that this will be verified independently by the police, who may also examine the land. Police contact with the landowner, agent or host may come as a surprise if you have not informed them in advance that there may be an approach. This can be embarrassing and may jeopardise your future stalking opportunities. It is also an offence to knowingly or recklessly make a false statement for the grant, renewal or variation of a certificate.

Storage of firearm and ammunition
You are required to give the address at which the firearms and ammunition concerned are to be stored and whether they are to be stored in a British standard (B.S.) gun cabinet.

Under the Firearms Rules, 1989, a safe-keeping condition is attached to all firearm and shotgun certificates. This stipulates that when not in use they must at all times be stored securely so as to prevent, so far as is reasonably practicable, access to the firearms or ammunition by unauthorised persons (the condition does not apply to shotgun ammunition other than solid slug).

The Firearms Rules do not prescribe how firearms must be kept securely. The Home Departments' guidance recommends that you store them in a locked gun cabinet or other similarly secure container. In some cases, if you do not have a gun cabinet, it may be acceptable to remove the firing mechanism from the firearm and store it in a secure container. A securely built gun room or cellar with a steel door that locks can be an acceptable form of secure storage. Ideally section 1 ammunition should be stored in a separate secure compartment within a gun cabinet or in its own secure container, such as a safe.

When considering whether your storage arrangements are secure enough, a chief officer must look at the circumstances of each case and at the overall security arrangements of the premises and, if relevant, the vehicle in which they are transported.

If you fit a gun cabinet you should ensure that it is bolted securely to the wall, sufficient to prevent it being prised off with a crow-bar or garden spade. Ideally it should be positioned in your property out of sight of ground-floor windows. It is not compulsory to have a cabinet which meets the British standard. However, advice on specification is published in the Home Departments' *Firearm Security* leaflet which can be obtained from your local licensing department, which will also offer crime-prevention advice if requested.

The police may wish to inspect your security arrangements, and whilst they do not have the power to do so there would appear little point in refusing to co-operate and delaying the processing of your application.

Security and storage in Northern Ireland

Police policy in relation to deer stalking under the Firearms (Northern Ireland) Order, 1981, should be noted. The bolt for a rifle must generally be stored separately from the weapon and, unless you are classed as a professional gamekeeper or stalker, it must be kept at a police station. You must then apply in writing to the Chief Constable if you intend to go stalking, stating dates, times and locations. Areas are then checked for safety and permission granted or refused. In effect this is the authority for the removal of the bolt from police safe-keeping.

There are some estates which have estate rifles and these can be used by anyone who is deemed competent to use them under supervision of estate employees. The competency qualification currently required is the Deer Stalking Certificate.[65]

65. See chapter 7, pages 142 and 143.

Referees
You must provide the names and addresses of two people who have agreed to act as referees for your application. If it is a new application then both referees must have known you for at least two years. They must be resident in Great Britain and must not be members of your immediate family. References must be given freely without payment. Applications for variation only do not require referees.

Renewal and variation of certificates

The renewal and variation procedures are similar to that for the grant of a certificate and as with the grant, form 101 must be completed. Prior to renewal it is usual practice for the issuing licensing department to send you a reminder. However, this is not obligatory and it remains your responsibility to ensure that you apply for renewal in good time. It can be expected, in normal circumstances, that on first renewal your territorial condition will be extended to include other land over which you have permission to shoot with that class of firearm. The onus is very much on you then to decide whether it is safe to shoot at a particular location.

If you wish to vary your certificate by the addition of other firearms or some other change, then provided this is done at the time of a renewal no fee will apply. A change to the quantities of ammunition attracts no fee at any time. However, when variations to increase the number of firearms held are applied for at times other than renewal, a fee will be charged, unless it is a 'one for one' transaction. Such a change would be free of charge provided both elements of the variation took place at the same time. If there is a significant gap between the removal of one firearm and its replacement by another, the second variation would be subject to the usual fee, as the number of firearms to which the certificate relates would be increased. The removal of a firearm from a certificate does not attract a fee.

REVOCATION OF CERTIFICATES

Firearm certificates can be revoked under section 30A, Firearms Act 1968 if the Chief Officer of Police has reason to believe –

a) that the holder is of intemperate habits or unsound mind or is otherwise unfitted to be entrusted with such a firearm: or
b) that the holder can no longer to be permitted to have the firearm or ammunition to which the certificate relates in his possession without danger to the public safety or the peace.

A shotgun certificate can be revoked under section 30C if the Chief officer of Police is satisfied that he cannot be permitted to possess a shotgun without danger to the public safety or the peace.

Breaches of security and safe-keeping continue to be one of the most common reasons for revocation.

SECURITY OF FIREARMS AND AMMUNITION

Do not underestimate your liabilities regarding the security of your firearms, ammunition and equipment, particularly if you are in the process of insuring them against loss. Whilst you may be able to safe-guard your interests by insuring against public liability, loss or theft, you cannot insure against the possible revocation of your firearm certificate through a breach of security conditions. There are also, of course, wider implications as the loss of firearms may result in their use by criminals, although the risk is not as great with sporting rifles as it is with handguns or shotguns.

Stalkers need to be security conscious. The safe-keeping condition that appears on firearm certificates gives clear guidance:

> The firearms and ammunition to which this certificate relates must at all times . . . be stored securely so as to prevent, so far as is reasonably practicable, access to the firearms or ammunition by an unauthorised person.

The courts are reluctant to convict defendants who have complied with Home Departments' guidance, and it would also be difficult to justify the revocation of a firearm certificate if the holder was seen to have followed the guidance. Nevertheless, any additional security above this minimum level must be beneficial. And the condition has wide-ranging implications, as stalking often involves being away from home in remote areas, where the normal security arrangements are not available.

It may be useful to consider the security implications for the average stalker who, on a typical day, may have to travel some distance to where he intends to stalk. It is likely that an early start will involve some preparation the night before. There is a temptation to take the rifle and ammunition out of their usual secure place and put them ready with other equipment. Our advice is to leave such items, together with other valuables, locked away until the last moment. Many burglaries are committed whilst the occupants are asleep, totally unaware of what is occurring.

If you have a long journey, be careful if you stop for refreshments at roadside services or hotels. The fitting of security devices in vehicles specifically for firearms is not a legal requirement, but you are nevertheless responsible for the safe-keeping of both firearms and ammunition and should they be stolen from your vehicle you would have to show that all reasonable steps had been taken to prevent theft. If possible, park your vehicle where you have sight of it during your break. You should also remove the bolt and ammunition and keep them in your possession. The rifle should be locked away out of sight in the boot – this may not be possible in a four-wheel drive vehicle, so cover it up.

There are a number of excellent devices on the market for securing weapons out of sight or in the boot of your vehicle. These offer a reasonable level of security but should not be viewed as totally satisfactory, as the vehicle itself may be stolen. A good alarm system to the vehicle is a deterrent and would certainly help keep your firearm safe. In circumstances where the vehicle is to be left for a prolonged period or overnight you must take the rifle with you, secure in its slip, and make alternative arrangements for its safe-keeping. Whatever arrangements you make, it is prudent to ensure that you keep the bolt and ammunition separate from the rifle if this is possible. Additionally, make sure that when you leave your vehicle, you lock away in the boot other valuable items such as binoculars or telescopes. Knives should not be carried about in public and should also be locked away out of sight. See chapter 7.

It is impossible to lay down hard and fast rules on security when you are away from home; individual circumstances dictate varying degrees of security. Should a problem arise, matters will be judged on whether you have taken reasonable measures in the circumstances.

You should remember, too, that the legal definition of 'possession' of firearms may extend beyond actual physical possession, as we saw earlier.

Security makes sense if you value your stalking equipment and future credibility. Whilst you may never be able to deter a determined thief, there is much that can be done to prevent this type of crime and fulfil your legal obligations.

FIREARM RELATED OFFENCES

The carrying of firearms in public places

Under section 19, Firearms Act, 1968 (England, Wales and Scotland), and article 20(1), Firearms (Northern Ireland) Order,

1991, it is an offence 'without lawful authority or reasonable excuse' to have a loaded shotgun or loaded air weapon or 'any other firearm, loaded or not', together with suitable ammunition for that firearm, in a public place.

A firearm is deemed to be loaded if ammunition is in either the chamber, or the magazine from where it is capable of being fed into the chamber. A 'public place' is defined as including any highway and any other premises or place to which at the material time the public have or are permitted to have access, whether on payment or otherwise.

It is important to note that this offence could apply to a stalker's rifle, whether loaded or not – e.g. if the rifle were in your vehicle and your ammunition were separate in a box or pouch. This is not an absolute offence, however, and if it could be shown that you had either lawful authority or reasonable excuse, such as dealing with an injured deer at the roadside or possession whilst travelling to your stalking area, there is no offence. So if your possession in a public place is questioned, the emphasis should be placed on whether you have lawful authority or reasonable excuse rather than whether the rifle is in a loaded state or not. Clearly, if it is in a loaded state you will have to explain why this is necessary, and this will form the basis of your reasonable excuse. In circumstances where you are travelling by vehicle to or from stalking areas, your rifle should be unloaded with the bolt open or removed.

It is not essential to establish that a person was actually carrying a firearm provided there is a close physical link with and immediate control of it. In cases involving shotguns it is not necessary to prove that the person knew the weapon was loaded.[66]

Discharging firearms near highways etc.

England and Wales
Section 161, Highways Act, 1980, states:

> It is an offence without lawful authority or excuse to discharge any firearm within 50 feet of the centre of the highway and in consequence of which a user of the highway is injured, interrupted or endangered.

This is not an absolute offence and requires an element of complaint from a road user – a walker, rider or motorist. Provided you do not injure, interrupt or endanger someone on the highway you are entitled to shoot adjacent to it.

The sudden shot of a high-calibre rifle close to a passing horse

66. R v. Harrison (1995) 1 Cr. App. R. 138.

could have serious consequences for the safety of the rider, and your suitability to be entrusted with a rifle may be also questioned. In addition you may find yourself having to defend a civil claim for damages. You should be mindful of the liabilities when considering the positioning of high seats near to highways. See chapter 7.

For this purpose a highway is a public road for vehicles. It is not an offence to shoot from or over a public footpath or right of way, or near buildings, unless you are found to be trespassing or are there with intent to endanger life.

Scotland

In Scotland it is a crime at Common Law to discharge a firearm anywhere in a culpable and reckless manner, even though no actual injury may be caused. The essence of this crime is the wanton disregard for the safety of others.

The case of Cameron v. Maguire 1998[67] is of interest to stalkers. The appellant had been convicted for recklessly discharging a loaded rifle in the direction of open woodland, to the danger of the lieges in the Isle of Mull. He had fired up to ten times from the yard of his house at a target in front of a high bank of earth which was about a foot from an open pathway leading into the woodland area, which was not obstructed by the bank. He argued that the Crown had not satisfied the test of recklessness which required there to be an utter disregard of the consequences of the act insofar as the public were concerned.[68]

The appeal was refused. It was held that the test of recklessness had been satisfied as the appellant had been firing a high-calibre rifle with a range of 3 miles, where there was a clear risk the bullet would miss the target and stray to the public footpath into the woodland area. Further to this the accuracy of the rifle was not known to the appellant as it was new and there was a risk of ricochet in the vicinity of houses and a public road. It was observed that the decision would have been the same even with the houses and public road disregarded.

Northern Ireland

Section 20(2), the Firearms (Northern Ireland) Order, 1981, provides that a person who discharges any firearm on any public road, or within 60 feet of the centre of any road, or in any street, passage of a town, church, churchyard or burial ground shall be guilty of an offence unless they establish to the satisfaction of the court that they did it for a purpose that was reasonable and lawful.

67. 1999 S.C.C.R. 44.
68. Quinn v. Cunningham 1956 S.L.T. 55 (1956).

Shooting from vehicles

In the absence of case law on this subject it is our opinion that the offences below relate to shooting from within a vehicle rather than the situation where the stalker is outside the stationary vehicle and using part of the bodywork as a 'lean' when taking the shot.

England and Wales
The Deer Regulatory Reform Order 2007 amended Section 4(4) Deer Act, 1991, to permit the shooting of deer from a mechanically propelled vehicle provided the vehicle is stationary and the engine switched off. A vehicle would include aircraft or boat.[69]

Northern Ireland.
Under Article 19 (3) (b) Wildlife (Northern Ireland) Order, 1981 it is an offence to shoot at deer from a mechanically propelled vehicle unless on enclosed land where deer are usually kept. A vehicle would include aircraft or boat.[70]

Scotland
Under section 20, Deer (Scotland) Act, 1996, it is an offence to shoot at deer from any *moving* vehicle, unless it is to prevent the suffering of an injured or diseased deer or calf about to be deprived of its mother. An exemption exists under section 41(2) for the taking of deer (alive) in any manner provided it does not cause unnecessary suffering.

Shooting from a stationary vehicle away from the highway has inherent dangers. Extra care is required to ensure the safety of the participants and the humane dispatch of the deer. In Scotland such shooting can take place at night under authorisation from the Deer Commission for the purposes of crop protection. The Code of Practice for Night Shooting should be strictly adhered to.[71]

The Act also restricts the driving of deer by vehicle on any land, for the purposes of taking or killing them, to those people with written authorisation from the Deer Commission. The Code of Practice on the Use of Vehicles for the Purposes of Deer Management issued by the Commission should be followed.[72]

---

69. See chapter 2.
70. See chapter 2 pages 51 and 53.
71. See page 72–75.
72. See page 68–71.

Trespassing with firearms

Under section 20(1) and (2), Firearms Act, 1968, it is an offence for a person to enter or be upon any land (including water) or building or part of a building as a trespasser whilst in possession of a firearm[73] without reasonable excuse. A similar offence exists in the Firearms (Northern Ireland) Order, 1981, under article 21(1) and (2), in which the proof of reasonable excuse lies on the accused.

As to whether following up a wounded beast would be considered a reasonable excuse would be for a court to decide. The aggrieved party might view the explanation as a cover for the poaching of deer. The criminal and civil liabilities of crossing your boundary in these circumstances are dealt with in chapter 7.

It is also worth noting that under section 21(5) of the Deer (Scotland) Act, 1996, any person who uses any firearm or any ammunition for the purpose of wilfully injuring any deer shall be guilty of an offence.

VISITS TO AND FROM ABROAD

Visits abroad

If you wish to stalk deer abroad and take your rifle, you must ensure that you are able to comply with the requirements the country may have for visiting stalkers. If the country to be visited is another E.U.

member,[74] you will need to obtain a European Firearms Pass (E.F.P.). These are obtainable without charge from the firearms licensing department of your local police force and can cover any section 1 firearm for which you have a certificate.

The E.F.P. will be valid for the duration of your current certificate, after which it can be renewed. You may also change or extend your E.F.P. to cover other firearms. Permission or

---

73. This means any firearm, including an air weapon.
74. Austria, Belgium, Denmark, Finland, France, Germany, Greece, the Republic of Ireland, Italy, Luxembourg, Netherlands, Portugal, Spain and Sweden.

authorisation from the authorities of the country to be visited should be obtained prior to your visit and put on your E.F.P. However, this is not normally required from an E.U. country if you are using the firearms for stalking, hunting or marksmanship activities. Certain categories of firearms, however, are prohibited by some states. These are laid down in the E.C. Directive on the Control of the Acquisition and Possession of Weapons, 91/477/E.E.C.

During your visit you must carry your E.F.P. whenever you have your rifle with you. You should be able to prove the reason for your trip and must produce your E.F.P. to the police or customs officers if requested.

An information leaflet entitled *The European Firearms Pass* is produced by the Home Departments and is normally available from your local police licensing department.

Visits to Northern Ireland

Stalkers wishing to take a rifle to Northern Ireland must first obtain a certificate of approval from the Royal Ulster Constabulary, Firearms Licensing Branch, Linasharragh, Montgomery Road, Belfast. There is no fee. Visiting stalkers are required to specify details of their firearms certificate and stalking arrangements whilst in the country. Applications must be made well in advance of your visit (at least a month). A copy of your firearm certificate must be sent with the application, together with a letter of permission or authority to stalk.

Firearms may be imported to Northern Ireland by a person normally resident outside the U.K. provided that either a Northern Ireland visitor's firearm certificate or a Northern Ireland three-year firearm certificate has been issued by the Chief Constable of the Royal Ulster Constabulary. Application must be made not less than two months before the proposed date of arrival. There is no fee payable for the visitor's firearm certificate.

Application forms together with other information that may be required, are obtainable from Royal Ulster Constabulary, Firearms Licensing Department, Knocknagoney House, Knocknagoney Road, Belfast BT4 2PP.

Visits to the Republic of Ireland

Over 3,000 overseas shooters visit Ireland each year, many of them for the purpose of deer stalking. The Republic has separate licensing arrangements and being a member of the E.U., visitors must first obtain an E.F.P., as described above. Deer stalkers should note that centre-fire calibres greater than .22 (5.56 mm) are prohibited and therefore they must first obtain a visitor's firearm certificate if they wish to take or use their own rifle. The minimum calibres for shooting deer are .22–250 centre-fire and the maximum is .270.

Application forms for firearms certificates can be obtained from the Department of Justice, Firearms Section, 72–76 St Stephens Green, Dublin. Certificates are granted on the basis of the issue of a hunting licence, for which there is no charge. This is obtainable from the Wildlife Service, Leeson Lane, Dublin. The licence must be forwarded with your application for the firearm certificate. It is stressed that applications should be made well in advance – at least a month before your visit.

Visits to Great Britain

The provisions for visitors are contained in the Firearms (Amendment) Act, 1988. Under section 17, all visitors who want to bring a firearm into Great Britain or possess one here must first obtain a visitor's firearm permit. The application for such permits must be made on the applicant's behalf by a sponsor or representative, to the chief officer of police for the area in which he lives. Application forms are available from police stations or the local licensing department. The sponsor or representative may be acting in a private capacity, or may be a professional stalker or an official or employee of a shooting organisation or agency. He does not necessarily need to have a firearm certificate himself. An information leaflet, *Permits for Visitors to Great Britain* is published by the Home Departments and is normally available from police licensing departments.

Section 18 of the Act provides that a permit is not required for the purchase of a firearm if it is exported without it coming into the visitor's possession in this country. You may only do this if you have not been in Great Britain for more than thirty days in the preceding twelve months. Additionally a permit is not required where an estate rifle is used by the visitor.[75]

Under E.U. Directive 91/477/E.E.C. there are special requirements for visitors from other E.U. states. In addition to the British visitor's permit they must also possess an E.F.P. issued by the authorities of their country of residence. When a sponsor or representative applies for a British visitor's permit the E.F.P. must be sent with the application to the chief officer of police. Both permits must be with the visitor when bringing the firearm into the country and at all times

---

75. See page 123.

when he is in possession of the firearm whilst here. They must be produced to a police or customs officer on demand.

The import and export of firearms

The import and export of firearms and ammunition are controlled in Great Britain and appropriate licences must be obtained from the Department of Trade and Industry (D.T.I.). The E.C. Weapons Directive (91/477/E.E.C.) applies only to movements of firearms between member states; other countries are subject to normal licensing procedures.

For commercial importations, D.T.I. import licences are only issued to importers authorised by the police as registered firearms dealers. Open individual licences may be issued for non-prohibited section 1 firearms and ammunition, or, in the case of an importation from another E.U. member state, a transfer licence issued by the member state.

As an extra statutory concession, certain firearms which are covered by a valid section 1 firearm certificate or a British visitor's firearms permit may be accepted in lieu of an import licence for the non-commercial importation of a section 1 firearm. If the firearm is being imported from another E.U. country, the importer must also hold an E.F.P. detailing the firearm being imported.

An export licence is not required if you are taking your rifle to another E.U. member state as part of your personal effects for a stalking holiday or competition, provided an E.F.P. is held and the firearm is not one of a restricted class. You cannot use your E.F.P. if you intend taking the rifle there on a permanent basis. To do this you will need a licence from the D.T.I.

You can obtain more information and advice about the licensing requirements from the Export Licensing Unit, Department of Trade and Industry, Kingsgate House, 66–74 Victoria Street, London SW1E 6SW. If you require more advice about the E.F.P., taking firearms abroad or buying firearms in other E.U. states, you should contact the firearms licensing department of your local police.

CHAPTER 7

Stalking Liabilities

As you travel to your stalking ground it is doubtful whether your thoughts will be on your responsibility to comply with the law. You are more likely to be thinking of the weather, the direction of the wind and conditions underfoot, which will ultimately dictate your stalking tactics. You may have a knife at your side and a high-calibre rifle with ammunition in the vehicle, yet as a prudent stalker with honest intentions you should pose no threat to public safety or the environment – unlike the 38-ton articulated lorry that has just overtaken you in the fast lane!

But whether you are stalking alone or as a guest, you must ensure that you do not contravene the law or put at risk your own or the public's safety. This can only be achieved with proper training and by having a thorough knowledge of the law. Minimising liabilities particularly in potentially dangerous situations should be everyone's aim.

RESPONSIBLE DEER MANAGEMENT

Whilst there is no substitute for hands-on experience gained over time and under the direct supervision of an experienced stalker, formal training courses are available that lay the foundations for safe and responsible stalking. Indeed, such qualifications may in the future be essential in assessing an individual's suitability to cull deer with a rifle.[76]

A progressive system of deer management qualifications relevant to both professional and recreational deer managers and stalkers has been developed. Known as the Deer Stalking Certificate (DSC), its aim is to set standards of competence for the efficient and humane culling of deer in line with the government's vocational qualifications. The certificate is awarded by Deer Management Qualifications Limited (D.M.Q.), a company set up by participating organisations from within the industry to develop, set and monitor the standards for wild deer management. Both the B.A.S.C. and the B.D.S. are assessment centres for this purpose.

A number of deer management courses are available including a B.D.S. Advanced Stalker's Course, BASC Sporting Rifle, Dogs for Deer, and preparatory courses for the Deer Stalking Certificates Level 1 and 2.

St Hubert Club members can undertake a training programme resulting in their Qualified Stalker Certificate recognised as a Lantra Customised Award.

Once a stalker has gained the appropriate qualifications,[77] or gained experience privately, there are a number of other requirements that should be satisfied prior to stalking.

Legal requirements relating to firearms

You should hold an appropriate firearm certificate covering both the weapon and ammunition. Your intended use of the weapon and ammunition must comply with the conditions of your certificate.[78] Of particular importance is the safe-keeping condition.

Game licences

Game licences are no longer required for the shooting of deer on unenclosed land in England and Wales:

Section 4 of the Game Licences Act, 1860, still applies in Scotland and states that such a licence is required by anyone who takes, kills or pursues, or assists in doing so, any game, woodcock, snipe, rabbit or deer. Section 5 provides an exemption for the taking and killing of

76. See chapter 6.
77. See pages 229–231 for contact details.
78. See chapter 6.

deer in enclosed lands by the owner or occupier or by those under his direction or permission. *Enclosed land* means land used for farming and enclosed by normal agricultural hedges in contrast to moorland where a licence would be required. In our view this would include fenced forestry blocks.[79]

Authority to be on the land

You may own the land or the sporting rights to the deer, in which case the authority is clear. Where this is not the case you may simply have verbal authority from the owner or occupier of the land. This is sufficient, provided he has a right to give such permission. Should the stalking rights be let[80] then such authority would need to be given by the holder of the rights.

Our advice is that all such authorities should ideally be in writing and should specify what you can and cannot shoot. Oral permission is a recipe for uncertainty and should anything go wrong the landowner could deny he gave you permission. We have assisted some major landowners in formulating their own firearms policy, and we advise that it should include guidance and the issuing of authorities to be on land with firearms. An identification system can be incorporated into the policy, in which users of section 1 firearms are issued with a personal document providing details of their authority. This can provide assurance to police and members of the public should the holder be challenged. It may also help prevent breaches of the law relating to armed trespass and poaching.

Knowledge of the land to be stalked

A good knowledge of the land is essential not only for safe shooting but also for efficient deer management. You should have an awareness of where footpaths and highways dissect the land, and knowledge of other sporting or farming activities. This information may make a difference to when and where you stalk. You should also have a clear understanding of where the boundaries lie. This is essential as ignorance will be a poor defence should you be found trespassing with a firearm. A number of liabilities arise in such situations and are elaborated upon in chapter 7.

79. Jemmison v Priddle 1971.
80. See chapter 1.

Making the landowner or occupier aware of your presence

This may not always be practical or useful in remote, isolated areas which are owned by absentee landlords. But in other areas arrangements should be made in advance where possible and the owner notified of your visit. Alternatively, some form of notice should be given from which it can easily be ascertained that you are stalking, such as a fax message, an advance list of dates, displaying red flags (often used on the open hill).

Identification of quarry

Even experienced stalkers can make a mistake in identification but the occasions should be rare and the error corrected before the trigger is squeezed. Mistaken identification may be grounds for mitigation but is no defence in law. The liabilities involved depend on whether what has been shot by mistake is protected at the time by close season.

Mistakes are more likely to be made in identifying the sexes rather than the species – an error in identifying the latter would be unforgivable. Care is required when shooting roe deer at the time when the bucks are casting antlers and in their close season. Time should be taken to ensure the correct sexing of immature deer that may not be showing obvious signs of antler development.

Stalker training and qualifications take account of the importance of identification but there is no substitute for experience in the field. As the late Ken Macarthur, the great roe expert in Scotland would say, 'Time has to be spent watching deer – without the rifle!'

The following sketches may be of assistance.

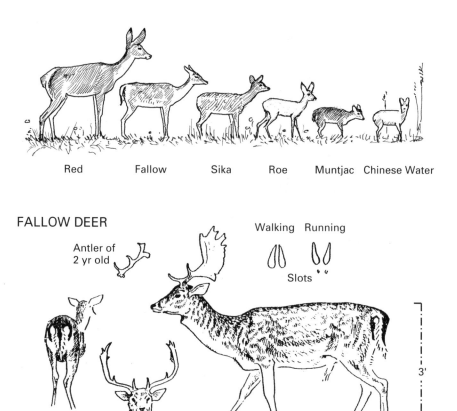

Red   Fallow   Sika   Roe   Muntjac   Chinese Water

FALLOW DEER

Walking   Running

Antler of
2 yr old

Slots

Doe

Buck

3'

Diana E. Brown.

Can be various colours. Antlers cast annually in April–May

RED DEER

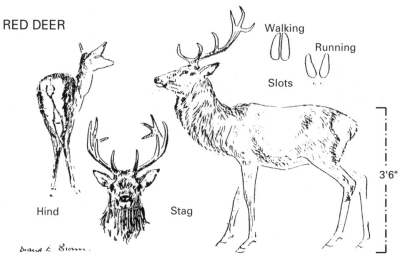

Walking

Running

Slots

Hind

Stag

3'6"

Diana E. Brown.

Antlers shed annually about March

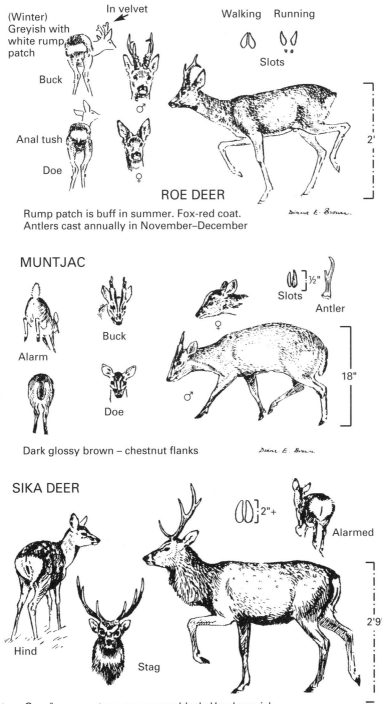

(Winter) Greyish with white rump patch

In velvet

Walking   Running

Slots

Buck

Anal tush

Doe

♂

♀

2'

ROE DEER

Rump patch is buff in summer. Fox-red coat.
Antlers cast annually in November–December

Diana E. Brown.

MUNTJAC

Alarm

Buck

Doe

♀

♂

Slots

½"

Antler

18"

Dark glossy brown – chestnut flanks

Diana E. Brown.

SIKA DEER

2"+

Alarmed

Hind

Stag

2'9"

Winter – Grey/brown – stags can appear black. Head greyish
Summer – Dappled chestnut. Head greyish
Antlers cast annually in March–May

Diana E. Brown

STALKING NEAR BOUNDARIES

One essential task prior to stalking any new ground is to gain a thorough knowledge of exactly where boundaries lie. If you have doubts you may become preoccupied when your full concentration should be on the job in hand. You should not be relying on the adjacent landowner, tenant or stalker to tell you that you have got it wrong. This is embarrassing and unprofessional – and not without liability. Clarification of boundaries can be an onerous task and in some cases may lead to disputes, but it must be set against the liabilities involved in ignoring them and the advantages it may bring. You should try and obtain a plan or large-scale ordnance survey map on which you can clearly mark boundaries once you have clarified them with the owner. On new ground you should ensure that you walk the boundaries, without your rifle and with the owner if this is possible.

Civil action for simple trespass may be taken by a landowner against anyone setting foot on his land without permission[81] (although in Scotland it is necessary to show that damage has occurred). If you are found on the wrong side of the fence you may be sued for damages in the civil court, although unless substantial damage or nuisance can be shown, any damages are likely to be minimal. However, if you are carrying your rifle at the time, loaded or not, and have no reasonable excuse, you may be prosecuted for the criminal offence of trespass with a firearm.[82] Where persistent trespass takes place an injunction may also be applied for to prevent further infringements.

Trespass is not confined to your own physical entry onto another's property but could extend to sending your dog or firing a shot over the boundary.

Shooting deer close to your boundary will inevitably lead to the dilemma of a shot beast running over the line before falling dead or continuing with an injury. For the responsible stalker this situation should not present a problem as agreements will previously have been made with the adjacent landowner or tenant to cater for this type of occurrence. The beast will be retrieved or followed up and a courtesy call made to inform the neighbour of the incident.

Where such amicable arrangements have not been or cannot be made then to retrieve the beast or go in search of it without first obtaining permission will incur liabilities. Claims over the ownership of a carcase, where boundaries are in dispute, can be difficult to assess

81. See chapter 8.
82. See chapter 6.

and ultimately would have to be decided by a court. However the Common Law principle is that property in a wild animal, should it fall dead, is vested in the owner of the land where it has died.

You may well consider you have a claim of ownership of the beast,[83] but in entering the land without permission you commit an act of trespass and have no legal right to be there, even if you are following up an injured animal. You may have to defend yourself against an allegation of trespassing with a firearm (contrary to section 20 of the Firearms Act, 1968), and you would have to convince the court that in pursuing the injured beast you had a reasonable excuse. At the very least an action could lie against you for simple trespass to land (England and Wales only). The obvious suspicion will be that you are a poacher and shot the deer over the boundary.

Liability may not be confined to the civil courts since the legislation protecting deer caters for offences of removing a carcase from land.[84] Although this legislation is designed to combat poachers returning to the land having killed deer the previous night, it may come into effect when a stalker's behaviour is suspicious and warrants legal action – e.g. when deer are being discreetly shot over a boundary and then retrieved on the excuse that they were legitimately shot but then crossed the boundary before falling dead.

We do not consider that proceedings are appropriate for the offence of removing a carcase from land if there is genuine evidence that the beast shot was legitimately on land where authority existed. In such cases careful examination of the area where the beast was shot should

83. See chapter 1.
84. See chapters 2 and 3.

be made in an attempt to reveal blood and hair (paint and pins) which may corroborate the evidence.

The case of Jemmison v. Priddle, 1971, involved the shooting of deer close to a boundary. One of the deer, a red hind, was shot on land where permission had been granted. The animal subsequently ran and dropped dead on the other side of the boundary. Although the case centred on whether the land was 'enclosed' for the purpose of exemption from the need for a game licence (elaborated upon above) it was accepted that deer shot legitimately on land where permission was granted may run and drop on land where no such permission existed. However, the case did not rule on the rights of ownership of the deer in question, which was seized by the owner of the land where it fell.

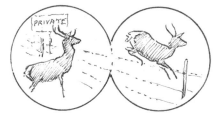

When there are disputes over where boundaries lie, there is a need to minimise the liabilities involved. Most situations are preventable, particularly if you resist pulling the trigger and wait for a better opportunity on another beast that is not so close to the boundary. Alternatively, it may be a case for getting in close and taking a neck shot, thereby preventing movement after the shot has been taken. Constructive trespass can also occur where your bullet travels on over the land where you do not have permission to shoot.[85] Liaison with neighbours is a matter of common courtesy and often mutually beneficial agreements can be achieved.

THE SHOOTING OF NON-TARGET SPECIES

Opportunities occasionally present themselves for the stalker to shoot non-protected species other than deer; wild goats, boar and foxes spring to mind. Authority for the shooting of other species should be obtained from the owner of the land (or the shooting rights). The firearm certificate for your stalking rifle should cater for such a

85. See chapter 8.

variation, i.e. that the conditions of use include wild goat, boar or fox control. The term 'vermin' may cover wild boar and foxes but you should clarify this with the licensing department of the issuing police force. If your certificate has been granted on the basis of deer stalking only, that is all you are legally entitled to shoot and therefore to shoot something other than a deer, irrespective of the circumstances, will render you liable for a breach of certificate conditions. These conditions are important, and you should be fully aware of exactly what is written there. Remember, you are at risk of revocation if you breach the conditions.[86]

Wild boar

Wild boar were once native to Britain and thought to have become extinct towards the end of the thirteenth century. In recent times the farming of wild boar has become popular and this has been promoted by the British Wild Boar Association (BWBA) who in the past have issued guidance on dealing with escapee boar. However, a number of escapees were never captured and together with suspected intentional releases by those with vested sporting interests in the species it was only a matter of time before a breeding population of feral wild boar were established. These are located mainly in the south of England.

DEFRA launched a public consultation on wild boar in England in 2005 . However, it was not until 2008 that a report was made public on the status, impact and management of feral wild boar by DEFRA's Wildlife Division.[87] This document sets out the policy that primary responsibility for feral wild boar management lies with local

86. See Chapter 6 Firearms.
87. *Feral Wild Boar in England* – A report on behalf of DEFRA European Wildlife Division 2008.

communities and individual landowners. Government will help facilitate this regional management through the provision of advice and guidance.

There are no specific legal restrictions governing how wild boar can be controlled at this present time. General protection is currently restricted to acts relating to cruelty and provided for by the Protection of Animals Act, 1911, Wild Mammals Protection Act, 1996, the Animal Welfare Act, 2006 and the Animal Health and Welfare (Scotland) Act 2006. Wild boar may only be kept under licence issued by local authorities, either under the Dangerous Wild Animals Act, 1976, in the case of private keepers or under the Zoo Licensing Act, 1981, for collections open to the public. The Wildlife and Countryside Act, 1981, prohibits their release or escape into the wild and the provisions of the Hunting Act 2004 or Protection of Wild Mammals (Scotland) Act 2002 would also apply in terms of the use of dogs. However no legislation exists in respect of their management and control once they become wild. There is clearly a need for further legislation to safeguard the welfare of wild boar and regulate how they are managed. Wild boar groups are matriarchal and the indiscriminate shooting of leading sows is likely to spread boar into unwanted areas making effective management difficult.

Where feral boar have become established in the wild they may be killed or taken by owners and occupiers of land or persons with their authority at any time using any type of firearm or ammunition. Now that DEFRA have declared their policy the once held view that their status could perhaps be classed as 'vermin' is doubtful, despite them being injurious to crops etc. Licensing Authorities are now requiring that wild boar be specifically listed on a firearms certificate if an individual wishes to shoot boar with a rifle. Therefore, where boar are shot with a firearm requiring a firearm certificate, unless the appropriate condition to shoot wild boar has been granted an offence may be committed relating to a breach of condition on the relevant certificate. A certificate will only normally be endorsed for shooting wild boar in this country if the calibre is deemed suitable (see below) and good reason is shown i.e. authority has been gained to shoot boar on land within an area known or thought to have boar present. Each application will be judged on its merits and assessed appropriately taking into account the most recent guidance from DEFRA and the Home Office.

DEFRA has proposed that consideration should be given to introducing a legal minimum firearms requirement as outlined below, a close season for sows from 1st March to 31st August, and the addition of wild boar and hybrids to Schedule 9 of the Wildlife and

Countryside Act, 1981 to prohibit their deliberate release into the wild. Following DEFRA's proposals further consultation will take place and it is anticipated that guidance will be issued. Of interest to those deer stalkers who may have the opportunity to shoot wild boar will be the recommended minimum calibre of rifle being .270W, with a bullet weight of at least 130grs, capable of delivering a muzzle energy in excess of 2,600ft/lbs.[88]

There has been a broad concensus on this recommended calibre and it is stressed this is viewed as the absolute minimum. The Forestry Commission, having risk assessed the impact of wild boar, propose to use no less than .30 calibre should there be a need for control by shooting. Further proposals relating to the use of shotguns specify their use in exceptional circumstances for damage prevention under similar provisions to those in Section 7 of the Deer Act, 1991. The proposal suggests the use of a 12 bore shotgun loaded with a single non-spherical projectile weighing not less than 22.68 grammes (350grns) where the boar are believed to be causing serious damage.

Deer stalkers operating in areas likely to be inhabited by wild boar should be aware that Natural England Wildlife Management and Licensing Service are monitoring any new reports of the presence of boar. Reports can be submitted to them by email or telephone. They are also interested in recording instances of agricultural damage attributed to wild boar.

CRUELTY AND HUMANE DISPATCH

Historically the law has not protected wild animals such as deer from acts of cruelty. Only in situations where wild deer could be considered as captive have they come within the legislation protecting animals against acts of cruelty. The provisions of the Protection of Animals Act, 1911, or the Protection of Animals (Scotland) Act, 1912, only provide protection for animals that are defined as 'domestic or captive'.[89] There may be circumstances in which wild deer may be deemed to be 'captive' and therefore the stalker needs to be aware of the liabilities involved.

In addition, the Welfare of Animals Act (Northern Ireland), 1972, and the Wild Mammals Protection Act, 1996, now provide protection in certain circumstances for deer in their wild state against acts of cruelty.

88. Police Home Office Guidance 2002 and BASC guidance.
89. The effect of these Acts in relation to farmed or wild deer kept in captivity are dealt with in detail in chapter 1.

The Protection of Animals Acts

The Protection of Animals Act, 1911, and the Protection of Animals (Scotland) Act, 1912, define a captive animal as 'any animal . . . which is in captivity, or confinement, or which is maimed, pinioned, or subjected to any appliance or contrivance for the purpose of hindering or preventing its escape'.

The Acts create offences of cruelly beating, kicking, ill-treating, over-riding, over-driving, torturing, infuriating or terrifying any animal, or causing the animal any unnecessary suffering by wantonly or unreasonably doing or omitting to do any act.

Two past cases, both considered by the Court of Appeal, involved allegations of cruelty to deer and are relevant in determining the circumstances in which deer may be viewed by the courts as being in captivity or a state of confinement.

The first of these is Rogers v. Pickersgill, 1910. At the time of this case it was a matter of great controversy as to whether the hunting of semi-captive animals should be allowed at all. An exception existed at the time (and still does under section 1(3)(b)) for the coursing or hunting of any captive animal, unless such animal is liberated in an injured, mutilated or exhausted condition. In addition the exception would not apply if the animal at the time was still in captivity, or had been recaptured or brought under control. The legislation catered here, amongst other hunting and coursing practices, for the hunting of 'carted' deer.[90]

The circumstances of the case were that a hind (previously released from a cart) was being hunted by hounds and twice took refuge in a yard, where it backed into a shed. It was poked and whipped to get it out. The hounds again gave chase. Eventually, after colliding with a barbed wire fence, by which it was injured, it was dragged in a state of exhaustion along a road, where it fell down and died.

The Master of Hounds was subsequently summoned to court for an offence of cruelty to the hind while *in captivity*. The case centred on whether, at the point when the hind had backed into the shed, the hunt was over and, if that was the case, the exemption under the above section did not apply. The magistrates initially dismissed the case on the basis that the acts were done at a time when the hunt was not at an end and during the course of the hunting of the animal, and therefore fell within the legal exemption.

Following an appeal it was apparent that the magistrates had not heard all the evidence. Hence the case as stated did not rule on whether cruelty offences were committed or whether the hunt had

90. See page 28 for a description of 'carted' deer.

ended. The judge was sufficiently satisfied that there was at least a *prima facie* case that what was done was done when the hunt was finished and therefore the case was remitted to the magistrates' court to hear evidence in answer to the facts proved.

The appeal court were of the opinion that hunting involved pursuit, and once an animal had taken refuge from being pursued any cruelty that was committed upon it may not be excused on the grounds that the hunt was still continuing (and therefore exempt).

The second case was Rowley v. Murphy, 1963. The circumstances of this case involved hunting a wild stag with hounds. The stag jumped over the hedge of a field onto a main road, slipped on the tarmac surface and went under a stationary van. The stag was dragged from beneath the van and carried into an enclosure nearby, where it was killed with a knife.

The Master of Hounds was summoned to court for the offence of cruelly terrifying an animal by cutting its throat with a knife, contrary to section 1(1)(a) of the Protection of Animals Act, 1911. The justices found that there was no case to answer on the basis that the stag was not an 'animal' within the meaning of the Act, i.e. not in captivity or confinement at the time of the incident. On appeal by the prosecutor it was contended that there was a case to answer and the case centred on whether the hunted stag at the point of killing was captive or in confinement. It was not of concern to the court whether what was done was cruel or not. The sole question was whether the stag in all the circumstances came within the scope of the legislation – i.e. was the animal in a state of captivity or confinement at the time the alleged cruelty was committed.

The court took due regard of the history of the legislation and a number of previous cases were referred to during the case, in particular Steele v. Rogers, 1912, in which it was stated that a mere temporary inability to get away was not a 'state of captivity' and that something more than mere captivity was necessary, such as some period of time during which 'acts of dominion' are exercised over the animal before it can be said to be in a state of captivity.

Judgement was made between whether 'captivity' starts the moment an animal is captured and hands are laid on the animal and prevented from escaping, or whether the words 'in captivity' denote a state of affairs in which domination is exercised over the animal beyond mere capture. In referring to the exemption for hunting and coursing of any 'captive' animal it was noted that *recapture* brings an animal into a state of 'captivity'. A clear distinction was drawn between 'in captivity' meaning a state of captivity and that of an animal being captive, i.e. subject temporarily to restraint by human beings.

It was subsequently held that a mere temporary inability to get away was not a state of captivity, and the words 'captive animal' meant by definition an animal in captivity or confinement, so the stag was not an animal within the meaning or protection of the Act. The appeal was dismissed.

Humane dispatch

There may be circumstances in which a stalker will have to dispatch deer that may be considered as 'captive' at the time by virtue of the fact that it is wounded and is prevented from escaping. Therefore the stalker's actions must not cause unnecessary suffering. Training in and experience of humane dispatch are therefore essential.

In a stalking situation a wounded beast should be dispatched with the rifle from a safe distance. There may be exceptional circumstances where this may not be possible or practical, in which case a knife can be used provided it is done in such a manner that it does not cause unnecessary suffering to the beast. It should be done in a swift and humane manner, which requires adequate training and experience on the part of the stalker, who should adhere to accepted practice and guidance given by such bodies as the British Deer Society and the B.A.S.C.[91] It is stressed that this should only be necessary in exceptional circumstances.

If a complaint is made against a stalker for the manner in which he has dispatched an injured deer, consideration would be given to whether a cruelty offence (Protection of Animals Act, 1911, Protection of Animals (Scotland) Act, 1912) had been committed. The first consideration would be whether in the circumstances the beast was captive or in a state of captivity, as discussed above. If this were the case and the actions of the stalker were considered to be unnecessary, matters could proceed to court. Two questions arise in establishing whether the act complained of was necessary and done with the minimum of suffering: what did the stalker do – e.g. cut the beast's throat with a sharp, suitable knife – and what was the reason for doing it – e.g. to prevent further suffering. If the reason is sufficiently important to justify the act, even if it is bodged through inexperience, then we do not consider an offence would be committed.

We are of the opinion that in normal stalking conditions, carrying handguns solely in case one needs to dispatch injured deer is neither practical nor necessary.[92] There is a case for some individuals, such

91. An advice note is available from the B.A.S.C.
92. See chapter 6.

as rangers and deer managers, who are regularly called out to deal with injured deer, often road casualties, to be licensed for the use of suitable handguns[93] or other slaughtering instruments for dispatching deer at close quarters. As explained in chapter 6, any firearm or shotgun can be used for humane dispatch but stalkers need to be aware that their Section 1 firearm certificate conditions must cover the use of the firearm in this situation .

It is worth noting that section 6(2), Deer Act, 1991, section 25 Deer (Scotland) Act, 1996, and article 20 The Wildlife (Northern Ireland) Order, 1985[94] provide legal exemptions against certain acts done for the purpose of preventing suffering of injured or diseased deer. It is stressed that these exemptions relate only to acts done that would otherwise be offences as specified within the Deer Acts. They do not exempt any act that may incur liabilities under other legislation. For example, shooting a deer during the close season is an offence but if done to prevent suffering no offence would be committed under the Deer Acts. However if a firearm was used in breach of the certificate conditions, for whatever purpose, an offence under the Firearms Act would be committed.

The Welfare of Animals Act (Northern Ireland), 1972

Sections 13 and 14 in Part III of the Act relate to offences of cruelty to any animal and are similar to the equivalent legislation in England, Wales and Scotland in describing the acts that will constitute cruelty offences. The key difference is that the legislation is not restricted to animals described as 'captive or domestic'. Hence any animal, wild or otherwise is included.

Section 15 provides for a number of exemptions to the offences of cruelty which may be of relevance to stalkers:

- acts done in the course of, or in the preparation for, the destruction of any animal as food for human consumption, unless unnecessary suffering is caused to the animal
- acts done in the course of the hunting, pursuit, coursing, capture or destruction of any wild animal, unless unnecessary suffering is caused to the animal
- the coursing or hunting of any animal, other than a domestic animal, which is released for that purpose and which is not under control, unless it was released in an injured, mutilated or exhausted condition

93. A single-shot .32 handgun is recommended by the R.S.P.C.A.
94. See chapters 2 and 3.

The Wild Mammals (Protection) Act, 1996

This Act, covering England, Wales and Scotland, represents the first legislation to protect all wild mammals from certain acts of cruelty. Pressure for its introduction was brought to bear on the government following a number of well-publicised cases of cruelty to wild animals, in situations where legal action was not possible against the offenders, e.g. the kicking to death of a hedgehog.

Section 1 provides that if any person mutilates, kicks, beats, nails or otherwise impales, stabs, burns, stones, crushes, drowns, drags or asphyxiates any wild animal (as defined below) with intent to inflict unnecessary suffering, he shall be guilty of an offence.

Section 2 gives certain exemptions:

A person shall not be guilty of an offence by reason of:

(a) the attempted killing of a wild mammal as an act of mercy if he shows that the mammal had been so seriously disabled otherwise than by his unlawful act and that there was no reasonable chance of its recovering;

(b) the killing in a reasonably swift and humane manner of any wild animal if he shows that the mammal had been injured or taken in the course of either lawful shooting, hunting, coursing or pest control activity;

(c) doing anything which is authorised by or under any enactment;

(d) any act made unlawful by section 1 if the act was done by means of any snare, trap, dog, or bird lawfully used for the purpose of killing or taking any wild animal; or

(e) the lawful use of any poisonous or noxious substance on any wild mammal.

The Act defines 'wild mammal' as any mammal which is not domestic or captive within the meaning of the Protection of Animals Act, 1911, or the Protection of Animals (Scotland) Act, 1912.

The exemptions listed at (a) and (b) are clearly relevant to the dispatch of injured deer. The key issues for the stalker are:

- The deer must not have been injured by the stalker's unlawful acts. A poacher would therefore not be able to claim this legal exemption in respect of a deer injured by him, but someone innocently coming across a deer in the road who attempted to put it out of its misery but bodged the killing through inexperience would not commit an offence under this Act.
- Such dispatch should be reasonably swift and humane and the deer

must have been injured or taken by lawful shooting etc. This exemption emphasises the point that the dispatch of deer should be done in the correct manner as described by the organisations responsible for competency qualifications.[95]

If allegations were made that such a killing was not swift and humane it would be important in any defence for the stalker to show that his actions were in accordance with accepted practice. It should be noted that the exemption would not apply if it could be shown that the activity you were involved in was unlawful – e.g. if you were trespassing or you were in breach of the conditions of your firearm certificate.

THE CARRYING OF KNIVES

No responsible deer stalker would set out without a sharp, suitable knife. It is an essential piece of equipment, its main use being to facilitate bleeding of the carcase and the gralloch. Good stalkers pride themselves on the quality of their knives and their safe use, but few stop to consider the liabilities involved in carrying them.

The increase in knife-related crime, particularly amongst young criminals, has led to substantial legislation restricting the possession of knives. There have been periodic amnesties; the one in 1996 yielding 38,000 weapons, including many formidable knives. The problem for the legislators over the years has been in framing the law to prevent the carrying of knives, which may be used for causing injury, and at the same time allow them to be routinely carried for wholly justifiable and innocent purposes, for example by stalkers.

The following legislation shows that the emphasis is on the prevention of crime, penalising the possession of knives in public places.

The Prevention of Crime Act, 1953 (England and Wales)

It is an offence to carry an offensive weapon in a public place without lawful authority or reasonable excuse (the onus is on the defendant to prove lawful authority or excuse). The term 'offensive weapon' includes any article made, adapted or intended for causing injury to a person. 'Public place' is defined as any place to which the public have access at the material time. This includes areas where an open access policy may apply.

95. See page 143.

The Restriction of Offensive Weapons Act, 1959 and 1961 (England, Wales and Scotland) and Criminal Justice (Northern Ireland) Order 1996

This legislation identifies certain specific weapons, including flick knives and gravity knives, and creates offences in respect of their manufacture and sale.

The Criminal Justice Act, 1988 (England and Wales) and Criminal Law (Consolidation) (Scotland) Act 1995

The provisions create an offence of possessing, in a public place, any article which has a blade or is sharply pointed, except a folding pocket knife with a blade not exceeding 3 inches, i.e. the cutting edge exceeds 7.62 centimetres. The exception does not extend to a lock knife of any length having a mechanism that must be physically activated to close the blade.

A defence is provided if the person can prove he had good reason or lawful authority for having the article with him in a public place or had it with him for use at work, for religious reasons or as part of any national costume. To 'have the knife with you' is wider than being attached to your belt or having it in your physical possession. It includes being to hand and ready for use. For example laid on the back seat of the car or even in the boot.

The Offensive Weapons Act, 1996 (England, Wales and Scotland)

This Act increases police powers of arrest and extended the law to cover school premises. It prohibits the sale of knives to persons under sixteen, and creates an indictable offence of carrying an offensive weapon, for which the offender can be sent for trial at the Crown Court.

Under the Act the offences described above – i.e. carrying offensive weapons such as knives without lawful authority or reasonable excuse (1953 Act) and having an article with a blade or point in a public place or school premises (1988 Act) – were made 'arrestable', giving the police (and civilians in certain circumstances) the power to make immediate arrests without warrant. The police may also arrest on suspicion.

The Knives Act, 1997 (England, Wales and Scotland)

This Act has two main objectives. The first is to create new criminal offences in relation to the possession, marketing and publishing of material about certain knives. The second is to confer powers on the police to stop and search people or vehicles for knives and other offensive weapons.

Under section 1 of the Act it is an offence to market a knife in a way that indicates or suggests that it is suitable for combat or is likely to stimulate or encourage violent behaviour involving the use of the knife as a weapon. Such a knife is described as being one 'suitable for use as a weapon for inflicting injury or causing fear, being an instrument with a blade or is sharply pointed'. Consequently any knife in the above circumstances may fall within the provisions of the Act.

The practical implications of the legislation

Whilst stalking it is unlikely that you will be in a public place and the carrying of a knife, should it ever be questioned, will be easily justified. Once in a public place – travelling in your car or visiting the local shop – the situation changes somewhat in that you may have to prove that you have a reasonable excuse or good reason for carrying your knife or, if you are a professional deer manager or ranger, that you have it for use at work.

Individual circumstances will dictate whether possession of a knife at a particular time and place can be justified. This is very much a matter of common sense, in that stalkers should be aware of the implications of carrying a knife overtly in a public place where concern or criticism may be expressed. Our advice is to remove them, if they are visible, prior to visiting places where concerns may be raised. Forgetting you are wearing a knife may not be an acceptable defence.

LIABILITIES THROUGH NEGLIGENCE OR LACK OF CARE

Stalkers

Stalking activities can be potentially hazardous and in civil law you owe a duty to others to take reasonable care so as not to cause them foreseeable injury. If you fail to exercise such care and your negligence results in injury to another person or damage to property, then you may be liable to the victim. If you are reckless then, in addition to incurring civil liabilities, you may find yourself facing a criminal prosecution.

The stalker who takes a reckless shot which results in someone being injured or killed may be liable in both criminal and civil law. If the court considered that he was grossly negligent or reckless the

161

consequences could be serious and a criminal charge may result in a term of imprisonment. There is a considerable amount of case law and difference of opinion about the extent of culpability in such circumstances and much would depend on the circumstances of each individual case.

Shots taken with no suitable back stop on the fringe of urban areas or near roads or public footpaths are obviously reckless. There is a risk of the bullet missing or going through its intended target and killing someone in its path, and consequently the stalker may be faced with a charge of manslaughter.

In 2004 a conviction for manslaughter followed an incident in which a young boy was accidentally shot dead with a .243 rifle having been mistaken for a fox.

Charges of manslaughter have also been brought when firearms which were thought to be unloaded have been pointed at people and gone off accidentally. So, serious criminal offences will be considered in cases where the reckless and negligent handling of a gun results in death or serious injury. In addition civil liability would apply, with a possible claim for loss of life or injury through negligence.

In some cases liability may be incurred by a corporate body, an employer or the owner of land, which could include a syndicate or deer management group, e.g. when such bodies have failed to take appropriate action to remedy situations where risks have been exposed. Even if they escape the rigours of the criminal law they may remain liable at civil law if their acts or omissions are negligent and in breach of a duty of care to the victim. The law is more likely to infer a breach where there is an employer/employee relationship, not least because of the normal obligations imposed on employers, including the provision of safe systems of work, proper equipment and training.

Whether a deer management group is a corporate body for this purpose will depend on its constitution. For example a group of adjoining landowners with a common interest in the deer cull who are not formally constituted as a club would be unlikely to have a corporate responsibility. However a group with a formal constitution which provides direction, training and guidance to stalkers and landowners may incur some liability, particularly if formal contracts exist.

Clearly there is a need for stalkers and management groups to seek advice in respect of their potential liabilities. Membership of organisations such as B.A.S.C. and the B.D.S. will provide access to such advice. It is also vital that management groups and individuals carry public liability insurance. Membership of organisations often provides insurance cover for individuals, who should ensure that the policy meets their needs.

Owners and occupiers of land

Owners and occupiers of land where stalking takes place should be aware of their liabilities in respect of visiting stalkers. They have a legal duty not to cause injury by negligence to anyone entering the land, including stalkers. In some circumstances it may also include uninvited guests. There may also be health and safety issues to be considered.[96] In certain circumstances the stalker may be treated as an occupier and therefore have certain responsibilities within the law.

The Occupiers' Liability Act, 1957 (England and Wales) imposes on the occupier of premises[97] a common duty of care to all visitors: that is to take such care as is reasonable in the circumstances to ensure the visitor's safety in using the premises for the purpose for which he is invited or permitted by the occupier to be there. In practical terms, this does not mean the occupier has to go to elaborate lengths, but if there are dangers on the property where stalkers have legal access, then he must take reasonable steps to safeguard them from the danger. This is particularly important where a danger is not obvious, e.g. a mine shaft or well hidden in the undergrowth.[98]

The Occupiers' Liability Act, 1984 (England and Wales) imposes on occupiers a duty of care to persons other than visitors and in some circumstances this may extend to those who may not have lawful authority to be on the land or premises where they may be exposed to danger. Owners may not place trespassers in deliberate danger from which they may be injured. For example, actions to deter deer poachers must be reasonable and the setting of any trap or device from which they are likely to be injured as a result will incur civil if not criminal liability. The test would be whether a humane person with the knowledge, ability and resources of the occupier could and would take steps to protect trespassers from any danger on the land.

---

96. See page 165.
97. 'Premises' means any property of the owner.
98. The Mines and Quarries Act, 1954, requires such dangers as quarries to be fenced and mines to be closed off etc.

The Occupiers' Liability (Scotland) Act, 1960, embraces similar principles to those in the Acts covering England and Wales and states that the care should in all circumstances of the case be reasonable to see that a person will not suffer injury or damage by reason of any such danger. The occupier owes the same duty of care to all classes of persons entering his premises, unlike in England and Wales where a distinction is drawn between visitors and trespassers.

In the case of McCluskey v. Lord Advocate damages were sought from the Forestry Commission for injuries caused resulting from a fall on a rocky path used as a short cut between two paths. The action was dismissed and the Commission absolved on the basis of the evidence the rocky path was clearly not part of the official path system, and its condition was obvious. It had been used for many years without accident and did not in terms of the Act constitute a danger. The Commission was under no duty to take steps to prevent members of the public from straying off the official path and the claimant had to be taken as having willingly accepted any risks in doing so.

High seats are an obvious source of danger and should be well maintained. They should be carefully sited to give an unobstructed field of shooting and a solid back stop. The rungs of wooden ladders should be properly secured and not just supported by nails or screws. Make sure your rifle is unloaded before climbing up or down the ladder and in winter be especially mindful of the problems of ice forming on the ladder rungs and rails.

Where there is public access to the area the ladder should be detached after use to prevent children from reaching the seat. You may also consider placing signs to warn of the danger.

Where a stalker falls from a seat through his own fault rather than because of a defective seat or ladder then the occupier is not liable.

The stalker has willingly accepted the risks involved and the occupier has a right to expect that such a person will appreciate and guard against any such risks involved in stalking.

If the stalker holds the sporting rights he may also be classed as an occupier, in addition to the landowner. Should a third party be injured then joint liability may exist in respect of any high seats erected by the stalker. Alternatively if the stalker is not classed as an occupier, the claim may be against the owner, who may then have a counter-claim against the stalker who erected the seat.

Liability may be incurred in situations where children play on high seats and become injured, even if the seats are safe and well maintained. The Act states that an occupier must be prepared for children to be less careful than adults and consequently in some circumstances occupiers may need to guard against their use by children. The Deer Initiative has issued an advice note on high seats for deer management and B.A.S.C. has a high seat building course.

Health and safety at work

Employers must take reasonable care to protect their employees from risks of foreseeable injury, disease or death at work. If they do not, an employee may be in a position to take civil action and sue for negligence under the common law or breach of a statutory duty under health and safety law. This is of particular relevance to deer stalking, where the risks involving the use of firearms and associated equipment can be high. The risk in some areas of contracting Lyme disease through tick bites should also be considered; employers have a responsibility to provide protective clothing. In addition employees also have responsibilities for their own health and safety and for that of other people who may be put at risk by their work or undertaking.

An employer's duties under common law were identified in general terms in the case of Wilson & Clyde Coal Co. Ltd v. English (1938).[99] All employers should provide and maintain a safe place of work, safe appliances and equipment, a safe system for doing the work and competent and safety-conscious personnel. These principles are now enshrined in statute law.

The legislation which now protects an employee's rights and general health and safety is considerable, and much of it applies to the recreational stalker with responsibilities for deer management, as well as to the professional stalker. We do not intend to deal here with this legislation in detail, but rather to raise the awareness of stalkers and employers of the aspects of their activities in which there may be health and safety considerations and provide reference to further reading.

The legislation would not generally apply to recreational stalkers who are not *employed* and have no responsibilities for deer management. However, stalkers who conduct an undertaking involving the

99. AC57 2AER 628.

use of firearms have a legal duty under the Health and Safety at Work etc. Act, 1974, to take all reasonably practical measures so that no one is put at risk. In this sense an 'undertaking' does not necessarily need to involve employment or commercial gain.

The duty may extend to a wide range of other individuals, including gamekeepers, beaters and guests. It is apparent that where the stalker has responsibility for the management of deer involving the use of firearms this will be classed as an undertaking within the legislation. Employers will also have responsibilities where equipment is loaned to a stalker – e.g. chain saws and brush cutters borrowed for clearing rides.

The Health and Safety Executive (H.E.S.) provides extensive guidance in many areas of the law and the use of equipment likely to be used by stalkers. Therefore, in the first instance, information and guidance should be sought from one of their regional branch offices, the B.A.S.C., the Deer Initiative or the B.D.S.

The Health and Safety at Work etc. Act, 1974

This Act covers employers, all people at work including the self-employed, and the suppliers of equipment to be used at work. It is aimed at people and their activities rather than premises and processes. As we have said, the legislation covers those who 'conduct an undertaking' and will therefore affect many deer stalkers.

The legislation includes provision for both the protection of people at work and the prevention of risks to the health and safety of the general public that may arise from work activities. The main provisions are as follows.

Section 2 states that it is the duty of every employer, so far as is reasonably practicable, to ensure the health, safety and welfare of employees. Provisions and steps that the employer is obliged to take to ensure this condition are detailed in the Act, and include such matters as: the provision and maintenance of equipment; the use, handling, storage and transport of articles; and the provision of information and training.

Section 2(3) provides that employers with five or more workers must have a written statement of their health and safety policy and this must be revised as appropriate. It must set out the general policy with respect to the health and safety at work of employees and the organisation.

Under sections 3 and 4, employers must ensure, as far as is reasonably practicable, that their business does not put at risk people who are not in their employment. Employers must ensure that premises under their control are safe and without risk to persons not in their direct employment.

Under section 6, any person who designs, manufactures, imports or supplies any article for use at work has a responsibility to ensure, as far as is reasonably practicable, that it is safe and without risk to health when properly used. Articles must be properly tested and supplied with appropriate information about their use.

Section 2(3) of the Health and Safety at Work etc. Act 1974 requires employers with five or more employees to prepare a written statement of their general policy on the health and safety at work of their employees.

The Management of Health and Safety at Work (MHSW) Regulations 1992 require employers and the self-employed to identify significant hazards arising out of their work activities, assess the risks and take steps to control those risks. If you employ five or more people you should record the significant findings of the assessment, i.e. those hazards which could result in serious injury or ill health, who is at risk from those hazards, what you are doing to control those hazards and what more (if anything) you need to do.

The following provision may be of interest to those erecting high seats. Any person who erects or installs any article for use at work must ensure, so far as is reasonably practicable, that nothing about the way it is erected or installed makes it unsafe or a risk to health when properly used. Additional responsibility to prevent falls from high seats is included in the Workplace (Health, Safety and Welfare) Regulations, 1992. Regulation 13 states that, so far as is reasonably practicable, suitable and effective measures shall be taken to prevent anyone falling a distance likely to cause personal injury.

Section 7 imposes a duty on all employees while at work to take reasonable care for their health and safety and that of others who may be affected by their acts or omissions, and section 8 provides that no one shall intentionally or recklessly interfere with or misuse anything provided for health and safety purposes.

The Noise at Work Regulations, 1989
These regulations, introduced in 1990, are accompanied by a number of guides by the H.S.E. They provide for the protection of workers against risks related to exposure to noise, which no doubt would include the blast from the stalker's rifle.

Under regulation 6 a general duty is placed on every employer to reduce the risk of damage to the hearing of their employees due to exposure to noise to the lowest level reasonably practicable. Regulation 8 deals with the provision of suitable and sufficient ear protection, which employers are obliged to supply where daily noise levels are likely to be a health risk. Varying noise levels, measured in decibels, determine the level of responsibilities placed on employers.

The Personal Protective Equipment at Work Regulations, 1992
These regulations cover all aspects of the provision, maintenance and use of personal protective equipment (P.P.E.) at work and in other circumstances. Under the regulation P.P.E. has a broad meaning and covers all equipment which is intended to be worn or held by a person at work to protect from the risks to health and safety. It includes clothing affording protection against the weather which may be of interest to professional stalkers.

Under regulation 4, every employer shall ensure that suitable P.P.E. is provided to their employees who may be exposed to a risk to their health and safety. It will not be considered suitable unless it is appropriate to the risks involved, takes account of ergonomic requirements and the state of health of the person and, so far as practicable, is effective when worn. This would apply to protective clothing required in deer larders.

Risk assessment

As referred to above a risk assessment is required by law in respect of many stalking situations. Many large landowners and estates now undertake full risk assessments which cover all aspects of work activities, including deer management. Stalkers with existing agreements or those taking on deer management for the first time should consider conducting a full risk assessment as part of their management plans, prior to embarking on shooting deer.

The following example takes account of a high risk location where deer have to be managed in an area subject to a high level of public access and close urbanisation. In cases where these conditions do not apply to the same extent the risk assessment can be amended appropriately.

OTHER STALKING LIABILITIES

There are also stalking liabilities involved in the following, which are elaborated upon in the relevant chapters as indicated:
- claims for compensation in respect of crop damage – chapter 4
- trespass – chapter 8
- firearm security and safekeeping – chapter 6
- disposing of animal by-products – chapter 5
- dealing with poachers – chapter 9.

Hazard	Location	Persons at risk	Risk level	Controls	Implementation and monitoring
Danger to public, estate workers and trespassers.	Woodland and adjacent property.	Stalkers and estate workers, visitors, unauthorised members of public, nearby residents and traffic.	Low	Avoid or control public access. Siting of appropriate signs at designated access points.	These should be reviewed annually and on renewal of FAC and insurance, membership.
Persons struck by bullet.				Maintain radio or phone contact.	All stalkers to hold minimum of DSC Level 1 certification. The stalking tenant [Your name] is responsible for any assisting stalkers who should hold copies of firearms certificates and insurance/membership insurance details. Stalkers to hold "Trained hunter qualification" to comply with food hygiene regulations.
Public access at sensitive times.				Identify safe routes.	
				Be aware of public, trespassers, estate workers and gardeners.	
				Stalkers and assistants to be briefed prior to stalking by tenant [Your name].	
				Use of firearms restricted to named competent individuals qualified as above.	Records to be kept of rifle maintenance and ammunition purchase.
				All stalking to be in accordance with recognised guidelines at all times.	
				Estate security and forester to be informed of all visits for the purpose of culling deer.	
				All stalkers should hold a minimum of NGO membership, BASC membership or similar insurance with public liability of £5m. [BASC now £10m.]	
				Stalkers to be fully aware of the topography of the land, motorways, roads and paths as shown on the maps provided and management plan. All stalkers should familiarise themselves with the ground, paying particular attention to footpaths, wire fences and pylons.	
				Stalkers should carry mobile phones and have the grid reference of the woodland access points in case emergency services are required.	

Hazard	Location	Persons at risk	Risk level	Controls	Implementation and monitoring
Use of firearms.	Estate	Stalkers and estate workers, visitors, unauthorised members of public, nearby residents and traffic.	Low	Follow safety procedures detailed in HSE leaflets Guns. Proven shooting ability as per recognised qualification e.g. DSC1. Rifle and scope to be cleaned regularly and serviced annually. Stalkers must only fire at identifiable targets. Rifles to be zeroed regularly. [Optional – No zeroing of rifles on the estate.] No shooting into or from pre-determined or designated areas. Control must be within conditions of FAC of each stalker. Lawful target species only. Compliance with close seasons unless legal exemption applies. No night shooting of deer except injured or diseased animal or where permitted by law under licence. Rifles to be unloaded when not stalking. E.g. when handling carcase.	Changes in legislation or FAC conditions to be implemented immediately.
Public access	Estate	Stalkers and estate workers, visitors, unauthorised members of public, nearby residents and traffic.	Low	No shooting into or from pre-determined or designated areas No shooting from the public road. Warning notices should be placed across car parks or footpath access as specified in the deer management plan. Safe and unsafe areas for control identified.	Annual review and immediate consideration of any incident reports.

Hazard	Location	Who is at risk	Risk level	Control measures	Review
Public confrontation	Estate	Stalkers and visitors, unauthorised members of public nearby, residents and motorists.	Low	Stalkers to anticipate persons who may be in restricted or prohibited areas at any time. Stalkers should immediately unload rifles. Stalkers to identify themselves and provide explanation for the action being taken in line with Estate policy. Referrals should be made to the Operations Manager of the Estate. All interactions with members of the public to be reported to the Operations Manager who will consider liaison with media consultants for the estate. The gralloch and all body parts of shot deer to be moved out of public sight and to be removed from the estate on day of cull. Further processing of carcases to be conducted away from the estate in accordance with hygiene requirements.	Annual review and immediate consideration of any incident reports.
Working alone. Danger if injured while working alone. Violence	Woodland	Stalkers	Low	Suitable footwear and weatherproof clothing. Co-workers to be aware of location and expected time of return. When it is not safe to carry out particular jobs alone work needs to be planned when assistance is available. Radio or mobile phone and map to be carried. First aid kit carried by tenant. Dealing with violence – stalkers should not endanger themselves in potentially violent situations. Stalkers should obtain support from colleagues or the police.	Annual review of working practices and equipment.

Hazard	Location	Persons at risk	Risk	Control measures	Review
Injury from wounded deer.	Estate	Stalkers or assistants.	Low	Dispatch of wounded animals to be carried out humanely and in accordance with recognised procedures/good practice guides.	Annual review.
Injury or disease through carcase handling.	Estate, location of shot deer, transport and larder.	Stalker or assistants, carcase handlers and processors, e.g. butchers and the public via the food chain.	Medium	Immunisation against tetanus.	Annual review. Reports to the Estate and District Veterinary Officer.
Tuberculosis and Lyme disease.				Immunisation against tuberculosis recommended.	
Tetanus				Be aware of other infections such as Weil's Disease [a form of Leptospirosis contracted from rats] and the tick borne Lyme disease.	
				Stalkers should have a good awareness of TB incidence in the local area and nationally.	
				If any notifiable disease e.g. TB is suspected the carcase should be isolated and the district veterinary officer and landowner informed without delay. Telephone number #########	
				Be aware of the risk of Lyme Disease and its symptoms. Try to keep your skin covered, especially legs. See GP immediately if symptoms occur. Stalkers must be aware of the presence of ticks that can be picked up from vegetation and deer carcases and the means to prevent infestation.	
				Culled animals to be gralloched on site [optional – gralloch removed for disposal away from the site.]	
				Gralloch to be removed where disease is suspected.	
				All carcases to be visually inspected by trained hunter as per legal requirements and guidance.	
				All stalkers should wear disposable gloves for handling and inspection of internal organs.	

All carcases visually inspected as per FSA guidelines. [Trained Hunter present.]

All stalkers should wear disposable gloves for handling and inspection of internal organs.

All stalkers should carry a mobile phone and have ready access to a first aid kit.

Confirm animal is dead and prior to handling be aware of the dangers of deer lashing out with hooves or antlers.

Use a sharp knife to gralloch with handles designed to prevent hand sliding onto the blade.

Always cut away from your body.

When gralloching wear disposable gloves and maintain good standard of personal hygiene to avoid infection.

Stalkers must be aware of the presence of ticks that can be picked up from vegetation and deer carcases.

All stalkers should be aware of the correct method of lifting and the use of appropriate equipment to aid extraction of carcases.

Try to avoid manual handling.

Consider use of winch and ramp.

Minimise height of the lift and distance carried or dragged – mechanical extraction to be used where possible e.g. 4x4 or quad type vehicle.

Avoid twisting and lifting situations.

Hazard	Location	Persons at risk	Risk level	Controls	Implementation and monitoring
Spread of notifiable contagious disease e.g. FMD and Blue Tongue.	Estate	Livestock owners	Low	Have an assistant available if possible. Stalkers to comply with DEFRA guidance/legislation when outbreaks occur and restricted zones are imposed.	Maintain awareness of national restrictions or spread of disease via DEFRA website and media coverage.
Noise and deafness	Estate and adjacent areas.	Stalkers and visitors, unauthorised members of public, nearby residents and motorists.	Low	All stalkers to be aware of the potential hazard, and the use of personal hearing protection as a matter of personal choice. The use of a rifle [if capable of being adapted] fitted with a moderator may be advantageous within or adjacent to urban areas to minimise disturbance. Shooting to take place at times and dates when low numbers of those at risk are in the area. e.g. Early and late parts of weekdays.	Annual review. Estate media policy to take account of public concern on the hearing of a rifle shot, reports to the police etc.
Use of vehicles Operating from inside vehicles.	All areas of the estate.	Stalkers and visitors, unauthorised members of public, nearby residents and motorists.	Low	All persons to adhere to estate safety procedure when operating from vehicles. Shooting from vehicle only when stationary with engine switched off in compliance with legislation. Rifle to be loaded and fired with muzzle out of the vehicle.	Annual review of method used and its effectiveness.
Injury from knives during carcase preparation.	Site of shooting and larder.	Stalkers and assistants.	Low	Gralloching and use of knives to be in accordance with recognised guidelines and training. Use of a sharp knife with handle designed to prevent hand sliding on to the blade and of type complying with Food Hygiene Regs. [non-porous.] Always cut away from your body. Guards to be placed on saw blade when not in use.	Stalkers must take responsibility for their own safety. Methods to be reviewed annually.

Hazard	Location	Persons at risk	Risk	Control measures
High seats – injury from fall or firearm discharge. Prevent unauthorised use or theft of the seat. Erection and maintenance of high seats.	Woodland or adjacent land.	Stalkers, members of the public, especially children.	Med-ium	Knives to be stored in sheaths. Knives to be retained and accounted for to prevent access by unauthorised persons. Awareness of proximity of assistants and other stalkers when using knives. Particular care to be taken on the removal of lower foreleg to guard against slipping of blade and when working within the enclosed area of the carcase e.g. ribcage. High seats will be used on a short-term temporary basis on and organised cull. They will be installed the day before the cull and removed within 24 hours of use. Ensure safe construction and erection of high seats. Consider use of two persons to erect seats. Any use of chainsaws should be subject to a specific risk assessment with regard to safe use, protective clothing/equipment and training. High seats should incorporate a suitable rifle rest to facilitate safe shooting. Location of high seats to provide unobstructed field of shooting and a safe backstop. Ladder rungs to be securely fastened. Removal of high seats after culling operation or prevent theft. Rifles to be unloaded prior to climbing up and down ladders of high seat. All high seats to be inspected prior to climbing by the stalker. All seats to be inspected regularly by the tenant and prior to each use.

Hazard	Location	Persons at risk	Risk level	Controls	Implementation and monitoring
				Notices should be placed at the bottom of each high seat forbidding unauthorised use.	
				Where high seats are to remain in situ steps to be taken to prevent unauthorised use e.g. removal of ladder or fitting of devise to prevent easy access to climbing rails.	

CHAPTER 8

Trespass and Deer

If you have responsibilities for deer management, have wild deer on your land or keep farmed deer, then the issues surrounding the civil wrongdoing known as trespass, will no doubt arise. Retrieving shot deer over boundaries, poachers, farmed deer escaping and deer hounds unlawfully encroaching onto land are just a few examples of situations involving trespass. Public consultation over the right to roam in the countryside may also lead in the future to increased public access in areas where deer management is necessary and therefore it is useful to have a clear understanding of the issues involved.

Legislation on access in Scotland is likely in the near future. After discussions in the Access Forum in December 1998, Scottish Natural Heritage advised the government on the shape of future legislation; the main features of the advice were that a new right of access to land should be created, to be exercised with responsibility, and that work should be done on drawing up a new Scottish Countryside Code to give definition to the duties and responsibilities of all concerned. Scotland has its own legislature and the anticipated introduction of access legislation will have implications for stalkers.

Simple trespass, which is known as a tort (a delict in Scotland) is an unlawful act under civil law. It is not a crime except in certain circumstances provided for by statute law, such as trespass on railway property. Generally, recourse for simple trespass is through the county courts, where compensation in appropriate cases may be awarded to the aggrieved party.

Trespass may take many forms. It is not confined to merely trespassing on land, but may also involve persons and property. Despite the myths that abound, many of the principles of trespass apply just as much to Scotland as they do to England and Wales, although some differences exist. Public debate about increased public access to the countryside in both Scotland and England has invited comparisons between the law in the two jurisdictions.

TRESPASS BY PEOPLE

Trespass is not restricted to a person's physical entry or presence on land where he has no right to be, but also to placing or throwing any material object upon the land. Land in this context includes not only the surface, but everything fixed to it such as buildings, everything beneath it and the air space above it. It also includes water. An act of civil trespass would even extend to the situation where someone makes a constructive, rather than physical, entry into land – e.g. a stalker firing a rifle from land where lawful authority is granted into land where permission has not been sought.[100] Trespass is still committed even if someone does not physically touch the land – e.g. driving a vehicle onto the land. In this latter example a criminal offence of driving a vehicle elsewhere than on a road may be committed, contrary the Road Traffic Act.

The term 'lawful authority' may embrace a number of different situations where someone may claim a right to be on the land if challenged. When in dispute it is usually the landowner or occupier who is approached to confirm whether permission has been granted and not withdrawn. Permission may also be conditional or relate to a number of persons – e.g. members of a deer management group viewing deer on a certain date. When gaining access to land for sporting purposes such as stalking, permission should ideally be in writing. Indeed the grant of a firearm certificate may depend on this.[101]

There will often be a sporting lease, and this should be carefully examined when it is taken up, to ensure that there are no misunderstandings which are likely to give rise to inadvertent trespass. It is advisable to make use of definitive maps with clearly marked

100. See chapter 7 on stalking the boundary.
101. See chapter 6.

boundaries of your area.[102] Stalkers who hold legal sporting rights over land which is let to a tenant have lawful authority to be on the land for those sporting purposes even if this is against the tenant's wishes.

'Lawful authority' also includes using private and public rights of way. These provide a right of access to the land without the express permission of the landowner. Private rights of way are granted to allow the owner of one property to cross another's land for reasons of access. There are several types of public rights of way. The most common are footpaths, bridleways and roads. All are referred to as 'highways' over which the public have a right to pass and repass. The responsibility for maintenance and signing rests with the highways authority, which may take legal action against anyone who causes obstruction or nuisance on the highway. Care should therefore be taken when erecting deer fencing or high seats to ensure that they are not placed on or near a footpath where obstruction or nuisance is likely to be caused.

Anyone using a right of way may have with them any article regarded as a 'usual accompaniment', such as a walking stick, binoculars or a dog.[103] Dogs should be under close control – at heel or ideally on a lead. Whatever the item carried or pushed it should not cause a nuisance or damage. Where rifles are being carried on a right of way to gain access to land where permission has been granted to stalk, it is advisable that they are carried within their slips and are unloaded (a rifle may still be deemed as loaded if bullets are left in the magazine).[104]

Poachers who claim they were on a highway or footpath when they indulged in their activities will find such a defence rejected by the courts. A number of past cases have held that using a right of way for an unlawful purpose may still be treated as trespassing. A footpath or right of way must be used for the purpose for which it is intended, i.e. to pass and repass as a means of communication.[105] Therefore a stalker who shoots a deer from a footpath on land where permission has not been granted would be trespassing with a firearm in addition to his poaching activities.[106] The latter situation is an example of where the tort of trespass to land forms an essential part of a criminal offence. However there are many situations in which trespassers may be acting unlawfully without the need to prove trespass.

102. See chapter 7.
103. R. v. Mathias, 1861. In this case a pram was referred to as such.
104. See chapter 6.
105. R. v. Pratt, 1855, and Harrison v. Duke of Rutland, 1893.
106. See chapters 6 and 9.

The fact that the criminal law makes exceptions for certain activities does not negate an individual's liability against trespass. For example, the picking of wild mushrooms is allowed in certain circumstances by the Theft Act, 1968, so you may not be stealing, but if you do so without the landowner's permission you are trespassing. A person who wanders aimlessly about the land, without lawful authority, searching for cast antlers for example, also commits a trespass, irrespective of the rights of ownership of the antlers found.[107]

Common Law in England and Wales

A person who enters or remains on land without lawful authority commits trespass against the holder of the land and this would include any interference with the land. This type of trespass would be actionable in itself, even if damage is not caused, as the landowner would be able to take civil action via the County Court.

Common Law in Scotland

The view has sometimes been expressed that in contrast to the position in England there is no law of trespass in Scotland. That view is wrong, but it may, perhaps, result from misunderstandings about the following points:

- In Scotland, trespass is a civil wrong at Common Law. The Scottish Common Law of civil wrongs is called the Law of Delict, and corresponds to the Law of Tort in England. Delict, in contrast to Tort, did not develop from the notion of trespass in the much wider sense in which it was historically used in English law; 'trespass to a chattel', for example, would not have any meaning in Scots law. However, the word 'trespass' was introduced from England to Scotland, and has been in common usage for perhaps two centuries.
- It is a general principle of the Law of Delict that so far as property is concerned, it is necessary to prove loss or damage in order to ground an action for damages. Thus, if trespass results in no loss or damage, no action for damages will lie. It must be stressed that this reflects a general principle of the law; it is not a condition special to the law concerning trespass.

An interdict in Scotland corresponds to an injunction in England. A lawful occupier may ask either the Sheriff or the Court of Session to

---

107. See chapter 1.

grant an interdict against a trespasser. But it must be kept in mind that it is a discretionary remedy, granted only when the action the pursuer (corresponding to the plaintiff in England) seeks to prohibit is of some consequence, or there is a danger of repetition which there is good reason to seek to prevent (for example, because there is reason to conclude that it could give rise to a disturbance).

Dealing with trespassers

People who persistently trespass can pose problems in terms of both deer management and safety. Deer change their habits when faced with too much human pressure. Some, especially fallow, can become almost nocturnal. They then become difficult to manage and so unwanted trespassers become a nuisance, particularly in areas where culling is necessary. Areas of natural beauty often hold large numbers of deer and people seeking recreation, particularly in the Highlands, often impede professional stalkers in achieving their culls. This can be a serious problem during the hind season on the lower ground when in January and February there is the opportunity to cull beasts emerging from cover.

Apart from the obvious disruption to stalking activities caused by someone being in the wrong place at the wrong time, the most serious potential risk is to human life itself, from a stray bullet. Whilst safe and responsible shooting should be a stalker's absolute priority, accidents can and do happen.[108]

Whilst the chances of such an accident may seem remote, keeping a watchful eye out for trespassers and dealing with them effectively will lessen the risks of accident or disruption. Some trespassers may simply be lost or unaware that they are trespassing on private property, others may pose an additional threat of poaching. Although poaching is generally done during the hours of darkness, reconnaissance is often done on foot during the preceding days.[109] You may recognise your local poacher, in which case your approach will be better informed, but on many occasions you will be dealing with someone you do not know and therefore your actions must be carefully considered, with the ultimate aim of an informal resolution.

Owners and occupiers of the land, and anyone acting with their authority, have certain powers to deal with trespassers personally. In the early 1900s one lawyer's advice was as follows:

108. Your liability in such a situation is discussed in chapter 7.
109. See chapter 9 for poaching methods.

> If you find a man walking down your glades doing no damage to the trees or fences, your only course is to show him the quickest path to the King's highway, and see that he takes it. Should he object to go, use as much force as is necessary, and if he shows fight, and you are strong enough to do so, knock him down, tie his hands and legs, and have him carried off.

Our advice today is rather different, inasmuch as that you should generally resist the temptation to take physical action to remove trespassers. To do so could lead to an argument and may end in violence, and it might invite a counter-claim by the trespasser, who may sue or prosecute for assault. You may request him to leave the land and should allow reasonable time for him to do so by the most convenient route to the right of way. The Common Law does allow you physically to remove trespassers who refuse to leave but, should you do so it is essential that you use no more force than is reasonable and necessary in the circumstances. You have no power to require them to supply their names and addresses, which presents obvious practical difficulties in pursuing any legal action.

Where legal action is taken in England and Wales, the landowner may apply to the court for both damages and an injunction. The effect of such an injunction is that the trespasser becomes liable for contempt of court should he trespass again. The court will need to be satisfied that there is a risk of further trespass before granting such an injunction. In Scotland, as referred to earlier, unless actual damage has been suffered, damages are not recoverable for simple trespass, particularly if innocent or unwitting. Interdicts are granted at the discretion of the court, which would have to be satisfied that there was reasonable apprehension that the trespass would be repeated in the future.

In cases which do not involve a crime the police, if called, are powerless. They can neither remove the trespassers nor demand their names and addresses, and if they do intervene they may not be acting in the execution of their duty. However, they may remain to ensure that there are no breaches of the peace. Landowners or persons acting on their authority must ensure that their own conduct is not threatening or violent towards trespassers, nor should they intimidate genuine ramblers on a right of way. Should they do so the police may be obliged to get involved, particularly where actual or threatened violence is used.

Criminal trespass

The Trespass (Scotland) Act, 1865, and the Public Order Act, 1986, create criminal offences of trespass by occupation of private property when taking up some form of residence such as camping. The offences are committed where the consent of the owner or occupier has not been given and they vary in respect of specific conditions that have to be met. The legislation provides the police with powers of arrest without warrant against those committing offences. A toleration policy is exercised in relation to traditional travelling people in areas where the provision of sites is inadequate, but this does not extend to large groups of people whose size, pattern and purpose of encampment are unrelated to established traveller movement, such as 'peace convoys'.

Aggravated trespass

The early nineties saw increasing concern over the activities of a number of groups and individuals intent on disrupting country sports. There were fears for the impact on rural economies of long-term disruption; for many people employed in rural areas their livelihood was at stake. Those concerns were not restricted to anti-blood sport campaigners; angling matches and even the Grand National had suffered disruption. There were frequent complaints that the police were uncertain of their powers or unwilling to use them, and that the law was inadequate. Hence legislation was seen as necessary to protect people who were conducting lawful activity in the countryside. What emerged was the Criminal Justice and Public Order Act, 1994, which not only created an offence of aggravated trespass but also addressed a number of other issues concerning trespass, including the problems caused by New Age travellers and ravers.

Under section 68 of this Act, a person commits the offence of aggravated trespass if, whilst trespassing on land, they do anything with intent to disrupt or obstruct a lawful activity, or seek to intimidate someone so as to deter him from engaging in a lawful activity. An 'activity' is lawful for the purposes of this section if those engaged in it do so without committing any offences and are themselves not trespassing.

Accidental or inadvertent trespass (including that by hunts) would not be an offence, even if it actually does cause disruption of a lawful activity, provided that the trespasser does not *intend* the disruption.

The trespass must be on land in the open air, and metalled roads are not included. However, it would apply if a footpath or other right of way was used for the purpose of disruption. It is quite possible that the offence of aggravated trespass may be committed by someone disrupting or attempting to disrupt deer management activity, particularly stalking, provided of course everything was lawful, i.e. the stalkers themselves were not trespassing, firearm certificates were correct and the deer being shot were in season. A case involving the disruption of a game shoot was dismissed on the grounds that the shoot did not have a written safety policy and risk assessment. It was argued that the shooting was therefore an 'unlawful activity'. Other cases have successfully argued that non-compliance with health and safety law did not make the activity unlawful in itself.

Section 69 gives the police powers to remove persons committing or participating in aggravated trespass. An offence is committed where a person fails to leave the land as soon as practicable or having left returns within a period of three months. The police have a power of arrest in these circumstances.

TRESPASS BY DEER

Deer that are truly wild, *ferae naturae* are ownerless[110] and therefore cannot trespass, since in the wild state they are free to roam where they please. However, concerns arise over damage to the natural environment and crops caused by unnaturally high wild deer stocks.

Historically an unchecked increase in deer numbers did not incur any liability on behalf of the occupier, even if resultant damage was caused to a neighbour's crops. However, in recent years the density of our wild deer populations has become acute in some areas of Scotland. Legislation has increased the powers of the Deer Commission for Scotland, enabling them to dictate cull levels and if necessary take action to reduce deer numbers. In these circumstances persons acting under such authority would not commit acts of trespass even if they were acting against the owner's wishes.[111] The owner of the land may also be liable for any expenses incurred by the Deer Commission in carrying out such action subject to certain conditions. The situation south of the border is also of concern, with a number of different bodies working towards maintaining a sustainable level of deer numbers in the interests of our natural environment.

Deer in captivity, whether from wild stock or captive-bred, can commit trespass and therefore their owners are liable in certain

110. See chapter 1.
111. See chapter 3.

184

circumstances. Where untagged captive deer have strayed onto the open hill rights of ownership may become difficult to prove.[112] It has long been established that landowners have a duty to ensure that any livestock, including captive deer are adequately fenced in.

The Animals Act, 1971 (England and Wales), and the Animals Act, (Scotland), 1987, make provision for strict liability for damage caused by animals including situations where livestock and other animals have strayed onto another's land. Deer are included in both Acts. Hitherto such liabilities were dealt with, in part, by old legislation and the Common Law. The latter still applies in respect of an ordinary duty of care upon owners to ensure their animals do not cause injury, damage or nuisance, including the death of, or injury to, any person. Such liabilities are dealt with in detail in chapter 1.

The Animals Act, 1971 (England and Wales)

This Act identifies liability in respect of the owners of trespassing livestock, which includes 'deer not in the wild state'. Under section 4, where deer belonging to any person stray onto another person's land and: a) damage is done by the deer to the land or any property on it which is in the ownership or occupation of the other person, or: b) any expenses are reasonably incurred by that other person in keeping the deer while they cannot be restored to the owner or while they are detained in pursuance of section 7 (see below) or in ascertaining to whom they belong, the person to whom the deer belong is liable for the damage and expense incurred. For the purposes of this section any deer 'belong' to the person in whose possession they are, but would not include the person detaining the trespassing deer.

An exemption from liability under this section would apply if it could be shown that the damage was due wholly to the fault of the person suffering it, but it would not include a failure by that person to fence their land adequately.

Under section 7, where it is clear that the deer are not from the wild state and have strayed onto land where they could be said to be trespassing and are not under the control of any person then the occupier of the land is entitled to detain the deer subject to the following conditions, unless ordered to return them by a court:

- where deer are detained in pursuance of this section the right to detain them would cease at the end of a period of forty-eight hours,

112. See chapter 1.

unless within that period notice of the detention has been given to the police and also to the owner of the deer, if known

- the right to detain them would cease when a sufficient amount of money is given to the person detaining the deer to satisfy any claim he may have
- if he has no such claim, the right would cease when the deer are claimed by the owner.

Where deer have been detained in pursuance of this section for a period of not less than fourteen days the person detaining them may sell them at a market or at public auction, unless proceedings are pending for the return of the deer or for any claim under section 4 (see above). Where deer are sold in these circumstances the proceeds of the sale, less the costs of the damage and expenses incurred, are recoverable by the original owner.

A person detaining trespassing deer is liable for any damage caused to them through a failure to treat them with reasonable care or supply them with adequate food and water while so detained.

Section 8 imposes a duty on those who own deer to take such care as is reasonable to ensure that damage is not caused by the animals straying onto a highway. Where damage is caused by animals straying from unfenced land they will not be regarded as having breached this duty of care if the land is common land or situated in an area where fencing is not customary or where a right exists to place them on that land.

The Animals (Scotland) Act, 1987

Section 1 of this Act provides that keepers of certain animals are liable for any damage caused by their foraging. Deer are included as being likely, unless controlled or restrained, to damage to a material extent land or the produce of land, whether harvested or not. However, under section 2, a person shall not be liable if the damage done was due wholly to the fault of the person sustaining it or if they had willingly accepted the risk as theirs.

Section 3 states that where animals stray onto any land, other than the highway, and are not under the control of any person, the occupier of the land may detain them for the purpose of preventing injury or damage. Part VI of the Civic Government (Scotland) Act, 1982, relating to lost and abandoned property applies in relation to any animals, other than stray dogs, which are detained in these circumstances, in the same way as to any property taken under section 67 of that Act and subject to some amendment of section 74.

Effectively this means that where such animals have been detained and it is reasonable to infer that they have been lost or abandoned the finder should take reasonable care of them and without un-reasonable delay report the fact to the owner or the police, who are obliged to take reasonable steps to ascertain the owner if he is not known. The Chief Constable may make such arrangements as he considers appropriate for the care and custody of the animals. Practically this may well involve the finder being requested to care and have custody of the animals. In this situation, under section 74, provided the animals have been detained for a period of two months and not claimed, the person shall become the owner of the animals. The rights of the original owners following disposal of animals, compensation and appeals are also detailed in the above Act.

DOGS AND TRESPASS

There are many situations involving trespass where the welfare of deer is jeopardised, particularly where dogs are involved. The owners of trespassing dogs can be liable for their animals' misdemeanours and there have been a number of successful civil actions in such cases.

In England, Wales and Scotland the use of dogs to take or pursue deer is prohibited.[113] As far as the civil law is concerned, those in charge of dogs are liable for their trespasses and also any followers who may have unintentionally found themselves on land where permission had not been obtained or illegal hunting is taking place.

Civil action against the masters of deer hounds prior to the banning of hunting was not uncommon, particularly in the West Country, where a number of private landowners, including the National Trust, refused hunts permission to go on their land. In 1985 the League Against Cruel Sports took civil action for trespass against the Devon and Somerset Staghounds following a number of invasions of one of their deer sanctuaries. An injunction was granted

113. See chapter 3.

at Bristol High Court and damages were awarded to the League. The judge defined trespass by hunts as follows:

> The Master will be liable for trespass if he intended to cause hounds to enter such land, or if by failure to exercise proper control over them he caused them to enter such land.[114]

This case has been followed by a number of similar actions. The legal definition of liability here could be applied to any individual who allows dogs to enter land where permission has not been granted, although it is doubtful whether civil action against someone merely exercising his dog would be worthwhile – there are other options that should be explored in this situation, as described earlier in respect of persons trespassing on land.

Shooting trespassing dogs

Taking summary action by shooting a trespassing dog rather than using the legal system may well put you at risk of court action. Dogs are classed as property and shooting a dog, even in the act of chasing a deer, may render you liable to prosecution for criminal damage or a civil claim – and the latter could be hefty if the dog is found to be a Crufts champion!

The Criminal Damage Act, 1971, covers offences of damage committed in England and Wales. In Scotland there is a Common Law offence of damage and an offence of vandalism under section 78 of the Criminal Justice (Scotland) Act, 1980; these are virtually identical to the offences contained in the English law.

Section 1 of the Criminal Damage Act, 1971, states:

> A person who without lawful excuse destroys or damages any property belonging to another intending to destroy or damage such property or being reckless as to whether any such property would be destroyed or damaged shall be guilty of an offence.

Shooting a dog chasing or attacking wild deer on your land would be difficult to defend as you would have to show lawful excuse for your actions – i.e. that you shot the dog to protect your property or a right or interest in it. (The defence is dealt with in detail later in respect of captive deer.) We know of one case that was successfully defended at Petworth Magistrates' Court in 1974, but this is not considered to be a sound authority.

---

114. League Against Cruel Sports v. Scott and others.

Generally wild deer are not classed as 'property' and therefore a defence would have to rely on convincing the court that the sporting rights to the deer were a right or interest in property, which includes 'any right or privilege in or over the land, whether created by grant, licence or otherwise'. It could be argued that killing a dog in these circumstances is an attempt to protect the wild deer which the holder of the sporting rights has a right to take and that a dog chasing or killing deer in these circumstances does not threaten that right since the sporting rights remain intact. A court may consider whether the action taken was reasonable in the circumstances.

Dogs worrying farm or park deer
There is no express legal right to shoot a dog in any circumstances, even if it is caught worrying livestock. However, under the Animals Act, 1971, which does not apply in Scotland, you are entitled to take action to protect livestock. Fortunately, deer that are not in the wild state are included in the definition of 'livestock', so effectively the following defence against any civil proceedings would apply in all cases where a dog was shot chasing deer that were captive in a park or farm. Similar provisions apply in Scotland under the Animals (Scotland) Act, 1987, which includes not only livestock but any animal whilst in captivity.

Under section 9(1) and section 4 (Scotland) there is a defence in any civil proceedings for those who shoot dogs worrying livestock, if the court is satisfied that:

- the person acted for the protection of any livestock
- he was entitled to do so
- the police were notified within forty-eight hours

Under section 9(2) a person is entitled to protect livestock if the livestock or the land belongs to him, or he is acting with the owner's authority. The entitlement does not extend to the killing of a dog worrying livestock which has strayed onto land and the dog belongs to the occupier of that land or is on the land with the occupier's permission.

Under section 9(3)(4), a person may only act for the protection of any livestock if he has reasonable grounds to believe that:

- the dog is worrying or is about to worry and there are no other reasonable means of ending or preventing the worrying
- the dog has been worrying livestock, has not left the vicinity and is not under the control of any person and there are no practical means of ascertaining to whom it belongs

189

The above only provides for protection against civil proceedings. Should a charge of criminal damage be made for shooting a dog then the defendant would need to prove he had a lawful excuse. This may be possible, since the deer in these circumstances would be classed as property and the criminal law provides for the protection of property in circumstances where it is at risk of being damaged or destroyed. In this situation the deer may be injured or killed by a chasing or attacking dog and you would have a lawful excuse under the Criminal Damage Act, 1971, to take action provided the following conditions were met:

- it was believed the consent of the owner of the dog had been given or would have been given in such circumstances
- your actions were taken in order to protect the deer or a right or interest in it and at the time you believed the deer were in immediate need of protection and the means of protection adopted were reasonable having regard to all the circumstances

This means you would have to justify your actions and if it could be shown that other means were at your disposal to stop the dog, rather than by shooting, then your defence might be weakened.

TRESPASS AND PROPERTY

A form of trespass can be committed against property, where perhaps the criteria for a criminal offence of either damage or theft are not satisfied. It is known as 'trespass to goods'. This is the intentional or negligent interference with the possession of another's property. The interference must be direct and forcible, although a mere touching, unless accidental, may constitute a trespass in some circumstances. Such trespasses are actionable *per se*, in that a case could be pursued at civil court.

There are many situations where those who manage deer or possess sporting rights may be affected by such trespass. The meaning of goods is very wide and would include any article in the possession or constructive possession of another.[115] This would include captive or farmed deer that are interfered with in some way or released. High seats and signs relating to deer management are often moved or interfered with, and all such acts constitute a trespass to goods. It is not

---

115. In a case at Peterborough in 1993, the County Court ruled that the blowing of a hunting horn to disrupt hounds amounted to a trespass to goods.

essential for the person to know his actions were wrong, provided they are intentional or negligent.

It is perhaps worth summarising a few general points about trespass.

- in practice, actions for damages for trespass are rare. If it happens that the lawful occupier of land can identify a trespasser as being responsible for loss or damage to his property, he may make a complaint of vandalism to the police where circumstances justify that course
- a lawful occupier of land may require any person who is on his land without legal right or permission to leave at any time. It is fair to say, however, that very few occupiers or land managers will require someone to leave their land without good reason
- questions are sometimes asked about the use of force to remove a trespasser. While there is some legal authority for saying that force may be used, general advice must be that in the absence of absolute necessity it should not. There are obvious risks involved; even with the best intentions, a situation may develop in a quite unexpected way, and get out of hand. If a trespasser will not respond positively to a polite request to leave, and there is a definite immediate need for him to go, the police should be asked for advice or assistance.

CHAPTER 9

Poaching

Poaching is one of the oldest professions, and centuries of experience have developed numerous methods of killing deer, including bows, snares, traps, dogs, firearms and even spikes on trees. The race to take deer before being discovered by the landowner or gamekeeper still results in immense cruelty. Indiscriminate poachers have no concern for the wellbeing of the deer or for risks to public health from ill-prepared venison. They have but one aim – a quick and easy profit.

POACHING PAST AND PRESENT

Until the tenth century, hunting in Britain was deemed as a necessity of life rather than a sport. The Saxons were keen to follow hounds on foot, mainly for the purpose of pest control. It was at this time that the kings started to designate areas of common folkland as hunting grounds and to strengthen game laws. The full nature of these laws is not known but Canute decreed that every man had the right to hunt on his land, establishing a principle which remains today.

The Normans enforced the Saxon laws after the invasion, but placed the forests under the sole jurisdiction of the King, preserving game for sport and feeding the royal household. William the Conqueror brought law and order to the land, 'so that a man could travel unmolested with his bosom full of gold and no man dare slay another'. Penalties could be extreme: a man who lay with a woman against her will was destined 'to forfeit those members with which he had disported himself'. Castration was not reserved for the rapist alone. William regarded hunting as a royal prerogative and imposed the strict continental forest laws to protect that right. Although the full nature of these laws is unknown he certainly introduced castration, amputation and blinding for 'venison trespass'.

The poacher's dog was not immune from such barbaric treatment either. As a preventative measure large dogs were 'lawed', a source of considerable grievance for people living in and near the forests. It is presumed the dogs were not too pleased either for those too tall to pass through the lawing ring, 18 inches and a barley corn high, had three toes of the front foot removed with a two inch chisel. Effectively lame, the dog could not chase and bring down the King's deer. There is a tale of one resourceful individual who trained a pig to retrieve game as a means of evading the forest laws against dogs.

Poaching with bow and arrow

The most common weapon over the years has undoubtedly been the bow. There have been many examples of its use, and not just against deer. In recent years a gamekeeper in North Yorkshire was shot in the chest with a bolt from a poacher's crossbow. Luckily he survived to tell the tale; others have not been so fortunate.

An early account of poaching with a longbow in England dates back to 1228, and took place in Rockingham Forest. The foresters, acting on information received, set an ambush and caught four out of five greyhounds that were hunting. On their return to the forest they saw four men with longbows and one with a crossbow, standing behind trees waiting for deer to be driven past them. They were challenged but made a fighting retreat. One of the foresters was killed by an arrow to the left breast 'to the depth of a hand slantwise'. The poachers escaped in the dark, and the villagers apparently all swore they did not recognise the dogs.

Thomas de Bromlegh, described as 'a very frequent malefactor of venison' was found armed in Kinver Forest. When challenged by the foresters he climbed into an oak tree and shot arrows at them. But this was a tactical error as they had him surrounded and outnumbered. Eventually he was taken by force and imprisoned in Bridgenorth Castle.

Both the longbow and the crossbow appear to have been in use for many years as weapons to take deer illegally. These have obvious advantages for poachers: they are almost silent when compared to the rifle, and the penalty for being caught in possession is minimal, as they are not classed as firearms. However the use of bow and arrow to take any animal or bird is outlawed in the U.K. under the Wildlife and Countryside Act, 1981, and the Wildlife (Northern Ireland) Order, 1985.

Bows are not as restricted in other countries. In the United States hunting deer with the conventional longbow and arrow has become increasingly popular, although it is strictly controlled and subject to appropriate licences in most states. A good deal of legal specification exists in relation to both the power of the bows and type of arrows used. Hunting with crossbows appears to be rather more restricted and in some states is completely banned.

It is the crossbow that in recent times has become the popular poacher's weapon. It is not difficult to imagine why as they can be accurate and extremely powerful. They are versatile and can be easily transported and carried without detection. During the 1980s there were many incidents involving their misuse; in one year there were eleven reported cases, which included two suicides and many pitiful injuries to animals.

Public pressure to legislate against the use of crossbows resulted in the Crossbows Act, 1987. It does not apply to crossbows with a drawn weight of less than 1.4 kilograms. It is an offence to sell or hire a crossbow to someone under the age of seventeen. If such a person buys or hires a crossbow or part of one, he also commits an offence. He may possess a crossbow, however, if supervised by someone who is twenty-one or over.

The Act gives various powers to the police to enable them to prove unlawful possession, including the searching of a suspect or vehicle and the power to enter land to conduct such a search. The courts are also given powers of forfeiture and disposal of crossbows in such cases brought before them.

The chances of any bow being used in a humane manner by unscrupulous poachers are remote. The vast majority just could not care less. If their ratio of success is one in five they are happy. Crossbows are still being used in some parts of the country and care should be exercised in approaching anyone suspected of their possession.

Gang poaching and the Waltham Blacks

The term poaching comes from the French verb *pocher*, to 'encroach' – to be on land where you have no right to be, in search of wild animals. Whilst the term is used to describe the purpose of some Acts relating to game, such as the Night Poaching Act, a definition does not exist in law.

Gang poaching has always been a threat to stocks of fish, game and deer. Two, three or more people may just have been looking to each other for mutual support when afraid of the dark, but at the other extreme might be a band of determined men, faces blackened, white bandages tied to their arms for identification, and armed with guns, sticks and swords. Such a gang was a formidable force in the darkness of a secluded wood, particularly when they had sworn to stand and fight or to shoot any deserting gang member.

One group of deer poachers which was active in 1723 was of such a violent nature that Parliament passed an Act specifically to deal with them. They were known as the Waltham Blacks, a band of thirty or more who met at a secluded inn, deep in Waltham Forest. Supper consisted of 'eighteen dishes of venison in every shape; boiled with broth, roasted, hashed collops, pasties, umble pies and a large haunch in the middle, larded'. Each man had a bottle of claret set at his elbow and the evening was spent merrily with singing and jollity until two in the morning.

Each man was disguised with a blackened face and their leader was known as the Black Prince or Prince Orinoko King of the Blacks. To enter the society one had to be seen drunk on two occasions to establish one's temperament in compliance with the old proverb, 'Women, children and drunken folks speak truth.' The Blacks also attracted criminals who had no settled employment but lived by their 'vices and indulged in all manner of wickedness, robbing, house breaking and in every species of depredation'.

Violence and intimidation became their trademarks. A magistrate committed one of the gang to prison and received a letter demanding the person's release or his house would be fired. The magistrate failed to bend to their will and the gang cut down young oaks to the value of £500. Landowners who refused to hand over money or venison would find cattle maimed, barns and haystacks burned down. One poacher caught in Windsor Park was fined and his gun confiscated. The Blacks assembled at the keeper's cottage and demanded the return of the weapon. The keeper's son looked out of the bedroom window and was shot dead.

The Black Act was a catalogue of the gang's excesses. It created a range of offences based specifically on their activities and included around 350 ways of securing an appointment with the hangman. To have a blackened face whilst thinking of poaching was virtually enough to be proved guilty and executed. The Act was also retrospective in that all persons who had committed such offences were required to surrender themselves and make a full confession giving the names of all accomplices, whereby a free pardon was granted. An order could be issued for their arrest and failing to comply resulted in instant conviction, confiscation of estates and execution.

To ensure a goodly flow of intelligence informers were promised free pardons and all inhabitants of a hundred (a community) were taxed to make good any damage done by offenders against the Act. But for all the power and ferocity of the law the authorities had to resort to subterfuge to trap the leaders. They were tricked into going to London, where they were subsequently arrested. Four were later executed and thirty-six other members were transported overseas.

That was the end of the Waltham Blacks, but not the Black Act. Although it was intended to last for three years, it was thought so useful that it remained in force until 1823 when Sir Robert Peel's Bill repealed nearly all the provisions. Its abrogation heralded a new approach to the problems of crime and punishment but one side-effect was the relegation of poaching offences to the bottom of the league in terms of penalties and enforcement.

The motivation behind poaching

Historically the poacher has been viewed as a romantic folk hero taking from the gentry to feed his family. To be fair, many fended off hunger with fur, fish or fowl and, to a degree, gamekeepers tolerated the 'one for the pot' character. Such minor losses were accepted as long as the poacher's activities were not obvious and did not attract the boss's attention.

Some still see poaching as a victimless rural pursuit, stocking the freezer or making a few pounds at no one's expense. They see wild animals as being ownerless, which they are, but overlook the legal principle that rights to take them are vested in landowners and occupiers. However, commercial poachers kept the London markets stocked with all forms of game, using carriers and the rail networks to speed their unlawful gains out of the county. Their aim was purely profit.

But profit and food are not the only motivation. It is often the thrill of the chase, putting dogs to the ultimate test and evading capture that lures poachers from their beds. We knew a farmer who bred and shot pheasants on his own land, yet on many an early morning his wife would find the kitchen floor littered with pheasants following poaching trips on his cycle. The only gain was the excitement of outwitting the keeper and perhaps getting something for nothing. We have also seen a video taken by a gang of deer poachers lamping for deer with dogs and four-wheel-drive vehicles, where the commentary is highly charged with emotion and the thrill of the chase. Perhaps the law will never overcome such excitement.

Modern trends

If poaching ever had a romantic image it has disappeared from today's country scene. The old village poacher, with a reputation as well known to the local gamekeepers as to his friends, is less evident. There

196

is a degree of admiration for these old characters, and there is a prolif-
eration of books describing their exploits and methods. But modern
technology has influenced the way deer are poached. The modern
rifle with its telescopic sight, the electric lamp and battery combination and the four-wheel-drive vehicle are the type of equipment now
used to poach deer.

Poaching methods vary across the country, depending on the
terrain, the species of deer and their availability. What may be a
common practice in the Highlands of Scotland may be rare in the
south of England. Poachers vary too; some are semi-professional and
others merely go out because they fancy a bit of venison, some extra
holiday money or simply the thrill of the chase. What is common to
all is their total disrespect for the welfare of deer. Dependent fawns
are often orphaned, killing methods are crude and carcases are never
bled correctly or inspected to detect disease.

Deer poaching in the remote areas of Scotland is more likely to be
done with rifles, either from the vehicle or by the poachers taking to
the hill on foot. They are opportunists who know that in such areas
they are difficult to detect, owing to the vastness and isolation of the
landscape. The rifle is stowed discreetly in the vehicle until deer are
spotted perhaps 200 or 300 metres from the roadside. They are then
shot out of the vehicle window, which provides not only a good lean
for the shooter but a degree of disguise. Unless the area is persistently
poached, the deer will not be too alarmed at the vehicle's presence.
Even if the shot is heard it is unlikely that it can be located quickly
enough to prevent the short drag of the carcase to the vehicle and
escape.

Where poachers take to the hill with rifles a more traditional style
is adopted. The wind, the lie of the ground and roaming sheep all
have to be considered in addition to someone who may be stalking
the poachers themselves. If they are disturbed the rifles will often be
hidden and the poachers will lie up, keep watch and await the
moment to depart or continue. If a deer is shot it is likely to be part
butchered on the spot rather than risk a lengthy and arduous drag
off the hill. The best cuts of venison will be loaded into a bag and
quickly carried back to the vehicle or a rendezvous point. These
poachers are undoubtedly in a different class from those who
operate out of the more industrialised areas of the country. They
will be good shots by necessity, fit and capable of good stalking
techniques.

Apart from these practices in the remote Highlands, the most
common method of deer poaching currently used is coursing by dogs
supported by four-wheel-drive vehicles. At night, with the minimum
use of a high-powered lamp to avoid detection, this cruel method can

be devastatingly effective. Unless you notice vehicle tracks on your land you may never know that deer have been taken until it is too late. This practice is commonly referred to as 'lamping', but unlike the normal practice for vermin control, firearms are rarely used. Access is gained to land via either gateways or insecure fencing. The deer are chased at high speed and lurchers slipped whilst still on the move. The deer are coursed and dragged down, the dogs are quickly called off and the deer are dispatched. Some gangs are even less refined and simply drive their vehicles at the deer, knocking them down and causing untold suffering.

Humane dispatch is rare, with deer being crudely killed by a variety of means. They are then thrown into the vehicle without being gralloched and the poaching continues in areas where deer have not been driven into cover. We know of one gang of poachers who record their exploits on video. It is not uncommon for six or seven deer to be taken per night by this method from one estate, with all gralloching and carcase preparation done elsewhere. They have a ready market for the venison via unscrupulous dealers, the hotel trade and their private outlets. Their own freezers are often full and so are their pockets, with a tax-free income.

These gangs are well organised and will get to know the ground. On the night they may also divert police resources by reporting or creating incidents away from the poaching area.

Not all poaching of deer is quite so blatant and more subtle methods are used – e.g. when a legitimate stalker shoots and takes deer over a boundary or stalks on an area owned by absentee landlords. If caught, such poachers rely on the defence that they were retrieving a wounded beast or were simply mistaken over the boundary location.[116]

The B.S.E. crisis generated a need for traceability of animals and foodstuffs to allay public health concerns. With wild game it is not possible to develop such detailed systems and being a natural product, it is attractive to those seeking leaner, healthier meat. Whilst consumers are prepared to accept that venison is a wild product they also have a right to expect that when it comes under human control it is processed to the highest standards. Poached venison may never see a licensed game dealer or be subject to inspection and hygienic conditions. In many cases it is processed in the poacher's outhouse and it has been known for a carcase to be left hidden in a field for several days awaiting collection.

---

116. See chapter 7.

POACHING OFFENCES

The poacher does not differentiate between wild and captive deer. Venison is venison whether it is poached or stolen. However, as discussed in chapter 1, where captive deer are taken they are considered to have been not poached but stolen, and stronger legislation exists to deal with those responsible. Here we consider the taking of wild deer and we must look to the poaching offences in the Deer Acts north and south of the border and across the Irish Sea. The offences are similar in England, Wales, Northern Ireland and Scotland. Note, too, that the legislation applies equally to someone who has a right to be on the land, but not to take deer, such as a tenant, an employee or someone on a public right of way.

In England and Wales the legislation defines deer as deer of any species and includes the carcase and any part thereof. In Northern Ireland deer means deer of any species and their hybrids, and includes those on enclosed land, where deer not in the wild state are usually kept. In Scotland deer means fallow, red, roe and sika deer, and any other species specified in an order by the Secretary of State, and includes hybrids of those species, and where appropriate, the carcase of any deer or any part of it. So all species of deer are covered in England, Wales and Northern Ireland, while in Scotland only red, fallow, sika, roe and red/sika hybrids are specified plus any others specified by the Secretary of State.

England, Wales and Northern Ireland

Poaching is covered by the Deer Act, 1991 (section 22 of the Wildlife (Northern Ireland) Order, 1985, contains similar offences). Under section 1(1), it is an offence, without the consent of the occupier, owner or other lawful authority, to enter any land in search or pursuit of any deer with the intention of taking, killing or injuring it, and under section 1(2), it is an offence, without the consent of the occupier, owner or other lawful authority, while on any land, to:

- intentionally take, kill or injure any deer or attempt to do so
- search for or pursue any deer with such intent
- remove the carcase of any deer

Under section 1(3), however, a person will not be guilty under sections 1(1) or (2) if:

- he believes he would have had the owner's or occupier's consent if he had known of the circumstances
- he believed he had a lawful authority

Scotland

Under section 17 of the Deer (Scotland) Act, 1996, is it an offence:

- without legal right or permission to take, wilfully kill or injure deer on any land
- to remove the carcase of any deer from any land without legal right or permission from someone having such legal right
- to wilfully kill or injure any deer otherwise than by shooting with the prescribed firearm and ammunition

There is a view based on the game laws that where deer are legitimately shot on land where authority exists, but fall dead over the boundary, they can be recovered. There remain however, the issues of trespass and ownership of the carcase at civil law.[117]

Consent or permission

Consent is normally proved in a statement after the incident by establishing the rights to take deer. It is wise to record stalking arrangements, even informal ones, in writing. Informal, unrecorded agreements can result in doubts over consent, as with the stalker who claims permission was granted by a previous occupier.

Shooting or sporting contracts can be a source of confusion and dispute. In the 'good old days' gentlemen's agreements, written or made on a handshake, were often understood by the parties, but as time and individuals pass on problems arise. A typical situation is where an estate lets the sporting rights over a tenanted farm to a third party. The farm may later be sold to the tenant, who may then sell it to another person. Existing rights should be identified at the time of purchase by the solicitor who does the conveyancing, but new owners often take matters for granted and attempt to exercise rights which have been removed from the land, restricting access, setting up their own shoot, catching up birds or taking deer. There is no simple answer to such a problem. To prove consent or permission means looking at the contracts and sporting licence under the civil law.[118]

117. See chapters 7 and 8.
118. See chapter 1.

Location

The relevant piece of land has to be identified. This aspect is particularly important when the incident is close to a boundary and is normally proved by eye-witness evidence. Expert evidence may be used to disprove a claim that a shot deer ran over the boundary before falling dead.

Time limits

There are limits to the time that can elapse between the offence being committed and the taking of a prosecution. The general rule is a maximum of six months unless the legislation includes special provisions.

Powers and penalties

The penalties for poaching are identical in all countries: on conviction a fine not exceeding level 4 on the standard scale and/or three months' imprisonment or both. The punishment can be applied to each deer taken. Powers to arrest and search vary, and they are covered in chapters 2 and 3.

OFFENCES ASSOCIATED WITH POACHING

The Deer Acts include numerous offences relating to illegal methods of taking deer, taking them at night and out of season, unlawful firearms and the possession of illegal venison. Poaching offences may sometimes be difficult to prove, but there are many others which can be considered, which may carry a greater penalty. The most obvious are cruelty and vehicle-related offences, including driving while disqualified, drink driving and document offences.

Cruelty[119]

There are offences under the Hunting Act 2004 [England and Wales] where dogs are used to poach deer. Section 1 states a person commits an offence if he hunts a wild mammal with a dog unless his hunting is exempt.

Also under the Wild Mammals (Protection) Act 1996 (England, Wales and Scotland), if someone, by his own actions or the use of a

119. See also chapter 7.

dog, mutilates, kicks, beats, nails, impales, stabs, burns, stones, crushes, drowns, drags or asphyxiates any wild mammal with intent to inflict unnecessary suffering he commits an offence. Any one of the above acts is sufficient and could easily be applied to deer poaching. The offences may be applicable where dogs are used to course and pull down deer. The Act was introduced following extreme acts of cruelty on wild mammals, notably nailing a vixen to a tree and using a hedgehog as a football. Before this Act wild mammals were not protected by the cruelty laws unless they were held in a state of captivity.

The Act contains exemptions which include:

- the humane dispatch of a disabled animal
- the humane and swift dispatch of an animal taken in the lawful course of shooting, hunting, coursing or pest control
- the lawful use of poison, a snare, trap, dog or bird for the purpose of killing or taking a wild animal

These exemptions only apply to *lawful* pursuits or the *lawful* use of certain methods. It follows therefore that activities which may be deemed unlawful, perhaps trespassing or acting without the owner's consent, may render someone liable to offences under this Act.

Driving on land (England, Wales and Scotland)

Under section 34 of the Road Traffic Act, 1988, it is an offence without lawful authority to drive a motor vehicle on common land, moorland, other land of any description not being part of a road, or on a public footpath or bridleway (except in emergencies or parking within 15 yards of a road). It is known for the police to dip the fuel tank for red diesel (fuel which is sold at a lower duty for non-road use). This is of great interest to Customs and Excise and often leads to the instant seizure of the vehicle and substantial penalties.

Firearms offences[120]

These offences include:

- use of section 1 firearms contrary to certificate conditions
- possession of firearms by young persons
- trespass with a firearm – all types of firearms, even air weapons
- possession of a loaded firearm in a public place

120. See also chapter 6.

Air weapons are also worth closer examination in case their power is such that they are classed as section 1 firearms. (Rifle exceeds 12ft/lb.)

Bows and crossbows are not classed as firearms but it is illegal to kill any bird or animal with them under the Wildlife and Countryside Act, 1981, in England, Wales or Scotland. In Northern Ireland it is illegal to take red, sika and fallow deer with any form of arrow.

Threats and intimidation

Encounters between poachers and deer managers are likely to result in threats and intimidation. Sometimes these may be directed at family members, homes, livestock and crops. Several pieces of legislation cover such behaviour, including the Public Order Act in England and Wales. Section 4 of this Act, for example refers to a person using towards another person threatening, abusive or insulting words or behaviour:

- with intent to cause that person to believe immediate violence will be used against him, or another, by any person
- with intent to provoke the immediate use of violence by the other person or another
- whereby that person is likely to believe that such violence will be used
- whereby it is likely that such violence will be provoked

Section 5 includes a person using threatening, abusive or insulting words or behaviour, or disorderly behaviour, within the hearing or sight of a person likely to be caused harassment, alarm or distress.

The offences can be committed in public or private places but not inside a house, and cater for confrontational situations. In a poaching situation, they apply equally to the gamekeeper and the poacher. It is necessary to prove the intent to create a fear of violence, harassment etc. which will rely on accurately recording the words and actions used by each individual. Only police officers have powers of arrest.

The intimidation of witnesses is covered by section 51 of the Criminal Justice and Public Order Act, 1994 (England and Wales), and similar offences apply in Scotland and Northern Ireland. The offence can be committed by any person who intimidates a person assisting in an investigation, a witness or juror. Threats need not be made in the presence of the person and may be financial as well as physical.

The Protection from Harassment Act, 1997 (the anti-stalking Act) contains offences of harassment and causing fear of violence.

Other offences

Criminal damage involves causing damage to buildings, fences, hedges, crops, captive or domestic birds or animals. It might include driving through hedges or across crops, injuring a keeper's dog or setting fire to buildings or haystacks.

Assault is the infliction of injury that amounts to severe bruising, cuts, broken bones or other discomforts.

Poachers may also be armed with **offensive weapons** or use an innocent object as a weapon when challenged. Under section 1 of the Prevention of Crime Act, 1953 (similar provisions apply in Scotland and Northern Ireland) it is an offence without reasonable excuse to have an offensive weapon in a public place. An offensive weapon is something made or adapted to cause injury, such as a baseball bat with a nail in it, a knuckle-duster or a cosh. It can also be anything which is used for the purpose – e.g. a walking stick or a hammer. Only the police can make an arrest.[121]

OBSERVATION AND IDENTIFICATION

Evidence requires an incident to be recorded from start to finish, and a written record, photograph, video or tape-recording are always more useful than your recollections. Always have a notebook and pen available to record details at the time or as soon as possible after the event – e.g. on return to your vehicle or when the police arrive. Tell the police about the notes, photographs, video or tapes to validate their authenticity.

The main principle of evidence-gathering is to present to a court the best evidence available – e.g. the actual carcase, the rifle or the dog used by the poacher. There are obvious difficulties with some of these and a photograph is the next best thing. If a car number is written on a cigarette packet it becomes an exhibit and should be preserved and presented to the court as the best evidence.

It is vital that you note what each individual did and said. Identify each one by his clothing – e.g. the one in the wax jacket and the one in the cammo trousers. Who was driving? Who had the dog, the lamp, the gun? If vehicles were involved try to identify the driver, the vehicle, the road and locations where they were driven.

---

121. See chapter 7 for legislation governing the carrying of knives.

Intention and wilfulness

Proving intention or wilfulness is sometimes difficult. We do not know what is going through someone else's mind and must base our evidence on the poacher's actions or words. Seeing the kill, finding the poacher with a carcase, seeing a dog slipped on a deer under the lamp or a high-speed chase in a four-wheel-drive vehicle are often sufficient to prove intent. Finding a suspect walking the land with a gun or dog may not be enough – even if it is 3 a.m. It is better to observe him until his actions give him away. The comments on intention are also applicable to attempts to commit offences.

The search or pursuit element of the offences in England, Wales and Northern Ireland require similar evidence to that which proves intention. Many excuses can be given for the poacher's actions: 'I'm exercising the dogs', 'I'm only after rabbits', 'I'm walking on to land where I have the stalking' etc. Once again it is better to watch and wait until his actions prove his intentions.

Scientific evidence

Scientific evidence in the form of DNA, blood, bone or hair on clothing, dogs or vehicles, can connect a deer carcase taken from the land to a gralloch, amputated legs or head, or a pool of blood at the scene. Knives and saws are also a source of flesh and bone fragments which can be compared with DNA from a carcase.

Videos

It is known for poachers to take photographs and videos of their activities which are often circulated amongst others with similar interests. Such evidence may be found in their vehicles but may also come to light when searching their homes for other evidence. Their activities

often cause disgust amongst their friends and relatives who have been known to hand them in to the police.

Photographs or videos taken by a witness provide damning evidence and should be brought to the attention of the police at the earliest opportunity. Evidence as to the time, date and location of the filming will be covered in a witness statement. In many cases the police will take possession of the film and process it.

One difficulty, however, can be in establishing the date and the location of the incidents on film. Poachers may claim that the acts caught on film took place in another country where such activities are lawful. It may also be claimed that the incidents were several months or years old.

Continuity and identification

These two factors are important in the prosecution of any offence. Continuity has two main aspects:

- the recording and handling of exhibits
- evidence which proves a continuous, unbroken chain of events

The handling of all exhibits must be traced back to each person who has been involved at any stage in the proceedings. This is normally done by referring to them in a written statement. For example, if a gamekeeper writes down a car number on a scrap of paper and later hands the paper to a police officer who may then pass it on to other officers, the details must be recorded in a statement each time possession changes. Months later in court the chain of evidence can then track the paper from the gamekeeper to the court.

Another important aspect of continuity is the observation of suspects. Let us assume that in the middle of the night you see a lamp in a field next to a public footpath. In the beam you see a dog running towards a deer, then the lamp goes out. You make your way to the footpath and find a man with a dog and a lamp walking towards you. You may be convinced that they are the ones you saw in the field, but the chain of events is broken and you cannot legally connect the man on the path with the man in the field. The facts amount to circumstantial evidence which is not as strong as direct evidence. An unbroken chain would necessitate the tracking of the man from the field to the path.

Identification is another critical area which is challenged in court. Eye-witness evidence is subjected to several tests:

- the distance involved
- the lighting conditions and position of any street lamps

206

- the weather conditions
- whether the witness was wearing spectacles
- any obstructions between the witness and the suspect
- the time and duration of the observation
- whether the witness knew the suspect

YOUR STATEMENT

It is vital that your statement to the police contains not only the evidence but also your justification for spending court time and money on what may, to some people, appear to be a trivial matter. Your statement can influence the decision to prosecute and the penalties. A poaching case must pass two tests before it can get to court: there must be sufficient evidence to have a good chance of securing a prosecution, and it must be considered worthy of prosecution in the public interest.

Many poaching cases fail when the details which justify prosecution and subsequent penalties are not included in the statement. Do not expect the police, the Crown Prosecution Services and magistrates to know how deer are managed, the economics involved or the effects of poaching.

The following is a suggestion for the basis of your statement. It includes numerous options to cater for different circumstances and offences. Once you have described the situation on your estate you can use it as the basis of your statement in future cases.

I am the [deer manager, stalker, gamekeeper, landowner, tenant, farmer, shooting tenant, etc.] in respect of land situated at [detail the area involved; consider providing an estate map].

Outline the responsibilities of the role, including:

- your employer (e.g. estate, syndicate, deer management group, forest owner)
- what you provide (e.g. stalking, trophies, venison production)
- who you provide it for (e.g. private owner, syndicate)
- how you do it (e.g. management by selective culling to promote healthy stock etc.)
- how you look after them (e.g. selective culling across an area in co-operation with other landowners, protection from poachers, night patrols etc.)
- if the estate is partly or wholly commercial what is meant by let days, stalking, trophies etc.

- how costs are calculated – what is charged per day, beats or trophy

Explain why you want the poachers prosecuted, including:

- the effect of poaching (an inability to provide the level of sport expected, the damage to stalking by disturbance the night before, loss of revenue, income tax and V.A.T., damage to the local economy in terms of income generated by way of equipment purchased, accommodation, food, etc., threat to employment, poor herd management)
- the public health risks from poached venison
- whether poaching affects proper deer management through indiscriminate killing
- the fact that poachers see a failure to prosecute as a sign of weakness, and that gamekeepers, their families and property are further exposed to violence, intimidation and financial loss
- why poaching is a problem in your locality

Describe what happened, including:

- what you saw and heard
- whether deer were injured or left to die
- whether livestock was worried or disturbed
- whether the poachers' acts were wilful – e.g. whether it was a gang from a city 100 miles away out to fill a van with venison or a couple of local youths taking pot shots with an air rifle, and whether there was any expression of regret
- if you were injured, details of injuries
- whether there were any threats of intimidation at the time or for the future and whether you have experienced any threats from these or other poachers in the past

COMPENSATION

Historically a realistic value has seldom been placed on fish, fur or feather and there has been a reluctance to claim compensation in poaching cases. Even in Roman times the principle of *ferae naturae* stated that wild animals were ownerless, but the right to take them has been jealously guarded through the centuries. Modern laws maintain this position on 'ownership' but rights to take sporting species remain enshrined in civil law. Sporting rights can change hands for vast sums of money and poaching can have a significant effect on the overall value of a piece of land.

The provision of sport for the leisure market has been phenomenal recently, and in many rural communities it is a financial lifeline through the jobs and money involved in providing accommodation, food, equipment and other local services. As we have said, you must assume that the police, magistrates, the Crown Prosecution Service and solicitors involved in a poaching case will be unaware of the significance to the local economy and the time, effort and investment which goes into a sporting estate – hence the detailed statement above.

Traditionally compensation has been based on the value of the venison at the game dealer's door but there is now an established legal authority for claiming compensation at the commercial value – Haslam v. C.P.S., Derby Crown Court, 1991. Although this case relates to poaching pheasants, its principles have been successfully applied to other species.

Haslam was found guilty of poaching thirty-six pheasants and the estate claimed the going rate at the time of £12 plus V.A.T. The keeper had to explain the process of managing an estate, of rearing and releasing birds into the wild, which he then tended by providing feed and protection from predators and poachers. Groups then rented out shooting by paying a fixed sum for each bird shot on the day. He explained what is obvious to those in the know: that birds were not released on the day of the shoot, so it was not possible to replace birds lost to poachers by buying in replacements from the game farm, and that such losses affected the number of birds which could be driven over the guns. Whilst there was no guarantee that the poached birds would have been shot and their value realised, the keeper drew a parallel with a baker, who does not sell all he bakes but must have bread for his customers to buy. The magistrates awarded £10 per bird, which went to the estate, in addition to a heavy fine for poaching and firearm offences.

It is difficult to apply a value to lamping hare and rabbit but you should be able to quantify the problems of poaching deer, in addition to the game and livestock, damage to fences, gates left open etc. For example, the stalking fee, trophy fee, carcase value, time taken to track an injured deer, potential damage to the herd.

In Derbyshire we successfully use a simple formula for the cost of poached trout: the total costs of running the club divided by the number of fish stocked. There are also figures available for rod-caught wild salmon, which often amount to several hundred pounds each.

The Haslam case has since been used successfully in other courts. Explain the grounds for your claim fully and include the following in your statement:

> I ask that compensation of . . . be awarded in accordance with Haslam v. C.P.S. Derby Crown Court, 1991, this being the value to my employer.

Here is a checklist for further action:

- Immediately after each incident write to the local police and the C.P.S. or Procurator Fiscal expressing your concerns.
- Emphasise that you wish to see a prosecution.
- Make a request for compensation.
- If you are able to attend court bring compensation to the notice of the C.P.S. prior to the start of the case.
- If you are injured ask for a Criminal Injuries Compensation form, even if the poacher was not arrested or identified.
- If you have concerns with the actions of the police or the prosecutor, write to the Chief Constable or head of the prosecution authority.

CITIZEN'S ARREST

There may be situations when dealing with poachers where serious criminal offences are involved. In certain circumstances you may be empowered to make what is commonly referred to as a 'citizen's arrest'. These powers are contained in the Police and Criminal Evidence Act,1984 as amended.
Any person can arrest a person who is:

- in the act of committing an indictable offence or
- whom he reasonably suspects to be committing such an offence, or
- where you know an indictable offence has been committed and you reasonably suspect someone of having committed it.

The powers of arrest above can only be exercised if it is not reasonably practicable for a constable to make the arrest instead and it is necessary to arrest the person to prevent the person:

- causing physical injury to himself or any other person;
- suffering physical injury;
- causing loss of or damage to property; or
- making off before a constable can assume responsibility for him.

An indictable offence is an offence that can be tried at Crown Court for example theft, burglary and criminal damage.
So if you come across someone stealing deer from an enclosed deer

farm or park, or damaging a high seat, then the persons responsible can be arrested if the conditions apply.

Remember, the police have more extensive powers and are specifically trained to make arrests so as to minimise the risk to personal safety. If you get it wrong, not only may you suffer injury but you may be sued for false imprisonment.

CHAPTER 10

Poaching Prevention

The prevention of poaching is vital to all those who have a vested interest in the welfare of deer. Historically poaching prevention was an essential element of the gamekeeper's role and had an impact on the occasional deer poacher. But poaching trends have changed, and deer are now more likely to be poached than game birds.

Knowing how to deal with poachers, identify offences and gather evidence are all important but ideally our efforts should be concentrated on tactics to prevent it occurring in the first place. Prevention remains far better than cure. However, it is a difficult concept to get over to people who may not think they have a problem in the first place, even though their livelihood may depend on a sustainable level of quality deer. The danger is that once poachers have been successful in finding and taking deer in a particular area, it becomes difficult to stop repeated intrusions. They are after all, the ultimate opportunists, being able to pick their own time, place and method. They will have a good knowledge of the area and a well-rehearsed story should they be caught. Despite this, much can be done to bring successful prosecutions and prevent further poaching.

Deterrence or prosecution

You must decide whether you are prepared to tackle poachers with a view to a prosecution or simply to deter them by driving them off your land. For a prosecution to have a good chance it is often better to observe quietly, gather the evidence and step in after the kill. Trying to prove a poacher's intentions whilst in pursuit is more difficult and provides numerous excuses e.g. I was only exercising my dog and it ran after a deer—

To let the pursuit continue, however, may cause more damage by disturbing deer and livestock. In these circumstances it may be better to show a presence and get them off the land.

Making best use of law enforcement

The police have the primary responsibility for enforcing deer legislation and it is in their interests to apply resources effectively to its prevention and detection.

Instigating successful action through the courts where punishment can be imposed can be a useful deterrent, and as we have seen, raising the awareness of the Crown Prosecution Service and magistrates of the realities of poaching and its effect on rural communities is essential to successful prosecutions. This is strengthened if the right levels of compensation are applied for and full use is made of publicity.[122]

Where poaching problems exist liaison with the local police is essential, as your own powers to deal with such situations are weak.[123] All police forces have appointed wildlife liaison officers and whilst this responsibility is often ancillary to their normal duties they are a good point of contact and may well have considerable experience in dealing with poaching matters. If you do not know the local officers and need to establish contact you may write to your area divisional commander, who should put you in touch with the right people and ideally arrange a meeting locally, at which you can outline the problems. Such action raises the profile of deer poaching and can lead to a more positive approach from local officers at your time of need. A number of initiatives may be suggested, some of which are elaborated

122. See pages 208 and 215.
123. See chapters 2, 3 and 9.

213

upon below.

Alternatively you could contact the B.A.S.C. for their help and advice.[124] They have successfully campaigned against deer poaching as a rural crime for some years. Their aim has been to raise awareness of the economic, conservation and social implications of poaching in all its forms. They continue to work in partnership with the police to promote watch schemes and provide training and information.

The Crime and Disorder Act, 1998, requires local authorities and the police to work together with other key agencies and the community at local level to develop and implement strategies for reducing crime and disorder. In rural communities this may well involve strategies to reduce deer poaching. The first step involves reviewing the patterns and levels of crime and disorder by consulting widely with the local community. The strategies must be published and kept under review. This legislation is a very useful way forward in some rural areas, giving the police the necessary impetus to provide resources to combat poaching problems. The development of countryside watch schemes may be the type of initiative included in a strategy to reduce rural crime.[125]

It is apparent that much of our poaching law fails to prevent poaching. Even if poachers are stopped by the police and are equipped for such purposes, perhaps with a lamp and dogs, there may be little that can be done; a 'going equipped' offence does not exist. The practice of leaving the deer to be transported from the land the following day in commuter traffic, emphasises the inadequacy of the legislation.

Successful use has been made of legislation which is some 600 years old, known as the Justice of the Peace Act, 1361. The police in Dorset were faced with an unprecedented level of deer poaching and found they were powerless to deal with the situation because of the difficulty of actually catching the offenders in the act or with deer in their vehicles. Lamping deer at night had become very prevalent, particularly during the winter months. It was occurring over a wide area on a large scale, and was relatively well organised. Eventually some of the offenders were caught in possession of a number of deer carcases. Further enquiries revealed that they had been checked by the police on five separate occasions in the early hours of the morning on what were suspected to be journeys to or from poaching expeditions. Large lurcher-type dogs were seen in their vehicle and on one occasion a search revealed lamping equipment.

---

124. See page 229 for contact details.
125. See page 220.

In addition to charges under the Deer Act, proceedings by way of complaint were also taken under the Justice of the Peace Act, 1361. The magistrates were sufficiently convinced, in view of all the circumstances, that the defendants could well continue their poaching activities. Orders were made binding them over in the sum of £200 to keep the peace and be of good behaviour for a period of two years. The circumstances of this case emphasise the need for the efficient gathering of intelligence concerning the movements of poachers, their associates and activities, all of which should be properly recorded at the time.

This ancient law is thought to have been used to combat poaching in the reign of George I, when a poacher on the Duke of Beaufort's estate was compelled to enter a bond not to take game or fish there. In more recent years it has been used in respect of a variety of offences, including kerb crawling for prostitutes. There is however a reluctance to use such legislation to overcome the inadequacies of modern legislation.

Enforcement of the legislation relating to venison dealers is an important step in poaching prevention.

Using the media as a deterrent

The potential for positive coverage of poaching cases in the press is often high, and it can easily be encouraged by involving the media at an early stage. But you need to co-operate with them.

Over the years we have sought to dispel the myths of the romantic image of poaching and the issue of class associated with country sports. The media are now keen to portray poaching as a cruel pursuit which has a detrimental economic and environmental impact on rural communities. Poachers are seen as criminals involved in a lucrative, illegal trade rather than as people taking from the rich to feed the poor.

The involvement of the media must be a benefit; they need a good story that will generate interest, and you need the exposure to deter poaching. But there are also risks. You may draw attention to the presence of deer in an area which was previously little known, and thereby attract unwelcome interest from a variety of sources, including poachers. However we believe the advantages of 'going public' outweigh the risks.

TV reporters will often need first-hand accounts by video interview. This may not be as daunting as you imagine and the interview not normally 'live'; if you make an error it can be done again. They will not want to rehearse matters with you too much, as this tends to spoil the spontaneity of the interview, but you should first check out the general areas of interest. Remember that they will not have first-hand knowledge of the issues and you should advise them accordingly. If you have a message to put across in the interview, for example inviting viewers to report suspicious incidents, then ensure that there is an opportunity for you to do so.

They will want to film the location if possible and any deer that may have been taken, and possibly at short notice. However, if a case is to go to court, the matter will be *sub judice* and any information or material must not be published until after the court proceedings. This is not unusual and should not be a bar to your co-operation, but you should seek the advice of the police officer dealing with the case.

Dealing with the media may be inconvenient, but the deterrent factor should not be underestimated. It is a valuable and powerful weapon in combating poaching by the exposure of antisocial behaviour and cruelty towards deer. Public interest is raised and may ultimately influence how such matters are viewed by the courts.

Physical deterrents

Unfortunately, for many poachers the thought of capture and conviction is a wholly inadequate deterrent compared to the sheer excitement and financial gains of further nightly raids. You need to concentrate on making your estate or stalking area a hard target. There are a number of practical measures you can take to achieve this.

First you must assess the level of poaching and how it is being done. If this is not known but you suspect it is likely, then consider the following. A key deterrent in lowland areas is to restrict vehicular access. Basic security can be relatively inexpensive and quite effective. You should restrict access to vehicles as far as possible in vulnerable areas – mainly those adjacent to the public roads or easily accessible from them. Closing and locking gates to private roads or access to fields is particularly important and wherever possible they should be chained and locked. Hedgerows and fences should be maintained and where they do not exist you should consider other means of preventing vehicular access. Many landowners have access to heavy plant which could be used to create small trenches at points where access would otherwise be easily gained by 4x4 vehicles.

In remote highland areas, where it is more common for deer to be poached by shooting from the road or taking to the hill on foot with a rifle, prevention is more difficult. In these situations good intelligence and observation are essential, with heavy covert patrolling. If

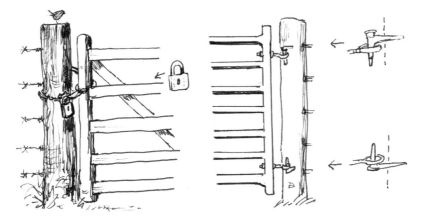

Restrict access by securing gates.

it is well co-ordinated with the police, this enables suspects to be stopped and searched at strategic locations.

Night-time surveillance is essential and can have a psychological effect on would-be poachers if they become aware that they have been seen. Gamekeepers have always practised 'night watching' in the past, and know its value as a deterrent. It involves active patrolling in the areas you consider most at risk. Good police liaison is essential and it is advisable to have established links with local officers prior to your night patrols. Record times and places where fences are damaged or vehicle tracks left, so that you know when there has been an unwanted presence on the land. This intelligence can then be used to target your patrols effectively. Good intelligence of the movements of suspected poachers and their vehicles is vital. Ideally you should have a system of communication by which information can be quickly circulated.

Vehicles are not always to be found discreetly hidden in gateways or farm tracks; you should bear in mind that where urban development is close by they may be left in pub car parks or secreted between residents' vehicles on housing estates. It is far more likely that poachers will not have left their vehicle and will be on the move, looking for areas to drive onto and lamp deer actually on the move. In the Highlands they may drive into remote areas with rifles on board ready to shoot from the vehicle if the opportunity presents itself. It is a difficult situation to deal with, as you do not have power to stop or search such vehicles on the road, even if you have previously seen them involved in poaching on the land. This power is restricted to

the police and you must be content with circulating the intelligence quickly and hoping that they may be stopped and searched by them.

Pursuing a poacher's vehicle on the public road is fraught with danger and should be avoided at all costs. You should content yourself with the knowledge that the poachers will know they have been seen and that their activities have been obstructed. You should have a good practical knowledge of your legal powers[126] and should guard against the temptation to act outside them. To do so will render you liable to counter-claims and actions through the criminal or civil courts.

If you are dealing with poachers at night you should involve the police early, when your suspicions are first raised. This is particularly important when you suspect firearms are involved. You should maintain observations from a safe distance until assistance arrives. Only police officers have powers to seize firearms and make arrests in respect of deer poaching, so improving police liaison and the setting up of watch schemes is a key element of your prevention tactics. Poachers quickly get to know the estates and areas where keepers and deer managers are active and vigilant. They do not like being watched or their whereabouts being noted. Eventually they will either be caught or go elsewhere, into areas which are not so well policed.

126. See chapters 2, 3 and 9.

Daytime vigilance and the value of observation

Maintaining vigilance during the day can be rewarding. It is common for poachers to undertake reconnaissance prior to night-time activities, and this type of intelligence can be invaluable. If you can see deer in the hot spots from the road, then so can the poachers. You may be able to move them or discourage them from visiting these visible areas. In crime prevention parlance this would be known as 'target hardening'.

It is a well-known practice for deer poachers to hide carcases in the night and return the next day when suspicions may not be aroused. A vehicle you think is a courting couple or a family on a picnic could be collecting the previous night's spoils. If you find a carcase you suspect has been hidden by poachers you should involve the police in any observations you mount, in the hope of the culprits returning. You must remain discreet in your activities and plans. Our experience in these situations suggest that observations can be worthwhile provided sufficient police resources are allocated. The legislation provides for offences of removing carcases from land.[127]

Two cases in Derbyshire emphasise the value of mounting such observations. The first involved a gamekeeper who found a fallow buck hidden in bracken, apparently shot with either a .22 or a crossbow. The police were involved and a decision taken to keep observation on the carcase that evening. As darkness fell three men arrived and attempted to remove the beast to a nearby vehicle. They were arrested and taken to the local police station before they had an opportunity to agree a line of defence. When they were interviewed the first man said his dog had accidentally chased and killed the beast. The second man said it was a mercy killing, as they had found the beast in a bad way caught in some baler twine. And the third man said, 'What deer?' The magistrates subsequently found all three guilty of removing a carcase from land.

The second incident highlights the need for patience and determination in obtaining evidence. A mature red stag had been brutally killed within the enclosed deer park of a stately home now owned by the National Trust. Part of the carcase was discovered, hidden in undergrowth and observations were kept for two days, but without success. The part-carcase was removed. On the third day a vehicle was seen in the vicinity in suspicious circumstances and details circulated to the police. The vehicle was later stopped and searched

127. See chapters 2 and 3.

some miles from the scene of the incident. To the officer's surprise, he found not only cutting equipment but part of the original red deer carcase taken on the night. The driver was arrested on suspicion of *theft* as the deer, having been taken from enclosed land, was treated as having been stolen rather than poached.[128] At court the man stated he had come by the venison innocently, having purchased it as dog meat from a man he had met in a lay-by. He was subsequently convicted of handling stolen property under the Theft Act, 1968.

Countryside watch schemes

Setting up poacher or deer watch schemes involving the police, landowners, keepers and stalkers can be extremely effective. Such schemes are not new and have had considerable success throughout the country. They are more successful if they involve the support of the wider community, not just those with an interest in deer. An essential element is the gathering, exchange and circulation of intelligence on suspected poachers, their vehicles, methods, and movements.

Other aspects of such schemes should include the determination of well-defined rendezvous points and the issue of standardised maps to all parties which clearly indicate boundaries and relevant information. Good communications are essential and can be achieved by the use of personal radios or mobile telephones. The latter are particularly useful where help is required urgently. The ability to ring for assistance from a remote area of woodland is an invaluable asset.

Remember that poachers have access to communication equipment, including radios on which they have been known to monitor other transmissions. Therefore in planning your operations you should include codes for identification and locations and supply relevant maps.

Watch schemes tend to encourage co-operation between neighbouring estates, which can be of mutual benefit. The pooling of resources affords greater personal safety, mobility and effectiveness. Night-vision equipment, although expensive, can give you the upper hand. By syndicating the purchase and use of such equipment the cost can be considerably reduced. There are a number of practical measures you can take, all of which contribute to making your area a hard target.[129] Basic security considerations are essential, particularly those restricting vehicular access points in vulnerable areas.

128. See chapter 1.
129. See page 191.

Let it be known that you are using night-vision equipment, radios etc. Publicise the watch scheme and the use of joint patrols. A high-powered lamp sweeping across a valley or along a wood side can be quite effective in demonstrating your presence. If you are short handed, carry two lamps each. Take the initiative; you have the advantage of local knowledge and assistance.

Watch meetings are key events that members should be encouraged to attend. They should be about developing future strategy rather than wasting time on anecdotal criticisms of the scheme or the police's response. Positive outcomes of such meetings include the opportunity to socialise, and presentations on associated topics such as law or deer management. A raffle in aid of a local charity also provides a good media opportunity.

Data protection
If you decide to organise a watch scheme or are already involved in one then you should be aware of the restrictions imposed by the Data Protection Acts of 1984 and 1998. There may be liabilities if you are involved in the circulation of intelligence concerning poachers.

The Acts give legal rights to individuals in respect of personal data held about them by others and places obligations on those who process information about individuals. The latter must be open about the use to which the information is put (through the data protection register) and follow sound and proper practices (the data protection principles). The legislation protects an individual's right to privacy and provides safeguards on the way personal information is used.

Unless a watch scheme is able to fulfil the conditions attached to an exemption from registration, it will need to register its intentions to process personal data.

However, having due regard for data protection and other legal obligations, the police may disclose limited details to watch schemes for the prevention or detection of crime. Such details will not normally be deemed 'personal data' within the terms of the Acts.

Where information such as the details of suspicious vehicles are circulated, it should be made clear that care must be taken in the subsequent use of that information, in that it may no longer be accurate. The vehicle may now be driven quite legitimately or have changed ownership. There is a good deal that can be circulated without the need for registration. Clearly personal details such as a poacher's name and address would contravene the Acts unless registration had been granted. But a watch scheme could circulate the following type of information, for example, without liability:

> Between 2 a.m. and 4 a.m. on Sunday, 4 January, the following vehicle was seen in the Peak Forest area in suspicious circumstances. Occupants are suspected of deer poaching. Toyota four-wheel-drive, red colour, registered number ABC 123D. The vehicle was seen to contain two white youths, both with short cropped hair and a number of lurcher-type dogs.

If you keep details of persons involved in the scheme, such as a fellow keeper or landowner, you may share information, but ensure that individuals know what is to be done with their personal information and that you gain their consent. You should only collect information that you can justify for the purposes of the scheme.

The registrar's staff are happy to assist with any queries you may have and can be contacted at the Office of the Data Protection Registrar, Wycliffe House, Water Lane, Wilmslow, Cheshire SK9 5AF.

List of Statutes

List of Cases

Bibliography

Chapman, Norma : *Deer*, Whittet Books
Chapman, Norma : *Fallow Deer*, The Mammal Society
Smith, J.C. : *The Law of Theft*, Butterworth
Everitt, Nicholas : *Shots from a Lawyer's Gun*, Gilbertson and Page Ltd
Haigh, J.C. : *Deer Magazine*, Vol. 10, No. 3
Stair Memorial Encyclopaedia, Vol. 11. 'Game'
Sandys-Winsch, B.A. Godfrey : *Animal Law*, Shaw & Sons
Sandys-Winsch, B.A. Godfrey : *Gun Law*, Shaw & Sons
Riddall, J.G. : *Land Law*, Butterworth
Riddall & Trevelyan : *Rights of Way – a guide to law and practice*, Ramblers'
    Ass.
Highways Agency : *The Prevention of Casualties Amongst Deer Populations*
    S.W.335/V2/08-97 Aug 1997
Radford, Mike : *Animal Cruelty and the Courts*, Justice of the Peace, Vol.
    162
Chenevix-Trench, Charles : *The Poacher and the Squire*, Longmans
Mead, Lawrence : *Oke's Game Laws*, Butterworth
Smith & Hogan : *Criminal Law*, Butterworth
Nature Conservancy Council : *The Capture and Handling of Deer*
Stranks, Jeremy : *Health & Safety Law*
Halsbury's Laws of England, 3rd ed.
Parkes, Charlie & Thornley, John : *Fair Game*, Pelham Books
Parkes, Charlie : *Law of the Countryside*, Countryside Management
    Association
Whitehead, G. Kenneth: *The Whitehead Encyclopaedia of Deer*, Swan Hill
    Press
Whitehead, G. Kenneth : *Half a Century of Scottish Deer Stalking* Swan
    Hill Press
Prior, Richard : *Roe Stalking*, Game Conservancy Ltd

Prior, Richard : *Modern Roe Stalking*, Tideline Books

Adams, John & Dannatt, Norman : *The Culling and Processing of Deer*

LACOTS : *Wild Game, Guidance on Recommended Standards for Wild Game*

Deer Commission for Scotland : *Codes of Practice for Driving and Night Shooting of Deer*. Policy for Sika Deer

Stones Justice's Manual: Butterworths

Wignall, Gordon : (August 1998) 'Handling nuisance claims', *Solicitors Journal*

Harwood, Michael : (June 1995) 'Litigation', *Solicitors Journal*

Lord Cullen : *Report of the Public Enquiry into the Shooting at Dunblane Primary School*

Bateson, P. : (1997) *The Behavioural and Physiological Effects of Culling Red Deer*, London: The National Trust

Broadbent, Graham : (August 1993) 'Problems with knives', *Justice of the Peace* Magazine

Warlow, T. A. : *Science and Justice* 1996

Frost, David : *Sporting Firearms and the Law*, Countryside Alliance

Archbold : *Criminal Pleading, Evidence & Practice*, 1999. Sweet & Maxwell

Deer Commission for Scotland: *Best Practice Guidelines*

Food Standards Agency: *Wild Game Guide*

Useful Addresses and Contacts

British Association for Shooting and Conservation
Marford Mill
Rossett
Wrexham
LL12 0HL
www.basc.org.uk
Tel. 01244 573000

British Deer Society
Burgate Manor
Fordingbridge
Hampshire
SP6 1EF

Northern Ireland Deer Society
Laurel Bank
Rugby Avenue
Newry Road
Banbridge
Co. Down
BT32 3NA

Deer Commission for Scotland
Great Glen House
Leachkin Road
Inverness
IV3 8NW

Natural England
Northminster House
Peterborough
PE1 1UA

Scottish Rural Property and Business Association
Stuart House, Eskmills
Business Park,
Musselburgh,
East Lothian
EH21 7PB
www.srpba.com

**The U.K. Association of
Professional Deer Managers**
PO Box 372
Exeter
EX5 5YL

**Humane Slaughter
Association**
The Old School
Brewhouse Hill
Wheathampstead
Hertfordshire
AL4 8AN

**British Wild Boar
Association**
38 Spring Street
London
W2 1JA

**National Game Dealers'
Association**
Pollards Farm
Clanville
Andover
Hants SP11 9JE

*Shooting Times and Country
Magazine*
IPC Media
Blue Fin Building
110 Southwark Street
London SE1 0SU

**National Gamekeepers'
Organisation (NGO)**
PO Box 107
Bishop Auckland
DL149YW.
Tel: 01388 665899. Website:
www.nationalgamekeepers.
org.uk

Forestry Commission
Great Eastern House
Tenison Road
Cambridge
CB1 2DU

The Game Conservancy
Fordingbridge
Hampshire
SP6 1EF

**British Shooting Sports
Council**
PO Box 11
Bexhill on Sea
East Sussex
TN40 1ZZ

**Country Land and Business
Association**
16 Belgrave Square
London
SW1X 8PQ

Countryside Alliance
The Old Town Hall
367 Kennington Road
London
SE11 4PT

Royal Ulster Constabulary
Firearms Licensing Branch
Linasharragh
Montgomery Road
Belfast

Royal Ulster Constabulary
Firearms Licensing Department
Knocknagoney House
Knocknagoney Road
Belfast
BT4 2PP

Department of Justice
Firearms Section
72-76 St Stephen's Green
Dublin

**Customs Directorate
Division**
Import of Firearms
Branch C
12th Floor
Alexander House
21 Victoria Avenue
Southend on Sea
SS9 1AD

Export Licensing Unit
Department of Trade and
Industry
Kingsgate House
66-74 Victoria Street
London
SW1E 6SW

RSPCA
Causeway
Horsham
Sussex
RH12 1HG

**British Deer Farmers'
Association**
Old Stoddah Farm
Penruddock
Penrith
CA11 0RY

**DEFRA Department for
Environment, Food & Rural
Affairs**
Nobel House
17 Smith Square
London
SW1P 3JR

The Deer Initiative
P O Box 2196
Wrexham
LL14 6YH

Lantra (www.lantra.co.uk)
Lantra House
Stoneleigh Park,
Nr Coventry,
Warwickshire CV8 2LG
Tel 024 7669 6996,
Fax 024 7669 6732

**St Hubert's Club of Great
Britain**
April Lodge
East Norton
Leicestershire
LE7 9XL

Index

The Rise and Decline of Nations

THE RISE AND DECLINE OF NATIONS

Economic Growth, Stagflation, and Social Rigidities

Mancur Olson

Yale University Press
New Haven and London

Table 7.1 is reprinted from *The Jacksonian Democracy* by
Peter Temin (New York: W. W. Norton, 1969) by permission
of the publisher.

Designed by James J. Johnson
and set in Times Roman type by
The Composing Room of Michigan, Inc.
Printed in the United States of America by
Courier Companies, Inc.

Library of Congress Cataloging in Publication Data

Olson, Mancur.
    The rise and decline of nations.

    Includes bibliographical references and index.
    1. Economic development.   2. Unemployment—Effect of
inflation on.   3. Caste–India.   4. Economics.
I. Title.
HD82.0565   1982   338.9′001   82–40163
ISBN 0–300–02307–3   AACR2
        0–300–03079–7 (pbk.)

20 19 18 17 16 15 14 13

For Ellika, Mancur Severin, and Sander

Contents

Preface

It may seem strange, at a time when so many find fault with economics, that an economist should claim to extend existing economic theory in a way that not only explains the "stagflation" and declining growth rates that have given rise to the recent complaints, but also provides a partial explanation of a variety of problems usually reserved for other fields—the "ungovernability" of some modern societies, the British class structure and the Indian caste system, the exceptionally unequal distribution of power and income in many developing countries, and even the rise of Western Europe from relative backwardness in the early Middle Ages to dominance of the whole world by the late nineteenth century. Yet the successful extension or improvement of something we have found unsatisfactory is commonplace: the technology that was impractical or full of bugs may after further development become economical and reliable. So also economics, even when it has encountered increasing skepticism, may with the aid of a new idea help to explain matters it could not explain before.

If we step back to gain perspective, we see not only the embarrassments of many economists in the last decade, but also more than two centuries of cumulative intellectual advance. I am fond of quoting Newton's assertion that, if he had seen farther than others, it was because he stood on the shoulders of giants. If Newton could say that in the seventeenth century, surely the trained economist today, however limited in stature, can claim at least as high a perch. The economist is the heir of several thinkers of recognized genius, such as Smith, Ricardo, Mill, Marx, Walras, Wicksell, Marshall, and Keynes, as well as of the yeoman labor of many hundreds of intelligent men and women. Indeed, since the giants of economics usually stood in turn on the shoulders of their predecessors, it is as though the economist today were standing atop a great pyramid of talent. Why, then, have so many economists failed to anticipate the emergence of new economic realities in the 1970s and 1980s? Perhaps it is because, wearing professional blinders, they have looked only straight ahead at phenomena economists have habitually examined. This book attempts to show that if we take the trouble to look to the side, at the domains of other disciplines, we shall gain a different conception of the entire landscape.

In part because this study encompasses several disciplinary domains, and even more because it aspires to reach policy-makers and students, I have worked hard to write this book in a language different from the one I use for articles in technical economic journals. This book is accordingly longer than it would need to be for the fellow economists who are my first concern, but I believe it is (with the exception of some notes and parenthetical expressions) also accessible to intelligent men and women in any profession. Luckily, most of the ideas I have come upon here turn out, once they are properly understood and explained, to be astonishingly simple.

I am indebted not only to the economists of the past, but also to an unusually large number of generous critics who have commented on drafts of this book and the papers out of which it has grown. These kind critics are so numerous and scattered that I have added a special acknowledgments section at the end of the book in an effort to do justice to them. The foundations and other organizations that have supported my research are less numerous, so I can mention them here. The most important source of support for my research has been the economics, social science, and policy research programs of the National Science Foundation—the Innovation Processes Research Program, the Economics Program, and the Measurement Methods and Data Resources Program. Despite their slender means and the manifold demands upon them, these programs have provided invaluable support for the research that underlies this and my other professional writings. I am also grateful to Resources for the Future, not only for support and stimulating hospitality, but also for patiently agreeing to wait when I delayed a book on their concerns to finish this book. The Environmental Protection Agency and the Sloan Foundation have also been helpful, and the Lehrman Institute, the Hoover Institution of Stanford University, and the Woodrow Wilson International Center for Scholars have also put me in their debt with fellowships that provided some months of freedom for my writing.

My thanks to the foregoing institutions are surpassed only by my gratitude to my family. A book such as this requires intense concentration over many years, and my wife and children have, above all else, given me the peace of mind that made such concentration possible. Since *The Logic of Collective Action* was dedicated to my wife, Alison, it is fitting that this book, a descendant of that one, is dedicated to our three children.

The Questions, and the Standards a Satisfactory Answer Must Meet

1

Many have been puzzled by the mysterious decline or collapse of great empires or civilizations and by the remarkable rise to wealth, power, or cultural achievement of previously peripheral or obscure peoples. The collapse of the Roman Empire in the West and its defeat by scattered tribes that would otherwise have been of no account is only one of many puzzling examples. On repeated occasions the imposing empires of China have decayed to the point where they could fall prey to far less numerous or sophisticated peoples like the Mongols or to uprisings by poor peasants in remote provinces. The Middle East provides several examples of such collapsed empires, and so do the Indian civilizations of MesoAmerica; even before the Aztec empire was destroyed by a small contingent of Spaniards there had been a succession of empires or cultures, each of which seems to have been supplanted by a previously obscure tribe, its grand pyramids or cities abandoned to the wilderness. The pattern was not greatly different in the Andes, or at Angkor Wat, or in still other places. It was evident among the Greek city-states at the time of Herodotus, who said that "the cities that were formerly great, have most of them become insignificant; and such as are at present powerful, were weak in olden time. I shall therefore discourse equally of both, convinced that human happiness never continues long in one stay."[1]

There are many examples of insignificant tribes and peripheral peoples rising to greatness. It was not in the awesome Egyptian empire that the Mediterranean achievement attained its fullest expression, but among the previously inconsequential peoples of the Ionian Peninsula. The empires of the great city-states of Greece were of course eventually

1

supplanted by the Romans, who before their amazing conquests had been a people of little note. The civilization of Western Christendom that had by the end of the nineteenth century come to dominate the entire world sprang from the backward and chaotic societies of Western Europe in the Middle Ages, which were usually unable even to defend themselves against the advances of the Moslems, the Magyars, and the Vikings. The parts of Western Europe that paced the advance of the West were often areas that had previously been peripheral or unimpressive; the center of growth in the seventeenth century was in the northern provinces of the Netherlands, which had never been important or wealthy before and had only lately escaped subjugation by Spain. In the eighteenth and early nineteenth centuries it was England, rather than the far larger and more imposing France, that gave us the Industrial Revolution. In the second half of the nineteenth century it was long-quiescent Germany and distant ex-colonies in North America, rather than the British Empire at its apogee, that carried that revolution farthest.

There will be no attempt here to account for the rise and fall of the ancient empires or civilizations in the manner of universalist historians like Spengler or Toynbee. If their disappointing experience is any guide, it is perhaps not even very fruitful to identify allegedly common patterns in the rise and decline of ancient civilizations or jurisdictions for which we have only scanty records. There will accordingly be no attempt here to draw universal inductive lessons from the historical experience of ancient societies.

By contrast, the suggestion here is that the hurried historical references indicate how little is understood of the rise and fall of nations and peoples. If the causes of the collapse of various ancient empires had been straightforwardly explained, the way we explain the conquest of a small and weak country in terms of an attack by a larger and stronger one, there would be no "mysterious" decay to attract continued speculation. Broad historical pageants of the kind painted by universal historians are, then, a better source of motivation for further inquiry than for immediate conclusions. But if other evidence, such as recent experience on which there is unprecedented quantitative evidence, or presumptions from oft-confirmed theory, should resonate with the familiar historical tales of the rise and decline of civilizations, then there would be a case for examining the universal histories in a systematic way, with precise questions and orderly procedures for weighing evidence. It is upon the other evidence that I shall rely here and it is to this that we now turn.

II

The economic history of the last century, and especially of the years since World War II, has its own examples of rise and decline. They are not so melodramatic as some accounts of ancient civilizations, but they are no less mysterious, and the rises and declines are probably more rapid. At the end of the Second World War the economies of Germany and Japan were devastated and observers of diverse persuasions and national origins wondered whether these abjectly defeated societies would be able to provide themselves with even the rudiments of survival. As everyone knows, the economies of West Germany and Japan have enjoyed "economic miracles" and are now among the most prosperous in the world. The German and Japanese economies not only grew substantially when these countries were rebuilding their factories and recovering to their prewar level of income, but also (and even more rapidly) after they had recovered and exceeded their previous levels of income. The problem of what we awkwardly but meaningfully call *stagflation,* or inflation combined with unusual levels of unemployment, has on the whole also been less serious in Germany and Japan than in most developed economies.

The last century also offers remarkable evidence of relative decline. The most notable case is that of Great Britain. Since World War II it has had one of the slowest growth rates of the developed democracies. Its growth rate has indeed lagged behind that of most developed countries since the last two decades of the nineteenth century. By now the per capita income in Great Britain is decidedly lower than in most of Western Europe. In the past decade, at least, Britain has also suffered relatively greater increases in both inflation and unemployment than comparable countries like Germany and Japan. The slow growth and other difficulties of the British economy have driven many people in Britain as well as in other countries to speak of the "British disease."

Within the United States there are dramatic examples of decline and at the same time notable instances of growth. The states of the Northeast and the older Middle West, and especially the great cities in these regions, have declined substantially in relation to the rest of the nation and the world. The near bankruptcies of New York and Cleveland are only extreme manifestations of a general loss in relative per capita income and outmigration in the industrial states of the Northeast and the Middle West. Most states in the West and the South, by contrast, have grown rapidly in the last few decades. These reversals of fortune have not been satisfactorily explained.

It might be thought that the examples of growth and decline that have been mentioned have been explained in the literature on the "sources" of economic growth. This literature is certainly impressive; Edward Denison's estimates of the relative contributions to growth of capital accumulation, of technical advance, and so on, have been altogether constructive, while Dale Jorgenson and many other economists have made herculean efforts to provide ever more sophisticated estimates. Yet estimates of the sources of growth, however meticulous, subtle, and useful, do not tell us about the ultimate causes of growth. They do not tell us what incentives made the saving and investment occur, or what explained the innovations, or why there was more innovation and capital accumulation in one society or period than in another. They do not trace the sources of growth to their fundamental causes; they trace the water in the river to the streams and lakes from which it comes, but they do not explain the rain. Neither do they explain the silting up of the channels of economic progress—that is, what I shall call here the "retardants" of growth.

The literature on the sources of growth helps to delineate another example of puzzlingly rapid growth. We know from this literature that capital accumulation, though considerably less important than the "advance of knowledge," is still a major source of economic growth. Since new technologies are often embodied in new capital equipment, some of the "residual" increase in productivity usually attributed to the advance of knowledge would not have occurred without investment in physical capital. Any uncertainty about economic policy, and especially political or military instability so great that it creates skepticism about whether any investment in durable capital goods will be protected, will tend to reduce productive investment. Of course, businessmen have a political incentive to exaggerate their need for stable and predictable public policies, but there can be no doubt that their insecurities can have some effect on both the level and the type of investment in new capital goods. Virtually all economists agree that events, or even expectations, that discourage investment or destroy productive capital will lower the level of income. Thus societies that are politically unstable or often subjected to foreign invasion are likely to have less productive investment and lower rates of growth than they would otherwise have had. There will be more flights of capital and fewer investments in plant or equipment that can pay off only in the long run. Savings are more likely to be hoarded in easily portable but socially unproductive assets such as gold.

In view of this, the rapid growth of the French economy in the postwar years is remarkable. It is not only that France was defeated and occupied in World War II: in less than two centuries that country has experienced some of the most profound and protracted revolutions in human history, has gone through constitutions almost as though they were periodical literature, and has suffered partial or total occupation four times. Even in the postwar period near-revolutions and fears of popular front government brought some capital flight. Given this extraordinary succession of political upheavals and foreign incursions, why did France in 1970 (the year for which we have the best adjustments for national differences in cost of living and thus the best real income comparisons)[2] have a per capita income decidedly above that of Great Britain, about the same as that of Germany, and only a fourth lower than the United States?

III

France and West Germany, with Italy and the three Benelux countries, founded the Common Market in 1957. It is remarkable how rapidly all six initial members of the European Economic Community have grown. A glance at table 1.1 reveals that in general they have grown more rapidly than Australia, New Zealand, the United Kingdom, and the United States, all of which had been spared the invasion and upheaval that "the Six" suffered. In some of these initia! Common Market countries growth was more rapid in the 1960s, when the Common Market took effect, than in the 1950s, even though by then recovery from the war had been completed and they had already caught up with some of the more secure societies. One of the questions this book will attempt to answer is why the Six enjoyed such rapid growth.

In the nineteenth century there were also remarkable examples of economic growth and national advance that have never been satisfactorily explained. In little more than a century, between the adoption of the Constitution and the outbreak of World War I, the United States became the world's largest economy with the highest per capita income. In the first part of the nineteenth century the German-speaking areas that were destined to become a united Germany were relatively poor, but after the creation of the Zollverein and the German Reich Germany

Table 1.1. Average Annual Rates of Growth of Per Capita Gross
Domestic Product at Constant Prices (in percent)

Country	1950–1960	1960–1970	1970–1978
Australia	2.0[a]	3.7[b]	2.4[c]
Austria	5.7	3.9	3.8
Belgium	2.0[d]	4.1	3.1
Canada	1.2	3.7	3.1
Denmark	2.5	3.9	2.2
Finland	3.3	4.2	2.5
France	3.5	4.6	3.0
Germany, Fed. Rep. of	6.6	3.5	2.4
Ireland	1.8	3.8	2.3[e]
Italy	4.9[f]	4.6	2.1[g]
Japan	6.8[h]	9.4	3.8
Netherlands	3.3	4.1	2.3
New Zealand	1.7[i]	2.2[j]	—[k]
Norway	2.7	4.0	3.9
Sweden	2.9	3.6	1.2
Switzerland	2.9	2.8	−0.1
United Kingdom	2.3	2.3	2.0
United States	1.2	3.0	2.0

NOTE: Data are from *Yearbook(s) of National Account Statistics* for 1969 and 1978,
Statistical Office of the United Nations, New York, published in 1970 and 1979,
respectively.
a. 1952–1960;   b. 1963–1970;   c. 1970–1976;   d. 1953–1960;
e. 1970–1977;   f. 1951–1960;   g. 1970–1977;   h. 1952–1960;
i. 1954–1960;   j. 1960–1968;   k. The statistics for New Zealand in this
period are not separated from those for "Oceania."

grew so rapidly that by 1914 it was overtaking Britain. In the mid-
nineteenth century the Japanese were desperately poor and could be
almost effortlessly humiliated by the warships of Western countries, but
within little more than a half-century after the Meiji Restoration in
1867–68, Japan had become the only industrialized country outside the
West and one of the world's significant powers. Another of my questions is, Why did these three countries figure so prominently in nineteenth-century economic growth?

There was a commercial revolution and considerable aggregate (if not per capita) growth in parts of Western Europe in the sixteenth and seventeenth centuries, followed by the Industrial Revolution that began in Britain in the second half of the eighteenth century. Some of this growth occurred in the northern provinces of the Netherlands just after they succeeded in gaining their independence from Spain. Much of it occurred in Britain and (to a lesser extent) in France after centralizing monarchs seized effective power from the baronies, manors, and towns that had enjoyed considerable autonomy in medieval times, and then began to eliminate local tolls and restrictions that stood in the way of nationwide markets. In the aggregate these episodes of economic growth transformed the Western Europe that had been relatively primitive in the "dark ages" into a civilization that by the nineteenth century dominated almost the entire world.

The rise of the West no doubt was due to a number of different factors, many of which are explained in the history textbooks, and it would be foolish to seek any monocausal explanation. The standard accounts do not, however, provide anything resembling a complete or compelling explanation for the rise of the West, much less of the specific advances of Holland, Britain, and France during the commercial revolution or of Britain during the Industrial Revolution. Something important must have been left out. Accordingly, one of my questions is, What has been left out or overlooked in the conventional accounts? Or more precisely, What has been left out that is so crucial that we cannot get a convincing and satisying account without it?

IV

There are several further questions that may seem unrelated to the foregoing questions about anomalous examples of economic growth or decline, but these further questions turn out to be answered by the same logic that explains the notable instances of growth and decline. The first of these questions is, Why does involuntary unemployment occur, and sometimes (as in the Great Depression of the 1930s) strike a large proportion of the work force? Those who are not economists naturally may suppose that this question had been adequately answered long ago; most leading economists today agree that it has not been. In the 1930s John Maynard Keynes offered a dazzling and influential account of unemployment and depression, but now leading Keynesian and anti-Keynesian economists agree that Keynes's contribution, however brilliant and important it might be, assumes certain types of behavior that are not reasonable or fully consistent with the interests of those individuals or firms that are assumed to engage in it. In other words, Keynesian *macro*economic theory (a theory of the economy in the aggregate) does not have an adequate basis in *micro*economic theory (a theory of the behavior of individual decision-makers in the particular markets or contexts in which each operates). The non-Keynesian theories of the "monetarist" and "rational-expectations equilibrium" economists do assume rational individual behavior, but these theories do not explain involuntary unemployment—indeed, one of the reasons many economists do not accept these theories is that they implausibly imply that all unemployment is voluntary. This book shows for the first time how involuntary unemployment, and also deep depressions, can occur even when each decision-maker in the economy acts in accordance with his or her best interests. As soon as we understand how involuntary unemployment can result from rational and well-informed individual behavior, it also becomes obvious how inflation and unemployment—which we once thought could not occur simultaneously—can be combined, as they have been in the recent stagflation.

At about the same time that the ugly word *stagflation* was introduced among economists, many political scientists began to describe certain modern societies as "ungovernable." The term *ungovernability* was used by various writers in Great Britain when the Heath government fell as it attempted to assert the authority of the government at the time of a miners' strike. The term was used in the United States to describe the politics that led to the virtual bankruptcy of New York City. It has also been invoked by observers of the failures of several administrations to obtain the legislation or authority to implement most of their programs, even when, as in the Carter administration, the president's party had a large majority in both houses of Congress. The concern about ungovernability in the United States often takes the form of complaints about "single-issue" politics and the limited influence and discipline of American political parties. Thus our next question is, Why are some modern societies to some degree ungovernable? That is, Why has it seemed that governments in some countries did not govern or control their societies as well as they had in the past?

There are also a couple of questions that it will not be possible to state even roughly until much of our analysis is complete, so I will make only an oblique reference to them here. One concerns what I have chosen to call the "top-heavy" societies, because of the unusual influence of the top firms and families in the largest cities. Such societies are most likely to arise where there is political instability and an underdeveloped economy, and lead to a great degree of inequality in the distribution of income.

The last major question is a bit different. It also requires the use of a controversy-laden and ill-defined concept, so this question cannot be stated as precisely as might be wished without tedious length. In a casual sense, though, the question is straightforward: What makes the class structure more rigid or exclusive in one country or period than in another? There may be some ambiguity partly because the word *class* is sometimes used to refer simply to differences in income or status, almost as a synonym for income brackets or educational levels; but here the concern will be with any exclusivity and barriers to entry in a social structure that at least to some degree limit opportunities and countervail meritocratic tendencies. The word *class* is used in approximately this sense fairly often in Great Britain, and the model offered in this book has striking implications about one important aspect of the evolution of class structure in that country. Those who believe that class rigidities in the sense described could not occur, or would never have much quantitative significance, will change their view the moment they think of the Indian caste system, an extreme form of class rigidity, which has limited untold millions of people to particular occupations. The same theory that generates testable answers to our other questions also happens, quite by accident, to generate an explanation of the Indian caste system as well as of class or group barriers.

V

Answers of sorts have been offered to many of the questions I have posed, and sometimes these answers are even established in the folklore. This is particularly true for the anomalous growth rates since World War II. The remarkably rapid economic growth in postwar Japan and West Germany, for example, is often ascribed to the wartime destruction of plant and equipment, which induced these countries to rebuild with the latest technology. It is similarly attributed to the exceptional industriousness of their peoples, while in the same spirit the slow growth of Great Britain is ascribed to the allegedly exceptional British taste for leisure.

Perhaps because Britain has had an anomalous growth rate for a longer time, its economic performance has been the object of an unusual number of such ad hoc explanations. Britain's slow growth is often laid to the strength or narrow-mindedness of British unions, to the resistance to change or the uncooperativeness of British workers, or to socialistic economic policies. Others emphasize a lack of entrepreneurial drive and willingness to innovate on the part of British managers; establishmentarian, anticommercial attitudes that keep the ablest and best-educated people away from business pursuits; and an addiction among the British ruling classes for Concorde-type purchases of national prestige. A common denominator of most of these explanations is that they emphasize some allegedly distinctive trait of one social class or another or the rigidities in the British class system.

The above folk wisdom is not set out as a straw man easily knocked down. On the contrary, I will argue that some of the folk wisdom is partly true, and I will endeavor to provide an intellectual foundation for some of the popular suppositions. The point is rather to make it clear that the foregoing arguments, like many others, are only ad hoc explanations, and ad hoc explanations cannot be sufficient.

One reason that ad hoc arguments are insufficient is that they are usually not testable against a broad enough array of data or experience to enable us to tell whether they are correct. Each country, region, historical period, and indeed each human being is unique in many ways. Thus the fact that a country with an unusually high growth rate has this or that distinctive trait provides no justification for the inference that there is a causal connection. Only the British have Big Ben and only the Germans eat a lot of sauerkraut, but it would of course be absurd to suggest that one is responsible for the slow British growth and the other for the fast German growth. No causal explanation can claim any more credence than the Big Ben/sauerkraut argument unless it identifies an attribute that explains a number of cases or phenomena or is logically derived from a theory that has wide explanatory power. Often explanations based on a unique attribute of a country provide in statistical terms a sample of the size of one; they are equivalent to concluding, from a single toss of a pair of dice that resulted in two ones, that tossing a pair of dice will always result in ''snake eyes.'' In some other cases where a unique attribute of a country is considered, this analogy is unfair; the unique trait may be present in different parts of the country in different degrees, or there may be enough variability or richness of other kinds to make an argument persuasive. This is what accounts for the appeal of the conclusions drawn in the better historical monographs. Nonetheless, only when a wide range of diverse phenomena is explained concisely can there be a compelling basis for belief.

Another reason we should be cautious about ad hoc explanations is that, when outcomes are already known, it is almost always possible to work out an irrefutable "explanation" if one can use any amount or type of information in constructing the explanation. Even if there should be no unique attribute to which appeal can be made, reality is normally so complex and variegated that any cases with different results are almost certain to differ in other ways as well. Any two countries, periods, or significant historical events differ in so many ways that if there is no limit to the amount or type of information that may be used, then it will almost always be possible to construct an explanation of any differences in outcome by appealing to one or more of the other ways in which the pair differ. Unless the differences that are invoked also apply to other cases, we are again back to making inferences from a sample of one. It is because it is so easy to rely on the unique attributes or distinctive sets of attributes that are likely to characterize any human or social phenomena that we must insist that any explanation fits some data or observations beyond those from which it was derived.

The seriousness of the shortcomings of ad hoc explanations is aptly illustrated by a set of photographs in a magazine I read as a child. The magazine article pointed out that some of those portrayed were convicted criminals and others were highly respected citizens, and the reader was invited to judge which was which before turning to the page with the answers. Neither my friends nor I did well in picking out the criminals—the most villainous-looking of the lot, I seem to remember, turned out to be a distinguished author. Yet it was remarkable how often, *after* looking up the answers, we would "discover" the sneaky eyes or suspicious chin that was, or should have been, a dead giveaway.

Now suppose that, after looking up the answers, we also received descriptions of the childhood and ancestry of each of the individuals. Would it not then also have seemed easy to explain why the criminals had turned to crime? This one fell on evil ways as a reaction against his severe and distant father, that one because he had no father, the next because he had too much of mother; yes, the successful businessman also had a severe and distant father, but he did not repress his hatred. Admittedly, the successful artist had no father and a doting mother, but this was the catalyst for his creativity. Whenever there is some astonishing behavior, be it a crime or a great achievement or whatever, there is someone ready to offer a confident psychological explanation based on one or the other of the special features of the astonishing person's history. Sometimes there are several different explanations by different experts. But few, if any, select those who will be so aberrant beforehand. One should be as suspicious of some of the historical and psychological explanations we hear as of the discoveries of evil features in the faces of men who have already been identified as criminal.

The limitations of ad hoc arguments also help to explain why the histories of each country and period are rewritten periodically and a different story told each time. Part of the explanation is that new sources are found, new interests emerge, and better analyses are developed; but partly, when there is no limit to the length of an explanation and no rules about which of the infinite number of outcomes is selected for explanation, an enormous—if not infinite—number of plausible stories can be told, and it is mainly a matter of taste which of these explanations is preferred. Scholar after scholar can then write plausible book after plausible book, but none need be definitive and there is no accumulation of knowledge of causes and effects.

We can begin to have confidence in an explanation when a large number of phenomena are explained—that is, when the explanation has "power"—and explained "parsimoniously." Since it is costly to acquire and remember information, parsimonious or concise and simple explanations must, other things equal, be preferred; the principle of Ockham's razor—that any inessential premises or complexities ought to be cut out of an argument—has been useful to philosophers, mathematicians, and scientists since the Middle Ages. But when the parsimony of an explanation is taken into account along with its power, it bears also on the likelihood that it is true. For one thing, if the explanation has both power and parsimony it is hard to see how its author could have resorted to unique or distinctive features to explain the outcomes. For another, when a simple explanation explains a great deal—when the ratio of power to parsimony is high—it is improbable that mere chance could explain its success. As Charles Darwin put it in the sixth edition of *The Origin of Species:*

> It can hardly be supposed that a false theory could explain, in so satisfactory a manner as does the theory of natural selection, the several large classes of facts above specified. It has recently been

objected that this is an unsafe way of arguing; but it is a method used in judging of the common events of life, and has often been used by the greatest natural philosophers.[3]

The persuasiveness of a theory depends not only on how many facts are explained, but also on how diverse are the kinds of facts explained. Darwin's theory offers insights into the origin and evolution of creatures as diverse as whales and bacteria, and this makes it more convincing than if it could explain only mosquitoes, however many millions of mosquitoes might be satisfactorily explained. If a theory explains facts of quite diverse kinds it has what William Whewell, a nineteenth-century writer on scientific method, called "consilience." Whewell argued that "no example can be pointed out, in the whole history of science, so far as I am aware, in which this consilience . . . has given testimony in favor of an hypothesis later discovered to be false."[4]

There is also a need to ensure that an explanation is not consistent with the evidence presented in support of it merely because those cases that happened to fit the theory were the only ones examined; there could, of course, be other cases to which the theory is supposed to apply that contradict it. Since it is usually impossible in practice to consider all relevant cases, the best approach is often to consider all the cases in one pre-established category or another; this rules out selection bias at least in this category. Possibly different principles apply to the category considered than to other categories, and this suggests examining other cases outside the test category as well. If the facts are not selected because they fit a theory, and they are also numerous and in very different classes, then it is most improbable that a false theory could explain them and at the same time remain parsimonious.

VI

The reader should accordingly not accept the argument in this book simply because he or she finds it plausible and consistent with known facts. Many plausible stories have been told before and often also widely believed, yet they failed to stand up. The reader should not place even a small degree of confidence in the argument here unless he or she finds that it explains a large number of facts in different categories and with such a limited set of "causes" or postulates that it is clear I could not consciously or unconsciously have been adding as many as were needed to cover every outcome I could have been aware of at the time I worked out the theory. (In fact, I did not know some of the facts this book explains when I developed the argument, but unless the reader knows me well, he or she, as a matter of scientific principle, ought not take this claim into account in deciding whether my explanation is right, for those who do not know me have no way, even indirectly, to test the truth of my assertion.) Finally, the reader should also be wary about whether the cases I have set out to explain are simply those that happen to fit the theory.

Lest the reader think I have been excessively sporting in emphasizing the need for high standards in judging the evidence in support of my theory, I should point out that it has occurred to me that intelligent people will judge all alternative explanations by the same high standards. And almost all of the competing explanations are separate and ad hoc explanations of each of the many phenomena at issue, and often explanations that focus on some unique alleged cultural or racial characteristic of each country, region, and historical period. In the aggregate these ad hoc explanations are anything but parsimonious, and even when they are partly right they do not take us far, or explain how the key causal attribute originated, or provide much guidance on public policies that might improve matters.

VII

Although we should not be satisfied with any theory that fails to explain a lot with a little, we need not of course expect any one theory to explain everything, or even the most important thing. Absolutely nothing in all of epistemology suggests that valid explanations should be monocausal. An explanation may be entirely valid, yet explain only a part (and even a small part) of the variation at issue. I am reminded by the pilot's announcement on the aircraft on which I am writing this paragraph that the groundspeed of the plane depends on the direction and the speed of the wind, and of course accurate navigation requires that they be taken into account, yet it is far more important whether the plane is at full throttle or idle, whether it has a jet or a piston engine, and so forth.

It is necessary to make this point here, since some readers of early drafts of my argument, perhaps beguiled by the simplicity of the explanation, have treated all other explanations of the same phenomena as wrong, or explicitly have supposed that the argument here said everything that needed to be said about the phenomena. Nothing could be farther from my intention than to provide a monocausal or complete explanation of social and economic phenomena, or even the particular historical phenomena analyzed here. At most—at the very most—the aspiration is to provide the equivalent of Sherlock Holmes's observation of the dog that didn't bark: to provide a missing clue that gives us a better understanding of the whole story.

Since no monocausal explanation is offered, one well-known test of validity is not applicable. It is often said in methodological discussions that every meaningful scientific theory must specify one or more possible events or observations, or experimental results, which would, if they occurred, refute the theory. This rule has no applicability to multicausal conceptions unless a perfect experiment is performed, or one so nearly perfect that we could be certain that it was the error in the theory rather than the flaw in the experiment that accounted for the result. In view of the limited possibilities for experiments in economics and other social sciences, the impossibility of controlled experiments on historical events, and the extreme improbability that nature or history will on its own provide anything resembling a perfect natural experiment, a search for a single decisive refutation is futile. I am told by some philosophers of science that even in the physical and natural sciences the rejection of theories usually occurs not because of a single negative experiment, but more often from a series of anomalous observations combined with the emergence of a better alternative theory. What we should demand of a theory or hypothesis, then, is that it be clear about what observations would increase the probability that it was false and what observations would tend to increase the probability that there was some truth in it. The theory set out in the next two chapters is clear in this sense: even though it is hard to foresee any one observation that would definitively refute it, it will be evident whether an observation tends to call the theory into question, and what types of observations in the aggregate would convince us it was false.

With multicausality, it is also conceivable that all (or almost all) of the facts that appear to corroborate the theory offered in this book could actually be due to a diversity of other causes. A number of other causes could, by coincidence, have produced the intricate patterns that the theory here predicts. The theory is evidently so consilient and powerful, and at the same time so parsimonious, that the chances of this are remote. Still, it is a possibility we should never forget.

Since the multiplicity of causal forces can make a false theory seem true or a true theory seem false, any single test of the theory may be weak, or far from decisive. Some of the tests of the theory offered here are weak, and the reader will be able to think of diverse causes that could have generated the observed results. At the same time, essentially all of the tests point in the same direction, so the results in the aggregate are incomparably stronger than the individual results. If, when we wake in the morning, we are surprised to see a patch or two of white outside, there could perhaps be uncertainty about the cause, but if every twig and piece of ground is freshly white, we know it snowed last night.

We turn now to the most crucial chapter in the book, which develops the logic needed to derive all the results and to make the rest of the book comprehensible.

The Logic

2

The argument of this book begins with a paradox in the behavior of groups. It has often been taken for granted that if everyone in a group of individuals or firms had some interest in common, then there would be a tendency for the group to seek to further this interest. Thus many students of politics in the United States for a long time supposed that citizens with a common political interest would organize and lobby to serve that interest. Each individual in the population would be in one or more groups and the vector of pressures of these competing groups explained the outcomes of the political process. Similarly, it was often supposed that if workers, farmers, or consumers faced monopolies harmful to their interests, they would eventually attain countervailing power through organizations such as labor unions or farm organizations that obtained market power and protective government action. On a larger scale, huge social classes are often expected to act in the interest of their members; the unalloyed form of this belief is, of course, the Marxian contention that in capitalist societies the bourgeois class runs the government to serve its own interests, and that once the exploitation of the proletariat goes far enough and "false consciousness" has disappeared, the working class will in its own interest revolt and establish a dictatorship of the proletariat. In general, if the individuals in some category or class had a sufficient degree of self-interest and if they all agreed on some common interest, then the group would to some extent also act in a self-interested or group-interested manner.

If we ponder the logic of the familiar assumption described in the preceding paragraph, we can see that it is fundamentally and indisputably faulty. Consider those consumers who agree that they pay higher prices for a product because of some objectionable monopoly or tariff, or those workers who agree that their skill deserves a higher wage. Let us now ask what would be the expedient course of action for an individual consumer who would like to see a boycott to combat a monopoly or a lobby to repeal the tariff, or for an individual worker who would like a strike threat or a minimum wage law that could bring higher wages. If the consumer or worker contributes a few days and a few dollars to organize a boycott or a union or to lobby for favorable legislation, he or she will have sacrificed time and money. What will this sacrifice obtain? The individual will at best succeed in advancing the cause to a small (often imperceptible) degree. In any case he will get only a minute share of the gain from his action. The very fact that the objective or interest is common to or shared by the group entails that the gain from any sacrifice an individual makes to serve this common purpose is shared with everyone in the group. The successful boycott or strike or lobbying action will bring the better price or wage for everyone in the relevant category, so the individual in any large group with a common interest will reap only a minute share of the gains from whatever sacrifices the individual makes to achieve this common interest. Since any gain goes to everyone in the group, those who contribute nothing to the effort will get just as much as those who made a contribution. It pays to "let George do it," but George has little or no incentive to do anything in the group interest either, so (in the absence of factors that are completely left out of the conceptions mentioned in the first paragraph) there will be little, if any, group action. The paradox, then, is that (in the absence of special arrangements or circumstances to which we shall turn later) large groups, at least if they are composed of rational individuals, will *not* act in their group interest.

This paradox is elaborated and set out in a way that lets the reader check every step of the logic in a book I wrote entitled *The Logic of Collective Action*.[1] That book also shows that the evidence in the United States, the only country in which all powerful interest groups were considered, systematically supported the argument, and that the scattered evidence that I was aware of from other countries was also consistent with it. Since the present book is an outgrowth of *The Logic of Collective Action* and in large part even an application of the argument in it, the most serious critics or students of the present book should have read that one. For the many readers who naturally would not want to invest the time needed to do so without knowing what might be gained, and for those with a more casual interest, the first part of this chapter will explain a few features of the argument in *The Logic* that are needed to understand the rest of the present volume. Other parts of the chapter, however, should not involve any repetition.

II

One finding in *The Logic* is that the services of associations like labor unions, professional associations, farm organizations, cartels, lobbies (and even collusive groups without formal organization) resemble the basic services of the state in one utterly fundamental respect. The services of such associations, like the elemental services or "public goods" provided by governments, if provided to anyone, go to everyone in some category or group. Just as the law and order, defense, or pollution abatement brought about by government accrue to everyone in some country or geographic area, so the tariff obtained by a farm organization's lobbying effort raises the price to all producers of the relevant commodity. Similarly, as I argued earlier, the higher wage won by a union applies to all employees in the pertinent category. More generally, every lobby obtaining a general change in legislation or regulation thereby obtains a public or collective good for everyone who benefits from that change, and every combination—that is, every "cartel"—using market or industrial action to get a higher price or wage must, when it restricts the quantity supplied, raise the price for every seller, thereby creating a collective good for all sellers.

If governments, on the one hand, and combinations exploiting their political or market power, on the other, produce public or collective goods that inevitably go to everyone in some group or category, then both are subject to the paradoxical logic set out above: that is, the individuals and firms they serve have in general no incentive voluntarily to contribute to their support.[2] It follows that if there is only voluntary and rational individual behavior,* then for the most part neither govern-

---

Rational need not imply *self-interested*. The argument in the text can hold even when there is altruistic behavior, although if particular types of altruistic behavior are strong enough it will not hold. Consider first altruistic attitudes about observable outcomes or results—suppose an individual would be willing to sacrifice some leisure or other personal consumption to obtain some amount of a collective good because of an altruistic concern that others should have this collective good. In other words, the individual's preference ordering takes account of the collective good obtained by others as

ments nor lobbies and cartels will exist, unless individuals support them for some reason *other* than the collective goods they provide. Of course, governments exist virtually everywhere and often there are lobbies and cartelistic organizations as well. If the argument so far is right, it follows that something *other* than the collective goods that governments and other organizations provide accounts for their existence.**

In the case of governments, the answer was explained before *The Logic of Collective Action* was written; governments are obviously supported by compulsory taxation. Sometimes there is little objection to this compulsion, presumably because many people intuitively understand that public goods cannot be sold in the marketplace or financed by

---

well as personal consumption. This assumption of altruism does not imply irrationality, or a tendency to make choices that are inconsistent with the maximal satisfaction of the values or preferences the individual has. Altruism also does not call into question the normal diminishing marginal rates of substitution between any pair of goods or objectives; as more of any good or objective (selfish or altruistic) is attained, other things being equal, the extent to which other goods or objectives (selfish or altruistic) will be given up to attain more of that good or objective will diminish.

A typical altruistic and rational individual of the sort described will not make any substantial voluntary contributions to obtain a collective good for a large group. The reason is that in a sufficiently large group the individual's contribution will make only a small and perhaps imperceptible difference to the amount of collective good the group obtains, whereas at the same time every contribution reduces dollar-for-dollar the amount of personal consumption and private-good charity, and the diminishing marginal rates of substitution entail that these sacrifices become progressively more onerous. In equilibrium in large groups there is accordingly little or no voluntary contribution by the rational altruist to the provision of a collective good.

Jarring as it is to the common-sense notion of rationality, let us now make the special assumption that the altruist gets satisfaction not from observably better outcomes for others, but rather from his or her own sacrifices for them. On this assumption we can secure voluntary provision of collective goods even in the largest groups. Here each dollar of personal consumption that is sacrificed can bring a significant return in moral satisfaction, and the problem that substantial personal sacrifices bring little or no perceptible change in the level of public good provided is no longer relevant. Even though this latter participatory or "Kantian" altruism is presumably not the usual form of altruism, I think it does exist and helps to account for some observations of voluntary contributions to large groups. (Yet another possibility is that the altruist is result-oriented but neglects the observable levels of the public good, simply assuming that his or her sacrifices of personal consumption increase the utility of others enough to justify the personal sacrifice.) My own thinking on this issue has been clarified by reading Howard Margolis, *Selfishness, Altruism, and Rationality* (Cambridge: At the University Press, 1982).

**This argument need not apply to small groups, which are discussed later in the chapter.

any voluntary mechanism; as I have already argued, each individual would get only a minute share of any governmental services he or she paid for and would get whatever level of services was provided by others in any event.

In the case of organizations that provide collective goods to their client groups through political or market action, the answer has not been obvious, but it is no less clear-cut. Organizations of this kind, at least when they represent large groups, are again not supported because of the collective goods they provide, but rather because they have been fortunate enough to find what I have called *selective incentives.* A selective incentive is one that applies selectively to the individuals depending on whether they do or do not contribute to the provision of the collective good.

A selective incentive can be either negative or positive; it can, for example, be a loss or punishment imposed only on those who do *not* help provide the collective good. Tax payments are, of course, obtained with the help of negative selective incentives, since those who are found not to have paid their taxes must then suffer both taxes and penalties. The best-known type of organized interest group in modern democratic societies, the labor union, is also usually supported, in part, through negative selective incentives. Most of the dues in strong unions are obtained through union shop, closed shop, or agency shop arrangements which make dues paying more or less compulsory and automatic. There are often also informal arrangements with the same effect; David McDonald, former president of the United Steel Workers of America, describes one of these arrangements used in the early history of that union. It was, he writes, a technique

> which we called . . . visual education, which was a high-sounding label for a practice much more accurately described as dues picketing. It worked very simply. A group of dues-paying members, selected by the district director (usually more for their size than their tact) would stand at the plant gate with pick handles or baseball bats in hand and confront each worker as he arrived for his shift.[3]

As McDonald's "dues picketing" analogy suggests, picketing during strikes is another negative selective incentive that unions sometimes need; although picketing in industries with established and stable unions is usually peaceful, this is because the union's capacity to close down an enterprise against which it has called a strike is clear to all; the early

phase of unionization often involves a great deal of violence on the part
of both unions and anti-union employers and scabs.*

Some opponents of labor unions argue that, since many of the
members of labor unions join only through the processes McDonald
described or through legally enforced union-shop arrangements, most of
the relevant workers do not want to be unionized. The Taft-Hartley Act
provided that impartial governmentally administered elections should
be held to determine whether workers did in fact want to belong to
unions. As the collective-good logic set out here suggests, the same
workers who had to be coerced to pay union dues voted for the unions
with compulsory dues (and normally by overwhelming margins), so that
this feature of the Taft-Hartley Act was soon abandoned as pointless.[4]
The workers who as individuals tried to avoid paying union dues at the
same time that they voted to force themselves all to pay dues are no
different from taxpayers who vote, in effect, for high levels of taxation,
yet try to arrange their private affairs in ways that avoid taxes. Because
of the same logic, many professional associations also get members
through covert or overt coercion (for example, lawyers in those states
with a "closed bar"). So do lobbies and cartels of several other types;
some of the contributions by corporate officials, for instance, to politicians useful to the corporation are also the result of subtle forms of
coercion.[5]

---

*The references to the often violent interaction between employers and employees in
the early stages of unionization should not obscure the consensual and informal "unionization" that also sometimes occurs because of employers' initiatives. This sort of labor
organization or collusion arises because some types of production require that workers
collaborate effectively. When this is the case, the employer may find it profitable to
encourage team spirit and social interaction among employees. Staff conferences and
work-group meetings, newsletters for employees, firm-sponsored employee athletic
teams, employer-financed office parties, and the like are partly explained by this consideration. In firms that have the same employment pattern for some time, the networks for
employee interaction that the employer created to encourage effective cooperation at work
may evolve into informal collusions, or occasionally even unions, of workers, and tacitly
or openly force the employer to deal with his employees as a cartelized group. This
evolution is unlikely when employees are, for example, day laborers or consultants, but
when stable patterns of active cooperation are important to production, the employer may
gain more from the extra production that this cooperation brings about than he loses from
the informal or formal cartelization that he helps to create. The evolution of this type of
informal unionization implies that there is more organization of labor than the statistics
imply, and that the differences between some ostensibly unorganized firms and unionized
firms are not as great as might appear on the surface.

Positive selective incentives, although easily overlooked, are also commonplace, as diverse examples in *The Logic* demonstrate.[6] American farm organizations offer prototypical examples. Many of the members of the stronger American farm organizations are members because their dues payments are automatically deducted from the "patronage dividends" of farm cooperatives or are included in the insurance premiums paid to mutual insurance companies associated with the farm organizations. Any number of organizations with urban clients also provide similar positive selective incentives in the form of insurance policies, publications, group air fares, and other private goods made available only to members. The grievance procedures of labor unions usually also offer selective incentives, since the grievances of active members often get most of the attention. The symbiosis between the political power of a lobbying organization and the business institutions associated with it often yields tax or other advantages for the business institution, and the publicity and other information flowing out of the political arm of a movement often generates patterns of preference or trust that make the business activities of the movement more remunerative. The surpluses obtained in such ways in turn provide positive selective incentives that recruit participants for the lobbying efforts.

III

Small groups, or occasionally large "federal" groups that are made up of many small groups of socially interactive members, have an additional source of both negative and positive selective incentives. Clearly most people value the companionship and respect of those with whom they interact. In modern societies solitary confinement is, apart from the rare death penalty, the harshest legal punishment. The censure or even ostracism of those who fail to bear a share of the burdens of collective action can sometimes be an important selective incentive. An extreme example of this occurs when British unionists refuse to speak to uncooperative colleagues, that is, "send them to Coventry." Similarly, those in a socially interactive group seeking a collective good can give special respect or honor to those who distinguish themselves by their sacrifices in the interest of the group and thereby offer them a positive selective incentive. Since most people apparently prefer relatively likeminded or agreeable and respectable company, and often prefer to associate with those whom they especially admire, they may find it costless to shun those who shirk the collective action and to favor those who oversubscribe.

Social selective incentives can be powerful and inexpensive, but they are available only in certain situations. As I have already indicated, they have little applicability to large groups, except in those cases in which the large groups can be federations of small groups that are capable of social interaction. It also is not possible to organize most large groups in need of a collective good into small, socially interactive subgroups, since most individuals do not have the time needed to maintain a huge number of friends and acquaintances.

The availability of social selective incentives is also limited by the social heterogeneity of some of the groups or categories that would benefit from a collective good. Everyday observation reveals that most socially interactive groups are fairly homogeneous and that many people resist extensive social interaction with those they deem to have lower status or greatly different tastes. Even Bohemian or other nonconformist groups often are made up of individuals who are similar to one another, however much they differ from the rest of society. Since some of the categories of individuals who would benefit from a collective good are socially heterogeneous, the social interaction needed for selective incentives sometimes cannot be arranged even when the number of individuals involved is small.

Another problem in organizing and maintaining socially heterogeneous groups is that they are less likely to agree on the exact nature of whatever collective good is at issue or on how much of it is worth buying. All the arguments showing the difficulty of collective action mentioned so far in this chapter hold even when there is perfect consensus about the collective good that is desired, the amount that is wanted, and the best way to obtain the good. But if anything, such as social heterogeneity, reduces consensus, collective action can become still less likely. And if there is nonetheless collective action, it incurs the extra cost (especially for the leaders of whatever organization or collusion is at issue) of accommodating and compromising the different views. The situation is slightly different in the very small groups to which we shall turn shortly. In such groups differences of opinion can sometimes provide a bit of an incentive to join an organization seeking a collective good, since joining might give the individual a significant influence over the organization's policy and the nature of any collective good it would obtain. But this consideration is not relevant to any group that is large enough so that a single individual cannot expect to affect the outcome.

Consensus is especially difficult where collective goods are concerned because the defining characteristic of collective goods—that they go to everyone in some group or category if they are provided at all—also entails that everyone in the relevant group gets more or less of the collective good together, and that they all have to accept whatever level and type of public good is provided. A country can have only one foreign and defense policy, however diverse the preferences and incomes of its citizenry, and (except in the rarely attainable case of a "Lindahl equilibrium")[7] there will not be agreement within a country on how much should be spent to carry out the foreign and defense policy. This is a clear implication of the arguments for "fiscal equivalence"[8] and of the rigorous models of "optimal segregation"[9] and "fiscal federalism."[10] Heterogeneous clients with diverse demands for collective goods can pose an even greater problem for private associations, which not only must deal with the disagreements but also must find selective incentives strong enough to hold dissatisfied clients.

In short, the political entrepreneurs who attempt to organize collective action will accordingly be more likely to succeed if they strive to organize relatively homogeneous groups. The political managers whose task it is to maintain organized or collusive action similarly will be motivated to use indoctrination and selective recruitment to increase the homogeneity of their client groups. This is true in part because social selective incentives are more likely to be available to the more nearly homogeneous groups, and in part because homogeneity will help achieve consensus.

IV

Information and calculation about a collective good is often itself a collective good. Consider a typical member of a large organization who is deciding how much time to devote to studying the policies or leadership of the organization. The more time the member devotes to this matter, the greater the likelihood that his or her voting and advocacy will favor effective policies and leadership for the organization. This typical member will, however, get only a small share of the gain from the more effective policies and leadership: in the aggregate, the other members will get almost all the gains, so that the individual member does not have an incentive to devote nearly as much time to fact-finding and thinking about the organization as would be in the group interest. Each of the members of the group would be better off if they all could be coerced into spending more time finding out how to vote to make the organization best further their interests. This is dramatically evident in the case of the typical voter in a national election in a large country. The gain to such a voter from studying issues and candidates until it is clear what vote is truly in his or her interest is given by the difference in the value to the individual of the "right" election outcome as compared with the "wrong" outcome, *multiplied by the probability a change in the individual's vote will alter the outcome of the election.* Since the probability that a typical voter will change the outcome of the election is vanishingly small, the typical citizen is usually "rationally ignorant" about public affairs.[11] Often, information about public affairs is so interesting or entertaining that it pays to acquire it for these reasons alone—this appears to be the single most important source of exceptions to the generalization that *typical* citizens are rationally ignorant about public affairs.

Individuals in a few special vocations can receive considerable rewards in private goods if they acquire exceptional knowledge of public goods. Politicians, lobbyists, journalists, and social scientists, for example, may earn more money, power, or prestige from knowledge of this or that public business. Occasionally, exceptional knowledge of public policy can generate exceptional profits in stock exchanges or other markets. Withal, the typical citizen will find that his or her income and life chances will not be improved by zealous study of public affairs, or even of any single collective good.

The limited knowledge of public affairs is in turn necessary to explain the effectiveness of lobbying. If all citizens had obtained and digested all pertinent information, they could not then be swayed by advertising or other persuasion. With perfectly informed citizens, elected officials would not be subject to the blandishments of lobbyists, since the constituents would then know if their interests were betrayed and defeat the unfaithful representative at the next election. Just as lobbies provide collective goods to special-interest groups, so their effectiveness is explained by the imperfect knowledge of citizens, and this in turn is due mainly to the fact that information and calculation about collective goods is also a collective good.

This fact—that the benefits of individual enlightenment about public goods are usually dispersed throughout a group or nation, rather than concentrated upon the individual who bears the costs of becoming enlightened—explains many other phenomena as well. It explains, for example, the "man bites dog" criterion of what is newsworthy. If the television newscasts were watched or newspapers were read solely to obtain the most important information about public affairs, aberrant events of little public importance would be ignored and typical patterns of quantitative significance would be emphasized; when the news is, by contrast, for most people largely an alternative to other forms of diversion or entertainment, intriguing oddities and human-interest items are in demand. Similarly, events that unfold in a suspenseful way or sex scandals among public figures are fully covered by the media, whereas the complexities of economic policy or quantitative analyses of public problems receive only minimal attention. Public officals, often able to thrive without giving the citizens good value for their tax monies, may fall over an exceptional mistake striking enough to be newsworthy. Extravagant statements, picturesque protests, and unruly demonstrations that offend much of the public they are designed to influence are also explicable in this way: they make diverting news and thus call attention to interests and arguments that might otherwise be ignored. Even some isolated acts of terrorism that are described as "senseless" can, from this perspective, be explained as effective means of obtaining the riveted attention of a public that otherwise would remain rationally ignorant.

This argument also helps us to understand certain apparent inconsistencies in the behavior of modern democracies. The arrangement of the income-tax brackets in all the major developed democracies is distinctly progressive, whereas the loopholes are more often tilted toward a minority of more prosperous taxpayers. Since both are the results of the same democratic institutions, why do they not have the same incidence? As I see it, the progression of the income tax is a matter of such salience and political controversy that much of the electorate knows about it, so populist and majoritarian considerations dictate a considerable degree of progression. The details of tax laws are far less widely known, and they often reflect the interests of small numbers of organized and usually more prosperous taxpayers. Several of the developed democracies similarly have adopted programs such as Medicare and Medicaid that are obviously inspired by the concerns about the cost of medical care to those with low or middle incomes, yet implemented or administered these programs in ways that resulted in large increases in income for prosperous physicians and other providers of medical care. Again, these diverse consequences seem to be explained by the fact that conspicuous and controversial choices of overall policies become known to the majorities who consume health care, whereas the many smaller choices needed to implement these programs are influenced primarily by a minority of organized providers of health care.

The fact that the typical individual does not have an incentive to spend much time studying many of his choices concerning collective goods also helps to explain some otherwise inexplicable individual contributions toward the provision of collective goods. The logic of collective action that has been described in this chapter is not immediately apparent to those who have never studied it; if it were, there would be nothing paradoxical in the argument with which this chapter opened, and students to whom the argument is explained would not react with initial skepticism.[12] No doubt the practical implications of this logic for the individual's own choices were often discerned before the logic was ever set out in print, but this does not mean that they were always understood even at the intuitive and practical level. In particular, when the costs of individual contributions to collective action are very small, the individual has little incentive to investigate whether or not to make a contribution or even to exercise intuition. If the individual knows the costs of a contribution to collective action in the interest of a group of which he is a part are trivially small, he may rationally not take the trouble to consider whether the gains are smaller still. This is particularly the case since the size of these gains and the policies that would maximize them are matters about which it is usually not rational for him to investigate.

This consideration of the costs and benefits of calculation about public goods leads to the testable prediction that voluntary contributions toward the provision of collective goods for large groups without selective incentives will often occur when the costs of the individual contributions are negligible, but that they will *not* often occur when the costs of the individual contributions are considerable. In other words, when the costs of individual action to help to obtain a desired collective good are small enough, the result is indeterminate and sometimes goes one way and sometimes the other, but when the costs get larger this indeterminacy disappears. We should accordingly find that more than a few people are willing to take the moment of time needed to sign petitions for causes they support, or to express their opinions in the course of discussion, or to vote for the candidate or party they prefer. Similarly, if the argument here is correct, we should not find many instances where individuals voluntarily contribute substantial sums of resources year after year for the purpose of obtaining some collective good for some large group of which they are a part. Before parting with a large amount of money or time, and particularly before doing so repeatedly, the rational individual will reflect on what this considerable sacrifice will accomplish. If the individual is a typical individual in a large group that would benefit from a collective good, his contribution will not make a perceptible difference in the amount that is provided. The theory here predicts that such contributions become less likely the larger the contribution at issue.[13]

V

Even when contributions are costly enough to elicit rational calculation, there is still one set of circumstances in which collective action can occur without selective incentives. This set of circumstances becomes evident the moment we think of situations in which there are only a few individuals or firms that would benefit from collective action. Suppose there are two firms of equal size in an industry and no other firms can enter the industry. It still will be the case that a higher price for the industry's product will benefit both firms and that legislation favorable to the industry will help both firms. The higher price and the favorable legislation are then collective goods to this "oligopolistic" industry, even though there are only two in the group that benefit from the collective goods. Obviously, each of the oligopolists is in a situation in which if it restricts output to raise the industry price, or lobbies for favorable legislation for the industry, it will tend to get half of the benefit. And the cost-benefit ratio of action in the common interest easily could be so favorable that, even though a firm bears the whole cost of its action and gets only half the benefit of this action, it could still profit from acting in the common interest. Thus if the group that would benefit from collective action is sufficiently small and the cost-benefit ratio of collective action for the group sufficiently favorable, there may well be calculated action in the collective interest even without selective incentives.

When there are only a few members in the group, there is also the possibility that they will bargain with one another and agree on collective action—then the action of each can have a perceptible effect on the interests and the expedient courses of action of others, so that each has an incentive to act strategically, that is, in ways that take into account the effect of the individual's choices on the choices of others. This interdependence of individual firms or persons in the group can give them an incentive to bargain with one another for their mutual advantage. Indeed, if bargaining costs were negligible, they would have an incentive to continue bargaining with one another until group gains were maximized, that is, until what we shall term a *group-optimal outcome* (or what economists sometimes call a "Pareto-optimal" outcome for the group) is achieved. One way the two firms mentioned in the previous paragraph could obtain such an outcome is by agreeing that each will bear half the costs of any collective action; each firm would then bear half the cost of its action in the common interest and receive half the benefits. It therefore would have an incentive to continue action in the collective interest until the aggregate gains of collective action were maximized. In any bargaining, however, each party has an incentive to seek the largest possible share of the group gain for itself, and usually also an incentive to threaten to block or undermine the collective action—that is, to be a "holdout"—if it does not get its preferred share of the group gains. Thus the bargaining may very well not succeed in achieving a group-optimal outcome and may also fail to achieve agreement on any collective action at all. The upshot of all this, as I explain elsewhere,[14] is that "small" groups can often engage in collective action without selective incentives. In certain small groups ("privileged groups") there is actually a presumption that some of the collective good will be provided. Nonetheless, even in the best of circumstances collective action is problematic and the outcomes in particular cases are indeterminate.

Although some aspects of the matter are complex and indeterminate, the essence of the relationship between the size of the group that would benefit from collective action and the extent of collective action is beautifully simple—yet somehow not widely understood. Consider again our two firms and suppose that they have *not* worked out any agreement to maximize their aggregate gains or to coordinate their actions in any way. Each firm will still get half the gains of any action it takes in the interest of the group, and thus it may have a substantial incentive to act in the group interest even when it is acting unilaterally.

There is, of course, also a *group external economy*, or gain to the group for which the firm acting unilaterally is not compensated, of 50 percent, so unilateral behavior does not achieve a group-optimal outcome.[15] Now suppose there were a third firm of the same size—the group external economy would then be two thirds, and the individual firm would get only a third of the gain from any independent action it took in the group interest. Of course, if there were a hundred such firms, the group external economy would be 99 percent, and the individual firm would get only 1 percent of the gain from any action in the group interest. Obviously, when we get to large groups measured in millions or even thousands, the incentive for group-oriented behavior in the absence of selective incentives becomes insignificant and even imperceptible.

Untypical as my example of equal-sized firms may be, it makes the general point intuitively obvious: other things being equal, *the larger the number of individuals or firms that would benefit from a collective good, the smaller the share of the gains from action in the group interest that will accrue to the individual or firm that undertakes the action. Thus, in the absence of selective incentives, the incentive for group action diminishes as group size increases, so that large groups are less able to act in their common interest than small ones.* If an additional individual or firm that would value the collective good enters the scene, then the share of the gains from group-oriented action that anyone already in the group might take must diminish. This holds true whatever the relative sizes or valuations of the collective good in the group.

There is a clear demonstration of this point in *The Logic of Collective Action*, a small part of which is included in the footnote to this sentence.* The fuller argument will make clear that the assumption in

---

*The cost (C) of a collective good is a function of the level (T) at which it is provided, i.e., $C = f(T)$. The value of the good to the group, V_g, depends not only on T but also on the "size," S_g, of the group, which in turn depends on the number in the group and the value they place on the good; $V_g = TS_g$. The value to an individual i of the good is V_i, and the "fraction," F_i, of the group value that this individual enjoys is V_i/V_g, and this must also equal F_iS_gT. The net advantage, A_i, that individual i obtains from purchasing an amount of the collective good is given by its value to him minus the cost, i.e., $A_i = V_i - C$, which changes with the level of T his expenditure obtains, so

$$dA_i/dT = dV_i/dT - dC/dT.$$

At a maximum $dA_i/dT = 0$. Because $V_i = F_iS_gT$ and F_i and S_g are constants

the preceding paragraphs of firms of equal size is unnecessary to the conclusion (though it is, I hope, helpful in obtaining a quick intuitive sense of the matter). Differences in size, or more precisely in the amount the different firms or individuals would be willing to pay for marginal amounts of the collective good, are of great importance and explain paradoxical phenomena like the "exploitation of the great by the small,"[16] but they are not essential to the argument in this book.

The number of people who must bargain if a group-optimal amount of a collective good is to be obtained, and thus the costs of bargaining, must rise with the size of the group. This consideration reinforces the point just made. Indeed, both everyday observation and the logic of the matter suggest that for genuinely large groups, bargaining among all members to obtain agreement on the provision of a collective good is out of the question.[17] The consideration mentioned earlier in this chapter, that social selective incentives are available only to small groups and (tenuously) to those larger groups that are federations of small groups, also suggests that small groups are more likely to organize than large ones.

The significance of the logic that has just been set out can best be seen by comparing groups that would have the same net gain from collective action, if they could engage in it, but that vary in size. Suppose there are a million individuals who would gain a thousand dollars each, or a billion in the aggregate, if they were to organize effectively and engage in collective action that had a total cost of a hundred million. If the logic set out above is right, they could not organize or engage in effective collective action without selective incen-

---

$$d(F_iS_gT)/dT - dC/dT = 0$$
$$F_iS_g - dC/dT = 0.$$

This gives the amount of the collective good that a unilateral maximizer would buy. This point can be given a common-sense meaning. Since the optimum is found when

$$dA_i/dT = dV_i/dT - dC/dT = 0,$$

and since $dV_i/dT = F_i(dV_g/dT)$

$$F_i(dV_g/dT) - dC/dT = 0,$$
$$F_i(dV_g/dT) = dC/dT.$$

Thus the optimal amount of the collective good for an individual to obtain occurs when the rate of gain to the group (dV_g/dT) exceeds the rate of increase in cost (dC/dT) by the same multiple by which the group gain exceeds the gain to the individual ($1/F_i = V_g/V_i$). In other words, the smaller F_i is, the less the individual will take, and (other things being equal) F_i must of course diminish as entry makes the group larger.

tives. Now suppose that, although the total gain of a billion dollars from collective action and the aggregate cost of a hundred million remain the same, the group is composed instead of five big corporations or five organized municipalities, each of which would gain two hundred million. Collective action is not an absolute certainty even in this case, since each of the five could conceivably expect others to put up the hundred million and hope to gain the collective good worth two hundred million at no cost at all. Yet collective action, perhaps after some delays due to bargaining, seems very likely indeed. In this case any one of the five would gain a hundred million from providing the collective good even if it had to pay the whole cost itself; and the costs of bargaining among five would not be great, so they would sooner or later probably work out an agreement providing for the collective action. The numbers in this example are arbitrary, but roughly similar situations occur often in reality, and the contrast between ''small'' and ''large'' groups could be illustrated with an infinite number of diverse examples.

The significance of this argument shows up in a second way if one compares the operations of lobbies or cartels within jurisdictions of vastly different scale, such as a modest municipality on the one hand and a big country on the other. Within the town, the mayor or city council may be influenced by, say, a score of petitioners or a lobbying budget of a thousand dollars. A particular line of business may be in the hands of only a few firms, and if the town is distant enough from other markets only these few would need to agree to create a cartel. In a big country, the resources needed to influence the national government are likely to be much more substantial, and unless the firms are (as they sometimes are) gigantic, many of them would have to cooperate to create an effective cartel. Now suppose that the million individuals in our large group in the previous paragraph were spread out over a hundred thousand towns or jurisdictions, so that each jurisdiction had ten of them, along with the same proportion of citizens in other categories as before. Suppose also that the cost-benefit ratios remained the same, so that there was still a billion dollars to gain across all jurisdictions or ten thousand in each, and that it would still cost a hundred million dollars across all jurisdictions or a thousand in each. It no longer seems out of the question that in many jurisdictions the groups of ten, or subsets of them, would put up the thousand-dollar total needed to get the thousand for each individual. Thus we see that, if all else were equal, small jurisdictions would have more collective action per capita than large ones.

Differences in intensities of preference generate a third type of illustration of the logic at issue. A small number of zealots anxious for a particular collective good are more likely to act collectively to obtain that good than a larger number with the same aggregate willingness to pay. Suppose there are twenty-five individuals, each of whom finds a given collective good worth a thousand dollars in one case, whereas in another there are five thousand, each of whom finds the collective good worth five dollars. Obviously, the argument indicates that there would be a greater likelihood of collective action in the former case than in the latter, even though the aggregate demand for the collective good is the same in both. The great historical significance of small groups of fanatics no doubt owes something to this consideration.

VI

The argument in this chapter predicts that those groups that have access to selective incentives will be more likely to act collectively to obtain collective goods than those that do not, and that smaller groups will have a greater likelihood of engaging in collective action than larger ones. The empirical portions of *The Logic* show that this prediction has been correct for the United States. More study will be needed before we can be utterly certain that the argument also holds for other countries, but the more prominent features of the organizational landscape of other countries certainly do fit the theory. In no major country are large groups without access to selective incentives generally organized—the masses of consumers are not in consumers' organizations, the millions of taxpayers are not in taxpayers' organizations, the vast number of those with relatively low incomes are not in organizations for the poor, and the sometimes substantial numbers of unemployed have no organized voice. These groups are so dispersed that it is not feasible for any nongovernmental organization to coerce them; in this they differ dramatically from those, like workers in large factories or mines, who are susceptible to coercion through picketing. Neither does there appear to be any source of the positive selective incentives that might give individuals in these categories an incentive to cooperate with the many others with whom they share common interests.* By contrast, almost

---

*Even groups or causes that are so large or popular that they encompass almost everyone in the society cannot generate very substantial organizations. Consider those concerned about the quality of the environment. Although environmental extremists are a

everywhere the social prestige of the learned professions and the limited numbers of practitioners of each profession in each community has helped them to organize. The professions have also been helped to organize by the distinctive susceptibility of the public to the assertion that a professional organization, with the backing of government, ought to be able to determine who is "qualified" to practice the profession, and thereby to control a decisive selective incentive. The small groups of (often large) firms in industry after industry, in country after country, are similarly often organized in trade associations or organizations or collusions of one kind or another. So, frequently, are the small groups of (usually smaller) businesses in particular towns or communities.

Even though the groups that the theory says cannot be organized do not appear to be organized anywhere, there are still substantial differences across societies and historical periods in the extent to which the groups that our logic says *could* be organized *are* organized. This, we shall argue, is a matter of surpassing importance for the nations involved, and it is to this that we now turn.

---

small minority, almost everyone is interested in a wholesome environment, and poll results suggest that in the United States, for example, there are tens of millions of citizens who think more ought to be done to protect the environment. In the late 1960s and early 1970s, certainly, environmentalism was faddish as well. Despite this, and despite subsidized postal rates for nonprofit organizations and reductions in the cost of direct mail solicitation due to computers, relatively few people pay dues each year to environmental organizations. The major environmental organizations in the United States have memberships measured in the tens or hundreds of thousands, with at least the larger (such as the Audubon Society, with its products for bird-watchers) plainly owing much of their membership to selective incentives. There are surely more than 50 million Americans who value a wholesome environment, but in a typical year probably fewer than one in a hundred pays dues to any organization whose main activity is lobbying for a better environment. The proportion of physicians in the American Medical Association, or automobile workers in the United Automobile Workers union, or farmers in the Farm Bureau, or manufacturers in trade associations is incomparably greater.

3 | The Implications

Although some of the implications of the logic in the preceding chapter were set out in that chapter, they were only the immediate implications of that logic alone. When we combine the argument in chapter 2 with some other logic and facts, and in particular with some standard findings from economics, we obtain a further set of implications. These second-level implications tell us what we should expect in certain types of societies and historical conditions if the theory we are now constructing is correct.

The validity or invalidity of our argument depends not only on the correctness of the preceding chapter, but also on what will be added. Fortunately, most of the economics we shall use is well-established; it is mainly the widely tested ''microeconomic theory'' of individual firms, consumers, and industries. Many laymen suppose that economists disagree about everything, but in fact this part of economics is mainly acceptable to almost all skilled economists, be they left-wing or right-wing, Keynesian or monetarist. To this we must add the less formal but invaluable ''Schumpeterian'' insight into innovation and entrepreneurship, which is also rather widely accepted, and a brief extension I have to the economist's usual analysis of the role of entry of outside firms into unusually profitable industries.

Unfortunately, it will not be possible to see how the further implications or theory we shall develop here relate to concrete problems in particular countries until we have first gone through the mildly abstract argument in this chapter—the rest of the book is not comprehensible by itself. Logical arguments that are not immediately related to practical experience do not seem important to some people, so there may understandably be readers who will wonder whether the abstract arguments of this chapter and the last one are of much practical significance. I can, without any fear of ultimate disagreement, promise the reader that, *if* the argument in this chapter and the preceding one is largely correct, it is indisputably of great practical importance.

Our initial second-level implication has to do with whether a society could achieve a rational or efficient economy through bargaining among organized groups. The last chapter pointed out that a small group of individuals or firms interested in a public good would have an incentive to continue bargaining with one another until they had maximized aggregate gains. There can be no confidence that bargaining even in a small group will work, much less have the complete success that is needed for group-optimality. But such an outcome is clearly a prominent possibility, and if everyone has participated in the bargaining the result might even be deemed fair to some degree. This reminds us to ask whether whole societies could achieve efficient results through comprehensive bargaining by leaders of all the groups in the society.

If the logic set out in the previous chapter is correct, a society that would achieve either efficiency or equity through comprehensive bargaining is out of the question. Some groups such as consumers, taxpayers, the unemployed, and the poor do not have either the selective incentives or the small numbers needed to organize, so they would be left out of the bargaining. It would be in the interest of those groups that are organized to increase their own gains by whatever means possible. This would include choosing policies that, though inefficient for the society as a whole, were advantageous for the organized groups because the costs of the policies fell disproportionately on the unorganized. (In the language of the game theorist, the society would not achieve a "core" or Pareto-efficient allocation because some of the groups were by virtue of their lack of organization unable to block changes detrimental to them or to work out mutually advantageous bargains with others.) With some groups left out of the bargaining, there is also no reason to suppose that the results have any appeal on grounds of fairness. On top of this there is the likelihood that the costs of bargaining and slow decision-making would make a society that made decisions by group bargaining inefficient in any case. Thus our first implication on this level is:

1. *There will be no countries that attain symmetrical organization of all groups with a common interest and thereby attain optimal outcomes through comprehensive bargaining.*

If such countries should emerge, that would mean that the argument in this book is probably wrong.

II

Our second implication relates to the emergence of organizations for collective action over time. The last chapter argued that collective action is difficult and problematical. In addition, there are normally some special start-up costs in creating any organization or new pattern of cooperation, including the fear of and resistance to the unfamiliar; as Machiavelli pointed out in another context, "There is nothing more difficult to arrange, more doubtful of success, and more dangerous to carry through, than to initiate a new order of things. . . . Men are generally incredulous, never really trusting new things unless they have tested them by experience."[1] Thus even those groups that are in situations in which they may be able to organize or collude, because their members are small or because some selective incentive could in principle be worked out, may not be able to organize until favorable circumstances emerge. Even in small groups there will often be difficulties in working out bargains for collective action; each party wants to bear the lowest possible share of the costs and in bargaining has an incentive to hold out, sometimes for an indefinitely long time. Thus some of the collective action that is attainable through bargaining in small groups will not be attained until some time has passed.

In larger groups, where collective action is attainable only through selective incentives, even greater difficulties must be overcome. If coercion is the selective incentive, the coercive force has to be arranged, and since people do not like to be coerced there is difficulty and even danger in this. Strong leadership and favorable circumstances will usually be required. The beginning of the union career of Jimmy Hoffa illustrates this. The young Hoffa was one of the workers in an unorganized warehouse in Detroit. On a hot summer day a large shipment of strawberries that would soon spoil arrived, and Hoffa then persuaded his coworkers to strike. The employer found it better to accept Hoffa's demands than to lose his perishable cargo. Usually the circumstances are not so favorable, and leaders with the cunning, courage, and lack of inhibition that characterized Jimmy Hoffa are not often on the scene.

When social pressure and social rewards are the selective incentives, there are also difficulties and delays. When a group that is already socially interactive needs a collective good, the problem may not be so difficult, although even here the social interaction must generate a sufficient surplus for the participants that they are willing to maintain it even after they are taxed for the cost of the collective good. Creating new patterns of social interaction is more difficult and surely time-consuming as well. Some late nineteenth-century American farm organizations, such as the Grange, managed to do this particularly well with relatively isolated farm families in recently settled areas, but attracting members away from previously established social networks, when possible at all, is likely to take exceptional leadership, and even then to evolve only over a considerable amount of time.

Positive selective incentives of a more tangible and material kind can also be found, if at all, only after a great deal of effort. Generating a surplus that can finance provision of a collective good or induce others to provide it is inherently chancy—there are failures as well as successes among those who attempt to create new businesses. And entrepreneurs who make money naturally often keep it for themselves. Thus usually some complementarity between the activity that can provide a collective good and that which produces income must be found or exploited; any lobbying power must be used in part to get favorable governmental treatment of the business activity, for example, or the reputation and trust of the lobbying organization among its beneficiaries must be exploited by the associated business activity. Even when such complementarities can be exploited, they may be discovered or worked out only after some time, and then only if there are imaginative leaders.

Scattered observation, at least, supports the hypothesis that organization for collective action takes a good deal of time to emerge. Though there was some earlier collective action by workers, it was not until 1851, or nearly a century after the start of the Industrial Revolution, that the first sustainable modern trade union emerged, the Amalgamated Society of Engineers in Great Britain. Though there was legal repression of combinations of workers at times during the Industrial Revolution, this cannot explain why unions did not become the norm in Britain until the decades just before World War I. Elsewhere unionization took place even later. In the United States a number of unions were established in the last half of the nineteenth century, but the fastest growth of union membership was in the period from 1937 to 1945, long after the country achieved the industrialized condition most favorable to unions. A study of unionization, industry by industry, in France similarly reveals "a lag between the initial appearance of an industry and the time its workers acquire an organizational capacity for collective action."[2] Farm organizations have taken even longer to develop. In the United States there was some farm organization in the second half of the nineteenth century, but it was not until the organization of the Farm Bureau (by the government-funded Agricultural Extension Service) after World War I that there was any really large or stable farm organization. Yet American farmers had significant common interests from the founding of the American republic. Many similar examples could be cited for other countries and other types of organizations.

The other side of the matter is that those organizations that have secured selective incentives to maintain themselves will often survive as organizations even if the collective good they once provided is no longer needed. As the sociologist Max Weber pointed out long ago,[3] the leader who is making a living out of an organization may keep it alive even after its original purpose has disappeared; an organization set up to represent the drivers of teams of horses, for example, will take on the task of representing drivers of trucks, and an organization set up to help the veterans of one war will outlive these veterans by representing veterans of subsequent wars. Selective incentives make indefinite survival feasible. Thus those organizations for collective action, at least for large groups, that can emerge often take a long time to emerge, but once established they usually survive until there is a social upheaval or some other form of violence or instability.[4]

If organizations and collusions for collective action usually emerge only in favorable circumstances and develop strength over time, a stable society will see more organization for collective action as time passes (unless, of course, constitutional and legal constraints on collective action, or on the changes in public policies lobbying is permitted to bring about, should leave little scope for such organizations). The more time that passes, the larger the number of those groups that are in situations in which collective action is a possibility will have enjoyed the favorable circumstances and innovative political leadership that they need to organize, and the greater the likelihood that the organizations that have been created will have achieved their potential. This, in combination with the fact that organizations with selective incentives in stable societies normally survive indefinitely, leads to our second implication:

2. *Stable societies with unchanged boundaries* tend to accumulate more collusions and organizations for collective action over time.*

III

The third implication is perhaps the hardest to relate to casual observation, so its meaning may not be clear until later. The source of this implication is, however, obvious: it is the finding in the last chapter that oligopolists and other small groups have a greater likelihood of being able to organize for collective action, and can usually organize with less delay, than large groups. It follows that the small groups in a society will usually have more lobbying and cartelistic power per capita (or even per dollar of aggregate income) than the large groups. The fact that small groups can usually organize with less delay than large ones implies that this disproportion will tend to be greatest in the societies that have enjoyed only a brief period of stability and least great in those societies that have been stable for a long time. Accordingly, our third implication is:

3. *Members of "small" groups have disproportionate organizational power for collective action, and this disproportion diminishes but does not disappear over time in stable societies.*

The reader may find it helpful to give this implication a skeptical examination after it has been put to practical use later in the book.

IV

If the extent and type of organization for collective action varies across societies and historical periods, then it is important to determine what impact such organization has on the efficiency and rate of economic growth of a society. Normally all such organizations, whatever their scale or form, have reason to want economic efficiency and growth, and good fortune generally, for the society in which they operate. Whatever type of goods or labor the members of an organization sell, normally the demand for it will be greater the more prosperous the society (there are

---

*The meaning and significance of the reference to "unchanged boundaries" will be made clear in a later chapter.

"inferior" goods on which more is spent if income falls, but they are exceptional). Similarly, the available technology will generally be better and the goods (though not the labor) that the members of the organization buy will generally be cheaper if they live in a more productive society. It might seem that one logical possibility, then, is that such organizations could in some circumstances serve their members' interests by helping to make the society in which they operate more productive.

Except for a special case we shall deal with later, the only other way in which such an organization could serve its members' interests is by obtaining a larger share of the society's production for the organization's members. In other words, the organization can in principle serve its members either by making the pie the society produces larger, so that its members would get larger slices even with the same shares as before, or alternatively by obtaining larger shares or slices of the social pie for its members. Our intuition tells us that the first method will rarely be chosen, but it is important to figure out exactly why this is so.

It will normally cost an organization something to make the society of which it is a part more efficient. Suppose a lobbying organization were to strive to eliminate the losses in economic efficiency that arise because of differential rates of tax on income from different sources (tax loopholes), or to attempt to reduce the losses from monopoly in the society. An effective campaign to achieve such goals would have significant costs that the organization sponsoring the campaign would have to bear. But the members of the organization would get only a part of the benefits that would result if they made the society as a whole more efficient; they would share in the lower prices or lower taxes or other gains from greater efficiency in the society, but so would most of the rest of society. This is important because in most cases each organization of the kind we are considering represents only a minute percentage of the population or other resources of a society. The typical trade association for an industry represents a small number of firms which, even though they may be large, own only a tiny share of the productive assets in a country; the typical labor union, even if it has tens or hundreds of thousands of members, includes only a minute percentage of the labor force of a country, and so forth. (There are exceptionally encompassing organizations for collective action in a few countries, and these are considered separately below.)

Suppose, for the sake of illustration, that an organization represents workers or firms that have 1 percent of the income-earning capacity in the country. This organization will have to bear the cost of whatever campaign it mounts to make the society more efficient, but its members will tend, on average, to get only about 1 percent of the resulting gain to the society. The organization's members would, on average, profit from devoting their resources to making the society more efficient only if those resources produced social gains one hundred times or more larger than the cost of obtaining those gains. (More generally, in the symbolic language of the footnote on page 31 in chapter 2, the benefit-cost ratio of the activity to make the society more efficient must equal or exceed $1/F_i$, or the reciprocal of the fraction of the income-earning capacity of the society that the organization represents.)

Thus there is a parallel between the individual in a group that would gain from provision of a collective good and the organization for collective action within the society. The organization that acts to provide some benefit for the society as a whole is, in effect, providing a public good for the whole society, and it is accordingly in the same position as an individual who contributes to the provision of a collective good for a group of which he or she is a part. In each case the actor gets only a part (and often only a tiny part) of the benefits of its action, yet bears the whole cost of that action.

Now suppose that our illustrative organization that represents 1 percent of the income-earning capacity in the country attempts to serve its members by getting a larger slice of the social pie. The resources that are diverted to seizing a larger share of the society's output will not, of course, produce the social output they produced in their previous employments, so this will reduce social output to some extent. More important, the pattern of incentives in the society will be changed by the redistribution, and (as we shall see) in ways that can vastly reduce the level of production. On the other hand, the members of the organization are part of the society, so they will also share in the loss of social output that results from the redistribution toward themselves. Self-interest alone will make them take these losses into account along with the gains from the redistribution to themselves. *But it will pay to go ahead with the redistribution, unless the reduction in the value of the society's output is a hundred or more times larger than the amount won by the organization's clients in the distributional struggle.* Exactly the same logic we have used all along suggests that the typical organization for collective action will do nothing to eliminate the social loss or "public bad" its effort to get a larger share of the social output brings about. The familiar image of the slicing of the social pie does not really capture the essence of the situation; it is perhaps better to think of wrestlers struggling over the contents of a china shop.

In short, the typical organization for collective action within a society will, at least if it represents only a narrow segment of the society, have little or no incentive to make any significant sacrifices in the interest of the society; it can best serve its members' interests by striving to seize a larger share of a society's production for them. This will be expedient, moreover, even if the social costs of the change in the distribution exceed the amount redistributed by a huge multiple; *there is for practical purposes no constraint on the social cost such an organization will find it expedient to impose on the society in the course of obtaining a larger share of the social output for itself.* (The ratio of the social cost or excess burden to the amount redistributed must equal or exceed $1/F_i$ before it will constrain the organization.) The organizations for collective action within societies that we are considering are therefore overwhelmingly oriented to struggles over the distribution of income and wealth rather than to the production of additional output— they are "distributional coalitions" (or organizations that engage in what, in one valuable line of literature, is called "rent seeking").[5]

There has long been some intuitive apprehension of this, if not of the extent of social losses that it would pay such organizations to impose on society in efforts to get a larger share of social output. This intuitive apprehension is perhaps suggested by the *special-interest group* label sometimes used for such organizations. Now that the incentives such organizations face have been set out starkly, I shall sometimes use the expression special-interest group as a synonym for distributional coalition, even though that expression has, as we shall see later, a somewhat narrower connotation in everyday language than is appropriate here. These coalitions may be cartels as well as lobbies and are often both. Any combination of individuals or firms for collusive action in the marketplace, whether a professional association, a labor union, a trade association, or an oligopolistic collusive group, will here be called a cartel, whatever term may be used to describe it in everyday language.

One of the obvious ways in which a special-interest group can increase the income of its members while reducing the efficiency and output of the society is by lobbying for legislation to raise some price or wage or to tax some types of income at lower rates than other income.

Although the effects may be different under certain initial conditions (because of "second-best" problems),[6] in general measures of this sort will not only increase the income of those favored by the legislation but also reduce efficiency. There will be an incentive for additional resources to move into the industry or activity that is favored by the higher price or lower tax, and this shift of resources will continue until the private post-tax returns are the same in the favored area as in the rest of the economy. But if the price is higher or the tax lower in the favored area simply because of special-interest legislation, then the extra resources that have been diverted into the favored area will be adding less to the value of society's output than they did in their previous employments. Whenever resources are free to move into the favored area, the private returns will eventually be the same in the favored area as in the rest of the economy, and this tends to make the gain to the special-interest group very small in relation to the cost to society. In this type of case the only gain to the clients of the distributional coalition is the capital gain on those assets that are specialized to the favored industry plus transitional profits during the time it takes other resources to move into the area. The situation is different if entry is not allowed into the favored area, but as I shall later show, barriers to entry usually impose substantial social costs of other kinds. The argument we have just used is extremely simple and leaves aside many fascinating questions, both technical and social.[7] The argument also has only a lesser applicability to any country in which constitutional and structural factors constrain the number and power of lobbying organizations, as appears to be the case in Switzerland. Nonetheless, as later parts of this book should show, the basic point that it makes is widely applicable and enormously important.

Another way in which a special-interest organization can increase the income of its members while reducing society's output is through cartelization—the members can agree to reduce output as a single monopolist would have done and thereby enjoy a higher price. The gains from cartelization and monopoly arise because less is sold to obtain a higher price, so naturally there is (in the absence of other distortions)[8] a reduction in social output; in general, the society will get a mix of goods that contains an inefficiently small proportion of those goods sold at a monopoly price and an inefficiently large proportion of those goods sold at a competitive price. Effective cartels must always block entry into the line of business in which they have raised the price, so the process described in the preceding paragraph, which made the coalition's gain small in relation to the cost to society, does not work in the same way. But the ubiquitous barriers to entry will make certain other social costs (which we shall examine later) even greater.

There is an interesting literature in economics, stemming mainly from a seminal article by Arnold Harberger,[9] suggesting that the social losses from monopoly and (as others have argued) from tariffs and certain other distortions of the price system are relatively small in relation to the national income. Later I will endeavor to show that these losses can sometimes be colossal, but for the moment it may be sufficient to point out that the foregoing analysis of the incentives faced by special-interest groups could make them impose very large costs indeed on the society as a whole. And, as the international trade theorist Jagdish Bhagwati has pointed out,[10] there is, alas, nothing in the laws of economics that requires that, if a society is inefficient, it must be inefficient in a small way.

One consideration that does limit the losses from distributional coalitions to some extent, however, is that occasionally some of them will nullify or offset the effects of others. A farmers' lobby may win the repeal of a tariff on farm machinery or automobile manufacturers may limit the protection given the steel industry. Note that, in cases such as these, the effort of the special-interest group can lead to an increase in the efficiency and income of the society, but that the gains are not diffused through the society so that the special-interest group gets a share approximated by the proportion of the income-earning capacity of the society it represents—instead, those in the special-interest group get a substantial share of the total social gain from their activity. Occasionally there are other types of situations in which the constituents of special-interest organizations seek to increase social efficiency because they would get a lion's share of the gain in output; this occurs when the special-interest organization provides a collective good to its members that increases their productive efficiency and also when it gets the government to provide some public good that generates more income than costs, yet mainly benefits those in the special-interest group. It certainly is not easy to find any significant percentage of special-interest organizations whose principal objective is some policy that has the special property that it will mainly benefit the clients of the organization and at the same time increase the efficiency and aggregate income of the society. Yet multiple causation and mixed motivation are usually evident in any area, including that of special-interest groups, so it is important not to lose sight of organizations or situations of this type. The largest proportion of the cases that this researcher has been able to find appear to consist of organizations whose clients suffer disproportionately from inefficiencies obtained by other distributional coalitions and who therefore oppose those inefficiencies. If the first of the implications in this chapter—that there is not and will not be a symmetrically organized society—is wrong, this situation is not or will no longer be a special case. But if, as the findings in later parts of this book and elsewhere suggest, that implication is true, then the great majority of special-interest organizations redistribute income rather than create it, and in ways that reduce social efficiency and output.

In addition, this focus on distribution makes the significance of distributional issues in political life relatively greater and the significance of widespread common interests in political life relatively smaller. The common interests that all or most of the people in a nation or other jurisdiction share can draw them together, as they are drawn together when they perceive a common interest in repelling aggression. In distributional struggles, by contrast, none can gain without others losing as much or (normally) more, and this can generate resentment. Thus when special-interest groups become more important and distributional issues accordingly more significant, political life tends to be more divisive. Moreover, as Dennis Mueller,[11] building on the work of Kenneth Arrow,[12] has shown, the increased emphasis on distributional issues due to accumulations of special-interest groups can also increase the likelihood that a democratic political system can repudiate its prior choices, even if all the individuals in the electorate have the same preferences as before—it can (for some reasons that cannot be explained briefly or without technical language) encourage intransitive or irrational and cyclical political choices. The divisiveness of distributional issues, and the fact that they may make relatively lasting or stable political choices less likely, can even make societies ungovernable.

Thus we have our fourth implication:

4. *On balance, special-interest organizations and collusions reduce efficiency and aggregate income in the societies in which they operate and make political life more divisive.*

V

There are also, in some countries, special-interest organizations that encompass a substantial portion of the societies of which they are a part.

A labor union that includes most of the manual workers in a country, for example, represents a large proportion of the income-earning capacity of that country. So does a lobbying organization that includes all the major firms in an industrialized country. How might the policies of such encompassing or inclusive organizations differ from the more common narrow special-interest groups discussed in the preceding section?

The incentives facing an encompassing special-interest organization are dramatically different from those facing an organization that represents only a narrow segment of society. If an organization represents, say, a third of the income-producing capacity of a country, its members will, on average, obtain about a third of the benefit from any effort to make the society more productive. The organization will therefore have an incentive to make sacrifices up to a point for policies and activities that are sufficiently rewarding for the society as a whole. The members of the highly encompassing organization own so much of the society that they have an important incentive to be actively concerned about how productive it is; they are in the same position as a partner in a firm that has only a few partners. Moreover, the organization whose clients own a third of the income-earning potential of the society will, on average, bear about a third of any loss in the society's output that results from the policies it obtains. Thus any effort to obtain a larger share of the national income for the clients of such an encompassing organization could not make sense if it reduced the national income by an amount three or more times as great as the amount shifted to its members. As the discussion in the previous section would suggest, the argument here is that this can be a constraint of great practical importance. Clearly the encompassing organization, if it has rational leadership, will care about the excess burden arising from distributional policies favorable to its members and will out of sheer self-interest strive to make the excess burden as small as possible.

The illustrative assumption that an encompassing interest group represents a third of the society is admittedly favorable to the distinction that has been drawn. But contrast an organization that represents even a tenth of the income-earning capacity of a country with one that represents, as most special-interest organizations do, only a minuscule segment of the whole society. The former sort of organization has not only an incentive at least to consider the effect of its policies on the efficiency of the society, but also an incentive to bargain with other substantial organized groups in the interest of a more productive society. The really narrow special-interest group usually does not have an incentive to do even that.

A special-interest organization that is minuscule in relation to a country may, however, be encompassing in relation to a particular firm or industry. Consider a labor union that represents all the workers in some firm (an "enterprise union," such as is common in Japan), or alternatively a union that represents all the workers in each of the firms in one industry. Such a union could be small in relation to society as a whole, but if (as is typical) about two-thirds of the value added of each firm is devoted to the wage bill, then the union is relatively encompassing in relation respectively to the firm or the industry. It is true that in principle greater prosperity for firms is supposed to result in higher profits, whereas the wages of labor in the firm are supposed to be explained instead by the general state of the labor market; if this is the whole story, a union has no reason to care whether its firm or industry is especially prosperous. But if the union has any real bargaining strength, it can force the unusually prosperous firms to raise wages well above the market level, whereas no amount of bargaining power can force a firm in a desperate financial situation to do this. Some of the workers may, moreover, have skills that are specific to the firm or industry for which they work, and the market value of these skills may rise if the firm or industry is profitable enough to expand. Thus a union that is encompassing in relation to the firm or industry for which its members work has a reason to help the host firm or industry prosper and expand. Contrast this with the situation of a craft union that controls the supply of some specialized skill a firm or industry needs, but controls only a minute percentage of the relevant employees. Such a union would have only a minute influence on the profitability of any firm and accordingly would have little incentive to avoid inefficient practices or to help the employer or industry in any other ways.

The foregoing logic therefore suggests that the efficiency of firms and industries can be influenced by whether or not the relevant institutions for collective action are encompassing in relation to them. It implies, for example, that enterprise and industry unions should usually agree to more efficient work practices than the narrower craft unions; the anecdotal evidence suggests that this is the case.

It would be a mistake, however, to suppose that any increase in the extent to which a special-interest organization is encompassing is necessarily desirable. The degree of monopoly power often increases as an organization becomes more encompassing. If an enterprise union becomes an industry-wide union, for example, it may, by striking against any firms in the industry that do not cooperate, make it easier for the firms to have an effective cartel, and thereby maximize the joint monopoly gain of the firms and the workers. The competition among firms also limits the premium that any one firm can pay its unionized workers, so the gains from monopolizing the supply of labor will usually be less for an enterprise union than for one that controls the labor force in the whole industry. There is, in addition, little or no gain in concern for the society as a whole when a special-interest organization expands from, say, firm to industry size; it is likely to be so small in relation to the society even after the expansion that it will not take account of its impact on the efficiency of the society. The circumstance in which an increase in the extent to which a special-interest organization is encompassing is likely to be most constructive is when it is already so substantial that it encompasses many different industries. At that stage further expansion may not affect the market or industrial action of the organization, but it would create an incentive to give greater weight to the organization's impact on social efficiency.

In the same way national confederations of business or labor organizations can also introduce a more nearly national perspective on political issues without affecting the degree of monopoly. These organizations, which political scientists sometimes call *peak associations,* frequently lack the unity needed to have any great influence on public policy, or even coherent and specific policies. Nonetheless, peak associations should on average take a somewhat less parochial view than the narrow associations of which they are composed, and this offers one way of empirically testing the argument that has just been put forth. The Norwegian sociologist Gudmund Hernes has found, in connection with some collaborative research he and I are doing on encompassing organizations in Scandinavia (where such organizations are unusually important), that Norwegian peak associations at least appear to fit the theoretical prediction very well.

The logic of the distinction between narrow and encompassing interests is not limited to special-interest groups. This is evident, for example, from an inference many political scientists have drawn from the observation of American politics. This is the inference that the United States would gain from stronger and more responsible political parties.[13] These political scientists observe that individual members of Congress are overwhelmingly influenced by the parochial interests of their particular districts and by special-interest lobbies, and that incoherent national policies are often the result. The leadership of whatever party is perceived to be in control usually is to some extent concerned about the aggregate national consequences of the policies chosen, since there is some connection between the state of the nation and the election prospects of the party deemed to be in control. Party discipline, however, is so weak that the influence of the party leadership and the concern about the party's fate in the next election exert only a marginal influence. The conclusion is that if party discipline could be strengthened and each party be held responsible for the policies it chose and their outcome, then national policies would tend to improve.

The logic set out in this book can help to explain and justify the political scientists' argument, if it is combined with an analysis of the electoral system. The United States does not use proportional representation or any other electoral system that gives candidates or parties that come in second, third, or worse in a general election some portion of the power; the winner in any given general election wins it all. Thus it does not make any sense to have a political party in the United States that would over the long run expect to get, say, a fourth of the votes in a presidential election; parties that expected to come in second or lower, however, could gain something by combining if that gave them a chance of winning. Thus the electoral system in the United States encourages a two-party system (as do some other factors that need not be discussed here). Given that, each of the parties will be quite encompassing; each will attempt to represent a majority of the electorate. A party whose clients comprise half or more of the society naturally is concerned about the efficiency and welfare of the society as a whole, particularly in comparison with lobbies for special-interest groups and congressmen accountable only to small districts. It is accordingly not surprising that systematic observers should note that American political parties were, on balance, more concerned about the welfare of the nation than were special-interest groups or individual congressmen, and therefore would favor stronger political parties.

The same logic shows up in a comparison of the behavior of congressmen and presidents over pork-barrel legislation, for example. A congressional district that contains about 1/435th of the United States will tend to gain from any project for the district financed with federal taxes, so long as the costs are not 435 or more times greater than the benefits. Obviously, congressmen are aware of this. A president, by contrast, will stand a much better chance of being able to win reelection on the ground that the voters never had it so good if he can reserve the public monies for undertakings with better cost-benefit ratios. Thus, year after year, with presidents and with congressmen of both party affiliations, we see presidents trying to limit pork-barrel projects and congressmen trying to promote them.

The applications of this logic naturally vary from country to country. In some countries with many small political parties, the logic is revealed in neglect of broad conceptions of the national interest by not-very-encompassing parties and disjointed policies of coalition governments. In other countries one sometimes sees labor or socialist parties that emerged from trade unions, but with leaders that sometimes take a less parochial view than the parent unions, presumably because the party leader has a more encompassing constituency. There are also parallel cases of conservative parties that draw their core support from business and professional associations, yet sometimes withhold certain favors from these lobbies in the interest of a thriving national constituency.

The occurrence of fragile coalition governments composed partly or wholly of many small parties, or of governments that are precarious for other reasons, also reminds us that the power of special-interest groups cannot be defined solely in terms of their organizational strength but should, strictly speaking, be defined in terms of a ratio of their power to that of more encompassing structures such as presidents or political parties. This nicety can probably be neglected in most cases, but it may be of decisive importance in understanding some countries with fragile governments.

Even though more encompassing organizations and institutions for collective action are systematically less likely to have an incentive to act in an antisocial way, it would be too hasty to conclude that more encompassing institutions should always be preferred. As I pointed out in the last chapter, information about collective goods is itself a collective good and accordingly there is normally little of it. When ignorance is often a rational strategy for constituents, there is a substantial possibility that an interest group or a political leader will not act in accord with the interest of constituents. If a political system is composed only of highly encompassing organizations and institutions, there also may be less diversity of advocacy, opinion, and policy, and fewer checks to erroneous ideas and policies. Encompassing organizations and institutions may therefore perform unusually badly in some cases or periods and unusually effectively in others. Accordingly, the idea of encompassing organizations and institutions is not necessarily always a guide for reform, but it is essential to a complete understanding of many important organizations and institutions.

So long as it is clear that our fifth implication refers to the incentives that face encompassing organizations rather than to their choices in particular cases, there should be no confusion. Thus:

5. *Encompassing organizations have some incentive to make the society in which they operate more prosperous, and an incentive to redistribute income to their members with as little excess burden as possible, and to cease such redistribution unless the amount redistributed is substantial in relation to the social cost of the redistribution.*

VI

We must now develop a point that may at first seem unimportant, and that in any case is obvious to anyone who has endured a committee meeting where it took a long time to make (or fail to make) a decision. The point is that special-interest organizations and collusions tend to make decisions more slowly than the firms or individuals of which they are composed. We shall see later that this trait is crucial to understanding phenomena as important as the business cycle and the rate of adoption of new technologies, and that the reasons for this slowness of decision-making are also very much worthy of our attention. The two main reasons why special-interest groups make decisions more slowly than the individuals or firms of which they are constituted is that they must use either *consensual bargaining* or *constitutional procedures*, or both of these methods, to make decisions.

Consensual bargaining is simply an expression to remind us that members of smaller groups who may hope to act collectively without selective incentives must bargain until they agree on a joint course of action and on how the costs of this action are to be shared. As the argument in the last chapter made clear, a group cannot achieve a group-optimal level of provision of a collective good through voluntary action unless everyone who would benefit from the collective good contributes to the marginal cost of providing it, so group-optimal provision requires unanimity, or what we have just called consensual bargaining.

In the case of collective action in the marketplace, this collective action normally requires consensus even if it does not reach a group-optimal level. Collusion among oligopolists to achieve a higher price entails an agreement to reduce the quantity sold so that a higher price can be achieved. If some of the firms in an industry, or even all but one of the firms, agree to restrict their sales in the interest of a higher price, then obviously whatever firm or firms are outside the agreement can gain by selling more than before, and normally so much more that the price will be driven down to a competitive level, so that the subset of firms that agreed to curtail sales is left with a competitive price and an unprofitably small quantity sold. There can be exceptional circumstances where this does not occur, as when the firm or firms outside the agreement lack the productive capacity to take full advantage in the short run of the cutbacks by other firms, but in general collusion to obtain a higher price will not work without consensus among the sellers.

The unanimous consent is made more difficult to achieve because the parties have a direct conflict of interest about how the costs of the collective action should be shared. In the case of firms agreeing on a higher price, there must be some agreement or arrangement that determines what cutback will be required of each firm. The consensus that is required also implies that it can be a rational strategy for each prospective participant to demand an altogether disproportionate share of the gains from the collective action in return for his indispensable cooperation. Threats to be a holdout in turn will not be credible unless they are sometimes carried out, and this means that it can take an extraordinary amount of time to achieve the necessary unanimity. The problem of resolving the conflict of interest about the costs of collective action naturally applies whatever the method of decision-making, so we shall need to return to this after considering decision-making by constitutional procedures.

When there are so many participants that bargaining is not feasible, collective action will require some decision-making rules or by-laws, which I call *constitutional procedures*. Groups that are small enough so that bargaining is feasible may also agree to some constitutional procedures on the ground that the individual members find it expedient to agree not to use their capacity to block unanimous action in return for the savings in bargaining costs and the greater likelihood of continuing collective action. Decision-making under constitutional procedures also takes time, especially in larger groups. Decisions may have to wait until everyone is talked out, or until the next board meeting or the next annual meeting, or even until those who favor a change in policy force out those officials who prefer the old policy. There is also the possibility that once decisions are made, they may be unmade or replaced by different decisions, even if none of the members has had a change of heart. That is, for reasons that were first fully explained by Kenneth Arrow[14] and that I discussed when showing that distributional coalitions could help to make societies ungovernable, there may be voting cycles, or situations in which an organization's democratic choices are intransitive or unstable. In my judgment, there probably is not as much instability in democratic choices as some students of voting cycles claim, partly because the typical procedural rules of democratic bodies tend to discourage reversals and to give the status quo an advantage over alternatives. But the very procedures that limit the extent to which democratic bodies reverse themselves, and especially the advantage given the status quo, tend to make democratic organizations slower in deciding how to adapt to new circumstances than their individual members are. Moreover, since the choices made by majority rule, elected leaders, or other devices for collective decisions may be harmful to some of those involved, participants often insist upon safeguards that protect them from arbitrary decisions by elected officers, or even by majorities, even though these safeguards slow decision-making further. The provision in the constitutions of some unions that a decision to strike, or to accept a contract, can be taken only by a vote (and sometimes more than a majority vote) of the membership or of some large representative body is an example of such a safeguard.

Whenever an organization for collective action is large, and sometimes even when it is not, it will have many different decisions to make. The combination of slow decision-making and multiple decisions usually leads to a crowded agenda. Everyday experience, even in organizations as small as departments in universities, suggests that some matters wait a long while to receive attention and that some never get on the agenda at all. Crowded agendas often delay decisions further. The importance of this phenomenon is also evident from the creation of committees and subcommittees, which are used mainly to relieve crowded agendas. Even the committees and subcommittees can have crowded agendas. When decisions are made by consensual bargaining, the word *agenda* is not usually used, but there is the same problem if a multiplicity of matters needs to be dealt with. Some matters may get on the bargaining table only after much delay and others not at all. Some agreements or contracts may be left unchanged, even when new circumstances make them no longer optimal, because of a concern about the time, trouble, and uncertainty involved in working out a new deal. There are dramatic examples of this. In a study of some legal agreements to fix prices in Denmark, Bjarke Fog found an extreme case in which the price of a product was unchanged for a decade, despite rising costs and disappearing profits.[15] Similarly, F. M. Scherer has pointed out that for a considerable time the International Air Transport Association was able to change decisions only on relatively peripheral matters such as jet surcharges, motion picture fees, and the definition of a sandwich: "Since the Association by-laws require that fare changes be approved unanimously, the result . . . was a perpetuation of the status quo."[16]

When there are crowded agendas or cluttered bargaining tables, resolving the conflict of interest about how to share the costs of collective action is even more difficult. This difficulty encourages organizations and collusions for collective action to seek impartial outsiders, simple formulas, or seniority rules that can apportion the costs of collective action among the participants. If there is a substantial reward to a group for collective action in the first place, then there is a likelihood that each prospective participant will gain from the collective action under a variety of reasonable rules or decisions about the allocation of costs, so there may be an incentive for each of the parties to agree to an impartial arrangement for decisions about the allocation of costs, rather than risk losing all the gains that the collective action is expected to bring.

Some observers of OPEC, for example, claim that the degree of collusion it occasionally achieved was due in part to the fact that the competition among the big international companies provided an approximate allocation of the costs of restriction of oil output among member nations. The OPEC nations could then agree on a price per barrel, and the amount that each nation could sell at that price was then the result of the relative success of the oil company or companies that pumped each nation's oil.[17] Similarly, labor unions usually stipulate that seniority rules, or even decisions by the employer, determine who gets the benefit of the higher wage the union negotiates, partly to insure that the union members do not have to fight as much about who has to work less, or who loses a job, because the employer now has an incentive to use less labor. Naturally, the favoritism to senior workers—and the neglect of the interests of potential entrants who are not hired because of the higher wage—also reflects the normally greater influence of senior workers in the union and the absence of any vote at all for potential entrants. Nonetheless, a seniority rule enables a union to settle the troublesome issue of how to allocate the benefits of the higher wage with one relatively straightforward vote.

It is partly because of this conflict of interest over the sharing of costs that a majority of cartels and lobbies seek to fix prices or wages, rather than the quantity that can be sold. Since the amount offered for sale determines the price or wage, a union or a cartel of firms can obtain whatever price it finds optimal, of course, simply by a sufficient restriction on the quantity that will be sold. Although other factors (like the greater ease in some cases of detecting cheating on price agreements than on quantity agreements) are also involved, one reason why prices and wages are fixed more often than quantities is surely that this makes it easier to leave the decision about the allocation of the costs to the market or to other impartial forces. At times, outside or impartial mechanisms will work in ways that are very harmful to dominant interests in the distributional coalition, and they then may be abandoned. If under a seniority rule, for example, a substantial majority of the workers would be laid off, there would naturally be pressure for job sharing, wage reductions, or other alternatives. In still other cases, entry restriction would be feasible but price-fixing would not be; there would be more resistance to increases in physicians' charges than to an increase in the qualifications demanded of entering physicians, even though these two measures would have similar effects.

After taking the time needed to arrive at their own decisions, cartels and lobbies sometimes then need more time to deal with their partners and antagonists. A labor union, for example, has to bargain with the employer as well as decide on its own policy. The lobbying organization must, besides agreeing on its own policies, go through the compromises and procedures needed to change government policy. All this makes decision-making still slower.

The combination of all the factors slowing decisions and the special-interest groups' typical preference for price-fixing rather than quantity-fixing results in relatively sticky or inflexible prices and wages in sectors where special-interest organization or collusion is important. If special-interest organizations usually specified the quantity that is made available, the prices and wages would vary with market conditions and the quantity sold would be given in the intervals between decisions. When they specify the price or wage, it remains unchanged over the intervals between decisions and the quantity then varies.

The foregoing considerations taken together provide the sixth implication:

> 6. *Distributional coalitions make decisions more slowly than the individuals and firms of which they are comprised, tend to have crowded agendas and bargaining tables, and more often fix prices than quantities.*

VII

If the environment in which the special-interest organization operates never changes, then the slow decision-making does not make much difference; once an optimal policy for the coalition is chosen, it will serve indefinitely. But the economic situation is changing all the time. Nowadays the most important source of change is perhaps the advance of scientific knowledge. The opportunities open even to the least dynamic economies in modern times are constantly changing, since they have access to a stream of innovations from abroad and from basic scientific discoveries. There are also changes in consumer tastes, resource discoveries, and even changes in the weather, to which an economy must adapt if it is to maintain its efficiency and exploit the opportunities for growth.

The environment in which special-interest groups operate also changes because of the incentives to innovate that face the firms in the economy, and particularly those firms in sectors that are not affected by cartels or lobbies. However, we cannot go very far into the incentives facing firms in the absence of special-interest groups without getting into old material that would already be familiar to economists, at least. An analysis of the incentives facing firms (or consumers) in the absence of special-interest groups would take us into the theory of unconstrained markets, which, as we know, is more than two hundred years old. And if such an analysis were to be complete, it would require a book far longer than this one. So I shall include only a few casual, impressionistic paragraphs on the effect of the incentives in unconstrained markets and how this in turn helps to change the environment in which special-interest groups operate. These paragraphs will focus on those respects in which my perspective on unconstrained markets differs a little from that of most other economists.

In this book, I do not assume there is perfect competition, even in the absence of special-interest groups. There are, of course, some purely competitive markets, particularly in agriculture. The perfectly competitive model admittedly also has a remarkable "robustness" (or capacity to generate valid predictions in many cases even when some of its assumptions are not satisfied). Nonetheless, the assumption here is that in most markets firms can choose the price at which they will sell their outputs, and that the quantity they sell will vary inversely with the price they charge—that is, that there are normally elements of monopoly power. This assumption is in accord with everyday observation of most firms and is also, unlike any straightforward model of perfect competition, consistent with a firm's decision to advertise. My argument, accordingly, does not imply that a market system in the absence of special-interest organization and collusion is ideally (Pareto) efficient. Neither does it assume the market system is static, as do most formal perfectly competitive and general-equilibrium models.

The assumption that drives the argument about unconstrained markets in this book is that, in the absence of cartelization or government intervention due to lobbies or other causes, there is normally no barrier to entry into any industry or line of economic activity and also no barrier to imitation of any profitable pattern of activity. This assumption is staggeringly powerful. If there are more than normal profits or returns of any kind in an industry or line of activity, there will be an incentive to enter that line of activity, and that incentive will remain until enough resources have moved into the area that profits are no longer above normal. In no area, in the absence of institutions such as those that this book examines, can abnormal profits or returns be secure in the long run. Free entry also entails that no firm has any shelter from a Darwinian struggle for survival, so none can remain lethargic or inefficient and survive. Free entry eventually eliminates all shelter and monopoly profits, but it need not bring about perfect competition (product differentiation may remain) nor does it ensure perfect (Pareto) efficiency. But the absence of barriers to entry and imitation does ensure that any product or service that generates abnormal profits will invite entry or imitation, so that there will be at least close substitutes for this good or service, and with close substitutes the degree of monopoly (the extent to which the demand curve is less than infinitely elastic) and the extent of any inefficiency in resource allocation will be limited.

It is sometimes supposed that the amount of capital needed to enter the industries in which there are giant companies is so great that these firms are protected against entry. This overlooks the desire for profits of other giant firms (and the imperial aspirations of some of their managers); these firms have the access to capital needed to enter any industry, and the prevalence of multiproduct and even conglomerate firms owes something to this willingness to enter industries with supranormal profits. In some smaller and medium-sized countries, especially less developed ones, it is said that there are only a few firms with the resources to enter certain industries, so entry is then not likely. But this argument depends on the tariffs and restrictions on foreign firms that organizations and domestic firms have normally obtained. In the absence of these restrictions there would be entry into areas of excessive profit by multinational firms. There are some markets in which the demand is small in relation to the scale at which a firm in that market must operate to be efficient, so that the industry can accommodate only a few firms, or even (as in the "natural monopoly" case) only one firm. But these markets are the exception rather than the rule, and (contrary to what economists used to believe) there is also the danger of entry in these markets;* they are also "contestable," to use an apt term borrowed from William Baumol et al.[18]

---

*In other words, even if only one or two firms can survive in the industry and these one or two could earn supranormal profits if assured there would be no entry, it does not follow that there will be no entry. If the established firm or firms make abnormal profits or become slack through lack of competition, another firm may still have an incentive to enter the industry; the entrant in this case must replace an existing firm, since the industry will not support them all, and this means increased risk for the entrant. But the established firm or firms in the industry also know that any entrant could lead to their own demise and are well advised to keep this in mind before seeking conspicuously large profits or letting their firm become lethargic. A few economists, perhaps too anxious to show the virtues of laissez faire, assume that there never can be abnormal profits even in the natural monopoly; but this goes too far, at least in cases where a great deal of fixed capital is needed to produce the good in question, because, among other reasons, the established firm might even build a plant of a size designed to discourage entry, rather than one that would maximize profits in the absence of entry.[19] The safer conclusion is that, in the absence of distributional coalitions, abnormal profits will eventually induce entry in the overwhelming majority of markets, and that even in markets that can support only one or two firms the existing firms are constrained to a significant extent by the possibility of entry.[20]

In the short run, and sometimes in the not-so-short run, there are often supranormal (and sometimes even colossal) rates of profit for some firms even with free entry. The reason is that it can take some time before the opportunity to get supranormal profits by entry or imitation is noticed, and still more time to learn the tricks of a new line of activity and to purchase or construct the capital needed for it. This is a matter that needs more research, but my judgment of the evidence is that temporarily supranormal profits (sometimes accompanied by high, if temporary, degrees of monopoly power) are very common indeed, so common that some readers may question the importance of the free entry condition. But what gives rise to these temporary profits? Most notably, innovations of one kind or another—discoveries of new technologies, previously unsatisfied demands of consumers, lower-cost methods of production, and so on. And the greater the extent of the profits due to difficulties of entry and imitation, the greater the reward to the innovations that mainly explain economic growth and progress!* Indeed, the rate of economic growth that can result from these incentives to innovate in an unconstrained economy is sometimes so rapid that, as I have argued in other publications,[21] there may be certain costs of social disruption. That is, however, a separate and complicated matter that will not substantially alter any conclusions in this book, so I will not go into it here.

VIII

It is at this point essential to remind ourselves that there are some factors that, in contrast to the incentives to innovate that have just been discussed, can affect the efficiency of an economy but *not* its rate of

---

*This account of the reward to innovation owes a great deal to the now-standard Schumpeterian analysis of innovation and entrepreneurship, but it differs in one respect. The Schumpeterian analysis emphasized that temporary monopoly was the reward to the entrepreneurs who introduced successful innovations. The rewards due to the delays in entry and imitation that are emphasized may, but need not, entail monopoly. Suppose that a farmer or a firm in any purely competitive industry discovers a new method of production that is significantly less expensive than any previously known, but suppose also that increasing costs, as the scale of the enterprise increases, ensure that the innovator will not take over the industry. The innovative firm then has no monopoly power—no capacity to influence the price of what it sells—but until others can successfully imitate the innovation it has supranormal profits. So it is disequilibrium rather than monopoly itself that is emphasized here as the reward to innovation.

growth. This seems counterintuitive to some people, so it will be necessary to compare two hypothetical economies that are identical in all but one respect. Suppose that the first of these economies had no distributional coalitions, but that the second had a large number that had obtained a larger share of that economy's output for their constituents by methods that greatly reduced that output. If the distributional coalitions reduced the second economy's output by a constant proportion in each period, this economy would have a lower per capita income but need *not* have a lower rate of growth. If special-interest groups did not interfere with the second economy's adaptation to change or its generation of new innovations, but simply kept it at all times a constant percentage below the income it would achieve without such groups, then this economy could grow just as fast as the first economy. Thus the argument that led up to our Implication 4, taken by itself, shows that special-interest groups lower the level of efficiency and per capita income, but it does not necessarily show that the rate of change of per capita income would be different. The gradual accumulation of such groups explained in Implication 2 would lower the rate of growth, but that is another matter.

In fact, as I implied in the discussion of barriers to entry, the distributional coalitions do interfere with an economy's capacity to adapt to change and to generate new innovations and therefore do reduce the rate of growth. A labor union, for example, sometimes has an incentive to repress a labor-saving innovation that would reduce the demand for the workers it represents, or to demand featherbedding or overmanning. Similarly, whenever a firm in a collusive group develops a product or productive process that its competitors cannot immediately copy, the other firms in the group have an incentive to use the collusive power to block or delay the innovation. Since a major technological advance will normally change the optimal policy for a cartelistic organization and the relative strength of its members, it will normally require difficult new rounds of bargaining which the special-interest organization or collusion might not survive. This in turn makes cartelistic groups cautious about innovation and change. When an industry is nationalized, regulated as a public utility, or for other reasons subject to political dictation, the pertinent lobbies may veto changes, or simply require consultation about them, and innovations and investments will take place less often and more slowly. In some cases even straightforward adaptations to new patterns of demand and the adoption of new machinery can be delayed, sometimes for generations, as the example of American railroads illustrates, so that a configuration of practices that might once have been optimal diverges ever farther from the current ideal arrangement.

The slow decision-making and crowded agendas and bargaining tables of distributional coalitions are important to understanding the delays in adapting to new technologies and other changes. If the required bargaining and consultation took place instantaneously, there might not be any delay. If a cost-saving innovation becomes available to a firm, the use of that innovation will mean that the difference between revenues and production costs will be greater, so that there is more money to divide between the firm and the workers; a sufficiently powerful union will therefore be able to get more for its members than if the firm did not adopt the innovation[22] (the firm and the union have an incentive to bargain with one another until they maximize the joint surplus, which is essentially the difference between revenues net of non-labor costs and the opportunity costs in the form of leisure and alternative employment of the workers). Of course, things do not always work out this way in practice. When there is one big innovation and no other changes to consider, there may be an agreement to use the new technology. When, as is more commonly the case, there are many changes and innovations, large and small, that must be adopted in each period to maximize efficiency, it is much less likely that there will be prompt agreement to adopt all of the efficient changes. The slowness of decision-making and the crowded agendas and bargaining tables prevent rapid adaptation, and the rational ignorance of constituents about collective action by the union makes matters worse. Whereas delays in adaptation involving labor unions are better known, the above logic applies also to lobbies and cartels of firms. Colluding firms, for example, sometimes obtain monopoly rights under public utility regulation which they are loathe to lose, even though the system of regulation and collusion is so slow-moving that there is not efficient adaptation to changing conditions. Trucking, railroads, and airlines in modern American economic history offer many examples of this.

Special-interest groups also slow growth by reducing the rate at which resources are reallocated from one activity or industry to another in response to new technologies or conditions. One obvious way in which they do so is by lobbying for bail-outs of failing firms, thereby delaying or preventing the shift of resources to areas where they would have a greater productivity. Some other policies that slow the rate of reallocation of resources are perhaps not so obvious. Consider a situation in which there is, for any reason, a large increase in the demand for labor in some industry or profession and where the labor is controlled by a single union or professional association. The cartelistic organization will be able to demand a higher rate of pay because of the shift in demand, and the new higher monopoly wage will reduce the amount of labor purchased by the booming sector and thereby reduce growth and efficiency.

Moreover, the movement of labor into the cartelized area may be restricted to a greater extent than would be supposed from the fact that there would be a rise in the monopoly wage. If there is a large upward shift in the demand for labor in the booming sector, those in the cartel may not want to supply as much extra labor as is wanted; the higher wage will increase the incentive to work, but the extra income it brings also means that the workers can afford to take more leisure, so at best there will be only a limited increase in the hours of work. Although there is a ''need'' for much more labor than those already in the cartel can provide, this need may not be met. Except for one special case,[23] adding additional members to the cartel would make the marginal product and wage of the old members lower than it would otherwise have been, so no additional members may be admitted. The movement into the booming area may, in other words, not only be constrained by the increase in the monopoly price, but even in some cases essentially limited to the amount the previous workers wish to supply.*

*An economist who neglects the effects of decision-making costs and delays might argue that there was a gain to be made from bringing extra labor into the sector and suppose that the cartel would bring in the labor to secure the gain; he might point out that, in the circumstances described, there would be a difference between the wage that suitable laborers outside the cartel would be willing to accept and the monopoly wage (marginal revenue) that the cartel could obtain from selling the outside labor to employers, so that the cartel would hire or admit additional workers, and the old members would pocket the difference between the wage paid to the newcomers and the marginal revenue obtained from selling this labor to the employers. Needless to say, this sequence is not usually observed. Decision-making costs and delays make it difficult for a cartelistic organization to buy and sell labor or to deal with different classes of membership. The cartel might let the employers hire the extra labor and pay the cartel members part of the profits obtained by doing so, but that would undercut the cartel's monopoly, so it happens only rarely, and then normally on a temporary basis. The argument that has just been put forth also makes it clear that the growth forgone because of increased monopoly prices in areas favored by rises in demand is not necessarily offset by decreased monopoly prices in the cartelized areas suffering from adverse shifts in demand.

Some economists have supposed that a given level of barriers to the reallocation of resources would reduce the level but not the rate of growth of income. In fact, as Sir John Hicks has rigorously proved in a paper that responded to an earlier version of my argument,[24] barriers to resource reallocation will in general also reduce the growth rate. Any increases in productivity in the different industries will normally change relative prices as well as income levels. There is the possibility that expenditures on each product, despite the income and price changes, might by chance be at just the level that induced all resources to remain in exactly the same employments. Unless expenditures happen to be at this special level, the increases in productivity will entail that resources must be reallocated if economic efficiency is to be maintained and the society is to take full advantage of the increases in productivity. The required resource reallocations will be prevented or delayed by the barriers to entry. Hicks has further demonstrated that the magnitude of the reduction in the growth rate will vary with the extent to which the new pattern of expenditures deviates from the old and on the size of the industries in which resources are wasted because of the changes growing out of the increases in productivity.[25] We can conclude that, even if there should be no accumulation of special-interest groups over time, the barriers to resource reallocation that such groups create would lower the rate of growth as well as the absolute level of income.

The argument that led to our fourth implication showed that, when there were lobby-induced price changes or other subsidies and no barriers to entry into the favored area, the gains to the special-interest group could be small in relation to the loss to society. We now see that when there are barriers to entry this slows the resource reallocations needed for rapid economic growth. When the slower adoption of new technologies resulting from special-interest groups is also taken into account, the reduction in growth rates can be considerable. The slower adoption of new technologies and barriers to entry can subtract many times more from the society's output than the special-interest group obtains, particularly over the long run.

So we now have the seventh implication, the dynamic or growth-oriented counterpart to the fourth implication about static efficiency:

7. *Distributional coalitions slow down a society's capacity to adopt new technologies and to reallocate resources in response to changing conditions, and thereby reduce the rate of economic growth.*

IX

At least after they reach a certain point, distributional coalitions have an incentive to be exclusive. In the case of collusive oligopolists or others that operate in the marketplace, the reason is simply that whatever quantity an entrant would sell must either drive down the price received by those already in the cartel, or alternatively force existing members to restrict their sales further.[26] When it is created, the cartel must, for reasons explained above, normally enlist all the sellers in the market if it is to succeed, but once it has done this there is a compelling incentive to exclude any entrant. Indeed, existing members even have a reason to hope that some of their number die or depart so that those who remain can each sell more at the monopoly price.[27]

If the number of physicians increases, for example, the earnings of physicians must decline if other things are equal, and in country after country one finds that the professional organizations representing physicians work to limit entry into the profession. As the high income-levels of physicians in many countries testify, these efforts often succeed. The educational credentials and qualifying examinations usually required of those who would enter the practice of medicine are, of course, explained as necessary to protect the patient against incompetence. But note that the examinations are almost always imposed only on entrants. If the limits were mainly motivated by the interest of patients, older physicians would also be required to pass periodic qualifying examinations to demonstrate that they have kept their medical knowledge up-to-date. Among lawyers and other professionals in many countries there are similar limitations on entry. In legal systems without much limitation on the initiation of litigation, however, additional lawyers can raise the demand for their colleagues by increasing the likelihood of legal disputes, and this makes control of entry less important.

In the case of those distributional coalitions that seek their objectives by political action, the reason for exclusion is that there will be more to distribute to each member of the coalition if it is a minimum winning coalition. A lobby, or even a military alliance seeking spoils, will have less to distribute to each member if it admits more members than are necessary for success. Just as a cartel must include all of the sellers, so the coalition operating politically or militarily must include enough members to win. In a world of uncertainty, the size of the minimum winning coalition may not be known in advance, in which case the coalition must, over a range, trade off lower payoffs per member against greater probabilities of success. There will nonetheless always be some point beyond which it must be in the interest of the existing members to exclude new entrants. In the terms of the dichotomy introduced in *The Logic of Collective Action,* distributionally oriented lobbies as well as cartels must be *exclusive* instead of *inclusive* groups.

A governing aristocracy or oligarchy can provide an interesting illustration of the exclusivity of special-interest groups that use political or military methods. Imagine a country or historical period in which some subset of the population, such as the nobility or the oligarchy, dominates the political system. This subset has an incentive to choose public policies that distribute more of the social output to its own members. Except in the case where the aristocracy or oligarchy would increase its security if new members (for example, powerful rivals) were added, it will be exclusive: every unnecessary entrant into the favored subset reduces what is left for the rest. The relevance of this argument is evident from the exclusiveness of governing nobilities throughout history. Any number of devices and emblems have been used to mark off ruling aristocracies from the rest of the population with the utmost clarity. The exclusivity is perhaps most dramatically evident when a ruling group is secure enough to pass its powers on to its descendants. In these cases there is, of course, great resistance to admitting anyone other than the children of the nobility or ruling group into the ruling group. Such exclusivity is so general that some people think of it as only ''natural,'' and find *any* explanation of it unsatisfying.

Let us nonetheless ask what institutions for marriage or child-rearing we would expect to emerge. If the sons and daughters of the ruling group marry outsiders, and both the sons and daughters and the spouses of these sons and daughters are in the ruling group in the next generation, the ruling nobility will tend to double in size in the next generation. In the next generation there will then tend to be half as much for each member. One possible solution is to allow only descendants of one sex and their families to be in the ruling class in the next generation, and probably some discriminatory rules against women in certain societies are explained in this way. But those members of the ruling group that have only or mainly daughters have reason to oppose such rules; even apart from natural concern about their daughters, they would lose their share of the future receipts of their ruling group. So how can all families in the ruling group bequeath their share of the group's entitlement to descendants without making the value of a share in the entitlement decline by half or more with each successive generation?

They can do this through rules or social pressures that enforce endogamy: if the sons and daughters of the ruling group are induced to marry one another, the growth of the ruling group can be constrained in ways that preserve a legacy for all the families in it. Again, the evidence that nobilities and aristocracies have resisted marriages to commoners and lower ranks generally is abundant, and from many diverse societies. In a similar spirit, the abhorrence in earlier times of royalty marrying commoners can be understood as a rule that helped to limit the losses that a multinational class such as European royalty would have suffered had their numbers expanded exponentially.

Of course, there are other factors that can encourage endogamy and one must be careful not to push the foregoing argument too far.[28] Yet later parts of this book do, I think, strongly suggest that we cannot ignore the logic that has just been set forth. We cannot conclude that endogamy is simply the result of general difficulties of marriages and other close social relationships among people of different backgrounds—that the nobility marry nobility and royalty marry royalty because they would not know how to get along with others. The disproportionate intermarriage within social groups of all kinds suggests there is something in this—that very often nobility would have married nobility, and so forth, even in the absence of any rules or mores that suggested that this was expected. But it still does not adequately explain legal or social condemnation of marriages of royalty and nobility to commoners; if the arrangement was uncomfortable for the couple, we still need to explain why *others* were so concerned. The rule of thumb that, in most cases, a person will be better off if married to someone of a similar background is not what is at issue. The mother from a family of average means who advises her daughter to marry within their social group does not usually want the daughter to discriminate against millionaires. Whatever might work out best in most cases, the individual has an interest in being able to follow the rule or not as circumstances dictate. Thus it is comprehensible that some noble families short on money should violate the mores of their group by marrying daughters of rich merchants. What needs explanation are legal and social rules that say a marriage outside the ruling group is to be condemned *by others* as a violation of *principle*. Such rules must be explained, as they are here, at least partly in terms of the interest of the group. Whatever may be the reaction to the possibly uncomfortable illustration that has been offered, the logic behind exclusion in distributional coalitions remains clear. Both in cartels and in special-interest organizations focused on the polity there are the further considerations mentioned in the last chapter. Collective action will be easier if the group is socially interactive, so there are social selective incentives. The fact that everyone in the relevant group gets a uniform amount and type of the collective good and must put up with the same group policies also argues that groups of similar incomes and values are more likely to agree. Thus our eighth implication:

8. *Distributional coalitions, once big enough to succeed, are exclusive and seek to limit the diversity of incomes and values of their membership.*

X

To achieve their objectives, distributional coalitions must use their lobbying power to influence governmental policy or their collusive power to influence the market. These two influences affect not only efficiency, economic growth, and exclusion of entrants in a society, but also the relative importance of different institutions and activities. Lobbying increases the complexity of regulation and the scope of government, and collusion and organizational activity in markets increase the extent of bargaining and what I call *complex understandings.* An increase in the payoffs from lobbying and cartel activity, as compared with the payoffs from production, means more resources are devoted to politics and cartel activity and fewer resources are devoted to production. This in turn influences the attitudes and culture that evolve in the society.

Lobbying increases the complexity of regulation and the scope of government by creating special provisions and exceptions. A lobby that wins a tax reduction for income of a certain source or type makes the tax code longer and more complicated; a lobby that gets a tariff increase for the producers of a particular commodity makes trade regulation more complex than if there were a uniform tariff on all imports and much more complex than it would be with no tariff at all. The limited incentive the typical citizen has to monitor public policy also implies that lobbies for special interests can sometimes succeed where matters are detailed or complex but not when they are general and simple, and this increases complexity still further.

The regulatory complexity that derives from lobbies is magnified by a dynamic process that Charles Schultze has described.[29] When regulations are established through lobbying or other measures, there is an incentive for ingenious lawyers and others to find ways of getting around the regulations or ways of profiting from them in unexpected ways. The interests behind the regulations and the officials who administer the regulations will often amend or extend the regulation to close the loophole and prevent the unexpected use of the regulation, but this will make the regulation still more complex. It does not, of course, follow that the more complex regulations cannot also be exploited. Indeed, the possibility of evasion and unintended consequences may sometimes even increase as the regulations become more complicated. So, as Schultze pointed out, there can be an unending process of loophole discoveries and closures with the complexity and cost of regulation continually increasing.

The more elaborate the regulation, the greater the need for specialists to deal with these regulations, such as lawyers, accountants, or other consultants on this or that aspect of governmental relations. When these specialists become significant enough, there is even the possibility that the specialists with a vested interest in the complex regulations will collude or lobby against simplification or elimination of the regulation. As the general argument here emphasizes, there is nothing easy, prompt, or automatic about the emergence of lobbies, but sometimes they will in time emerge. When lobbies of this kind emerge, the effects they have are aptly illustrated by the successful opposition of trial lawyers in many American states to "no-fault" automobile insurance laws that would greatly reduce the extent of litigation about automobile accidents. In the political system in the United States, at least, there is a sense in which even legislators can come to have a vested interest in the complexity of regulations, as Morris Fiorina and Roger Noll pointed out.[30] Congressmen and senators can gain exceptional support by helping constituents to obtain particular services or exceptions from the government, since the legislator is obviously linked more closely with these favors than with general legislation that can pass only if many legislators voted affirmatively. For this reason, Fiorina and Noll have argued, legislators seek more bureaucratic or manipulatable legislation that further increases the importance of the constituent services that help them to be re-elected. Interestingly, the proportion of incumbents getting re-elected has increased over time. I recall, in support of the Fiorina–Noll hypothesis, that when I was an official in the U.S. Department of Health, Education and Welfare, then-President Lyndon Johnson placed a general moratorium on a class of construction projects particularly favored by the Congress, allegedly in an attempt to pressure the Congress into supporting administration legislation. According to reports I heard, congressmen often privately were pleased with the moratorium, apparently because those exceptions to it that they were able to obtain brought them substantial credit with constituents.

Someone has to administer the increasingly complex regulations that result from the lobbying and the related processes that have been described. This increases the scale of bureaucracy and government. Lobbying obviously also adds in another way to the scope of government when it leads to government expenditures and programs to serve special-interest groups. Although lobbying on the whole undoubtedly tends to increase the extent of government activity, it would probably be claiming too much for the present argument to attribute most of the increase in the role of government around the world in the last generation or so to the growth of special-interest groups. The interwar depression, World War II, and other developments led to profound ideological changes that increased the scope of government, and developments like the cold war and pollution, to mention only two, also increased the demands upon governments. A great many factors have to be taken into account to explain the growth of government, and all that is asserted here is that the accumulation of special-interest organizations is one of these factors.

The increase of collusion and cartelistic organization similarly increases the amount of bargaining and organizational activity in the marketplace. There must be transactions between buyers and sellers in any market, but cartelization, as was argued earlier, also requires either a demanding type of bargaining or constitutional procedures for associational politics. The cartelistic organizations and collusions must sometimes also bargain with each other, as happens when there are negotiations between organizations of employers and labor unions. Given the slow decision-making, crowded agendas, and cluttered bargaining tables, it takes some time before negotiators agree on anything. But once agreements are reached, the same considerations suggest that they should not be changed without compelling reason. Thus, in time, work rules, customary market shares, or established ways of doing things emerge that cannot easily be changed. As time goes on, these arrangements often become rather complex. The complexity can be codified in legal contracts, as is often the case in labor-management bargains in the United States, or embodied in a network of customs, understandings, and habits, as is commonly the case in British industrial relations and in collusive activities among oligopolistic firms. Whether the agreements or understandings are written or not, they become more elaborate over time, and this is what is meant by increasingly complex understandings. Increasing complexity of understandings implies, for example, that employers dealing with labor unions would sometimes want to move to new locations, even if they would confront other equally powerful and aggressive unions in the new situations, because they would not there be hindered by a heritage of complex and out-of-date understandings.

The growth of coalitions with an incentive to try to capture a larger share of the national income, the increase in regulatory complexity and governmental action that lobbying coalitions encourage, and the increasing bargaining and complexity of understanding that cartels create alter the pattern of incentives and the direction of evolution in a society. The incentive to produce is diminished; the incentive to seek a larger share of what is produced increases. The reward for pleasing those to whom we sell our goods or labor declines, while the reward for evading or exploiting regulations, politics, and bureaucracy and for asserting our rights through bargaining or the complex understandings becomes greater.

These changes in the patterns of incentives in turn deflect the direction of a society's evolution. Some observers might suppose that the accumulation of distributional coalitions would make societies evolve in ways that favor the less talented, the weak, and the poor, but this is wrong. In every environment, those who are best fitted for that environment are most likely to thrive, survive, and multiply. There is evolution in the zoo as there is in the jungle, as those animals that are able to adapt to cages and keepers outlast those that cannot. So also with cultural evolution and evolution in human societies. Every society, whatever its institutions and governing ideology, gives greater rewards to the fittest—the fittest for *that* society. What it takes to be favored varies from society to society, but no society rewards those who are least fit to thrive under its arrangements.

If a society mainly rewards production or the capacity to satisfy those with whom one engages in free exchange, it stimulates the development of productive traits. It does this particularly through cultural or Lamarckian evolution, whereby learned or acquired behavior can be passed on to descendants. If the accumulation of distributional coalitions increases the incentive for distributional struggle, augments regulatory complexity, encourages the dominance of politics, stimulates bargaining, and increases the complexity of understandings, this encourages the development of different attitudes and attributes. What we loosely call intelligence, or aptitude for education, will probably be favored as much as or more than before because the articulate and educated have a comparative advantage in regulation, politics, and complex understandings. This, in turn, probably limits the extent to which intellectuals oppose their elaboration.

The competition is not any gentler because it takes a different form. The gang fight is fully as rough as the individual duel, and the struggle of special-interest groups generates no magnanimity or altruism. Competition about the division of income is not any nicer than competition to produce or to please customers. The new competition is, in part, less individualistic, so in certain areas the rewards to individual effort are diminished and the relative attractiveness of leisure enhanced. But the weaker groups still suffer. The poor and the unemployed have no selective incentives to enable them to organize, whereas small groups of great firms or wealthy individuals can organize with relative ease. Thus life is not any gentler because of special-interest groups, but it is less productive, especially in the long run.

So, with thanks to the reader for patiently waiting until the next chapter before getting to the main practical applications of the argument, we come finally to the ninth and last implication.

9. *The accumulation of distributional coalitions increases the complexity of regulation, the role of government, and the complexity of understandings, and changes the direction of social evolution.*

To make later reference to them more convenient, all of the implications are listed on the next page.

Implications

1. There will be no countries that attain symmetrical organization of all groups with a common interest and thereby attain optimal outcomes through comprehensive bargaining.

2. Stable societies with unchanged boundaries tend to accumulate more collusions and organizations for collective action over time.

3. Members of "small" groups have disproportionate organizational power for collective action, and this disproportion diminishes but does not disappear over time in stable societies.

4. On balance, special-interest organizations and collusions reduce efficiency and aggregate income in the societies in which they operate and make political life more divisive.

5. Encompassing organizations have some incentive to make the society in which they operate more prosperous, and an incentive to redistribute income to their members with as little excess burden as possible, and to cease such redistribution unless the amount redistributed is substantial in relation to the social cost of the redistribution.

6. Distributional coalitions make decisions more slowly than the individuals and firms of which they are comprised, tend to have crowded agendas and bargaining tables, and more often fix prices than quantities.

7. Distributional coalitions slow down a society's capacity to adopt new technologies and to reallocate resources in response to changing conditions, and thereby reduce the rate of economic growth.

8. Distributional coalitions, once big enough to succeed, are exclusive, and seek to limit the diversity of incomes and values of their membership.

9. The accumulation of distributional coalitions increases the complexity of regulation, the role of government, and the complexity of understandings, and changes the direction of social evolution.

The Developed Democracies
Since World War II

4

In the preceding chapters I have argued, among other things, that associations to provide collective goods are for the most fundamental reasons difficult to establish, and that therefore even those groups that are in situations where there is a potential for organization usually will be able to organize only in favorable circumstances. As time goes on, more groups will have enjoyed favorable circumstances and overcome difficulties of collective action. The interest of organizational leaders insures that few organizations for collective action in stable societies will dissolve, so these societies accumulate special-interest organizations and collusions over time (Implication 2). These organizations, at least if they are small in relation to the society, have little incentive to make their societies more productive, but they have powerful incentives to seek a larger share of the national income even when this greatly reduces social output (Implication 4). The barriers to entry established by these distributional coalitions and their slowness in making decisions and mutually efficient bargains reduces an economy's dynamism and rate of growth (Implication 7). Distributional coalitions also increase regulation, bureaucracy, and political intervention in markets (Implication 9).

If the argument so far is correct, it follows that countries whose distributional coalitions have been emasculated or abolished by totalitarian government or foreign occupation should grow relatively quickly after a free and stable legal order is established. This can explain the postwar ''economic miracles'' in the nations that were defeated in World War II, particularly those in Japan and West Germany. The everyday use of the word *miracle* to describe the rapid economic growth in these countries testifies that this growth was not only unexpected, but also outside the range of known laws and experience. In Japan and West Germany, totalitarian governments were followed by Allied occupiers determined to promote institutional change and to ensure that institutional life would start almost anew. In Germany, Hitler had done away with independent unions as well as all other dissenting groups, whereas the Allies, through measures such as the decartelization decrees of 1947 and denazification programs, had emasculated cartels and organizations with right-wing backgrounds.[1] In Japan, the militaristic regime had kept down left-wing organizations, and the Supreme Commander of the Allied Powers imposed the antimonopoly law of 1947 and purged many hundreds of officers of zaibatsu and other organizations for their wartime activities.[2] (In Italy, the institutional destruction from totalitarianism, war, and Allied occupation was less severe and the postwar growth "miracle" correspondingly shorter, but this case is more complex and will be discussed separately.)* The theory here predicts that with continued stability the Germans and Japanese will accumulate more distributional coalitions, which will have an adverse influence on their growth rates.

Moreover, the special-interest organizations established after World War II in Germany and Japan were, for the most part, highly encompassing. This is true of the postwar labor union structure of West Germany, for example, and of the business organization, Keidanren, that has played a dominant role in economic policymaking in Japan. The high growth rates of these two countries also owe something to the relatively encompassing character of some of the special-interest organizations they did have (and this organizational inclusiveness in turn was sometimes due to promotion by occupation authorities).[3] At least in the first two decades after the war, the Japanese and West Germans had not developed the degree of regulatory complexity and scale of government that characterized more stable societies.

The theory also offers a new perspective on French growth experience.[4] Why has France had relatively good growth performance for much of the postwar period (achieving by about 1970 levels of income

---

*In Italy the evolution of political competition since World War II appears to have resulted in progressively weaker governments and less stable governing coalitions. Thus, apart from the growing strength of distributional coalitions, the *ratio* of the strength of these coalitions to that of the government appears to have increased. Another element of the Italian postwar experience is mentioned in the next chapter.

broadly comparable with other advanced countries) when its investment climate has often been so inclement? The foreign invasions and political instability that have hindered capital accumulation have also disrupted the development of special-interest organizations and collusions. The divisions in French ideological life must have deepened as one upheaval after another called into question the country's basic political and economic system. The intensity of these ideological divisions must have further impaired the development of at least the larger special-interest organizations in that country. Most notably, the development of French labor unions has been set back by periods of repression and disruption and by ideological fissures that divide the French labor movement into competing communist, socialist, and catholic unions. The competition among these semideveloped unions, often in the same workplaces, in most cases prevents any union from having an effective monopoly of the relevant work force. French unions accordingly have only a limited capacity to determine work rules or wage levels (or to make union membership compulsory, with the result that most French union members do not pay dues). Smaller groups such as trade associations and the alumni of prestigious schools (as Implication 3 predicts) have been better able to organize. But their effects on growth rates in the last two decades have been limited by considerations discussed in the next chapter, which will develop another reason why the French economy has performed better in the 1960s than its troubled history would lead us to expect.[5] The foregoing argument about France has some applicability to other continental countries as well.

II

The logic of the argument implies that countries that have had democratic freedom of organization without upheaval or invasion the longest will suffer the most from growth-repressing organizations and combinations. This helps to explain why Great Britain, the major nation with the longest immunity from dictatorship, invasion, and revolution, has had in this century a lower rate of growth than other large, developed democracies. Britain has precisely the powerful network of special-interest organizations that the argument developed here would lead us to expect in a country with its record of military security and democratic stability. The number and power of its trade unions need no description. The venerability and power of its professional associations is also striking. Consider the distinction between solicitors and barristers, which could not possibly have emerged in a free market innocent of professional associations or government regulations of the sort they often obtain; solicitors in Britain have a legal monopoly in assisting individuals making conveyances of real estate and barristers a monopoly of the right to serve as counsel in the more important court cases. Britain also has a strong farmers' organization and a great many trade associations. In short, with age British society has acquired so many strong organizations and collusions that it suffers from an institutional sclerosis that slows its adaptation to changing circumstances and technologies.

Admittedly, lobbying in Britain is not as blatant as in the United States, but it is pervasive and often involves discreet efforts to influence civil servants as well as ministers and other politicians. Moreover, the word *establishment* acquired its modern meaning there and, however often that word may be overused, it still suggests a substantial degree of informal organization that could emerge only gradually in a stable society. Many of the powerful special-interest organizations in Britain are, in addition, narrow rather than encompassing. For example, in a single factory there are often many different trade unions, each with a monopoly over a different craft or category of workers, and no one union encompasses a substantial fraction of the working population of the country. Britain is also often used as an example of ungovernability. In view of the long and illustrious tradition of democracy in Britain and the renowned orderliness of the British people, this is remarkable, but it is what the theory here predicts.

This explanation of Britain's relatively slow postwar growth, unlike many other explanations, is consistent with the fact that for nearly a century, from just after the middle of the eighteenth century until nearly the middle of the nineteenth, Britain was evidently the country with the *fastest* rate of economic growth. Indeed, during their Industrial Revolution the British invented modern economic growth. This means that no explanation of Britain's relatively slow growth in recent times that revolves around some supposedly inherent or permanent feature of British character or society can possibly be correct, because it is contradicted by Britain's long period with the fastest economic growth. Any valid explanation of Britain's relatively slow growth now must also take into account the *gradual* emergence of the "British disease." Britain began to fall behind in relative growth rates in the last decades of the nineteenth century,[6] and this problem has become especially notable since World War II. Most other explanations of Britain's relatively slow growth in recent times do not imply a temporal pattern that is consistent with Britain's historical experience with dramatically different relative growth rates,[7] but the theory offered here, with its emphasis on the gradual accumulation of distributional coalitions (Implication 2), does.

III

There cannot be much doubt that totalitarianism, instability, and war reduced special-interest organizations in Germany, Japan, and France, and that stability and the absence of invasion allowed continued development of such organizations in the United Kingdom. My colleague Peter Murrell systematically recorded the dates of formation of those associations recorded in *Internationales Verzeichnis der Wirtschaftsverbande*.[8] This is, to be sure, an incomplete source, and is perhaps flawed also in other ways, but it was published in 1973 and thus cannot have been the result of any favoritism toward the present argument. Murrell found from this source that whereas 51 percent of the associations existing in 1971 in the United Kingdom were founded before 1939, only 37 percent of the French, 24 percent of the West German, and 19 percent of the Japanese associations were. Naturally, Britain also had a smaller proportion of its interest groups founded after 1949—29 percent, contrasted with 45 percent for France and 52 percent for Germany and for Japan. Britain also has a much larger number of associations than France, Germany, or Japan, and is exceeded in this category only by the far larger United States. Of course, we ought to have indexes that weight each organization by its strength and its membership, but I know of none.

Murrell also worked out an ingenious set of tests of the hypothesis that the special-interest groups in Britain reduced that country's rate of growth in comparison with West Germany's. If the special-interest groups were in fact causally connected with Britain's slower growth, Murrell reasoned, this should put old British industries at a particular disadvantage in comparison with their West German counterparts, whereas in new industries where there may not yet have been time enough for special-interest organizations to emerge in either country, British and West German performance should be more nearly comparable. Thus, Murrell argued, the *ratio* of the rate of growth of new British industry to old British industry should be higher than the corresponding *ratio* for West Germany. There are formidable difficulties of definition and measurement, and alternative definitions and measures had to be used. Taking all of these results together, it is clear that they support the hypothesis that new British industries did relatively better in relation to old British industries than new German industries did in relation to old German industries. In most cases the results almost certainly could not have been due to chance, that is, they were statistically significant. Moreover, Murrell found that in heavy industry, where both industrial concentration and unionization are usually greater than in light industry, the results were strongest, which also supports the theory.[9]

IV

Of the many alternative explanations, most are ad hoc. Some economists have attributed the speed of the recoveries of the vanquished countries to the importance of human capital compared with the physical capital destroyed by bombardment, but this cannot be a sufficient explanation, since the war killed many of the youngest and best-trained adults and interrupted education and work experience for many others. Knowledge of productive techniques, however, had not been destroyed by the war, and to the extent that the defeated nations were at a lower-than-prewar level of income and needed to replace destroyed buildings or equipment, they would tend to have an above-average growth rate. But this cannot explain why these economies grew more rapidly than others after they had reached their prewar level of income and even after they had surpassed the British level of per capita income.[10]

Another commonplace ad hoc explanation is that the British, or perhaps only those in the working classes, do not work as hard as people in other countries. Others lay the unusually rapid growth of Germany and Japan to the special industriousness of their peoples. Taken literally, this type of explanation is unquestionably unsatisfactory. The rate of economic growth is the rate of *increase* of national income, and although this logically could be due to an *increase* in the industriousness of a people, it could not, in the direct and simple way implied in the familiar argument, be explained by their normal level of effort, which is relevant instead to their *absolute* level of income. Admittedly, when the industriousness of those who innovate is considered, or when possible connections between level of effort and the amount of saving are taken into account,[11] there could be some connection between industriousness and growth. But even if the differences in willingness to work are part of the explanation, why are those in the fast-growing countries zealous and those in the slow-growing countries lazy? And since many countries have changed relative position in the race for higher growth rates, the timing of the waves of effort also needs explaining. If industriousness is the explanation, why were the British so hard-working during the Industrial Revolution? And by this work-effort theory the Germans evidently must have been lazy in the first half of the nineteenth century when they were relatively poor, and the impoverished Japanese quite lethargic when Admiral Perry arrived.

One plausible possibility is that industriousness varies with the incentive to work to which individuals in different countries have become accustomed. These incentives, in turn, are strikingly influenced, whether for manual workers, professionals, or entrepreneurs, by the extent to which special-interest groups reduce the rewards to productive work and thus increase the relative attractiveness of leisure. The search for the causes of differences in the willingness to work, and in particular the question of why shirking should be thought to be present during Britain's period of slower-than-average growth but not when it had the fastest rate of growth, brings us to economic institutions and policies, and to the more fundamental explanation of differences in growth rates being offered in this book.

V

Some observers endeavor to explain the anomalous growth rates in terms of alleged national economic ideologies and the extent of government involvement in economic life. The "British disease" especially is attributed to the unusually large role that the British government has allegedly played in economic life. There is certainly no difficulty in finding examples of harmful economic intervention in postwar Britain. Nonetheless, as Samuel Brittan has convincingly demonstrated in an article in the *Journal of Law and Economics*,[12] this explanation is unsatisfactory. First, it is by no means clear that the government's role in economic life has been significantly larger than in the average developed democracy; in the proportion of gross domestic product accounted for by government spending, the United Kingdom has been at the middle, rather than at the top, of the league, and it has been also in about the middle, at roughly the same levels as Germany and France, in the percentage of income taken in taxes and social insurance.[13] Perhaps in certain respects or certain years the case that the British government was unusually interventionist can be sustained, but there is no escaping Brittan's second point: that the relatively slow British growth rate goes back about a hundred years, to a period when governmental economic activity was very limited (especially, we might add, in Great Britain).

Some economists have argued that when we look at the developed democracies as a group, we seem to see a negative correlation between the size of government and the rate of growth.[14] This more general approach is much superior to the ad hoc style of explanation, so statistical tests along these lines must be welcomed. But the results so far are weak, showing at best only a tenuous and uncertain connection between larger governments and slower growth, with such strength as this relationship possesses due in good part to Japan, which has had both the fastest growth rate and the smallest government of the major developed democracies. A weak or moderate negative relationship between the relative role of government and the rate of growth is predicted by Implication 9.

VI

One well-known ad hoc explanation of the slow British growth focuses on a class consciousness that allegedly reduces social mobility, fosters exclusive and traditionalist attitudes that discourage entrants and innovators, and maintains medieval prejudices against commercial pursuits. Since Britain had the fastest rate of growth in the world for nearly a century, we know that its slow growth now cannot be due to any *inherent* traits of the British character. There is, in fact, some evidence that at the time of the Industrial Revolution Britain did not have the reputation for class differences that it has now. It is a commonplace among economic historians of the Industrial Revolution that at that time Britain, in relation to comparable parts of the Continent, had unusual social mobility, relatively little class consciousness, and a concern in all social classes about commerce, production, and financial gain that was sometimes notorious to its neighbors:

> More than any other in Europe, probably, British society was open. Not only was income more evenly distributed than across the

Channel, but the barriers to mobility were lower, the definitions of status looser. . . .

It seems clear that British commerce of the eighteenth century was, by comparison with that of the Continent, impressively energetic, pushful, and open to innovation. . . . No state was more responsive to the desires of its mercantile classes. . . . Nowhere did entrepreneurial decisions less reflect non-rational considerations of prestige and habit. . . . Talent was readier to go into business, projecting, and invention. . . .

This was a people fascinated by wealth and commerce, collectively and individually. . . . Business interests promoted a degree of intercourse between people of different stations and walks of life that had no parallel on the Continent.

The flow of entrepreneurship within business was freer, the allocation of resources more responsive than in other economies. Where the traditional sacro-sanctity of occupational exclusiveness continued to prevail across the Channel . . . the British cobbler would not stick to his last nor the merchant to his trade. . . .

Far more than in Britain, continental business enterprise was a class activity, recruiting practitioners from a group limited by custom and law. In France, commercial enterprise had traditionally entailed derogation from noble status.[15]

It is not surprising that Napoleon once derided Britain as a "nation of shopkeepers" and that even Adam Smith found it expedient to use this phrase in his criticism of Britain's mercantilistic policies.[16]

The ubiquitous observations suggesting that the Continent's class structures have by now become in some respects more flexible than Britain's would hint that we should look for processes that might have broken down class barriers more rapidly on the Continent than in Great Britain, or for processes that might have raised or erected more new class barriers in Britain than on the Continent, or for both.

VII

One reason that only remnants of the Continent's medieval structures remain today is that they are entirely out of congruity with the technology and ideas now common in the developed world. But there is another, more pertinent reason: revolution and occupation, Napoleonism and totalitarianism, have utterly demolished most feudal structures on the Continent and many of the cultural attitudes they sustained. The new families and firms that rose to wealth and power often were not successful in holding their gains; new instabilities curtailed the development of new organizations and collusions that could have protected them and their descendants against still newer entrants. To be sure, fragments of the Middle Ages and chunks of the great fortunes of the nineteenth century still remain on the Continent; but, like the castles crumbling in the countryside, they do not greatly hamper the work and opportunities of the average citizen.

The institutions of medieval Britain, and even the great family-oriented industrial and commercial enterprises of more recent centuries, are similarly out of accord with the twentieth century and have in part crumbled, too. But would they not have been pulverized far more finely if Britain had gone through anything like the French Revolution, if a dictator had destroyed its public schools, if it had suffered occupation by a foreign power or fallen prey to totalitarian regimes determined to destroy any organizations independent of the regime itself? The importance of the House of Lords, the established church, and the ancient colleges of Oxford and Cambridge has no doubt often been grossly exaggerated. But they are symbols of Britain's legacy from the preindustrial past or (more precisely) of the unique degree to which it has been preserved. There was extraordinary turmoil until a generation or two before the Industrial Revolution[17] (and this probably played a role in opening British society to new talent and enterprise), but since then Britain has not suffered the institutional destruction, or the forcible replacement of elites, or the decimation of social classes, that its Continental counterparts have experienced. The same stability and immunity from invasion have also made it easier for the firms and families that advanced in the Industrial Revolution and the nineteenth century to organize or collude to protect their interests.

Here the argument in this book is particularly likely to be misunderstood. This is partly because the word *class* is an extraordinarily loose, emotive, and misleadingly aggregative term that has unfortunately been reified over generations of ideological debate. There are, of course, no clearly delineated and widely separated groups such as the middle class or the working class, but rather a large number of groups of diverse situations and occupations, some of which differ greatly and some of which differ slightly if at all in income and status. Even if such a differentiated grouping as the British middle class could be precisely delineated, it would be a logical error to suppose that such a large group as the British middle class could voluntarily collude to exclude others or to achieve any common interest.[18] The theory does suggest that the unique stability of British life since the early eighteenth century must have affected social structure, social mobility, and cultural attitudes, but *not* through class conspiracies or coordinated action by any large class or group. The process is far subtler and must be studied at a less aggregative level.

We can see this process from a new perspective if we remember that concerted action usually requires selective incentives, that social pressure can often be an effective selective incentive, and that individuals of similar incomes and values are more likely to agree on what amount and type of collective good to purchase. Social incentives will not be very effective unless the group that values the collective good at issue interacts socially or is composed of subgroups that do. If the group does have its own social life, the desire for the companionship and esteem of colleagues and the fear of being slighted or even ostracized can at little cost provide a powerful incentive for concerted action. The organizational entrepreneurs who succeed in promoting special-interest groups, and the managers who maintain them, must therefore focus disproportionately on groups that already interact socially or that can be induced to do so. This means that these groups tend to have socially homogeneous memberships and that the organization will have an interest in using some of its resources to preserve this homogeneity. The fact that everyone in the pertinent group gets the same amount and type of a collective good also means, as we know from the theories of fiscal equivalence and optimal segregation,[19] that there will be less conflict (and perhaps welfare gains as well) if those who are in the same jurisdiction or organization have similar incomes and values. The forces just mentioned, operating simultaneously in thousands of professions, crafts, clubs, and communities, would, by themselves, explain a degree of class consciousness. This in turn helps to generate cultural caution about the incursions of the entrepreneur and the fluctuating profits and status of businessmen, and also helps to preserve and expand aristocratic and feudal prejudices against commerce and industry. There is massive if unsystematic evidence of the effects of the foregoing processes, such as that in Martin Wiener's book on *English Culture and the Decline of the Industrial Spirit, 1850–1980.*[20]

Unfortunately, the processes that have been described do not operate by themselves; they resonate with the fact that every distributional coalition must restrict entry (Implication 8). As we know, there is no way a group can obtain more than the free market price unless it can keep outsiders from taking advantage of the higher price, and organizations designed to redistribute income through lobbying have an incentive to be minimum winning coalitions. Social barriers could not exist unless there were some groups capable of concerted action that had an interest in erecting them. We can see now that the special-interest organizations or collusions seeking advantage in either the market or the polity have precisely this interest.

In addition to controlling entry, the successful coalition must, we recall, have or generate a degree of consensus about its policies. The cartelistic coalition must also limit the output or labor of its own members; it must make all the members conform to some plan for restricting the amount sold, however much this limitation and conformity might limit innovation. As time goes on, custom and habit play a larger role. The special-interest organizations use their resources to argue that what they do is what in justice ought to be done. The more often pushy entrants and nonconforming innovators are repressed, the rarer they become, and what is not customary is "not done."

Nothing about this process should make it work differently at different levels of income or social status. As Josiah Tucker remarked in the eighteenth century, "All men would be monopolists if they could." This process may, however, proceed more rapidly in the professions, where public concern about unscrupulous or incompetent practitioners provides an ideal cover for policies that would in other contexts be described as monopoly or "greedy unionism."[21] The process takes place among the workers as well as the lords; some of the first craft unions were in fact organized in pubs.

There is a temptation to conclude dramatically that this involutional process has turned a nation of shopkeepers into a land of clubs and pubs. But this facile conclusion is too simple. Countervailing factors are also at work and may have greater quantitative significance. The rapid rate of scientific and technological advance in recent times has encouraged continuing reallocations of resources and brought about considerable occupational, social, and geographical mobility even in relatively sclerotic societies.[22]

In addition, there is another aspect of the process by which social status is transmitted to descendants that is relatively independent of the present theory. Prosperous and well-educated parents usually are able through education and upbringing to provide larger legacies of human as well as tangible capital to their children than are deprived families. Although apparently the children of high-ranking families occasionally are enfeebled by undemanding and overindulgent environments, or even neglected by parents obsessed with careers or personal concerns, there is every reason to suppose that, on average, the more successful families pass on the larger legacies of human and physical capital to their children. This presumably accounts for some of the modest correlation observed between the incomes and social positions of parents and those that their children eventually attain. The adoption of free public education and reasonably impartial scholarship systems in Britain in more recent times has disproportionately increased the amount of human capital passed on to children from poor families and thereby has tended to increase social mobility. Thus there are important aspects of social mobility that the theory offered in this book does not claim to explain and that can countervail those it does explain.

I must once again emphasize multiple causation and point out that there is no presumption that the process described in this book has brought *increasing* class consciousness, traditionalism, or antagonism to entrepreneurship. The contrary forces may overwhelm the involution even when no upheavals or invasions destroy the institutions that sustain it. The only hypothesis on this point that can reasonably be derived from the theory is that, of two societies that were in other respects equal, the one with the longer history of stability, security, and freedom of association would have more institutions that limit entry and innovation, that these institutions would encourage more social interaction and homogeneity among their members, and that what is said and done by these institutions would have at least some influence on what people in that society find customary and fitting.[23]

VIII

The evidence that has already been presented is sufficient to provoke some readers to ask rhetorically what the policy implications of the argument might be and to answer that a country ought to seek a revolution, or even provoke a war in which it would be defeated. Of course, this policy recommendation makes no more (or less) sense than the suggestion that one ought to welcome pestilence as a cure for overpopulation. In addition to being silly, the rhetorical recommendation obscures the true principal policy implications of the logic that has been developed here (which will be discussed later). Those readers who believe that the main policy implication of the present theory is that a nation should casually engage in revolutions or unsuccessful wars should read the remaining chapters of the book, for some of the further implications of the logic that has already been set out are sure to surprise them.

This is really too early in the argument to consider policy implications. There is much more evidence to consider. Let us proceed, as the lovely expression used by Mao Tse Tung's more pragmatic successors says, "to seek truth from facts," and to do so without the preconceptions that a prior knowledge of policy implications sometimes can generate. Let us look first at the other developed democracies that, although lacking as long a history of stability and immunity from invasion as Britain, have nonetheless enjoyed relatively long periods of stability and security—namely, Switzerland, Sweden, and the United States.

As a glance at table 1.1 reveals, Switzerland has been one of the slowest growing of the developed democracies in the postwar period; it has grown more slowly than Great Britain. Such slow growth in a long-stable country certainly is consistent with the theory. We should not, however, jump to the conclusion that Switzerland necessarily corroborates the argument I have offered, because Switzerland for some time has had a higher per capita income than most other European countries and therefore has enjoyed less "catch-up" growth. Those countries that had relatively low per capita incomes in the early postwar period presumably had more opportunities to grow than Switzerland had, so probably we should make an honorary addition to Switzerland's growth rate to obtain a fairer comparison. Even though no one knows just what size this honorary addition should be, possibly it would be large enough to classify Switzerland as having a relatively successful postwar growth performance. This is, in effect, the assumption made in "Pressure Politics and Economic Growth: Olson's Theory and the Swiss Experience" by Franz Lehner,[24] a native of Switzerland who is a professor of political science at the University of Bochum in Germany. Lehner shows that the exceptionally restrictive constitutional arrangements in Switzerland make it extremely difficult to pass new legislation. This makes it difficult for lobbies to get their way and thus greatly limits Switzerland's losses from special-interest legislation. The high per capita income that the Swiss have achieved is then, by Lehner's argument, evidence in favor of the present theory.

Since cartelistic action sometimes requires government enforcement, the Swiss constitutional limitations undoubtedly also limit the losses from cartelization. On the other hand, there can also be cartelistic action without government connivance, and so I would hypothesize that Switzerland ought to have accumulated some degree of cartelistic organization. The extraordinary Swiss reliance on guest workers from other countries for a considerable period would suggest that this cartelization mainly would not involve the unskilled or semi-skilled manual workers that are strongly unionized in some other countries, but rather business enterprises and the professions. The theory here also would predict that, by now, stable Switzerland would have acquired at least a few rigidities in its social structure. The private cartelization and some attendant class stratification should have offset to at least a slight extent some of the growth Switzerland has enjoyed from the limitations on the predations of lobbies and governmentally enforced cartels. Another consideration is that Switzerland has enjoyed not only the normal encouragement for long-run investment that stability provides but also the special gains that accrue from its history as a haven of stability and its permissive banking laws in a historically unstable and restrictive continent. Just as Las Vegas and Monaco profit more from gambling than they would if similar gambling were legal everywhere, so Switzerland has profited more from its stability and permissiveness than it would have if its neighbors had enjoyed a similar tranquility and liberalism. If there had not been capital flights and fears about the stability and economic controls of other continental countries, Switzerland would not have received so much capital or had such an impressive role in international banking. Of course, this factor must not be exaggerated; Britain has profited from being a center of international finance for much the same reasons. When all these factors, and another factor that will emerge in a later chapter, are taken into account, it is difficult to be utterly certain how the theory fares in the test against Swiss experience. The hope must be that the example of Lehner's useful study will stimulate additional expert investigations of the matter.

IX

If we also make a large enough honorary addition to Sweden's growth rate to adjust for its relatively high per capita income, that country then seems at first sight to contradict the theory. Although it industrialized late, Sweden has enjoyed freedom of organization and immunity from invasion for a long time, and it does not have the constitutional obstacles to the passage of special-interest legislation that Switzerland has. The strength and coverage of special-interest organizations in Sweden are what our model would predict. Why then did Sweden (at some times during the postwar period, at least) achieve respectable growth even though it already had a high standard of living? In particular, why (despite some severe recent reverses) has Sweden's economic performance been superior to Britain's when its special-interest organizations are also uncommonly strong? Similarly, why has neighboring Norway done as well as it has? Even though Norway's stability was interrupted briefly by Nazi occupation during World War II, it has relatively strong special-interest organizations. Does the experience of these two countries argue against our theory?

Not at all. The theory lets us see this experience from a new perspective. As we recall from chapter 3, the basic logic of the theory implies that encompassing organizations face very different incentives than do narrow special-interest organizations (Implication 5). Sufficiently encompassing or inclusive special-interest organizations will internalize much of the cost of inefficient policies and accordingly have an incentive to redistribute income to themselves with the least possible social cost, and to give some weight to economic growth and to the interests of society as a whole. Sweden's and Norway's main special-interest organizations are highly encompassing, especially in comparison with those in Great Britain and the United States, and probably are more encompassing than those in any other developed democracies. For most of the postwar period, for example, practically all unionized manual workers in each of these countries have belonged to one great labor organization. The employers' organizations are similarly inclusive. As our theory predicts, Swedish labor leaders, at least, at times have been distinguished from their counterparts in many other countries by their advocacy of various growth-increasing policies, such as subsidies to labor mobility and retraining rather than subsidies to maintain employment in unprofitable firms, and by their tolerance of market forces.[25] Organized business in Sweden and Norway has apparently sought and certainly obtained fewer tariffs than its counterparts in many other developed countries. It is even conceivable that the partial integration for part of the postwar period of the Norwegian and Swedish labor organizations with the even more encompassing labor parties (on a basis that contrasts with corresponding situations in Great Britain) has at times accentuated the incentive to protect efficiency and growth,[26] although any definite statement here must await further research.

Why Sweden and Norway have especially encompassing organizations also needs to be explained. This task will in part be left for another publication,[27] but one hypothesis follows immediately from my basic theory: smaller groups are much more likely to organize spontaneously than large ones (Implication 3). This suggests that many relatively small special-interest organizations (for example, British and American craft unions) would be a legacy of early industrialization,[28] whereas special-interest organizations that are established later, partly in emulation of the experience of countries that had previously industrialized, could be as large as their sponsors or promoters could make them.[29] The improvement over time in transportation and communication and in the skills needed for large-scale organization could also make it feasible to organize larger organizations in more recent than in earlier times. Small and relatively homogeneous societies obviously would be more likely to have organizations that are relatively encompassing in relation to the society than would large and diverse societies.

It might seem that the gains from encompassing—as compared with narrow special-interest—organizations would ensure that there would be a tendency for such organizations to merge in every society, in much the way large firms come to dominate those industries in which large-scale production is most efficient. This is not necessarily the case. When there are large economies of scale, the owners of small firms usually can get more money by selling out to or merging with a larger firm and thereby can capture some of the gains from creating a firm of a more efficient scale. The leaders of a special-interest organization, by contrast, cannot get any of the gains that might result from the mergers that could create a more encompassing organization by ''selling'' their organization; a merger is indeed even likely to result in the elimination or demotion of some of the relevant leaders. There is, accordingly, no inexorable tendency for encompassing organizations to replace narrow ones.

Inclusive special-interest organizations, however, sometimes can break apart. There are significant conflicts of interest in any large group in any society. For example, these arise among firms in different industries or situations over government policies that harm some firms while helping others, or between strategically placed or powerful groups of workers and groups of workers with less independent bargaining power when uniform wage increases (or diminished wage differentials) are sought by an encompassing union.

As the discussion of Implication 5 pointed out, the extent to which a special-interest organization is encompassing affects the incentives it faces when seeking redistributions to its clients and when deciding whether to seek improvements in the efficiency of the society; but the link between incentives and policies is not perfect. A special-interest organization's leaders may be mistaken about what policies will best serve their clients; they may not immediately see the gains their clients will obtain from more rapid economic growth, for example, or may be mistaken about what policies will achieve such growth. Since, as chapter 2 pointed out, information about collective goods is itself a collective good, the chances of mistakes about such matters are perhaps greater than they are for firms or individuals dealing with private goods. And even if most of the firms in a market make mistaken decisions, one or more may make correct ones and these will accordingly profit, expand, and be imitated, so the errors before very long will be corrected. In a society with encompassing special-interest organizations, by contrast, there are not many entities making choices, and these may be *sui generis* organizations without direct competitors, so there may be no corrective mechanism apart from the reaction to the setbacks the society suffers. Thus there is no guarantee that encompassing organizations will always operate in ways consistent with the well-being of their societies, or that the societies with such organizations will necessarily always prosper.

Nonetheless, the society with encompassing special-interest organizations does have institutions that have some incentive to take the interest of society into account, so there is the possibility and perhaps the presumption that these institutions in fact generally do so. Sweden and Norway (and sometimes other countries, such as Austria) at times have been the beneficiaries of such behavior. There is not even the possibility that such behavior can be general among the narrow special-interest organizations and collusions that prevail in some other countries.

X

Since it achieved its independence, the United States has never been occupied by a foreign power. It has lived under the same democratic constitution for nearly two hundred years. Its special-interest organizations, moreover, are possibly less encompassing in relation to the economy as a whole than those in any other country. The United States has also been since World War II one of the slowest growing of the developed democracies.

In view of these facts, it is tempting to conclude that the experience of the United States provides additional evidence for the theory offered here. This conclusion is, however, premature, and probably also too simple. Different parts of the United States were settled at very different times, and thus some have had a much longer time to accumulate special-interest organizations than others. Some parts of the United States have enjoyed political stability and security from invasion for almost two centuries. By contrast, the South was not only defeated and devastated in the Civil War—and then subjected to federal occupation and ''carpet-bagging''—but for a century had no definitive outcome to the struggle over racial policy that had been an ultimate cause of that war.

There are other complications that make it more difficult to see how well aggregate U.S. experience fits the theory offered here. The United States, like the other societies of recent settlement, has no direct legacy from the Middle Ages. The feudal pattern that seems to have left less of a mark on the chaotic Continent than on stable Britain has never even existed in the United States, or in most of the other societies settled in postmedieval times. Few of the earliest immigrants from Britain to the thirteen colonies were people of high social status, and it was often impossible to enforce feudal patterns of subordination, or to enforce contracts with indentured servants, on a frontier that sometimes offered a better livelihood to those who abandoned their masters. The social and cultural consequences of the non-feudal origins of American society were presumably enhanced by the relatively egalitarian initial distribution of income and wealth (except, of course, in the areas with slavery), which in turn must have owed something to the abundance of unused land. A vast variety of foreign observers, of whom Tocqueville is the best known, testified to this greater equality, and there is quantitative evidence as well that the inequality of wealth was less in the American colonies than in Britain.[30] This point has not been seriously disputed by historians (though there has been a good deal of disagreement about the timing and extent of the apparent increase in inequality sometime during the nineteenth century and about the estimates showing some reduction in inequality since the late 1920s).[31] The implication of the absence of a direct feudal inheritance and the unusually egalitarian beginnings of much of American society, according to the model developed earlier, is that the United States (and any areas of recent settlement with similar origins) should be predicted to be less class-conscious and less condescending toward business pursuits than are societies with a direct feudal inheritance, or at any event less than those with a feudal tradition and a long history of institutional stability.

Obviously, the United States and comparable countries can have no special-interest organizations or institutions with medieval origins. The theory predicts that countries that were settled after the medieval period, and that have enjoyed substantial periods of stability and immunity from invasion, would more nearly resemble Great Britain in their labor unions and in modern types of lobbying organizations than in any structural or cultural characteristics that had had medieval origins. It would also suggest that, other things being equal, the societies of recent settlement would have levels of income or rates of growth at least a trifle above those that would be predicted using only the length of time they had enjoyed political stability and immunity from invasion.

Just as it is hard to say exactly what growth performance the theory offered here would predict for the United States, so it is also difficult to say exactly how bad or good the country's growth performance has been. In at least most of the postwar period, the United States has had the highest per capita income of all major nations, partly because (at least in the earlier decades) it had a higher level of technology than other countries. This means that, at least for part of the postwar period, other countries have had the opportunity to catch up by adopting superior technologies used for some time in the United States, as well as the opportunity to adopt those developed in the current period, whereas in most industries in the United States any technical improvements could be only of the latter variety. Thus the U.S. growth rate should probably be adjusted upward for a fair test of the model offered here, but no one knows by just how much.

XI

The very fact that the United States is a large federation composed of different states, often with different histories and policies, makes it possible to test the theory against the experience of the separate states.

It is indeed doubly fortunate that such a test is possible, because it helps compensate for the fact there are only a handful of developed democracies with distinctive growth rates. As we shall see later, the theory offered here explains at least the most strikingly anomalous growth rates among the developed democracies, and no competing theory developed so far can do this. Although this is an important argument in favor of the present theory, my impression is that many readers of early drafts of the argument have been too easily convinced by it. Intellectual history tells us that there is a considerable susceptibility to new theories when the old ones are manifestly inadequate, and this is as it should be. Yet, just as it is understandable that a drowning man should grab at a straw, so it is also unhelpful. We should look skeptically at the theory offered here, however it may compare with the available alternatives. This skepticism is all the more important because of the aforementioned small number of developed democracies with distinctive growth rates. When the number of observations or data points is so small, it is always possible that the relative growth rates are what they are because of a series of special circumstances, and that these special circumstances have, simply by chance, produced a configuration of results that is in accord with what the theory predicts. The timing and gradual emergence of Britain's relatively low ranking in growth rates is somewhat reassuring, because special circumstances are unlikely to have generated the particular profile of relative growth rates observed over such a long period. So are Murrell's results in his comparison of old and new British and West German industries; since he compared so many industries, his results are almost certainly not due to chance. Nonetheless, there are so many ways in which the facts can mislead us that it is important to remain skeptical and to be thankful for the additional observations that can be obtained from the separate states (and from the other countries and developments to be considered in later chapters).

The number of observations is emphasized partly because it is so often neglected. It is neglected both by those who draw strong generalizations out of a few observations (for example, those who write of the "lessons" drawn from only one or two historical experiences), and also by those whose beliefs remain unaltered by even massive statistical evidence (for example, those who still doubt the compelling statistical evidence on the harmful effects of smoking). If prior reactions to earlier drafts are any guide, this book will probably illustrate both problems—a small number of dramatic illustrations will generate more belief in the theory than is warranted, whereas the statistical evidence will generate less conviction than it should. Psychologists have also shown through experiments that vivid or dramatic examples tend to be given more weight as evidence than they deserve, whereas extensive statistical evidence tends to be given less credence than is justified.[32]

Admittedly, one reason why statistical arguments sometimes fail to persuade is that different statistical methods may produce varying results, and investigators are suspected of choosing the method most favorable to their arguments. The range of statistical techniques available to the modern econometrician is so wide that the zealous advocate can often "torture the data until it confesses." But I will in the following tests use only the most obvious and elementary procedures. A rudimentary approach is appropriate as a first step and also offers the reader a small degree of protection against the selection of methods favorable to the theory offered here.

Although the statistical methods that will be used are among the simplest, they may still seem forbidding to those readers who have never studied the principles of statistical inference. Partly in the interest of those readers, and partly to provide a guide to the statistical material that follows, I shall endeavor in the next three paragraphs to offer a glimpse of the statistical tests and findings in everyday language.

The theory here cannot say very much about state-to-state variations in economic growth in earlier periods of American history. One reason is that, until more recent times, even the oldest states had not been settled long enough to accumulate a great deal of special-interest organization, so such organizations could not have caused large variations in growth rates across states. Another reason is that until fairly recently the United States had frontier areas that were growing unusually rapidly, and it would bias any tests in favor of the theory offered here if the rapid growth of these frontier areas were attributed solely, or even mainly, to their lack of distributional coalitions; through most of American history the newer, more westerly areas have tended to grow more rapidly, and the center of gravity of the American economy has moved steadily in a westerly and southwesterly direction. This is entirely consistent with the theory but is due partly to other factors. Accordingly, the theory is most appropriately tested against recent experience; the following tests consider the period since World War II, and most often the period since the mid-1960s.

The statistical tests reveal that throughout the postwar period, and especially since the early 1960s, there has been a strong and systematic relationship between the length of time a state has been settled and its rate of growth of both per capita and total income. The relationship is negative—the longer a state has been settled and the longer the time it has had to accumulate special-interest groups, the slower its rate of growth. In the formerly Confederate states, the development of many types of special-interest groups has been severely limited by defeat in the Civil War, reconstruction, and racial turmoil and discrimination (which, until recently, practically ruled out black or racially integrated groups). The theory predicts that these states should accordingly be growing more rapidly than other states, and the statistical tests systematically and strongly confirm that this is the case. The theory also predicts that the recently settled states and those that suffered defeat and turmoil should have relatively less membership in special-interest organizations, and although comprehensive data on state-by-state membership in such organizations have not been found, the most pertinent available data again strongly support the theory. Moreover, as expected, the higher the rate of special-interest organization membership, the lower the rate of growth. All of the many statistical tests showed that the relationships are not only always in the expected direction, but virtually without exception were statistically significant as well. The statistical significance means that the results almost certainly are not due to chance, but it does not rule out the possibility that some obscure factor that happens to be correlated with the predictions of the theory could have made the results spurious. There is an independent tendency for relatively poorer states to catch up with relatively more prosperous ones, but the hypothesized relationships hold even when this tendency is taken into account. A variety of tests with other familiar or plausible hypotheses about regional growth show that these other hypotheses do not explain the data nearly as well as the present theory. Strongly significant as the statistical tests are, it is nonetheless clear that many other factors also importantly influence the relative rates of growth of different states. Accordingly, the theory here is not nearly sufficient to serve as a general explanation of differences in regional growth rates. There is also a need for massive historical and statistical studies (especially on the South) that would search for heretofore unrecognized sources of variation in regional growth rates and then take them into account along with the present theory. Only then could we rule out the possibility that there are obscure but systematic factors that somehow have happened to generate the pattern of results that the theory leads one to expect.

It is possible to follow the remaining chapters of this book even if one skips the rest of this chapter, but I hope that even readers who have never studied statistical inference will persevere. They will rarely find easier or more straightforward examples of statistical tests. And the evidence is important; it is not simply the experience of one country, but of forty-eight separate jurisdictions, each of which provides additional evidence.

XII

The statistics we are about to consider lend themselves especially well to straightforward treatment. The theory specifies a connection that goes primarily or entirely in one direction: the length of time an area has had stability should affect its rate of growth, but there is (for a first approximation) not much reason to suppose that the rate of growth of a region would on the whole greatly change the rate at which it accumulates distributional coalitions. On the one hand, a booming economy may make strikes and barriers to entry more advantageous, but on the other, adversity can give a threatened group a reason to organize to protect customary levels of income. This suggests that simple and straightforward tests (nonstructural regressions) should not only be sufficient, but perhaps even better than any more subtle method (such as a simultaneous equation specification) apparent now.

Since the theory predicts that the longer an area has had stable freedom of organization the more growth-retarding organizations it will accumulate, states that have been settled and politically organized the longest ought, other things being equal, to have the lowest rates of growth, except when defeat in war and instability such as occurred in the ex-Confederate states destroyed such organizations. The length of time a state has been settled and politically organized can roughly be measured by the number of years it has enjoyed statehood. Thus, if we exclude erstwhile members of the Confederacy, a simple regression between years since statehood and rates of growth should provide a preliminary test of our model.

If carried back into the nineteenth century, however, this test might be biased in favor of the model, since some states were then still being settled. The westward-moving frontier must have created disequilibria (the California gold rush might be the most dramatic example) with unusual rates of growth of total, if not per capita, income. The frontier is generally supposed to have disappeared by the end of the nineteenth century, but where agriculture and other industries oriented to natural resources are at issue, some disequilibria may have persisted into the present century. Thus, the more recent the period, the more likely that frontier effects are no longer present. In large part for this reason, we begin by looking at the years since 1965. Great disequilibria are unlikely three-quarters of a century after the frontier closed, especially since many of the great agricultural areas in most recently settled states suffered substantial exogenous depopulations during the agricultural depression of the 1920s, the dust bowl of the 1930s, and the massive postwar migration from farms to cities. The two newest states may, however, still be enjoying frontier or similar disequilibria and thus bias the results in favor of the theory, so we shall consider only the forty-eight contiguous states.

Another reason for concentrating on relatively recent experience arises from the ease of mobility of capital and labor within the United States. If the theory offered here is correct, there ought to be some migration of both firms and workers from those states with more distributional coalitions to those with fewer. The extent of this migration should be given by the extent of the *differential* in the degree of special-interest organization across states. There could not have been any substantial differential in the earliest periods of American history, but if the theory is right there should be significant differentials in more recent times. This will be explored more specifically later, but it is already evident that the states which the theory predicts should grow most rapidly should do so in periods when the differential in levels of special-interest organization across states is greatest.

The aforementioned regressions and a variety of other statistical tests were done with my former student Kwang Choi, who has undertaken more detailed inquiries that complement the present study, and are to be published separately.[33] We found that there is the hypothesized negative relationship between the number of years since statehood for all non-Confederate states and their current rates of economic growth, and that this relationship is statistically significant. This holds true for income from manufacturing only, for private nonfarm income, for personal income, and for labor and proprietors' income from all sources.*

In a country with no barriers to migration of workers, migration should *eventually* make real per capita incomes much the same everywhere, so the regressions use measures of total rather than per capita income as dependent variables. When the corresponding measures of growth of per capita income by state are used, however, the relationship remains negative and statistically significant.** Conceivably, the duration of statehood and political stability should not be measured on a ratio scale, and nonparametric tests focusing only on rank orders should be used instead, to guard against the possibility that the result might be an artifact of states at the far ends of the distribution or of other spurious intervals. Accordingly, Choi ran nonparametric tests on the same variables, and these equally supported the hypothesis derived from the theory.[34]

Happily, there is a separate test that can provide not only additional evidence but also insight into whether it is the duration of stable freedom of organization and collusion, rather than any lingering frontier effect, that explains the results. Several of the defeated Confederate

---

*LPI = 10.896 − 0.0160 STAHOD
   (1965–80)   (4.02) $R^2 = 0.32$
PN = 11.699 − 0.0218 STAHOD
   (1965–78)   (6.25) $R^2 = 0.53$

The first dependent variable, *LPI*, is the growth rate of income (but not transfer payments) received by labor or by proprietors, irrespective of source. The other, *PN*, measures only nonfarm income from private sources. STAHOD is years since statehood. The absolute value of the *t* statistic is given in parentheses beneath the coefficient. Unfortunately, there are no data on what proportion of the profits of corporations operating in more than one state were generated in each state, so both measures exclude undistributed corporate profits. There are data on dividends, interest, and rents received by state, but these factor payments will often have been generated by activity in states other than states where the recipient lived—indeed, if the most profitable corporations are in the fastest growth areas and their stockholders are dispersed across states in proportion to absolute levels of income, attributing dividends or other corporate profits to the state of the stockholder's residence will tend to understate the growth of production in the rapid-growth states. Corporate profits should vary roughly in accordance with wage and proprietary income by state. Thus *LPI* should be a better measure for testing the hypothesis here than any comprehensive measure of "national income" by state that could be estimated.

**PCLPI = 8.538 − 0.0060 STAHOD
         (3.19) $R^2 = 0.22$
PCPN = 9.744 − 0.0142 STAHOD
       (6.24) $R^2 = 0.53$

states were among the original thirteen colonies, so they are as far from frontier status as any parts of the United States, and, of course, all the Confederate states had achieved statehood by 1860. Yet the political stability of these Deep South states was profoundly interrupted by the Civil War and its aftermath, and even at times by conflicts and uncertainties about racial policies that were settled only with the civil rights and voting rights acts of 1964 and 1965. If the model proposed here is correct, the former Confederate states should have growth rates more akin to those of the newer western states than to the older northeastern states. Although we shall soon turn to earlier periods, we shall start with the southern rates of growth since 1965. In earlier years there were episodes of instability, lynchings, and other lawlessness that complicate the picture, but after the passage of the voting rights and civil rights acts there was clearly a definitive answer to the question of whether the South could have significantly different racial policies than the rest of the nation and unambiguous stability. In earlier years there is also the greater danger of the lingering frontier effects even in the South, so including it will not serve so well as protection against the possibility of these effects in the West; there is also a lesser differential in special-interest accumulation across states, not to mention other complexities. So we briefly postpone our consideration of earlier periods and ask if the former Confederate states have a higher average growth rate than the other states in the years since 1965.

They definitely do. The exponential growth rate for the ex-Confederate states is 9.37 percent for income from labor and proprietorships (LPI), and 9.55 percent for private nonfarm income (PN), whereas the corresponding figures are 8.12 percent and 8.19 percent for the thirty-seven states that were not in the Confederacy. If variations in growth rates are normally distributed, the probabilities that these two samples are from different populations can be calculated. Choi found that the difference in growth rates on this basis was statistically significant. A nonparametric test, the Mann-Whitney U-test, also indicated that the difference in average growth rates between the South and the rest of the United States was statistically significant. Again, this result holds true whether the growth of total or per capita income is at issue. These findings obviously argue in favor of the model offered in this book and should also allay any fears that regression results involving years since statehood for the non-Confederate states were due to any western frontier settlement that might have taken place since 1965.

XIII

Because the southern and western results are essentially the same and the parametric and nonparametric tests yield about the same results, it is reasonable to consider the data on all the forty-eight states together and use only standard ordinary-least-squares regression techniques. This has been done with the few score of Choi's regressions shown in the following tables. Although more elaborate tests might possibly produce different conclusions, the results are nonetheless remarkably clear and consistent.

As the results with the separate treatment of the South and the other states suggest, any regressions that use the year of statehood for the non-Confederate states to establish the earliest possible date for special-interest groups, and *any* year after the end of the Civil War to establish when the Confederate states came to have stable freedom of organization, will provide a statistically significant explanation of growth rates by state (table 4.1). Since organizations that could most directly constrain modern urban and industrial life have had more time to develop in states that have been urbanized longer, the level of urbanization in 1880 was also used as an independent variable. This variable again tends to have a significant negative influence on current growth rates. In combination with a dummy variable for defeat in the Civil War, it explains a fair amount of the variance, but it is apparently not as significant as the duration of freedom of organization. The same patterns hold for income from manufacturing, and for all of our broader measures of income as well, and apply whether total or per capita income is at issue.

The theory predicts that distributional coalitions should be more powerful in places that have had stable freedom of organization, so we can get an additional test of its validity by looking at the spatial distribution of the memberships of such organizations. The only special-interest organizations on which we have so far found state-by-state membership statistics are labor unions. In view of the widespread neglect of the parallels between labor unions and other special-interest organizations, it is important not to attribute all the losses caused by such organizations and collusions to labor unions. They are, however, certainly the most relevant organizations for studying income from manufacturing, and for reasons that will be explained later are appropriate for tests within a country in which manufacturers are free to move to wherever costs of production are lowest. In addition, many other types of distributional

Table 4.1. Determinants of Growth since 1965

(1)	$MFG = 12.6802 - 5.5427$ STACIV1			
	(7.34)			$R^2 = 0.54$
(2)	$LPI = 11.227 - 3.051$ STACIV1			
	(4.74)			$R^2 = 0.33$
(3)	$PN = 11.988 - 4.018$ STACIV1			
	(7.25)			$R^2 = 0.53$
(4)	$MFG = 11.5575 - 4.3148$ STACIV2			
	(6.89)			$R^2 = 0.51$
(5)	$LPI = 10.742 - 2.592$ STACIV2			
	(5.18)			$R^2 = 0.37$
(6)	$PN = 11.248 - 3.248$ STACIV2			
	(7.37)			$R^2 = 0.54$
(7)	$MFG = 10.5131 - 2.9334$ STACIV3			
	(5.60)			$R^2 = 0.41$
(8)	$LPI = 10.172 - 1.866$ STACIV3			
	(4.75)			$R^2 = 0.33$
(9)	$PN = 10.493 - 2.266$ STACIV3			
	(6.20)			$R^2 = 0.45$
(10)	$MFG = 10.2920 - 0.0626$ UR1880			
	(5.89)			$R^2 = 0.43$
(11)	$LPI = 9.796 - 0.029$ UR1880			
	(3.27)			$R^2 = 0.19$
(12)	$PN = 10.192 - 0.042$ UR1880			
	(5.22)			$R^2 = 0.37$
(13)	$MFG = 10.2450 + 0.1067$ CIVWAR $- 0.0616$ UR1880			
	(0.21)		(5.25)	$R^2 = 0.43$
(14)	$LPI = 9.545 + 0.573$ CIVWAR $- 0.023$ UR1880			
	(1.39)		(2.45)	$R^2 = 0.22$
(15)	$PN = 10.033 + 0.363$ CIVWAR $- 0.039$ UR1880			
	(0.96)		(4.38)	$R^2 = 0.38$
(16)	$MFG = 12.2885 - 4.0418$ STACIV1 $- 0.0284$ UR1880			
	(4.17)		(2.32)	$R^2 = 0.59$
(17)	$LPI = 11.141 - 2.722$ STACIV1 $- 0.006$ UR1880			
	(3.12)		(0.56)	$R^2 = 0.33$
(18)	$PN = 11.776 - 3.206$ STACIV1 $- 0.015$ UR1880			
	(4.39)		(1.66)	$R^2 = 0.56$
(19)	$MFG = 10.6865 - 1.6460$ STACIV3 $- 0.0397$ UR1880			
	(2.51)		(2.92)	$R^2 = 0.50$

(*continued*)

Table 4.1. (*Continued*)

(20)	LPI =	10.198	−	1.674 STACIV3	−	0.006 UR1880		
				(3.13)		(0.53)		$R^2 = 0.33$
(21)	PN =	10.581	−	1.620 STACIV3	−	0.020 UR1880		
				(3.38)		(2.01)		$R^2 = 0.50$
(22)	PCMFG =	10.7060	−	4.2147 STACIV1				
				(6.06)				$R^2 = 0.44$
(23)	PCLPI =	8.833	−	1.129 STACIV1				
				(3.95)				$R^2 = 0.25$
(24)	PCPN =	10.014	−	2.690 STACIV1				
				(7.02)				$R^2 = 0.52$
(25)	PCMFG =	9.0864	−	2.2829 STACIV3				
				(4.97)				$R^2 = 0.35$
(26)	PCLPI =	8.495	−	0.987 STACIV3				
				(5.50)				$R^2 = 0.40$
(27)	PCPN =	9.067	−	1.616 STACIV3				
				(6.79)				$R^2 = 0.50$
(28)	PCMFG =	9.0063	−	0.0529 UR1880				
				(5.96)				$R^2 = 0.44$
(29)	PCLPI =	8.314	−	0.016 UR1880				
				(3.92)				$R^2 = 0.25$
(30)	PCPN =	8.907	−	0.033 UR1880				
				(6.49)				$R^2 = 0.48$
(31)	PCMFG =	8.9810	+	0.0575 CIVWAR	−	0.0523 UR1880		
				(0.14)		(5.33)		$R^2 = 0.44$
(32)	PCLPI =	8.103	+	0.481 CIVWAR	−	0.012 UR1880		
				(2.64)		(2.74)		$R^2 = 0.35$
(33)	PCPN =	8.769	+	0.314 CIVWAR	−	0.030 UR1880		
				(1.35)		(5.44)		$R^2 = 0.50$

NOTE: Explanation of and for the Variables Used in the Regressions
The absolute values of the *t* statistic are given in parentheses beneath the coefficients.

Statehood, Civil War, Length of Time:

CIVWAR: Dummy variable 1 for defeated (Confederate) states and 0 for non-Confederate states
YEAR: For Confederate—100
    For non-Confederate—length of time since statehood
YEAR2: For Confederate—50
    For non-Confederate—length of time since statehood
YEAR3: For Confederate—0
    For non-Confederate—length of time since statehood
STACIV1 = YEAR/178 STACIV2 = YEAR2/178 STACIV3 = YEAR3/178

Table 4.1. *(Continued)*

178   = 1965–1787 (earliest year of statehood)
STAHOD: Years since statehood

SOURCE: Date of Statehood: Council of State Governors, *The Book of the States,* 1976; Civil War Information: Peter J. Parish, *The American Civil War* (New York: Holmes and Meier, 1975).

Growth Rates of Income:
  MFG: Exponential rate of growth of manufacturing income during 1965–1978
  LPI: Exponential rate of growth of income of labor and proprietors during 1965–80
  PN: Exponential rate of growth of private nonfarm income during 1965–1978
  PCLPI: Exponential rate of growth of per capita labor and proprietors' income during 1965–1980
  PCPN: Exponential rate of growth of per capita private nonfarm income during 1965–1978

SOURCE: Information from the Regional Economic Information System Branch, Bureau of Economic Analysis, U.S. Department of Commerce. These data have income by state of employment rather than state of residence, which is better for present purposes. Essentially the same results were obtained using published data on personal income from the *Survey of Current Business* and the *Statistical Abstract.*

Urbanization: UR1880 and UR1970: the percentage of people who resided in cities in the corresponding year.
SOURCE: U.S. Department of Commerce, Bureau of Census, *Historical Statistics of the U.S.—Colonial Times to 1970,* 1976.

coalitions, such as trade associations of manufacturers, are likely to obtain special-interest legislation or monopoly prices that can enrich the states in which they are located at the expense of the rest of the nation. Thus labor unions are the main organizations with negative effects on local growth, and their membership should also serve as a proxy measure of the strength of such other coalitions that are harmful to local growth.[35] We will nonetheless also consider the number of lawyers per 100,000 of population, on the debatable assumption that the need for lawyers would probably show *some* tendency to increase with the extent of lobbying and the complexity of legislation and regulation it brings about.

Table 4.2 suggests immediately that union membership as a percentage of nonagricultural employment is greatest in the states that have had stable freedom of organization longest. Urbanization in 1880 is also

Table 4.2. Special Interest Organizations

A. *Membership as Dependent Variable*

(1) UNON64 = 18.536 + 0.262 UR1880		
(3.64)		$R^2 = 0.22$
(2) UNON70 = 18.842 + 0.212 UR1880		
(3.21)		$R^2 = 0.19$
(3) UNON74 = 16.586 + 0.234 UR1880		
(3.79)		$R^2 = 0.24$
(4) UNON64 = 9.820 + 0.223 UR1970		
(2.25)		$R^2 = 0.10$
(5) UNON74 = 9.663 + 0.185 UR1970		
(2.16)		$R^2 = 0.09$
(6) UNON64 = 22.924 − 9.974 CIVWAR + 0.167 UR1880		
(3.28)	(2.34)	$R^2 = 0.38$
(7) UNON74 = 19.922 − 7.584 CIVWAR + 0.162 UR1880		
(2.82)	(2.57)	$R^2 = 0.35$
(8) UNON64 = 17.687 − 11.780 CIVWAR + 0.143 UR1970		
(4.01)	(1.63)	$R^2 = 0.30$
(9) UNON74 = 15.984 − 9.465 CIVWAR + 0.122 UR1970		
(1.55)		$R^2 = 0.29$
(10) UNON64 = 12.107 + 0.104 STACIV1		
(3.06)		$R^2 = 0.17$
(11) UNON64 = 12.178 + 0.114 STACIV2		
(4.36)		$R^2 = 0.32$
(12) UNON64 = 15.441 + 0.094 STACIV3		
(5.19)		$R^2 = 0.37$
(13) UNON74 = 14.044 + 0.081 STACIV3		
(5.19)		$R^2 = 0.37$

a statistically significant predictor of union membership in the period from 1964 on. Indeed, the crucial importance of the duration of freedom of organization is shown by the fact that urbanization in the 1880s is a better predictor of union membership in the 1960s and 1970s than urbanization in 1970. The number of years of freedom of organization is often an even better predictor. There is a similar connection between the length of time a state has enjoyed political stability and the number of lawyers, although this relationship is less strong and sometimes not statistically significant.

Table 4.2. (*Continued*)

B. *Membership in Special-Interest Organizations and Growth*

(1)	MFG =	11.223	− 0.0953	UNON64	
			(4.49)		$R^2 = 0.31$
(2)	LPI =	10.420	− 0.053	UNON64	
			(3.22)		$R^2 = 0.18$
(3)	PN =	10.898	− 0.067	UNON64	
			(4.33)		$R^2 = 0.29$
(4)	MFG =	11.3033	− 0.102	UNON70	
			(4.19)		$R^2 = 0.28$
(5)	LPI =	10.525	− 0.058	UNON70	
			(3.20)		$R^2 = 0.18$
(6)	PN =	11.001	− 0.074	UNON70	
			(4.19)		$R^2 = 0.28$
(7)	PCMFG =	9.171	− 0.0773	UNON64	
			(4.28)		$R^2 = 0.29$
(8)	PCLPI =	8.703	− 0.031	UNON64	
			(4.18)		$R^2 = 0.27$
(9)	PCPN =	9.390	− 0.050	UNON64	
			(4.84)		$R^2 = 0.33$

NOTE: UNON64 and UNON70 are union memberships as a percentage of employees in nonagricultural establishments in 1964 and 1970.
SOURCE: Same as in table 4.1 and Bureau of Labor Statistics, U.S. Department of Labor, *Directory of National Unions and Employee Associations,* 1967 and 1971. Bureau of the Census, U.S. Department of Commerce, *Statistical Abstract of the United States,* 1976.

As the previous results and the theory suggest, there is also a statistically significant negative relationship between special-interest organization membership in 1964 and 1970 and rates of economic growth since 1965. This result holds for income from manufacturing and for all measures of income and for both total and per capita changes in those measures (table 4.2, part b). Thus there is not only statistically significant evidence of the connection between the duration of stable freedom of organization and growth rates predicted by our model, but also (at least as far as labor unions are concerned) distinct and statistically significant evidence that the process the model predicts is going on, that is, that the accumulation of special-interest organization is occurring, and that such organizations do, on balance, have the hypothesized negative effect on economic growth. A negative relationship between the proportion of lawyers and the rate of growth also is evident, but again this relationship is somewhat weaker.

XIV

A number of possible problems should be considered. One of these is that changing responses to climate may explain the results. The advances in airconditioning presumably have induced migration toward some of the more rapidly growing states (although other rapidly growing states in the Northwest are among the coldest in the country). Accordingly, Choi regressed the mean temperature for January for each state's principal city, and also the average temperature in the city over the entire year, against growth rates by state. These variables were positively correlated with growth rates, but usually less strongly than our measures of the length of time a state has had to acquire distributional coalitions.

Another possibility is that the rapidly growing states happened to contain the industries that have been growing most rapidly, and that such an accident of location explains our results. To test for this possibility, Choi regressed the rate of growth of ten major (one-digit) industries, and also a subclassification (two-digit) of eighteen manufacturing industries that existed in more than a score of states, against our measure of the time available in each state for the formation of special-interest groups. In all these industries but one (agricultural services, forestry, and fisheries), all or almost all of the signs were consistent with the theory, and in a large proportion of cases the results for each separate industry were statistically significant as well.[36]

A third possible problem is that the forty-eight states might be, for the purposes of the present argument, essentially three homogeneous regions—the South, the West, and the Northeast–Midwest. If that is true, we do not have forty-eight observations but only three, and thus too few for statistically significant results. To test for this possibility, Choi and I examined each of the three regions separately and also considered the thirty-seven non-Confederate states as a separate unit. The same pattern shows up within each region; the pattern is weak within the West and to some extent in the ex-Confederate states but very strong within the Northeast–Midwest region and for the thirty-seven non-Confederate states.

Still another possibility is that the results are a peculiarity of the recent past and considering a longer period would give different results. If we take the longest possible period, the whole of American history, we see a massive movement in a westerly (even somewhat southwesterly) direction. This movement has been greatly slowed at times by the rapid relative decline in agriculture (which abated only in the 1970s), but its existence and continued rapid pace long after the disappearance of the frontier is consistent with the theory.

XV

The picture in the South over the longer run, although it also appears in a general way consistent with the theory, is more complex and more difficult to sort out. If my highly preliminary investigation of southern history is at all correct, the first important special-interest coalitions that emerged in the South during and after Reconstruction were small, local, and white-only coalitions, sometimes without formal organization. All these small groups were by no means always against the advancement of the black population, but many were, and there was an undoubted susceptibility of the majority of the white southern population at that time to racist demagogues. The much weaker black population was in essence denied political organization and often the opportunity to vote through extra-legal coercion, which included at times widespread lynchings. The electoral consequence of the disproportion in organized power between the races and the susceptibility of the white population to racist appeals was the *gradual* emergence of the "Jim Crow" pattern of legalized segregation and racial subordination. This was apparently augmented by informal exclusion and repression by some of the white-only coalitions. Many have supposed that the segregationist patterns in the South emerged promptly after Reconstruction or even earlier, but the historian C. Vann Woodward has shown that decades passed before most of the Jim Crow legislation was passed and that it was in the twentieth century that this system reached its full severity.[37] In other words, the collective action of the white supremacists took some time to emerge in each of the many southern communities and states.

The low productivity of black sharecroppers predates the full development of the Jim Crow system and cannot be blamed entirely upon it. The causes of this low productivity and the widespread poverty of the black population after the Civil War are the subject of a vast and controversy-laden literature that this book could by no means resolve. Yet it is not on the surface astonishing that the deprivations of the black population under slavery, their lack of education and limited access to credit, and the vast and sudden change from the large-scale slave-plantation to small-scale independent sharecropping should have resulted in low productivity in black agriculture, and that this should have had adverse effects on the southern economy as a whole.

The lack of industrial development is another matter. Although I must postpone any conclusions for a separate publication that may emerge from some further research that I hope to do,[38] my very tentative hunch now is that many of the organized interests in many of the southern communities realized that any substantial outside investment or in-migration from the North would disrupt or at least endanger the Jim Crow system and the lattice of vested interests intertwined with it. There certainly was a lot of intensely agrarian, chauvinistic, anti-industrial, and anti-capitalist rhetoric for a long time in the South.[39] The large-scale efforts to attract business from afar, moreover, emerged mainly after the old system was already breaking down. Outside investors and potential in-migrants must at times also have been put off by the extra-legal violence and the uncertain stability of the system. The old pattern of coalitions in the South was eventually emasculated by New Deal and postwar federal policies, by cosmopolitan influences due to better communication and transportation, by increased black resistance, by adaptation to new technologies and methods of production, and perhaps by still other factors. These changes and a variety of favorable exogenous developments permitted rapid change and growth. A new pattern of coalitions, such as racially integrated labor unions, has begun to form in the South, but this new pattern of coalitions has been emerging only gradually, and thus has not had any massively adverse impact on economic development.

The tentative and heuristic character of the foregoing conjectures cannot be emphasized too strongly. Even if the foregoing speculation is largely correct, clearly it could be only one part of a complex and multicausal story. Another possible source, for example, of the increasing tempo of the southern (and western) growth in recent years is the growing relative importance of "footloose" industries. These industries, unlike the "resource-based" industries like iron and steel, and unlike the other heavy industries for which transportation costs are substantial, can locate in many different areas and thus can more easily avoid environments with inefficient institutional arrangements. High technology and other footloose light industries have become increasingly important in the United States in recent times. It is perhaps also significant that transportation costs have not been very significant for a long time in textiles; this was the first manufacturing industry of importance to move to the South.

As later chapters of this book should make clear, labor unions are often only a small part of the story of distributional coalitions, and sometimes not part of the story at all, but they are the most important coalitions where the migration of footloose manufacturing is concerned. The manufacturers, even if they are cartelized, will have lower profits if they face higher costs of production due to restrictive work rules or supracompetitive wages. If the theory offered in this book is right, the location of manufacturing activity, at least to the extent that the location of natural resources does not constrain it, should be influenced by differences in the strength of unions across areas. The most rapid growth of American labor unions began in 1937 and proceeded rapidly through World War II, so it is during the postwar period that differences in union strength across the states have been really important. Implication 6 suggests, moreover, that distributional coalitions cause more inefficiency when they are old than when they are first organized, because slow decision-making means that work rules become archaic after a long period of organization; only in the postwar period were there great differentials in the extent of mature unionism. A test of the present theory on the whole of the postwar experience is accordingly appropriate, especially for manufacturing output, and so we turn to this now.

The results, as we can see from table 4.3, are again strongly in favor of the theory. Separate regressions indicate that they also support the theory in each major part of the postwar period—before the mid-1960s as well as after. The relation is not as strong in early postwar years as it is later, however; it is also perhaps slightly less strong in the last few years, perhaps because the differential in union membership across states is diminishing somewhat.

XVI

The above tests focus on growth-retarding influences and assume that opportunities for growth in different states are randomly distributed.

Table 4.3. Growth Since World War II

A. *Value Added by Manufacturers, 1947–1977*

$(1)\ VAM = 11.0097 - 4.8402\ STACIV1$
(7.07) $R^2 = 0.52$

$(2)\ VAM = 10.1951 - 4.0375\ STACIV2$
(7.70) $R^2 = 0.56$

$(3)\ VAM = 8.8613 - 0.0518\ UR1880$
(5.23) $R^2 = 0.37$

$(4)\ VAM = 9.7758 - 0.0848\ UNON64$
(4.50) $R^2 = 0.31$

B. *Value Added by Manufacturers, 1947–1963*

$(1)\ VAM = 9.5861 - 4.3589\ STACIV1$
(4.26) $R^2 = 0.28$

$(2)\ VAM = 8.8401 - 3.6157\ STACIV2$
(4.47) $R^2 = 0.30$

$(3)\ VAM = 7.6063 - 0.0447\ UR1880$
(3.24) $R^2 = 0.19$

$(4)\ VAM = 7.9001 - 0.0528\ UNON64$
(1.99) $R^2 = 0.08$

C. *Total Personal Income, 1946–1978*

$(1)\quad PI = 8.5767 - 1.8469\ STACIV1$
(3.25) $R^2 = 0.19$

$(2)\quad PI = 8.3399 - 1.6609\ STACIV2$
(3.76) $R^2 = 0.24$

$(3)\quad PI = 7.6575 - 0.0153\ UR1880$
(2.00) $R^2 = 0.08$

$(4)\quad PI = 8.1406 - 0.0338\ UNON64$
(2.50) $R^2 = 0.12$

D. *Per Capita Personal Income, 1946–1978*

$(1)\ PCPI = 8.3012 - 0.6911\ STACIV1$
(2.92) $R^2 = 0.16$

$(2)\ PCPI = 8.4394 - 0.8618\ STACIV2$
(5.29) $R^2 = 0.38$

$(3)\ PCPI = 8.1811 - 0.0123\ UR1880$
(4.52) $R^2 = 0.31$

$(4)\ PCPI = 8.3574 - 0.0184\ UNON64$
(3.52) $R^2 = 0.21$

E. *Summary and Additional Regressions*

	Total Personal Income 1946–1978		Per Capita Income 1946–1978		Mfg. Value-Added 1963–1977		Mfg. Value-Added 1947–1977	
	t	R^2	t	R^2	t	R^2	t	R^2
STACIV1	3.25	0.19	2.92	0.16	6.03	0.44	7.07	0.52
STACIV2	3.76	0.24	5.29	0.38	6.54	0.48	7.70	0.56
STACIV3	3.65	0.22	6.56	0.48	5.82	0.42	6.68	0.49
UR1880	2.00	0.08	4.52	0.31	4.89	0.34	5.23	0.37
CIVWAR	1.62	0.13[a]	5.23	0.57	1.27	0.37	1.33	0.40
UR1880	1.21		3.07		3.99		4.26	
STACIV1	2.43	0.19	0.28	0.31	3.41	0.48	4.22	0.55
UR1880	0.06		3.15		1.76		1.73	
STACIV2	3.11	0.24	2.74	0.41	3.76	0.50	4.63	0.58
UR1880	0.67		1.46		1.24		1.14	
STACIV3	2.92	0.23	4.11	0.50	3.19	0.46	3.84	0.53
UR1880	0.37		1.11		1.82		1.83	
CIVWAR	3.30	0.25	7.10	0.54	5.16	0.50	6.58	0.63
STAHOD	3.02		2.15		5.72		7.05	
STAHOD	1.90	0.07	0	0	3.47	0.21	4.26	0.28
UNON64	2.50	0.12	3.52	0.21	5.87	0.43	4.50	0.31
UNON70	2.36	0.11	3.03	0.17	5.74	0.42	4.14	0.27

a. When there are two independent variables, the R^2 values appear on the lines between the two variables.

NOTE: Explanation of Variables

VAM: Exponential growth rate of value added by manufactures

PI: Exponential growth rate of total personal income

PCPI: Exponential growth rate of per capita personal income

SOURCE: Same as in table 4.1 and U.S. Department of Commerce, *Survey of Current Business,* April 1965, April 1967, and April 1981. Bureau of the Census, U.S. Department of Commerce, *1977 Census of Manufactures—General Summary,* April 1981.

There is, however, at least one systematic difference in the opportunities for growth across states. This difference arises because the economies in some states had not come close to exploiting the full potential of modern technology or of their own natural and human resources, at least at the beginning of the period of growth we are studying. The areas that have many unexploited opportunities can, other things being equal, grow faster than those that have very few, and thus we once again come upon the well-known hypothesis that poorer and technologically less advanced areas can grow faster, as they catch up, than richer and technologically more advanced areas.[40] I have argued elsewhere that the catch-up argument is a particularly congenial partner for the present theory and that there are sometimes severe specification problems if the two are not tested together.[41] Obviously the catch-up hypothesis cannot explain, for example, the differences between German and Japanese rates of growth, on the one hand, and British rates of growth, on the other. But it does not mean that the catch-up process was not operating;[42] its impact may have been obscured by stronger forces working in the opposite direction.

The forty-eight states provide a uniquely rich and comparable data base for testing the present theory and the catch-up model together. Choi has calculated how much the per capita income deviated, in terms of each of our measures of income, from the average for the forty-eight states in a given year. If the catch-up hypothesis is true, this deviation should then be negatively associated with the state's growth rate. In all the equations reported in table 4.4, the catch-up coefficient has the hypothesized negative sign, and in several regressions it has statistical significance as well. The catch-up factor appears to have less significance than the length of time a state has had to develop organizations pertinent to modern urban conditions,[43] but since the two theories are compatible, it would be absurd to reject one simply because it may have less significance than the other.

XVII

When we look at cities and metropolitan areas we see the same tendency for relative decline in the places that have had the longest time to accumulate special-interest groups. The best-known manifestation of this and of the ungovernability brought about by dense networks of such coalitions is the bankruptcy that New York City would have suffered in the absence of special loan guarantees from the federal government. Interestingly, Norman Macrae of the *Economist* was sufficiently impressed by the parallels between his own country and New York City that he wrote a section entitled ''Little Britain in New York'' in his book on the United States.[44] But New York is only a prototypical case.

Table 4.4. Growth with Catch-Up Variables Added

(1) MFG = 3.8973 + 9992.38 INVLPI
             (3.96) R^2 = 0.25
(2) LPI = 7.03 + 4231.00 INVLPI
             (2.15) R^2 = 0.09
(3) PN = 6.69 + 3848.44 INVPN
             (3.96) R^2 = 0.25
(4) MFG = 8.4112 + 0.0025 DEVLPI
             (4.02) R^2 = 0.26
(5) LPI = 8.92 − 0.0011 DEVLPI
             (2.37) R^2 = 0.11
(6) PN = 8.83 − 0.0019 DEVPN
             (4.88) R^2 = 0.34
(7) MFG = 8.8894 − 2.5009 STACIV3 + 2767.57 INVLPI
             (3.53)   (0.91) R^2 = 0.42
(8) LPI = 11.41 − 2.196 STACIV3 − 2113.81 INVLPI
             (4.13)   (0.93) R^2 = 0.34
(9) PN = 9.72 − 1.999 STACIV3 + 951.89 INVPN
             (4.20)   (0.88) R^2 = 0.46
(10) MFG = 8.5228 − 0.0533 UR1880 + 3117.81 INVLPI
             (3.93)   (1.11) R^2 = 0.45
(11) LPI = 9.37 − 0.0269 UR1880 + 746.11 INVLPI
             (2.34)   (0.31) R^2 = 0.19
(12) PN = 9.03 − 0.0339 UR1880 + 1456.76 INVPN
             (3.21)   (1.26) R^2 = 0.39
(13) MFG = 10.0981 − 2.4533 STACIV3 − 0.0008 DEVLPI
             (3.51)   (1.04) R^2 = 0.42
(14) LPI = 10.34 − 2.0585 STACIV3 − 0.0003 DEVLPI
             (3.89)   (0.55) R^2 = 0.33
(15) PN = 10.02 − 1.7219 STACIV3 − 0.0008 DEVPN
             (3.59)   (1.71) R^2 = 0.49
(16) MFG = 9.9302 − 0.0531 UR1880 − 0.0008 DEVLPI
             (3.87)   (1.09) R^2 = 0.44
(17) LPI = 9.65 − 0.0253 UR1880 − 0.0003 DEVLPI
             (2.17)   (0.53) R^2 = 0.19
(18) PN = 9.63 − 0.0276 UR1880 − 0.0010 DEVPN
             (2.62)   (2.11) R^2 = 0.43
(19) MFG = 7.9862 + 5088.80 INVLPI − 0.0671 UNON64
             (1.64)   (2.48) R^2 = 0.34

Table 4.4. (*Continued*)

(20)	LPI =	9.98	+ 687.38 INVLPI	− 0.0485 UNON64	
			(0.28)	(2.28)	$R^2 = 0.19$
(21)	PN =	8.72	+ 3421.65 INVPN	− 0.0487 UNON64	
			(1.49)	(2.43)	$R^2 = 0.32$

NOTE: Explanation of Variables

INVPN, INVLPI: Inverse of per capita private nonfarm income and labor and proprietors' income in 1965, respectively.

DEVPN, DEVLPI: Deviation of per capita private nonfarm income and labor and proprietors' income in 1965, respectively, from U.S. average in 1965.

SOURCE: Same as in table 4.1.

As Felix Rohatyn has pointed out, all the great cities to the north and east of a crescent extending from just south of Baltimore to just west of St. Louis and Milwaukee are in difficulty. In general, the newer cities of the South and the West are in incomparably better shape. Statistical tests like those used here have much the same success in explaining the relative growth of what the Census Bureau calls the "Standard Metropolitan Statistical Areas." The results also hold true when the biggest cities—which might perhaps be in decline because of crowding or lack of space—are omitted, and when the independent effect of city size is allowed for in other ways.[45]

Casual observation also suggests that the "older" manufacturing industries in the United States, such as the railway, steel, automobile, and farm machinery industries, are often in relative decline. Newer American industries, such as the computer, aircraft, and other high-technology industries, are doing much better. Because of the lack of any one unambiguous measure of industry age, statistical tests in this case are more difficult and problematic, and I have so far not attempted any. Peter Murrell, however, has looked at the pattern of exports of the United States and various other major trading countries and found that the pattern of comparative advantage exhibited by the U.S. economy resembles that of Britain more than that of Germany and Japan.[46] This is surely consistent with the hypothesis that the United States as well as Britain does relatively badly in older industries and heavy industries that are especially susceptible to oligopolistic collusion and unionization. No doubt other factors are also relevant, but the fact that wage rates in the troubled U.S. automobile and steel industries have been very much higher than the average wages in American manufacturing tends to confirm Murrell's hypothesis that the present theory is part of the explanation. I would also not be surprised if in these troubled industries there have also been excessive numbers of vice-presidents and other corporate bureaucrats with handsome perquisites.

XVIII

All the statistical tests that have been reported (and many others that have not been discussed in the interest of brevity) are consistent with the theory and almost all are statistically significant as well. In this complex, multicausal world, it is hard to see how the data could have fitted the theory much better. Still, the case is not yet compelling. Less elementary and straightforward tests, for example, might yield somewhat different results, or an alternative model that is inconsistent with the theory could produce still better results. Any alternative model should, however, also be tested against international and historical experience of the kind considered earlier in this chapter. As I argued in the first chapter, the presumption must be in favor of the theory that explains the most with the least, so a model that could not explain anything else but the growth experience of the states of the United States, or could not do so without losing its parsimony, is out of the running.

Partly because the credibility of a theory depends on how much it can explain (without losing parsimony) and partly because of its intrinsic interest, we shall present more evidence—much more. This evidence will relate to different countries and different historical periods. But the theory remains unchanged, so the later evidence will strengthen the argument made in this chapter in the same way that the evidence in this chapter adds strength to later results.

5

Jurisdictional Integration and Foreign Trade

As we know from table 1.1, the original six members of the European Economic Community have grown rapidly since World War II, particularly in comparison with Australia, New Zealand, the United Kingdom, and the United States, and for some of the member countries the growth was fastest in the 1960s when the Common Market was becoming operational. Although I have offered some explanation of the most anomalous or puzzling cases of rapid growth in Germany and France, there has been no analysis of the rapid growth of the other four members of the Six. Such an analysis is necessary not only to complete the coverage of the developed democracies, but also to show that there was a further factor contributing to the growth of France and Germany that complements the explanation in the previous chapter. In addition, the analysis of the Common Market will also help us to understand why New Zealand's postwar growth performance has been about as poor as that of the United Kingdom, and why Australia's growth has also been unimpressive, especially in view of the valuable natural resources it has discovered in the postwar period.

Looking at the timing of the growth of most of the Six, one is tempted to conclude, as many casual observers have, that the Common Market was responsible. This is *post hoc ergo propter hoc* reasoning and we obviously cannot rely on it, especially in view of the fact that most, if not all, of the careful quantitative studies indicate that the gains from the Common Market were *very* small in relation to the increases in income that the members enjoyed. The quantitative studies of the gains from freer trade, like those of the losses from monopoly, usually show far smaller effects than economists anticipated, and the calculations of the gains from the Common Market fit the normal pattern. The studies of Edwin Truman and Mordechai Kreinen, for example, while maintaining that trade creation overwhelmed any trade diversion, imply that the Common Market added 2 percent or less to EEC manufacturing consumption.[1] Bela Balassa, moreover, argues that, taking economies of scale as well as other sources of gain from the Common Market into account, there was a "0.3 percentage point rise in the ratio of the annual increment of trade to that of GNP," which was probably "accompanied by a one-tenth of one percentage point increase in the growth rate. By 1965 the cumulative effect of the Common Market's establishment on the Gross National Product of the member countries would thus have reached one-half of one percent of GNP."[2] Careful studies by other skilled economists also suggest that the intuitive judgment that large customs unions can bring about substantial increases in the rate of growth is not supported by economists' typical comparative-static calculations.

II

There is a hint that there is more to the matter in the instances of remarkable economic growth in historical times discussed in chapter 1. The United States, we know, became the world's leading economy in the century or so after the adoption of its constitution. Germany similarly advanced from its status as a poor area in the first half of the nineteenth century to the point where it was, by the start of World War I, overtaking Britain, and this occurred after the formation of the Zollverein, or customs union, of most German-speaking areas and the political unification of Germany. Both situations, I shall argue, were similar to the Common Market because they shared three crucial features. These common features are sometimes overlooked because the conventional nomenclature calls attention to the differences between the formation of governments and of customs unions.

The Common Market created a large area within which there was something approaching free trade; it allowed relatively unrestricted movement of labor, capital, and firms within this larger area; and it shifted the authority for decisions about tariffs and certain other matters from the capitals of each of the six nations to the European Economic Community as a whole. When we consider these features, we immediately recognize that the creation of a new or larger country out of many smaller jurisdictions also includes each of these three fundamental features.

The establishment of the United States of America out of thirteen independent ex-colonies involved the creation of an area of free trade and factor mobility, as well as a shift in the institutions that made some of the governmental decisions. The adoption of the Constitution did, in fact, remove tariffs that New York had established against certain imports from Connecticut and New Jersey. Similarly, not only the Zollverein but also the creation of the German Reich itself included the same essential features. Until well into the nineteenth century, most of the German-speaking areas of Europe were separate principalities or city-states or other small jurisdictions with their own tariffs, barriers to mobility, and economic policies, but an expanding common market and a shift of some governmental powers resulted from the Zollverein, and even more from the formation of the German state, which was complete by 1871.

There was a much earlier development elsewhere in Europe that also created vastly larger markets, established far wider domains for factor mobility, and shifted the locus of governmental decision-making. The centralizing monarchs of England and France in the late fifteenth and sixteenth centuries tried to create nation-states out of the existing mosaic of parochial feudal fiefdoms; there had been nominal national kingdoms before, but the real power customarily rested with lords of various fiefs, or sometimes with virtually self-governing walled towns. Each of these mini-governments tended to have its own tolls and tariffs; a boat trip along the Rhine, where toll-collecting castles are sometimes only about a kilometer apart, is sufficient to remind one how numerous were local tolls in medieval Europe. The nationalizing monarchs, with their mercantilistic policies, strove to eliminate these local authorities and their restrictions and in turn imposed highly protectionist policies at the national level. In France many of the feudal tolls and restrictions to trade and factor mobility were not removed until the Revolution, but in Britain the creation of nationwide markets took place much more rapidly. Whether there was any causal connection or not, we know that the creation of effective national jurisdictions in Western Europe was followed by the commercial revolution, and in Britain ultimately by the Industrial Revolution.

In many respects, and possibly the most important ones, the creation of meaningful national governments is very different from the creation of customs unions, however effective the customs union might be. Nonetheless, in all the cases we have considered, a much wider area of relatively free trade was established, a similarly wide area of relatively free movement of factors of production was created, and the power to make at least some important decisions about economic policy was shifted to a new institution in a new location. There was in each case a considerable measure of what I shall call here *jurisdictional integration*. It would be much better if we could avoid coining a new phrase, especially such a ponderous one, but the familiar labels obscure the common features that concern us here.

Since there are several cases of jurisdictional integration followed by fairly rapid economic progress, it is now even more tempting to posit a causal connection. That would still be premature. For one thing, we should have some idea just how jurisdictional integration would bring about rapid growth, and statistical studies such as those cited above for the Common Market suggest that the gains from the freer trade are not nearly large enough to explain substantial economic growth. For another, the number of cases of jurisdictional integration is still not large enough to allow confident generalization. We must therefore look at the specific *patterns* of growth *within* jurisdictions as well as across them to see if they provide corroborating evidence. In addition, we must present a theoretical model that could explain why jurisdictional integration should have the observed effects.

III

One of the most remarkable and consistent patterns in the advancing economies of the West in the early modern period was the relative (and sometimes absolute) decline of many of what used to be the major cities. This decline of the major cities is paradoxical, for the single most important development moving the West ahead was surely the Industrial Revolution, and Western society today is probably more urbanized than any society in history. The commercial and industrial revolutions created new cities, or made great cities out of mere villages, instead of building upon the base of the larger existing medieval and early modern cities. Major capitals like London and Paris grew, of course, as administrative centers and as consumers of part of the new wealth, but they were by no means the sources of the growth. As the French economic historian Fernand Braudel pointed out, ''The towns were an example of deep-seated disequilibrium, asymmetrical growth, and irrational and unproductive investment on a nationwide scale. . . . These enormous urban formations are more linked to the past, to accomplished evolutions, faults and weaknesses of the societies and economies of the *Ancien Regime,* than to preparations for the future. . . . The obvious fact was that the capital cities would be present at the forthcoming industrial revolution in the role of spectators. Not London, but Manchester, Leeds, Glasgow, and innumerable small proletarian towns launched the new era.''[3]

M. J. Daunton shows that, at least for Great Britain during the Industrial Revolution, Braudel was right. Of the six cities deemed to have been the largest in England in 1600, only Bristol, a port that profited from the economic growth, and London were among the top six in 1801. Manchester, Liverpool, Birmingham, and Leeds completed the list in 1801. York, the third largest city in 1600, was the seventeenth in 1801; Newcastle, the fifth largest city in 1600, was the fourteenth in 1801, as indicated by table 5.1.[4]

Even before 1601 there was concern about the ''desolation of cytes and tounes.'' Charles Pythian-Adams's essay on ''Urban Decay in Late Medieval England'' argues from a mass of detailed, if scattered, figures and contemporary comments that the population and income of many English cities had begun to decline before the Black Death. Though Pythian-Adams finds that the decline of certain cities may be offset by the expansion of others, we are left wondering why so many towns declined while others grew. During the late fifteenth and early sixteenth centuries, and especially between 1520 and 1570, Pythian-Adams finds that most of the more important towns were ''under pressure,'' if not in an ''acute urban crisis,'' often involving significant loss of economic activity and population.[5]

On the Continent, towns were not so likely to be substantially autonomous institutions operating within relatively stable national boundaries. Partly because of this, and partly because the Continent did not experience the rapid changes of the Industrial Revolution until later, the situation there is not so striking. Nonetheless, there were many similar replacements of older urban centers with newer towns or rural industry. One example is the partial shift of the medieval woolen industry from the cities of Flanders to nearby Brabant and the decline of Flemish woolen production generally in relation to that of the North Italian cities, which in their turn declined as well. Another is the decline

Table 5.1. English Cities Ranked by Size

1600		1801	
Rank	*Population*	*Rank*	*Population*
1. London	250,000	1. London	960,000
2. Norwich	15,000	2. Manchester	84,000
3. York	12,000	3. Liverpool	78,000
4. Bristol	12,000	4. Birmingham	74,000
5. Newcastle	10,000	5. Bristol	64,000
6. Exeter	9,000	6. Leeds	53,000
		8. Norwich	37,000
		14. Newcastle	28,000
		17. York	16,000

of Naples, on the eve of the French Revolution probably Europe's fourth largest city. Domenico Sella concludes that "throughout Europe, none of the old centers of early capitalism (whether Antwerp or Venice, Amsterdam or Genoa, Bordeaux or Florence) played a leading role in the advent of modern industrialization." In seventeenth-century Spanish Lombardy, whose economy Sella studied in great detail, he finds that the cities "had few of the traits that we associate with modern industrialization and in fact some that were diametrically opposed to it. . . . The cities were thus clearly ill-suited to serve as the cradle of large-scale industrialization; far from being the vanguard of the modern economy, they must be viewed as anachronistic relics of a rapidly fading past. To find the harbingers of the modern economy, it is to the countryside that we must turn."[6] It was also commonplace that suburbs should grow at the expense of central cities.[7] A classic case is the decline of the central city of Aachen, which Herbert Kisch has chronicled in detail.[8]

IV

Medieval towns and cities were small by modern standards. Their boundaries usually were precisely defined by city walls and they often had a substantial degree of autonomy (and in some cases were independent of any larger government). Within these small jurisdictions there would be only a few merchants in any one line of commerce and only a limited number of skilled craftsmen in any one specialized craft, even if the population of the town was in the thousands. The primitive methods of transportation and the absence of safe and passable national road systems also tended to segment markets; a handful of merchants or skilled craftsmen could more easily secure a monopoly if they could cartelize local production. When the merchants in a given line of commerce had more wealth than the townspeople generally, it seems likely that they would have interacted with one another more often than with those of lesser means. To some extent, this also would have been true of skilled craftsmen.

The logic set out in chapter 2 implies that small groups have far greater opportunities to organize for collective action than large ones and suggests that, if other things are equal, there will be relatively more organization in small jurisdictions than in large ones. The logic also implies that small and homogeneous groups that interact socially also have the further advantage that social selective incentives will help them to organize for collective action. These considerations entailed Implication 3, that small groups are better and sooner organized than large ones. If the logic set out earlier was correct, it follows that the merchants in a given line of commerce and practitioners of particular skilled crafts in a medieval city would be especially well placed to organize collective action. If the city contained even a few thousand people, it is unlikely that the population as a whole could organize to counter such combinations, although in tiny villages the population would be small enough for this to occur.

V

The result of these favorable conditions for collective cartelistic action was, of course, the guilds. The guilds naturally endeavored to augment the advantages of their small numbers and social homogeneity with coercive civic power as well, and many of them did indeed influence, if not control, the towns in which they operated. This outcome was particularly likely in medieval England, where the national monarchies found it expedient to grant towns a substantial degree of autonomy. In what is now Germany, guilds would more often confront small principalities more jealous of their power and would need to work out symbiotic relationships with territorial rulers and the nobility. In France, especially, guilds would often be given monopoly privileges in return for special tax payments, in part because of the cost of wars and the limits on tax collections due to the administrative shortcomings of government. The city-states of North Italy extended well beyond the walls of the town, and in such cases the guilds would have a wider sphere of control if they shared power, but at the same time they were thereby exposed to instabilities in the North Italian environment that must sometimes have interrupted their development or curtailed their powers. In spite of all the variation from region to region, guilds of merchants and master craftsmen, and occasionally journeymen, became commonplace from Byzantium in the East to Britain in the West, and from the Hanseatic cities in the North to Italy in the South.

Although they provided insurance and social benefits for their members, the guilds were, above all, distributional coalitions that used monopoly power and often political power to serve their interests. As Implications 4 and 7 predicted, they also reduced economic efficiency and delayed technological innovation. The use of apprenticeship to control entry is demonstrated conclusively by the requirement in some guilds that a journeyman could become a master only upon the payment of a fee, by the rule in some guilds that apprentices and journeymen could not marry, and by the stipulation in other guilds that the son of a master need *not* serve the apprenticeship that was normally required. The myriad rules intended to keep one master from advancing significantly at the expense of others undoubtedly limited innovation. (Since masters owned capital and employed journeymen and apprentices, it is important not to confuse guilds of masters, or those of merchants, with labor unions—they usually are better regarded as business cartels.)

VI

What should be expected when there is jurisdictional integration in an environment of relatively autonomous cities with a dense network of guilds? Implication 2 indicated that the accumulation of special-interest organization occurs gradually in stable societies with *unchanged* borders. If the area over which trade can occur without tolls or restrictions is made much larger, a guild or any similar cartel will find that it controls only a small part of the total market. A monopoly of a small part of an integrated market is, of course, not a monopoly at all: people will not pay a monopoly price to a guild member if they can buy at a lower price from those outside the cartel. There is free movement of the factors of production within the integrated jurisdiction, providing an incentive for sellers to move into any community in the jurisdiction in which cartelization has brought higher prices. Jurisdictional integration also means that the political decisions are now made by different people in a different institutional setting at a location probably quite some distance away. In addition, the amount of political influence required to change the policy of the integrated jurisdiction will be vastly larger than the amount that was needed in the previous, relatively parochial jurisdictions. Sometimes the gains from jurisdictional integration were partly offset when financially pressed monarchs sold monopoly rights to guilds in return for special taxes, but in general the guilds lost both monopoly power and political influence when economically integrated, nationwide jurisdictions replaced local jurisdictions.

The level of transportation costs is also significant. If transportation costs are too high to make it worthwhile to transport a given product from one town to another, the jurisdictional integration should be less significant, even though there would still be a tendency for competing sellers to migrate to the cartelized locations in the integrated jurisdiction. The time of the commercial revolution was also a time of improved transportation, especially over water, which led to the development of new routes to Asia and the discovery of the New World. The growth in the power of central government also reduced the danger of travel from community to community by gradually eliminating the anarchic conflict among feudal lords and the extent of lawlessness in rural areas, and it brought road building and eventually the construction of canals. If the countryside is relatively safe from violence, not only is transportation cheaper but production may also take place wherever costs are lowest.

When jurisdictional integration occurs, new special-interest groups matching the scale of the larger jurisdiction will not immediately spring up, because, as we know from Implication 2, such coalitions emerge only gradually in stable situations. It will not, however, take small groups as long to organize as large ones (Implication 3). The great merchants involved in larger-scale trade, often over longer distances, were among the first groups to organize or collude on a national scale. They were often extremely successful; as Adam Smith pointed out, the influence of the "merchants" gave the great governments of Europe the policy of "mercantilism," which favored influential merchants and their allies at the expense of the rest of the nation. Often this involved severely protectionist policies that protected the influential merchants from foreign competitors—mercantilism is, to this day, nearly synonymous with protectionism.

It might seem, then, that the gains from jurisdictional integration in early modern Europe were brief and unimportant, since the mercantilist policies followed close on the heels of the decaying guilds in the towns. Not so. The reason is that tariffs and restrictions around a sizable nation are incomparably less serious than tariffs and restrictions around each town or fiefdom. Much of the trade will be *intra*national, whether the nation has tariffs at its borders or not, because of transport costs and the natural diversity of any large country. Restrictions at national borders do not have any direct effect on this trade, whereas trade restrictions around each town and fiefdom reduce or eliminate most of it. Moreover, as Adam Smith pointed out, "the division of labor is limited by the extent of the market," and thus the widening markets of the period of jurisdictional integration also made it possible to take advantage of economies of scale and specialization. Another way of thinking of the matter emerges when we realize that the shift of trade restrictions from a community level to a national level reduces the length of tariff barriers by a vast multiple. I believe the greatest reductions of trade restrictions in history have come from reducing the mileage rather than the height of trade restrictions.

VII

Since the commercial and the industrial revolutions took place during and after the extraordinary reduction in trade barriers and other guild restrictions and occurred overwhelmingly in new cities and suburbs relatively free of guilds, there appears to have been a causal connection. Yet both the timing of growth and the fact that guilds were regularly at the locations where the growth was obstructed could conceivably have been coincidences. Happily, there are additional aspects of the pattern of growth which suggest that this was not the case.

One of these is the "putting out system" in the textile industry, which was then the most important manufacturing industry. Under this remarkable system, merchants would travel all over the countryside to "put out" to individual families material that was to be spun or woven and then return at a later time to pick up the yarn or cloth. Clearly such a system required a lot of time, travel, and transaction costs. There were uncertainties about how much material had been left with each family and how much yarn or cloth could be made from it, and these uncertainties provoked haggling and disputes. The merchant also had the risk that the material he had put out would be stolen. Given the obvious disadvantages, we must ask why this system was used. The answer from any number of accounts is that this system, despite its disadvantages, was cheaper than production in towns controlled by guilds. There may have been some advantages of production scattered throughout the countryside, such as cheaper food for the workers, but this could not explain the tendency at the same time for production to expand in suburbs around the towns controlled by guilds. (Adam Smith said that "if you would have your work tolerably executed, it must be done in the suburbs, where the workmen have no exclusive privilege, having nothing but their character to depend upon, and you must then smuggle it into town as well as you can.")[9] Neither can any possible inherent advantages of manufacturing in scattered rural sites explain the objections of guilds to the production in the countryside; Flemish guilds, for example; even sent expeditions into the countryside to destroy the equipment of those to whom materials had been put out.

By and large there was more economic growth in the areas of early modern Europe with jurisdictional integration than in the areas with parochial restrictions, and the greatest growth in the areas that had experienced political upheaval as well as jurisdictional integration. Centralized government came early to England; it was the first nation to succeed in establishing a nationwide market relatively free of local trade restrictions. Though comprehensive quantitative evidence is lacking, the commercial revolution was by most accounts stronger in that country than in any other country except the Dutch Republic. In the seventeenth century, and even to an extent in the early eighteenth century, Britain suffered from civil war and political instability.[10] Undoubtedly the instability brought some destruction and waste and, in addition, discouraged long-run investment. But within a few decades after it became clear that stable and nationwide government had been re-established in Britain, the Industrial Revolution was under way. It is also generally accepted that there was much less restriction of enterprise of trade in mid-eighteenth century Britain than on most of the Continent, and for the most part probably better transportation as well.

Similarly, the Dutch economy enjoyed its Golden Age, and reached much the highest levels of development in seventeenth-century Europe, just after the United Provinces of the Netherlands succeeded in their struggle for independence from Spain. At least some guilds that had been strong in the Spanish period were emasculated, and guilds were not strong in most of the activities that were important to Dutch international trade.[11] As a lowland coastal nation with many canals and rivers, the Dutch enjoyed unusually easy transportation.

France apparently enjoyed very much less economic unification than did Great Britain; it did not eliminate many of its medieval trade restrictions until the French Revolution. Yet France did enjoy some jurisdictional integration well before the Revolution. Most notably under Louis XIV and Colbert, there was some economic unification and improvement of transportation. At the same time, Louis XIV, short of money for wars and other dissipations, often gave monopoly rights to guilds in return for special taxes, and a powerful special-interest group, the nobility, was generally able to avoid being taxed. Notwithstanding Colbert's tariff reforms, goods from some provinces of France were treated as though they came from foreign countries. Still, within the *cinq grosses fermes,* or five large tax farms, at least, there was a measure of unification; this area had a population as large as or larger than that of England. Thus France probably did not have as much parochial restriction of trade as the totally Balkanized German-speaking and Italian-speaking areas of Europe, and its economic performance also appears to have been better than that in those areas, however far short it fell of the Dutch and British achievement.[12] It was not until the second half of the nineteenth century that the German-speaking and Italian-speaking areas enjoyed much jurisdictional integration, and when that occurred these areas, and particularly Germany, also enjoyed substantial economic growth.

Of course, thousands of other factors were important in explaining the varying fortunes of the different parts of Europe, so it would be preposterous to offer the present argument as a monocausal explanation. It is, nonetheless, remarkable how well the theory fits the pattern of growth across different nations as well as the pattern of growth within countries.

In the United States, there was not only the constitutional provision mentioned earlier that prohibited separate states from imposing barriers to trade and factor mobility, but also more than a century of westward expansion. Any cartel or lobby in the United States before the present century had to face the fact that substantial new areas were regularly being added to the country. Competition could always come from these new areas, notwithstanding the high tariffs at the national level, and the new areas also increased the size of the polity, so that ever-larger coalitions would be needed either for cartelization or lobbying. Vast immigration also worked against cartelization of the labor market. In addition, the United States, like all frontier areas, could begin without a legacy of distributional coalitions and rigid social classes. In view of all these factors, the extraordinary achievement of the U.S. economy for a century and more after the adoption of the Constitution is not surprising.

VIII

The case with which we began, the rapid growth in the 1960s of the six nations that created the Common Market, also fits the pattern. The three largest of these countries—France, Germany, and Italy—had suffered a great deal of instability and invasion. This implied that they had relatively fewer special-interest organizations than they would otherwise have had, and often also more encompassing organizations. In France and Italy the labor unions did not have the resources or strength for sustained industrial action; in Germany the union structure growing out of the occupation was highly encompassing.

As Implication 3 tells us, small groups can organize more quickly and thoroughly than large groups, so even in the countries that had suffered the most turbulence those industries that had small numbers of large firms were likely to be organized. In Italy the Allied occupation had not been as thorough as it was elsewhere, and some industries remained organized from fascist times. In all the countries, organizations of substantial firms, which were often manufacturing firms, would frequently have an incentive to seek protection through tariffs, quotas, or other controls for their industry, and in at least some of these countries they were very likely to get it. Once imports could be excluded, the home market could also be profitably cartelized; as an old American adage tells us, "The tariff is the Mother of the Trust."[13] If foreign firms should seek to enter the country to compete with the domestic firms, the latter could play upon nationalistic sentiments to obtain exclusionary or discriminatory legislation against the multinationals. Sometimes, in some countries such as postwar Germany at the time of

Ludwig Erhard, there would, because of economic ideology or the interests of exporters, be some determined resistance to protectionist pressures, but in other countries like France and Italy in the years just before the creation of the Common Market the capacity or the inclination to resist these pressures was lacking.

In France and Italy and to some extent in most of the other countries, the coalitional structure and government policy insured that tariffs, quotas, exchange controls, and restrictions on foreign firms were the principal threat to economic efficiency. In France, for example, as Jean-François Hennart argues in "The Political Economy of Comparative Growth Rates: The Case of France,"[14] exchange controls, quotas, and licenses had nearly closed off the French market from foreign competition; raw materials were often allocated by trade associations, and trade and professional associations fixed prices and allocated production in many important sectors. In such situations the losses from protectionism and the cartelization it facilitates could hardly have been small. If a Common Market could put the power to determine the level of protection and to set the rules about factor mobility and entry of foreign firms out of the reach of each nation's colluding firms, the economies in question could be relatively efficient. The smaller nations among the Six were different in several respects, but they would also gain greatly from freer trade, in part because their small size made protectionist policies more costly for them. Most of the founding members of the European Economic Community (EEC), then, were countries with coalitional structures, protectionist policies, or small sizes that made the Common Market especially useful to them. This would not so clearly have been the case if the Common Market had chosen very high tariff levels against the outside world, but the important Kennedy Round of tariff cuts insured that that did not happen.

It does not follow that every country that joins any institution called a common market will enjoy gains comparable to those obtained by most of the Six. Whether a nation gains from a customs union depends on many factors, including its prior levels of protection and (to a lesser extent) those of the customs union it joins. In the case of France and Italy, for example, the Common Market almost certainly meant more liberal policies for trade and factor mobility than these countries otherwise would have had. In the case of Great Britain, where the interests of organized exporters and the international financial community in the City of London have long been significant, the level of protection was perhaps not so high, and it is not obvious that joining the Common Market on balance liberalized British trade. When many high-tariff jurisdictions merge there is normally a great reduction in tariff barriers, even if the integrated jurisdiction has equally high tariffs, but a country with low tariffs already is getting most of the attainable gains from trade.

The coalitional structure of a society also makes a difference. In Britain the professions, government employees, and many firms (such as "High Street" or downtown retail merchants) that would have no foreign competition in any case are well-organized; joining the Common Market could not significantly undermine their organizations through freer trade, although a shift of decision-making to a larger jurisdiction could reduce their lobbying power. More foreign competition for manufacturing firms can reduce the power of unions, since manufacturers whose labor costs are far out of line must either cut back production or hold out for lower labor costs, but even here the influence is indirect and presumably not as significant as when imports directly undermine a cartel of manufacturing firms.

Common markets have even been tried in or proposed for developing countries with comparative advantage in the same goods and thus little reason to trade with one another, but this cannot promote growth. For these and other reasons, it is not possible to say whether a customs union will be good for a country's growth. One has to look at the prior level of protectionism, the coalitional structure, the potential gains from trade among the members, and still other factors in each individual case.

IX

The growth rates of Australia and New Zealand, we recall, were not greatly different from those of Britain. In spite of the exceptional endowments of natural resources in relation to population that these two countries possess, their levels of per capita income lately have fallen behind those of many crowded and resource-poor countries in Western Europe. If we examine the tariff levels of Australia and New Zealand in the spirit of the foregoing analysis of jurisdictional integration, and remember that these countries have also had relatively long histories of political stability and immunity from invasion, we obtain a new explanation of their poor growth performance.

There are problems in calculating average tariff levels for different countries. Tariffs on important commodities should receive greater weight than tariffs on minor commodities, but the importance of each commodity for a country cannot be determined by the amount of its imports, since the country would not import much of any commodity, however important, if its tariff against that commodity were sufficiently high. Fortunately, there have been some calculations of average tariff levels that determine the weight to be attributed to the tariff on each commodity by the magnitude of the trade in this commodity among all countries that are important in world trade. The latest such calculations that I have been able to find were prepared by the Office of the United States Trade Representative. These calculations have not previously been published; they are shown in the columns labeled "World Weights" in table 5.2. Unfortunately, the average tariff levels given in the table probably underestimate the true level of protection, for they take no account of quotas and other nontariff barriers and are based on what international trade theorists call the *nominal* rather than the *effective* rate of protection. The table is nonetheless an approximate guide to relative levels of protection on industrial products in the different countries. One reason is that nontariff barriers are generated by the same organizational and political forces as tariffs and in the developed nations, at least, seem to vary across countries in similar ways. It is probably also significant that the different types of calculations listed in different columns of table 5.2 show broadly similar results, as do earlier calculations by other institutions.

Table 5.2 shows that Australia and New Zealand—especially New Zealand—have far higher tariffs than any of the other countries described. Their levels of protection are two to three times the level in the EEC and the United States and four to five times as high as those of Sweden and Switzerland. As might be expected from the level of its tariffs, quotas on imports are also unusually important in New Zealand. The impact of protection levels that are uniquely high by the standards of the developed democracies is made even greater by the small size of Austrialian and New Zealand economies; larger economies such as those of the United States or Japan would not lose nearly as much per capita from the same level of protection as Australia and New Zealand do.

The theory offered in this book suggests that manufacturing firms and urban interests in Australia and New Zealand would have organized to seek protection. When this protection was attained, they would some-

Table 5.2. Average Industrial Tariff Levels

	No trade weighting:[a] simple average		Own country import weighting:[b]		"World" Weights[c] Import weights on BTN aggregates[d]		Import weights on each BTN commodity[e]	
	1976 Ave.	Final[f] Ave.	1976 Ave.	Final Ave.	1976 Ave.	Final Ave.	1976 Ave.	Final Ave.
Australia								
Dutiable[g]	28.8	28.0	29.1	28.1	27.8	26.7	26.4	25.2
Total[h]	16.9	16.5	15.4	15.1	13.3	12.8	13.0	12.6
New Zealand								
Dutiable	31.4	28.3	28.6	25.5	33.0	30.4	30.2	27.5
Total	24.3	21.9	19.7	17.6	20.5	18.7	18.0	16.3
EEC								
Dutiable	8.8	6.0	9.8	7.2	9.5	7.0	9.6	7.1
Total	8.0	5.5	6.3	4.6	7.0	5.2	6.9	5.1
United States								
Dutiable	15.6	9.2	8.3	5.7	9.2	5.5	7.6	4.8
Total	14.8	8.8	6.2	4.3	7.1	4.1	5.6	3.5
Japan[i]								
Dutiable	8.1	6.2	6.9	4.9	8.0	5.7	7.9	5.5
Total	7.3	5.6	3.2	2.3	6.1	4.4	5.8	4.1
Canada								
Dutiable	13.7	7.8	13.1	8.9	12.0	7.3	12.9	8.3
Total	12.0	6.8	10.1	6.8	8.9	5.5	9.4	6.1
Austria								
Dutiable	14.2	9.8	18.8	14.5	15.9	12.0	17.0	13.3
Total	11.6	8.1	14.5	11.2	10.5	7.9	10.9	8.5
Finland								
Dutiable	17.0	14.6	11.6	9.2	11.2	9.0	11.5	9.1
Total	14.3	12.3	8.2	6.5	6.7	5.3	6.7	5.3
Norway								
Dutiable	11.1	8.2	10.5	8.0	10.2	7.4	10.0	7.5
Total	8.5	6.3	6.4	4.9	5.8	4.3	5.8	4.4
Sweden								
Dutiable	7.8	6.1	7.7	5.9	7.4	5.3	7.1	5.2
Total	6.2	4.9	6.3	4.8	4.6	3.3	4.5	3.3
Switzerland								
Dutiable	3.7	2.7	4.1	3.3	4.2	3.1	4.0	3.1
Total	3.7	2.7	4.0	3.2	3.3	2.4	3.2	2.4

times have been able to engage in oligopolistic or cartelistic practices that would not have been feasible with free trade. With high tariffs and limitations on domestic competition, firms could survive even if they paid more than competitive wages, so there was more scope for labor unions and greater gains from monopolizing labor than otherwise. Restrictions on Asian immigration would further facilitate cartelization of labor. Stability and immunity from invasion would ensure that few special-interest organizations would be eliminated, but more would be organized as time went on (Implication 2). The result would be that frontiers initially free of cartels and lobbies would eventually become highly organized, and economies that initially had exceptionally high per capita incomes would eventually fall behind the income levels of European countries with incomparably lower ratios of natural resources to population.

There is a need for detailed studies of the histories of Australia and New Zealand from this theoretical perspective. The histories of these countries, like any others, are undoubtedly complicated and no mono-causal explanation will do. Final judgment should wait for the specialized research. But preliminary investigation into Australia and New Zealand suggests that the theory fits these countries like a pair of gloves.

A comparison with Australia and New Zealand puts the British

Table 5.2. (*Continued*)

SOURCE: Dr. Harvey Bale, Office of the United States Trade Representative.

a. An average of tariff levels on the assumption that all commodities are of equal significance.

b. The relative weight attributed to each tariff is given by the imports of that commodity by that country.

c. The significance of each tariff determined by world imports of the commodity, or aggregate of commodities, to which the tariff applies. World imports are the imports of the countries listed and the EEC.

d. "BTN" means Brussels Tariff Nomenclature. The weight attributed to each tariff is given by the world imports of the BTN class of commodities in which it falls.

e. Each tariff weighted by world imports of that particular commodity—the maximum attainable disaggregation.

f. "Final" means after the Tokyo Round of tariff reductions.

g. Average tariff rates considering only those commodities on which tariffs are levied.

h. Average tariff levels of duty-free commodities as well as those to which duties apply.

i. Some anecdotal evidence, as well as casual impressions of the relatively high costs that Japanese consumers must pay for many imported goods, and the fact that agriculture tariffs are not included raise the question whether these figures may give the impression that the level of protection is lower than it actually is. This is a matter in need of further research.

economy in a more favorable light. The less restrictive trade policies that Great Britain has followed, presumably because of the importance of the organized power of industrial exporters and its free trade inheritance from the nineteenth century, probably mean that parts of its economy are open to more competition than corresponding sectors in Australia or New Zealand, notwithstanding Britain's still longer history of stability. Australia, like Britain, is an industrialized country with the overwhelming proportion of its work force in cities. But how many readers in competitive markets outside Australia and its environs have ever purchased an Australian manufactured product? Transport costs from Australia to the United States and Europe are high, but so are they high from Japan. Australia probably does not have comparative advantage in many kinds of manufactures, so we might not see many Australian manufactured goods even if Australia had different trade policies. Nonetheless, with a large part of Australia's healthy and well-educated population devoted to the production of a wide range of manufactured products, the paucity of sales of manufactures abroad is evidence of a serious misallocation of resources. British manufacturing exports, by contrast, are fairly common, although of diminishing relative significance. Social manifestations of distributional coalitions, on the other hand, are more serious in Britain, with its inheritance from feudal times, than in Australia or New Zealand.

The present argument also casts additional light on some other variations in economic performance. Consider Sweden and Switzerland, which have enjoyed somewhat higher per capita incomes than most European countries. As table 5.2 reveals, Sweden and Switzerland, and especially the latter, have had unusually low levels of protection. Note also that the Japanese economy grew more rapidly in the 1960s than in the 1950s, despite the fact that Japan could gain more from catching up by borrowing foreign technology in the earlier decade than the later. As Alfred Ho emphasizes in *Japan's Trade Liberalization in the 1960's*,[15] between 1960 and 1965 the Organization for Economic Cooperation and Development (OECD) ''liberalization rate'' measure for Japan improved from 41 percent to 93 percent. Finally, note that Germany, which considerably liberalized its economic policies before entering the Common Market, grew more rapidly in the 1950s than in the 1960s, in contrast to EEC partners like Belgium, France, and the Netherlands. Although again I want to emphasize that many different causes are normally involved, it is certainly not difficult to find instances in which freer trade is associated with growth and prosperity.

X

The paradox arising from the frequent association of freer trade (whether obtained through jurisdictional integration or by cutting tariff levels) and faster growth, and the skillful calculations suggesting that the gains from trade creation are relatively small, remains. Indeed, since we now have a wider array of cases where freer trade is associated with more rapid growth and several aspects of the patterns of growth suggest that the freer trade is connected with the growth, the paradox is heightened. If freer trade leads to more rapid growth, why does it not show up in the measures of the gains from the transactions that the trade liberalization allows to take place?

The reason is that there is a further advantage of freer trade that escapes the usual comparative-static measurements. It escapes these measurements because the gains are *not* direct gains of those who take part in the international transactions that the liberalization permitted, but *other* gains from increases in efficiency in the importing country— increases that are distinct from and additional to any that arise because of comparative advantage.

In the interest of readers who are not economists, it may be helpful to point out that the conventional case for freeing trade rests on the theory of comparative advantage. This theory goes back at least to David Ricardo, one of the giants on whose shoulders the economist is fortunate to stand. The theory of comparative advantage is lucidly and rigorously stated in many excellent textbooks, so there is no need here to go into it, or into certain exceptional circumstances that could make tariffs possibly advantageous. The literature on comparative advantage is so valuable and fascinating that it ought to be part of everyone's education. Only one point in that rich literature, however, is indispensable to what follows. This is the point that *differences in costs of production* drive the case for free trade because of comparative advantage. These differences are conventionally assumed to be due to differences in endowments of natural resources among countries, to the different proportions of other productive factors such as labor and capital in different economies, or to the economies of scale that sometimes result when different economies specialize in producing different products. If there is free trade among economies and transport costs are neglected, producers in each country will not produce a product if other countries with their different endowments of resources can produce it at lower cost. If each country produces only those goods it can produce at costs as low as or lower than those of other countries, there will be more production from the world's resources. A country that protects domestic producers from the competition of imports gives its consumers an incentive to buy from more costly domestic producers, and more resources are consumed by these producers. These resources would, in general, yield more valued output for the country if they were devoted to activities in which the country has a comparative advantage and the proceeds were used to buy imports; normally with freer trade a country could have more of all goods, or at least more of some without less of any others.

The argument offered here is different from the conventional argument for comparative advantage, although resonant with that argument. To demonstrate that there are gains from freer trade that do not rest on comparative advantage or differences in cost of production, let us look first at the case of a country that has comparative advantage in the production of a good and exports that good, but that also is subject to the accumulation of distributional coalitions described in Implication 2. Suppose that the exporters who produce the good in question succeed in creating an organization with the power to lobby and to cartelize. It might seem that the exporters would have no interest in getting a tariff on the commodity they export, since their comparative advantage ensures that there will not be lower-cost imports from abroad in any case. In fact, exporters often do not seek tariffs. To illuminate the logic of the matter, and also to cover an important, if untypical, class of cases, we must note that they might gain from a tariff. With a tariff they may be able to sell what they sell on the home market at a higher price by shifting more of their output to the world market (where the elasticity of demand is usually greater), because they do not affect the world price that much (in other words, the organized exporters engage in price discrimination and thereby obtain more revenue than before). Even though the country had, and by assumption continues to have, comparative advantage in producing the good in question, eliminating the tariff will still increase efficiency. The reason is that the tariff is necessary to the socially inefficient two-price system that the organized exporters have arranged. This example is sufficient to show gains from freer trade that do not flow from the theory of comparative advantage or differences in costs across countries, but rather from the constraints that free trade and factor mobility impose on special-interest groups. To explore a far more important aspect of this matter, assume that a number of countries have comparative advantage in the same types of production. Their natural resources and relative factor endowments are by stipulation *exactly* the same, and there are by assumption no economies of scale. Suppose that these countries for any reason have high levels of protection and that they have been stable for a long while. Then, by Implication 2, they would each have accumulated a dense network of coalitions. These coalitions would, by Implication 4, have an incentive to try to redistribute income to their clients rather than to increase the efficiency of the society. Because of Implications 6, 7, 8, and 9, they will entail slower decision-making, less mobility of resources, higher social barriers, more regulation, and slower growth for their societies.

Now suppose the tariffs between these identical countries are eliminated. Let us assume, in order to insure that we can handle the toughest conceivable case, that even the extent of distributional coalitions is identical in each of these countries, so there is no case for trade even on grounds of what I might call "institutional comparative advantage." Even on these most difficult assumptions, however, the freeing of trade can make a vast contribution. We know from *The Logic of Collective Action* and from Implication 3 that it is more difficult to organize large groups than small ones. When there are no tariffs any cartel, to be effective, would have to include all the firms in all the countries in which production could take place (unless transport costs provide natural tariffs). So more firms or workers are needed to have an effective cartel. Differences of language and culture may also make international cartels more difficult to establish. With free trade among independent countries there is no way the coercive power of governments can be used to enforce the output restriction that cartels require. There is also no way to obtain special-interest legislation over the whole set of countries because there is no common government. Individual governments may still pass inefficient legislation for particular countries, but even this will be constrained if there is free movement of population and resources as well as free trade, since capital and labor will eventually move to jurisdictions with greater efficiency and higher incomes.

Given the difficulties of international cartelization, then, there will be for some time after the freeing of trade an opportunity for firms in each country to make a profit by selling in *other* countries at the high cartelized prices prevailing there. As firms—even if they continue to follow the cartel rules in their own country—undercut foreign cartels, all cartels fall. With the elimination of cartelization, the problems growing out of Implications 4, 6, 7, 8, and 9 diminish, efficiency improves, and the growth rate increases.

Economic theory, I have argued earlier, has been more like Newton's mechanics than Darwin's biology, and there is a need to add an evolutionary and historical approach. This also has been true of that part of economic theory called the theory of international trade. The traditional expositions of the theory of international trade that focus on the theory of comparative advantage are profound and valuable. The world would be a better place if they were more widely read. They also must be supplemented by theories of change over time of the kind that grew out of the analysis in chapter 3. The failure of the comparative-static calculations inspired by conventional theory to capture the increases in growth associated with freer trade is evidence that this is so.

XI

In the last chapter the question arose of what the policy implications of the present argument might be. Some commentators on early drafts of the argument had suggested that its main policy implication was that there should be revolution or other forms of instability. Concerned that ideological preconceptions, both left-wing and right-wing, would distort our reading of the facts and the logic, I belittled that conclusion and promised readers who thought it was the main policy implication of my argument that they were in for some surprises. Now that a gentler and more conventional policy prescription is close at hand, it may not frighten most readers away from the rest of the book to say that, yes, if one happens to be delicately balancing the arguments for and against revolution, the theory here does shift the balance marginally in the revolutionary direction.

Consider the French Revolution. It brought about an appalling amount of bloodshed and destruction and introduced or exacerbated divisions in French political life that weakened and troubled France for many generations, perhaps even to the present day. At the same time, if the theory offered here is correct, the Revolution undoubtedly destroyed some outdated feudal restrictions, coalitions, and classes that made France less efficient. To say that the present theory adds marginally to the case for revolution, however, is for many readers in many societies similar to saying that an advantage of a dangerous sport like hang gliding is that it reduces the probability that one will die of a lingering and painful disease like cancer; the argument is true, but far from sufficient to change the choice of people who are in their right minds.

Now that we are all, I hope, reminded of the overwhelming importance of other considerations in most cases, it should not be misleading to point out that this "revolutionary" implication of the present argument is not *always* of minor importance. We can now see more clearly that the contention of *some* conservatives that if social institutions have survived for a long time, they must necessarily be useful to the society, is wrong. We can also appreciate anew Thomas Jefferson's observation that "the tree of liberty must be refreshed from time to time with the blood of patriots and tyrants."[16] Let us now put this unduly dramatic matter aside and turn to a policy implication of vastly wider applicability.

The policy prescription is not in any way novel or revolutionary. Indeed, in keeping with my general emphasis on the contributions of my predecessors and professional colleagues, I would say that this policy recommendation has been shared by nearly every scholar of stature who has given the matter specialized thought. The recommendation unfortunately has far more often than not been ignored, and when it has been taken into account it almost always has been followed only to a limited degree. The policy implication, as readers of this chapter have long foreseen, is that there should be freer trade and fewer impediments to the free movement of factors of production and of firms.

Any readers who doubt that this policy recommendation has more often than not been ignored should note that most of the great examples of the freeing of trade and factor mobility have come about not because the recommendations of economists were followed, but wholly or largely as an incidental consequence of policies with other objectives. I have attempted to show in this chapter that the most notable reductions in barriers to the flow of products and productive factors have been reductions in the length rather than in the height of barriers—that they have resulted from jurisdictional integration. The jurisdictional integration brought about by the centralizing monarchs of early modern Europe was not inspired by liberal teaching, but by the monarchs' lusts for power and pelf. The jurisdictional integration of the United States and Germany owed more to nationalistic, political, and military considerations than to economic understanding; the mainly inadvertent character of the massive liberalization these two countries brought about is proven by the tariffs, trusts, and cartels they accepted at a national level. Even the creation of the Common Market owed more to fears of Soviet imperialism, to a desire to insure that there would not be yet another Franco-German war, and to imitation of and uneasiness about the United States, than it did to a rigorous analysis of the gains from freer trade and factor mobility. Specialists have long known that a country could get most or all of the gains from freer trade without joining a customs union simply by reducing its own barriers unilaterally, and would indeed often gain much more from this than from joining a customs union. Unilateral tariff reductions are nonetheless rare.

Although the textbooks explain the other reasons for liberal or internationalist policies, such policies can draw additional support from the theory offered here, because free trade and factor movement evade and undercut distributional coalitions. If there is free international trade, there are international markets out of the control of any lobbies. The way in which free trade undermines cartelization of firms, and indirectly also reduces monopoly power in the labor market, has already been discussed. Free movement of productive factors and firms is no less subversive of distributional coalitions. If local entrepreneurs are free to sell equities without constraint to foreigners as well as to borrow abroad, those with less wealth or inferior connections at home will be better able to get the capital needed for competition with established firms, and may even be able to marshall enough resources to break into collusive oligopolies of large firms in industries where there are substantial economies of scale. If foreign or multinational firms are welcome to enter a country to produce and compete on an equal basis with local firms, they will not only often bring new ideas with them but also make the local market more competitive and perhaps destroy a cartel as well. That is one reason why they are usually so unpopular—the consumers who freely choose to buy their goods and the workers who choose to accept the new jobs they offer do not lose from the entry of the multinationals, but these consumers and workers may be persuaded that this foreign entry is undesirable by the propaganda of those who do.

The resistance to labor mobility across national borders has a similar inspiration. Whereas rapid and massive immigration obviously can generate social tensions and other costs, these costs are not the only reason for the barriers against foreign labor. The restrictions on immigration and guest workers in many countries and communities are promoted mainly by special-interest organizations representing the groups of workers who have to compete with the in-migrants; labor unions obtain limitations on the inflow of manual workers, medical societies impose stricter qualifying examinations for foreign-trained physicians, and so on. The separate states of the United States, for example, not only control admission into most professions, but often also into such diverse occupations as cosmetology, barbering, acupuncture, and lightning-rod salesmen. These controls are frequently used to keep out practitioners from other states. The nations of Western Europe also vary greatly in the proportion of migrants and guest workers they have admitted. Many other factors are involved, but the initial impression is that countries with weaker labor unions have accepted relatively larger inflows of labor.

The law of diminishing returns suggests that the growth of income per capita or per worker would be reduced when an already densely populated country imports more labor. However, as Charles Kindleberger has argued,[17] the developed industrial economies in which per capita income has grown most rapidly are often those which have absorbed the most new labor. Kindleberger explains this in terms of Arthur Lewis's famous model of growth with "unlimited supplies of labor," and this hypothesis deserves careful study.

Another part of the explanation is that the size of the inflow of labor affects the strength of special-interest groups of workers. If a large pool of less expensive foreign labor may easily be tapped, and unions have significantly raised labor costs for domestic firms, then it will be profitable to set up new firms or establishments employing the outside labor. The competition of these new undertakings will in turn reduce the gains from monopoly over the labor force in the old establishments. Union co-optation of the outside workers will be at least delayed by cultural and linguistic differences or by the temporary status of guest workers. Similar freedom of entry for foreign professionals, of course, will undermine the cartelization that is characteristic of professions.

We are finally in a position to assess the ad hoc argument that Britain's economic plight is due to its trade unions. This argument is in part profoundly wrong, and in part right and important. It is profoundly wrong because combinations of firms (being fewer in number) can and often do collude in their common interest more than larger numbers of employees can. The ad hoc anti-union argument also overlooks the professions, whose cartelization is generally older, and probably more costly to British society per person involved, than the average union. It also neglects the class structure and the anti-entrepreneurial and anti-business attitudes which grow in large part out of the same logic and history that underlie the British pattern of trade unions.

Despite its shortcomings, the blame-it-on-the-unions argument does have one important merit (if the professional associations are counted as unions). That arises because the net migration of labor into the United Kingdom has been relatively modest and was quickly restricted when it promised to become great (as was the case with Commonwealth immigrants from South Asia and the Caribbean). If we take a long-run or historical view, we can probably conclude that, relative to many other countries, Britain has not had especially high levels of protection or unusually restrictive legislation against foreign capital or multinational firms. Postwar multilateral tariff-cutting agreements, the Common Market, and falling transport costs have brought about a substantial increase in international trade. Thus many firms that export or that compete with importers are denied most of the gains from collusion, except in those cases where they have been able to form international cartels. The firms that provide international financial and insurance services in the City, for example, must be roughly as efficient as the foreigners with which they compete. This suggests that the British disease is most serious for goods and services and factors of production that do not face foreign competition and are at the same time in a situation where they are susceptible to organization for collective action. Those major "High Street" merchants who resist suburban shopping centers and hyper-markets, for example, can lobby and collude without any real fear that their customers will go overseas to shop. Thus relatively parochial industries and services, construction, government, the professions, and (as the ad hoc argument states) the unions probably account for a large share of the inefficiencies in the British economy. Since wages absorb most of the national income and much of British labor is organized, the unions also have great quantitative significance.

Unfortunately, as British experience in the late nineteenth and early twentieth centuries shows, free trade alone is not enough. Even in combination with free factor mobility it would not come close to being a panacea or complete solution. Freedom of trade and of factor mobility have to be used in combination with other policies to reduce or countervail cartelization and lobbying. But even with other policies, there are no total or permanent cures. This is because the distributional coalitions have the incentive and often also the power to prevent changes that would deprive them of their enlarged share of the social output. To borrow an evocative phrase from Marx, there is an ''internal contradiction'' in the development of stable societies. This is not the contradiction[18] that Marx claimed to have found, but rather an inherent conflict between the colossal economic and political advantages of peace and stability and the longer-term losses that come from the accumulating networks of distributional coalitions that can survive only in stable environments.

6

Inequality, Discrimination, and Development

When testing any theory, it is by no means enough to find a few cases that seem to support it. If the predictions of the theory apply to a large number of cases and only a small number of those cases are discussed, then there is always the possibility that only those cases that happen to be consistent with the theory have been considered and that a thorough analysis of the available evidence would indicate that the theory was false. Unfortunately, the present theory has implications for such an incredibly wide array of phenomena in different countries and historical periods that a thorough and meticulous testing is out of the question here. It would not only make this book impossibly long, but it would also require vastly more knowledge than I have or could hope to acquire. There is, however, protection against the possibility that I have considered only unrepresentative cases in the fact that we have looked at the growth rates of *all* of the developed democracies in the years since regular estimates of national income were first prepared, shortly after World War II (see table 1.1, p. 6 above). Thus, so far as the postwar developed democracies are concerned, there is no possibility that only those cases that happen to fit the theory have been considered. It may be a matter of dispute whether the theory is consistent with all of the major variations in growth rates in this subset or just with most of them, but since the importance of other causal factors is emphasized, there is *some* support for the theory in the postwar experience of the developed democracies on even the most skeptical reading of this evidence.

It is, on the other hand, still possible that the developed democracies since the war are unrepresentative in ways that are crucial to deciding what claim to credence, if any, the theory has. One real pos-

146

sibility is that the data on these countries fit the argument purely by chance, although the collateral evidence on industry comparisons and temporal patterns of growth and the mass of corroborative data on the forty-eight states make this extraordinarily unlikely. Another possibility is that there is some altogether different causal mechanism operating that has much the same results as the theory here predicts. A third possibility is that the theory is true or largely true for these countries but does not apply to other types of societies, such as the developing nations or the communist countries.

There is some protection against all these possibilities in the way the theory appears to fit the experience of Britain, Holland, and France in the early modern period, the patterns of growth within European countries in that period, and the growth of the United States and Germany in the nineteenth century. Indeed, as we shall see in the last chapter, the theory is consistent with some dramatic features of the interwar period also, so the claim that it fits the most striking departures from normal economic experience among the nations of the West since the late Middle Ages has some basis.

No matter how much additional evidence might substantiate the findings on the developed democracies and on the modern economic history of the West, it still would not support compelling conclusions about non-Western societies (except perhaps Japan). Possibly different causal processes are operating in non-Western areas. Erudite scholars like Max Weber have argued that certain features of Western European christendom, and especially of puritanism, were uniquely favorable to capitalism and economic progress. Although the historical support for Weber's fascinating argument is at best mixed, we must ask whether the coalitional processes described in this book are dependent on certain cultural or religious attitudes and confined more or less to Western civilization. We should not conclude that the same tendencies are at work in other civilizations unless there is evidence of similar coalitional processes in several other cultural traditions.

II

There is, in fact, massive evidence of coalitional processes in a variety of non-Western societies. There have been guilds, for example, in Moslem countries (and even in Mecca),[1] in Byzantium, in China, in Hellenistic times, and even in Babylonia.[2] These guilds, moreover, bear the same dead-giveaway signs of cartelistic purposes: restrictive membership, price-fixing, long apprenticeships from which the sons or relatives of members are often exempt, and rules limiting output and innovation. As might be expected from the many modern studies finding similar motivations and responses to prices and profit opportunities in developed and developing nations,[3] the eager acceptance of the gains from cartelization and political power seems much the same in very different cultural and religious traditions. Whereas those parts of the world that have never developed very far cannot show us quite the contrasts that European economic history offers, it is still clear that guilds and other distributional coalitions have normally had the same harmful effects on economic efficiency and growth, whatever the culture.

The Chinese economy in the latter part of the nineteenth century offers a good example. Even though some guilds had been destroyed in the instability associated with the Taiping rebellion in the mid-nineteenth century, guilds were powerful, especially in the latter part of the century. Hosea Ballou Morse, a leading scholar on China (and Commissioner of Chinese Maritime Customs for a time during the "treaty ports" period), wrote in *The Guilds of China* (1909) that "all Chinese trade guilds are alike in interfering with every detail of business and demanding complete solidarity of interest of their members, and they are alike also in that their rules are not a dead letter, but are actually enforced. The result is tyranny of the many over the individual, and a system of control which must by its nature hinder freedom of enterprise and independence of individual initiative."[4]

Some economists argue that there cannot be much monopoly or cartelistic power unless the coercive power of government is brought into play, but Chinese guilds provide unusually clear evidence that this view is wrong. There were, to be sure, symbiotic relations between guilds and government officials in which the coercive power of government was brought to bear in the common interests of the guild and the officials. Nonetheless, as Morse stated it, "The trade guilds have grown up apart from and independent of the government; they . . . devised their own regulations, and enforced them in their own way and by their own methods."[5] He argued that Chinese guilds could enforce their regulations.

> Partly because of the enormous impulsive power of a mediaeval form of public opinion and the development of the boycott by

centuries of practical use, the guilds have in fact obtained an enormous and almost unrestrained control over their respective trades. . . . Their jurisdiction over their members is absolute, not by reason of any charter or delegated power, but by virtue of the faculty of combination by the community and of coercion on the individual. . . . The craftsman who is not a guild member is as one exposed to the wintry blast without a cloak.[6]

Even individual appeals to the government on matters of interest to the guild were excluded, unless the guild had first considered the matter. Another observer, Daniel J. Macgowan, cites guild rules specifying that if a "complainant have recourse to the [government] official direct, without first referring to the guild, he shall be subject to a public reprimand, and any future case he may present for the opinion of the guild will be dismissed without a hearing."[7]

Guild power could be used even *against* the government. There is a ghastly illustration of this in Macgowan's reports of the gold beaters guild, which provided gold leaf that the emperor purchased in large quantities. The rule of the trade was that no employer could have more than one apprentice at a time, but one member of the craft represented to the magistrate that, if he were allowed to take on a number of apprentices, the work would be expedited. He received permission to do so and engaged a great many apprentices. This output-increasing, price-reducing conduct infuriated the craft. The word was passed around that "biting to death is not a capital offence," apparently on the gruesome theory that no one of the morsels taken is fatal, and the cartel-buster was soon dead from the fiendish efforts of 123 of his fellows.[8] None of the guild members was allowed to leave the shop until his teeth and gums attested to what, in more delicate settings, might be called his "professional ethics." Although the man who took the first bite was, it turns out, discovered and executed, one can well imagine that the squeamish, at least, must have been made apprehensive about increasing output or cutting prices, even when the emperor was the buyer.

The effect of guilds was no doubt increased by the fact that China, ostensibly a unified nation, had tariffs or transit taxes on trade within the country.[9] In addition, there was effectively a prohibition against foreign trade (because all imports had to go through a single guild in Canton), until the Western powers imposed treaties on the Chinese that opened certain ports and commercial opportunities to foreigners. After these treaties there were many efforts to introduce various types of production with modern Western technology, many of which were defeated by boycotts or governmental discouragements organized by guilds of competitors. Guilds blocked or delayed the use of modern technologies in silk reeling, coal mining, soybean-oil pressing, steamboat transportation, and railways, for example. Chinese as well as foreign businessmen were discouraged from investing in new technologies, and the most successful Chinese businessmen were concentrated in the treaty port cities under European jurisdiction.[10]

China, though possessed of an extraordinarily ancient and rich culture, did not of course industrialize. Only a few decades ago it was often taken for granted, even by the most erudite and sympathetic observers, that something in the Chinese spirit or culture was inherently unsuited to modern economic life.[11] This is nearly the opposite of the conventional wisdom now. In the last three decades the most rapidly growing areas in the world have been Chinese or profoundly influenced by Chinese culture. Consider the communities that I. M. D. Little has called the "gang of four": Hong Kong, Korea, Taiwan, and Singapore. All four, it is worth noting, have recent histories that have been inimical to the development of distributional coalitions and have had relatively liberal trade policies as well. Korea and Taiwan did not have the freedom to develop independent interest groups while they were colonies of Japan, Singapore had little to gain from lobbies when it was run by Britain, and Hong Kong is still a colony run along nineteenth-century British free-trade lines.[12]

III

Western observers usually greatly underestimate the differences between Chinese and Japanese cultures, but Japan can nonetheless also be considered an area that has been profoundly influenced by Chinese culture. The rapid growth of Japan since World War II has already been analyzed, but there is also the exceptional growth Japan enjoyed for a couple of generations after the Meiji restoration in 1867–68. This earlier phase of Japanese growth also stands in sharp contrast to what occurred in China, and for that matter to what happened at that time in all other non-Western areas of the world.

Many accounts of Japanese growth attribute it mainly to special characteristics of the Japanese culture or people. The Japanese were not, however, always considered economic supermen. Western visitors in the mid-nineteenth century were often struck with the utter poverty of the people and even with the number of families that were reduced to infanticide. Although the rate of literacy was quite high by the standards of poor societies at that time, and the society had been progressing in certain respects,[13] it was pathetically weak both technologically and militarily and subject to humiliation by even the most casual efforts of Western navies. In those days the conventional wisdom among Western observers was far different than it is today, with some alleging that Japanese character or culture was intrinsically incapable of economic development.[14]

Before Admiral Perry's gunboats appeared in 1854, the Japanese were virtually closed off from the international economy; foreign trade was largely confined to one port and trade through that port was severely limited. A central government of sorts under the shogun had maintained peace and stability for several centuries, but much of the power to determine economic policies remained in the hands of more than 200 separate *daimyo,* or feudal lords. The tolls, tariffs, regulations, and legal monopolies of these separate fiefs, with their own coinages and currencies, drastically limited trade within Japan.

As we know, the theory offered here predicts that protected markets enjoying a period of stability will become cartelized, at least if the number of enterprises in the market is small enough to allow each individual enterprise to get a significant share of the gain from collective action. This prediction fits Japan no less than other societies; there were any number of powerful *za,* or guilds, and the shogunate or the daimyo often strengthened them by selling them monopoly rights. Various guilds controlled major markets, although there were also independent enterprises in rural areas and even merchants who used the "putting-out" system. Of course, Japanese guilds fixed prices, restricted production, and controlled entry in essentially the same way as cartelistic organizations elsewhere.

The reader may be weary of seeing the same story over and over again in different settings, but since the causes of Japanese growth are shrouded by tenacious myths, it is perhaps best to be explicit. The upheaval that led to the Meiji restoration not only deposed the shogun and effectively dispossessed many of the vested interests tied to the shogunate, but soon also abolished the domains of the feudal daimyo as well and all of the restrictions on trade and enterprise that went with them. At about the same time that the Meiji government eliminated the barriers to a national market, Britain and other Western powers imposed treaties upon the Japanese that required something approaching free trade with the rest of the world. In particular, a treaty of 1866 restricted the Japanese to a revenue tariff of not more than 5 percent, which lasted until 1899. It was the military, technological, and economic weakness of the Japanese that forced them to accept the provisions of this and similar agreements, which the Japanese are accustomed to describing as "humiliating."

Lo and behold, the Japanese were humiliated all the way to the bank. Trade immediately expanded and economic growth apparently picked up speed, particularly in the 1880s and 1890s, and just after the turn of the century a new Japan was able to triumph in the Russo-Japanese War. Once again, multiple causation must be emphasized. For example, the government subsidized industries that were deemed important for military purposes and also promoted education effectively. Quantitatively speaking, however, the overwhelmingly important source of Japanese growth in the nineteenth century was the progress of small-scale private industry and agriculture, such as exports of silk and tea. Interestingly, most of the important Japanese entrepreneurs in this period do not trace their origins to the merchant houses belonging to the guilds of the pre-Meiji period; but rather, they came disproportionately from the ranks of impoverished lesser samurai (who, by the precepts of traditional Japanese culture, were not supposed to engage in commerce at all) or from rising farm and trading families in rural areas that were more likely to be beyond control by guilds or officials. It is said that when markets opened up, many of the houses that had belonged to guilds were disoriented and at a loss what to do.[15]

IV

It is natural to turn from East Asia and the countries that have been most influenced by China to South Asia and particularly to India. Like China, India has an unusually ancient history, a rich culture, and a huge impoverished population. Yet there are also colossal and oft-neglected differences between these two countries. China was among the earliest, if not the earliest, of the nation-states, and, in spite of the several occasions when its empires have collapsed, it has an extremely long history as (more or less) a single country. India, of course, did not have a single government over the whole of the subcontinent, or over all of what is now India, until it fell under British control. The Indian subcontinent is also geographically divided, by deserts, jungles, and mountains, to a greater extent than the populous parts of China are. The conquest of formative areas of Indian civilization by Aryan-speaking peoples about 1500 b.c. also introduced a further disparity into Indian life that has no counterpart in Chinese history—the Mongol conquerors of China did not impose their religion, for example, on Chinese society but were instead thoroughly assimilated by it. For these and no doubt other reasons, India is in several important respects more diverse than China. It does not have a single language common to its many peoples, whereas China (despite the vast differences in its dialects) has at least a common written language. Even a glance at the physical appearances of people from the two nations suggests much less diversity among the Chinese than among the Indians. This great diversity suggests that it is wise to be skeptical about any generalizations concerning India, including those that will be offered here.

The mosaic of jurisdictions that covered the Indian subcontinent in the pre-British era changed many times. Thus there was often a good deal of instability and war, as some warlords or dynasties expanded and others retreated or were defeated. In many periods of Indian history, however, there was what the British called "indirect rule." The British in India and throughout their empire usually did not seek to impose their government down to a local level, much less require every community or tribe to follow uniform rules. They would often rule indirectly by letting traditional authorities, decision-making arrangements, and customs prevail, provided there was no insurrection or outrage against British sensibilities or interests. As time went on or conditions changed, there might be somewhat more obtrusive government, but the British never attempted to eliminate the traditional religion or social structure of India or to remake all of Indian society along British lines; they deliberately kept out all missionaries, for example, until 1813.[16] Indirect rule was also characteristic of the Moghuls who earlier ruled the more northerly parts of India, although some of these rulers did encourage or require conversions to Islam. The Moghuls did not have bureaucracies akin to those of modern governments, or even to those of the Chinese emperors, and could not impose detailed or uniform government at a village level. Often supporters were given a *jagir* (a right to tax a collection of villages), but they would not normally own land or manage the daily life in these villages. Sometimes Hindu nobles, or *zamindars,* retained hereditary control of village revenues, and some Hindu princes continued to rule and collect taxes in autonomous states within the Moghul empire.[17] The diverse rulers of the various parts of India before the Moslems did not appear to have the bureaucracy and efficiency needed to administer vast areas in a uniform way and also appear to have taxed villages as units rather than separately taxing the individuals in the village. In general, traditional India did not have individual ownership of land, and both the different groups in the village and the rulers would share in the output resulting from the cooperative effort and division of labor in the village. At local and especially village levels, then, life could often continue without great change or instability even when new rulers came to exact taxes and tribute.

V

My thoughts about how the theory offered in this book relates to India occurred when, quite by chance, I was reading Jawaharlal Nehru's *The Discovery of India.* This remarkable book was written in only five months in 1944, while Nehru was confined by the British to Ahmadnagar Fort prison. Even though I had previously read accounts of how profoundly Nehru had been influenced by his English education and experience, I nonetheless expected that Nehru—who was after all a political figure who already may have hoped to become the leader of an independent India—would celebrate the glories of India's ancient civilization and place almost all of the blame for the country's problems on the British. Nehru naturally did point with pride to many of the great achievements of India and Indians, but what was most notable was that his praise was confined almost exclusively to certain periods of Indian history, whereas Indian society and institutions in other periods were criticized if anything more seriously than he criticized the rule of his British jailers.

Nehru was impressed, as everyone must be, by the precocious civilization in the Indus valley, one of the world's earliest societies with settled agriculture and what can fairly be called civilization. He cites, for example, the impressive houses, baths, and drainage systems evident in the excavations of the ancient city of Mohenjo-daro and quotes Western authorities who compare aspects of this Indus valley civilization favorably with contemporary civilizations in Egypt and Mesopotamia. He also points out that what the West calls "Arabic" numerals came originally from early India and that the discoveries of the concept of zero in a number system and of symbolic, algebraic notation were further examples of the creativity of early Indian civilization. Western Europe in the Dark Ages, he argues, was backward by the standards of Asia at that time.

He offered a very different view of Indian civilization at the coming of the Moslems and at the conquest of India by the Europeans. India in this epoch was "drying up and losing her creative genius and vitality"; it was the "afternoon of a civilization." This "stagnation and decay" was pervasive: "There was decline all along the line—intellectual, philosophical, political, in technique and methods of warfare, in knowledge of and contacts with the outside world, in shrinking economy." It was true, Nehru conceded, "that the loss of political freedom leads inevitably to cultural decay. But why should political freedom be lost unless some kind of decay has preceded it? A small country might easily be overwhelmed by superior power, but a huge, well-developed and highly civilized country like India cannot succumb to external attack unless there is internal decay, or the invader possesses a higher technique of warfare. That internal decay is clearly evident in India." Most of the above quotations from *The Discovery of India* relate to India at the time much of it was conquered by the Moslems, but he is clear that the same stagnation was evident when the Europeans conquered India a few centuries later and points out that they were able to capture the subcontinent "with remarkably little effort"; there was "a certain inevitability in what happened."

Nehru attributed the decay to "the static nature of Indian society which refused to change in a changing world, for every civilization which resists change declines." He reasoned that "probably this was the inevitable result of the growing rigidity and exclusiveness of the Indian social system as represented chiefly by the caste system." The caste system, he wrote, was a "petrification of classes" that "brought degradation" and is "still a burden and a curse."[18] Nehru did not claim any originality for this diagnosis and it is fairly common. There are also limits to the reliance that can be placed upon the hurried writings of a jailed political leader without the best access to sources and specialists. Nonetheless, I think that the account must have resonated with the experience and observations of many educated Indians, for the book as well as the author have been widely celebrated in India as elsewhere.

Quite apart from its effects on efficiency, the caste system is also a source of profound inequality, both in opportunities and in results. In India today there have been changes, but one must remember that in the traditional caste system groups in the population were condemned for life, and their descendants in perpetuity after them, to such tasks as the cleaning of latrines and the removal of dead carcasses. Their very touch, and in some cases even their nearness, was deemed to be polluting, their presence in temples defiling. Apart from slavery, it is hard to think of a system with greater inequality of opportunity, and the results are also most unequal. This inequality was, of course, also of great concern to Nehru.

VI

It is not sufficient to explain the decline of India by the era of the Moslem and European invasions in terms of the caste system. That, too, is an untestable ad hoc explanation; Indian history is unique in countless ways, and there is no way to determine whether a given unique trait was in fact the source of the decline Nehru noted. We have not reached home until we have explained *why* India acquired the caste system when it did and have comprehended the caste system in a theory that is testable against the experience of many countries.

The sources for the distant past of India are scanty and so little is known that agnosticism is very much in order. There is general agreement that India did not always have the caste system. It is not normally thought to have been part of the civilization in the Indus valley that preceded the Aryan conquests. Neither do the Vedas of the Aryan invaders speak of the ritual purity and pollution or the prohibitions against intermarriage or change in rank that characterized the caste system. How then did the caste system emerge?

One of the most common hypotheses is that the castes emerged out of guilds or similar organizations; most castes bear the names of occupations and there is evidence of guilds in earlier Indian history. Another common hypothesis is that visible racial differences among the indigenous peoples of India and between these peoples and the Aryan-speaking invaders were the source of the caste system; there are visible differences among some caste groups to this day, and the English word *caste* stems from the Portuguese *casta,* meaning race. Yet another familiar explanation ascribes the castes to common descent; a crucial feature of the caste system is endogamy or the prohibition against marriage outside the basic unit of caste grouping, the *jati,* and many tribes have been incorporated into the caste system. It might seem that the theory here would focus exclusively on the hypothesis that the castes grew out of guilds, but the other two hypotheses are also important, if the theory offered here is right, and we shall return to them shortly.

Castes traditionally have behaved like guilds and other distributional coalitions. With modernization many new occupations have emerged and the caste system has changed for other reasons as well, so the caste need not be primarily an occupational or guild-type classification for the educated Indian today. Traditionally, however, caste groups were not only mainly occupational, but also exhibited all the features of cartels and other special-interest organizations. They controlled entry into occupations and lines of business, kept craft mysteries or secrets, set prices monopolistically, used boycotts and strikes, and often bargained on a group rather than an individual basis.

The caste system also had several features that would be expected of distributional coalitions. One of these is that often groups rather than individuals change status. A caste group that enjoys prosperity will rise gradually to a higher status and also may decide collectively to adopt more restrictive ritualistic rules, thereby rising even in terms of the religious concepts of purity and pollution. Another feature is that Hinduism emphasizes the concept of *dharma,* the duties appropriate to the caste or group. Morality, in other words, is defined not in a universalistic way, but in terms of obedience to the rules of one's caste or station, so it is similar to professional ethics that rule out competition in a profession. Even the murderous thugs or other criminal castes were behaving consistently with their dharma when they carried on their caste's activities. A reward for fidelity to the rules of the caste or group into which one is born is a favorable reincarnation. Finally, the one way in which those born into humbler castes can rise in religious status during one lifetime is by leaving the system of group competition and forgoing material satisfactions and affiliations; higher religious status, such as that of Brahmins, is associated with privilege, and any rise in religious status that does not involve renunciation threatens other groups.

VII

None of the preceding, however, is an explanation of the prohibition against marriage out of the group that is such a basic feature of the caste system, nor does it explain any correlation of caste with racial or ethnic differences. For that we must turn to Implication 8, which is that distributional coalitions are characteristically exclusive and seek to limit the diversity of their memberships. We must ask how that implication would apply over a multigenerational time span.

Consider the situation of an older member of a profitable guild. As one of the co-owners of an advantageous coalition, the older member would have an interest in how he or his descendants might share in the future returns. One logical possibility is that he could upon his death or retirement bequeath his share of the future returns of the coalition to his children; his son, for example, could take his place in the craft. But some of the members of the coalition will have daughters and some only daughters. Suppose that the coalition is a guild with only male workers, and that the members with daughters then offer access to the profitable cartel as part of a marriage bargain with sons-in-law. That will offer the old member a way of getting something for his share of his coalition's worth, but we must ask what will happen if both sons and sons-in-law enter the trade. Even with a steady-state population *the number in the craft will double if both sons and sons-in-law are allowed to enter, and normally a doubling of the craft's membership would eliminate the gains of the cartelistic output restriction that gave the guild its value in the first place.* The same problem will occur if both sons and daughters practice a craft that was previously restricted to one sex. The multigenerational guild can be successful only if it can keep its membership from increasing faster than can be justified by any expansion in its market, which will depend on such things as the growth of population and income in the areas in which it is located. Unless some sons are left out, the *only* way those members who have only or mainly daughters can gain their share of the value of the cartel, without making the cartel valueless, is to restrict the sons allowed to enter the trade to marriages with daughters of members of the trade.

The same is true of a coalition that has, say, disproportionate rights to the village harvest. The greatest distributional gains come from a minimum winning coalition. Thus if the favorable share of the harvest is divided up among more families, there is less for each family. But if each family has on average two surviving children who marry, then there will be two families in the next generation for every family in the first generation, and in a few generations even the grandest entitlement will provide very little per family. The only way the distributional coalition can retain its value over several generations is by restricting the children of members to marriages with one another or by disinheriting a large portion of the children. I hypothesize that the Indian castes mainly used the first method. The English nobility used this method to a great degree and combined it with primogeniture as well (thus it is not astonishing that some great fortunes were passed on for several generations in the English aristocracy).

This reference to the British nobility brings us back to the discussion of Implication 8 in chapter 3, where the nobility and royalty of Europe were used to illustrate the exclusiveness of marriages (or bequests) that is essential to any successful multigenerational special-interest group. Those who have a chauvinistic turn of mind or who are convinced that fundamentally different processes must operate at different levels of wealth or status no doubt will be surprised by this alleged similarity of motivation in groups as different in wealth and background as the European nobility and the Indian castes. Those who have done a lot of empirical and historical research in economics would, I think, be surprised by anything else. Those who have studied barriers to intergenerational mobility across social classes in any societies with significant class barriers will also, I conjecture, find incipient castes.

Just as the origin of the caste system is often ascribed to guilds, so is it often related to the racial diversity of India at the time of the Aryan migrations and also to descent groups. Given the repeated emphasis on multicausality and the complexity of reality in this book, we should examine these hypotheses sympathetically. They are, as it turns out, also very much in keeping with the logic behind Implication 8. If a racially distinct distributive coalition is formed by alien conquerors, it will be able to preserve itself over many generations only by arbitrary rules of bequest such as primogeniture or through endogamy. If it is largely endogamous the differences in appearance will be preserved.

Indeed, it will be far easier for a racially, linguistically, and culturally distinctive group to maintain a multigenerational coalition. The linguistic and cultural similarities will reduce differences in values and facilitate social interaction, and, as chapters 2 and 3 show, this reduces conflict and makes it easier to generate social selective incentives. Moreover, any special-interest group that uses endogamy to preserve its benefits over a multigenerational period must be large enough to avoid inbreeding. As the endogamous group gets larger, however, the difficulty of enforcing endogamy rises. How is this or that son to be restrained from marrying some especially appealing girl outside the group, or how are his parents to be prevented from making an especially advantageous marriage contract for him with relatively wealthy or powerful people outside the group? How can the astute outsider be kept from marrying into the coalition? If exogamy is not prevented, at least some of the families must lose their share of the coalition's future gains. If there are visible differences, it will be easier to determine who is in the group and who is not and to enforce the endogamy rule. Differences in speech, culture, and lifestyle are also shibboleths that make it harder for the outsider to blend in. Unfortunately, *the promotion of prejudices about race, ethnicity, culture, and intergroup differences in lifestyle will also make the coalition work better.* The inculcation of these prejudices will increase the probability that the members will follow the rule of endogamy and strengthen selective incentives by interacting socially only with their own group, of their own accord.

Though multigenerational distributional coalitions foster inefficiency, inequality, and group prejudice, it is nonetheless important to realize that some individuals and groups outside the society containing these coalitions may improve their positions by joining that society, even if they enter at the bottom. Tribes without settled agriculture, for example, might in some circumstances have found that they would be better off joining Indian society than by staying out of it, even though they were accorded the lowest status and were victims of special-interest groups to boot. There have been many observations of such assimilation of tribal groups into India's caste system, and they must help to account for its great diversity.

This diversity, once again, reminds us of the complexity of the matter. Because of this complexity and the limited sources on the early years of the caste system, we must not jump to any conclusions. The hypotheses that emerge from the theory here should be considered primarily a stimulus to further research. There has been no theoretical consensus on caste and class: a fresh perspective could provide some help. It is, I submit, worth doing serious research on whether multigenerational processes of the sort the theory suggests have in fact emerged over the millennia of Indian history. This exceptionally long history of settled agriculture and civilized life was combined for the most part with indirect or parochial rulers who could not or did not challenge the power or usurp all the gains of the distributional coalitions. It was combined also with racial diversity and geographical segmentation of markets favorable to the coalition formation by small groups. If the processes of the kind described above did not occur, then how do we explain what happened?

VIII

In keeping with the scientific principle that the theory that explains the most with the least is most likely to be true, any alternative explanation of the Indian caste system should also be capable of explaining some developments outside India, as the present theory does, or at least parsimoniously explain a good deal more about the caste system. By the same token, the explanation offered here of the Indian caste system will be stronger if the theory in the book explains not only diverse developments outside India, but also developments outside India that are similar to the Indian developments. To some extent the previous analysis of class rigidities was in that category, but there is still the problem that the Indian caste system is unique, so that developments in other countries do not provide the close parallelism we seek. In particular, in most other countries any class rigidities usually do not involve rigid requirements of endogamous marriage and group or race prejudice. Since the theory here implies that over a sufficiently long run distributional coalitions will stimulate group prejudice and promote endogamous marriage, it is wise to look for countries other than India where this is occurring. Other societies will not have the extraordinary antiquity and cultural richness of India, but perhaps some of them will in certain respects resemble India in the era when the caste system emerged. We should particularly look for societies with racial and cultural differences.

The extraordinary system of apartheid in South Africa is a relatively recent development. The more severe forms of racial segregation and discrimination do not go back to the early days of the Boers in South Africa. On the contrary, there was more than a small amount of interbreeding between the Boers or other Europeans and the Africans. There is, after all, a large population of "Coloured" or mixed-race people in South Africa today; the South African government treats them as a separate category and segregates them from Africans and Asians as well as from Europeans.

A distinguished South African economist, W. H. Hutt, in *The Economics of the Colour Bar,*[19] has written a startling history of the evolution of progressively tighter systems of racial segregation and discrimination in South Africa. Although Hutt is perhaps insufficiently detached about his classical liberal ideology and may offend some readers of other persuasions, my checks with other specialists on South Africa suggest that even those who do not share his interpretation are generally in agreement on his rendition of the historical facts.

Hutt's account focuses closely on the mining industry in South Africa early in the present century. The mine owners and management needed labor and naturally preferred to secure it at low wages rather than high wages. Since Africans had few other opportunities outside the traditional sector of African society, they were often available at low wages. The mine owners also drew upon the huge pool of low-wage labor in Asia and for a time used indentured Chinese labor. European workers were employed in the mines mainly as foremen and skilled and semi-skilled laborers. It was clear that that the far-cheaper African laborers could at very little cost soon be taught the semi-skilled jobs and the employers naturally coveted the savings in labor cost that this would bring.

The competition of cheaper African and Asian labor did not appeal to the higher-paid workers of European stock or their recently formed unions. There were strikes. In part because of these strikes there were changes in labor policy in South Africa. The Mines and Works Act of 1911, also called the "Colour Bar Act," was passed. On a superficial reading relatively innocuous, as administered it constrained employers in their use of African labor in semi-skilled and skilled jobs. The regulations promulgated under the act prevented Africans in the Transvaal and the Orange Free State from entering a wide variety of mining occupations. They even specified *ratios* between foremen (whites) and mining laborers (Africans).[20]

Disagreement about the ratios emerged. After World War I, the mine employers asked for a ratio of 10.5 Africans per white worker, whereas the labor union demanded 3.5 to 1. A general strike in the Rand followed in 1922. This strike and the agitation that followed became a common cause of conservative Afrikaaners and communist and socialist leaders, with all of them supporting the efforts to deny opportunities to the poorer Africans who were competing with white labor. The South African Labour Party, modeled more or less after its British counterpart, prospered in the wake of the strike and joined with the mainly Afrikaaner, white supremacist Nationalist Party in a coalition government. The Nationalist-Labour "Pact" government soon introduced the second "Colour Bar Act," the Mines and Works Act of 1926. Hutt calls this "probably . . . the most drastic piece of colour bar legislation which the world has ever experienced."[21] It was accompanied by a "civilized labour policy," which limited opportunities for Africans still further. One of the devices used to keep African laborers out of jobs where they would compete with whites was the requirement of "the rate for the job." If the wage for a given job is fixed at a level attractive to Europeans, the employer has no incentive to seek African workers who would work for less. Apprenticeship rules under the "civilized labour policy" also had the effect of excluding Africans.

These and similar policies drastically limited opportunities for African workers. The denial of various skilled and semi-skilled jobs to Africans not only raised the wages of the European (and sometimes Coloured and Asian) workers, but it also crowded more labor into the areas that remained open to Africans, making the wages there lower than they would otherwise be. It is important to remember, though, that there was a continuing demand of Africans from farther north to enter, notwithstanding the policies against them. They came in at the bottom and were victimized by the rules, but it was still better than the alternatives some of them had in the traditional sector. The analogy with the tribes that have been assimilated into the bottom of the Indian caste system is striking.

Since firms that could hire unusually inexpensive African labor had an advantage over foreign or domestic competitors without such opportunities, they would often be profitable even if they were forced to pay more for certain skills because only whites could be employed, to hire more foremen than needed, and so on. There were efforts of firms to move to areas where restrictions on the use of African workers were fewer, but this too was curtailed, as were some African entrepreneurs. Thus the system, while it forced employers to adopt less profitable and more discriminatory policies than they preferred, brought substantial gains to organized white (and sometimes Coloured and Asian) workers.

The theory offered in this book suggests that the employers would have been just as interested in excluding competitors as the workers were, and would as small groups have been better able to organize to do so than the workers. But the competitors of the employers were other firms or capitalists, often in other lands; the employers were not competing against African laborers, as the white workers were, so the employers were not a principal source of the racial exclusion and discrimination that the Africans suffered. South African consumers of all races paid higher prices because of the higher costs growing out of the discriminatory policy, but, as in other countries, they were not organized.

Let us now ask what necessary conditions must be met if the South African system, and the cartelistic gains it provides for many, are to be preserved over the long run. There is a need for police and military power, but this is widely understood and discussed, so it need not be considered here. The system could not possibly survive for many generations unless the demarcation between the races was preserved. If less-favored groups could enter the more-favored groups, as they would have massive incentives to do, wage differentials could not be maintained. A continuation of the processes that generated the Coloured population would make the system untenable in the long run, and even in what (by the standards of Indian history) would be the medium run.

That is not only an implication of the present theory but evidently the conclusion of the South African government as well. Just as the restrictions on the use of African labor in skilled and semi-skilled jobs increased over time, so did the rules separating the population into rigid racial categories and forbidding sexual relations, in marriage or otherwise, between them.

Undoubtedly any number of other causal factors have been at work in South Africa, and any account as brief and monocausal as this must be in many respects misleading. The purpose, however, is not to give a complete account, but to induce reflection on the sources of racial and other forms of discrimination. As others have argued before, the individual as a consumer, employer, or worker finds it costly to discriminate. The consumer who discriminates against stores owned by groups he finds offensive has to pay higher prices or suffer a lesser selection by shopping elsewhere. The employer who discriminates against workers of a despised group has higher labor costs, and his business may even bankrupt itself competing against other firms that do not let prejudice stand in the way of profit. Similarly, the worker who does not accept the best job irrespective of the group affiliation of the employer essentially is taking a cut in pay. A similar logic applies to individual social interactions of other kinds. The fact that *individuals* find discrimination costly means that, if individuals are free to undertake whatever transactions they prefer, there will be a constraint on the extent of discrimination.

Distributional coalitions of individuals, on the other hand, can sometimes gain enormously from discrimination. Any group difference that facilitates exclusion, by Implication 8, will be advantageous. For periods of only a generation or two in length, the group differences can usually be considered as given, but over the centuries and certainly the millennia they cannot. In the long run, then, multigenerational special-interest groups must tend toward endogamy. This is equally true of the South African whites, the Indian castes, and the European nobility.

IX

This book has not even touched upon societies of the soviet type. The declines in the growth rates of these societies over the stable postwar years are quite as notable as in other countries. Unfortunately, the way the present theory applies to societies of this type cannot be set out briefly; the theory of collective action by small groups needs to be elaborated and the limited role of markets in these societies analyzed. It would be digressive to go into these issues now, and so an account of how the present theory applies to these societies must be left for another publication.

The other class of contemporary societies that has so far been ignored is the characteristically unstable countries. Instability in France and on the Continent were discussed earlier, but nothing has been said about the depressingly large number of less developed countries, in Latin America, Africa, and elsewhere, that have been persistently unstable.

The dense network of distributional coalitions that eventually emerges in stable societies is harmful to economic efficiency and growth, but so is instability. There is no inconsistency in this; just as special-interest groups lead to misallocations of resources and divert attention from production to distributional struggle, so instability diverts resources that would otherwise have gone into productive long-term investments into forms of wealth that are more easily protected, or even into capital flights to more stable environments. On the whole, stable countries are more prosperous than unstable ones and this is no surprise. But, other things being equal, the most rapid growth will occur in societies that have lately experienced upheaval but are expected nonetheless to be stable for the foreseeable future.

The characteristically unstable countries are usually governed part of the time by dictators or juntas; they have intervals of democratic or at least relatively pluralistic government. The policies of the dictators or the juntas obviously will depend dramatically on the interests, the ideology, and sometimes even the whims of the dictator or the leadership group. Experience and common sense tell us that dictators and juntas may be right-wing or left-wing, this or that, although they are systematically more likely to be specialists in violence than in economics. The theory here cannot tell us what policies the dictators and juntas will have. As the better historians remind us, much of what happens in history is due to chance and must remain beyond the explanatory powers of any theory.

Fortunately, something of a systematic or theoretical nature can be said about the influences and pressures that will be brought to bear on the changing governments of the unstable societies, and about their intervals of democracy or pluralism. Implication 3 states that small groups are more likely to be organized than large ones, but that (since small groups organize less slowly) the disproportionate organizational and collusive power of small groups will be greatest in lately unstable societies. The theory here predicts that the unstable society will have fewer and weaker mass organizations than stable societies, but that small groups that can collude more readily will often be able to further their common interests. The groups may be at any level, but usually those which can gain from either lobbying or cartelizing at a national level are small groups of substantial firms or wealthy and powerful individuals.

The tendency for small groups to be better organized than large ones is further accentuated in unstable societies by two other factors. One is that large groups are more likely to be a threat to a dictator or a junta than small ones. If there were an association that included most of the peasants, or a labor union that represented most of the workers, in an unstable country with a dictator, that organization could pose a threat to the dictator. The sheer numbers of the membership of the mass organization would give it some coercive power. (Actually, this point holds for undemocratic regimes whether they are unstable or not—even the stable totalitarian state does not like the threat inherent in independent mass organizations. Unobtrusive small groups accordingly also play a leading role in the application of the theory to totalitarian societies.)

The second factor is that the small group can be discreet and inconspicuous during the dictatorial periods, whereas the organized large group cannot. Dictators, juntas, and totalitarian leaders are not enthusiastic about independent organizations of any kind, but they cannot repress collusions they do not know about. The likelihood that a group will be exposed by an indiscretion of one of its members must rise with its size and becomes a virtual certainty with a large group. Thus if a small group should feel threatened in a repressive society, it can often retain its coherence by becoming invisible to the authorities and then be able to act promptly when there is relaxation or elimination of the repression. (This point, too, applies to stable despotisms as well as unstable ones.)

The most basic implication of the theory for unstable societies, then, is that their governments are systematically influenced by the interests, pleas, and pressures of the small groups that are capable of organizing fairly quickly. Admittedly, the policies of unstable countries may shift wildly, with each coup d'etat bringing new policy preferences. The economic policy of such countries is similar to a leaf blowing in the wind—a gust may blow it suddenly in any direction, but over time gravity still will pull it to the ground.

The small groups that can organize or collude in the unstable societies will have different interests in different countries at different times. In one period they might be landed oligarchs, in another manufacturing firms; in one country they might have a vested interest in exports, in another, in import substitution. Again, it is important to respect the diversity and detail of actual experience and not to push this theory, or any other general theory, farther than it can go. The only general point so far about the unstable societies is that one must look at the vested interests of the small groups capable of relatively prompt collective action to understand one systematic element in economic policies.

X

By bringing additional information to bear we can make more specific predictions. One fact is that, since almost all the unstable governments are in developing nations, they usually do not have anything like a complete modern system of transportation and communication, at least in the rural areas. This makes it more costly and difficult for those in rural areas to mobilize political power to influence the government and gives the residents of the major metropolitan areas, especially the capital city, a disproportionate influence. Before the Industrial Revolution and the railway, transportation was slow and expensive everywhere, and this presumably explains why in his time Adam Smith observed that farmers were unable to organize to gain monopoly or political influence, whereas businessmen rarely met without conspiring against the public interest. In the developing nations today the rural interests are at a similar disadvantage, and the residents of the capital city obtain an altogether disproportionate share of governmental favors.

Although this was not always true, in most developing nations the largest firms and the wealthiest individuals are involved in producing import substitutes and goods that can also be provided by foreign firms. That is, they produce goods and services that are also available at lower cost on the world market or that could be provided more economically by local branches of foreign firms. The enterprises engaged in import substitution will in some developing countries include heavy industry, but in others they may only manufacture textiles or brew beer. Sometimes the wealthiest families will own banks or insurance companies that provide services that foreign firms could also provide. Of course, nowadays these enterprises and families will also tend to be located in the great cities with the easiest access to the government.

When the most substantial firms are in the import-substitution and foreign-replacement sectors, and especially when there is poor transportation in the rural areas, a special *perverse policy syndrome* develops in the "top-heavy" society. The key to this policy syndrome is the markedly disproportionate strength of small groups in the unstable societies.

The large enterprises and wealthy families in the situations described above have an obvious interest in protection against imports and discriminatory legislation against the foreign or multinational firms with which they compete. This drives up prices for consumers, but consumers are in latent groups that cannot organize, and many of them are out in the provinces as well. The most drastic forms of protection, such as quotas and exchange controls that deny citizens foreign currency for the purchase of imports for which there are domestic substitutes, are often used. These methods of protection are not readily subject to measurement. But in many cases, the level of protection is staggeringly high and quite beyond comparison with the levels of protection in the major developed democracies.

Let us look at the effects of these protective policies on the distribution of income. The imports and foreign firms are normally a source of competition because they have lower costs. In other words, the unstable developing country and its firms do not have a comparative advantage in the types of production in question. If they did, in most cases they would not care for protection.[22] Most developing countries do not have comparative advantage in many manufactured import substitutes because these types of production involve large proportions of capital and technical expertise, which are usually scarce and therefore tend to be relatively expensive.

When the goods and services that are intensive in capital and technical expertise are protected, the price of capital and technical expertise in the developing nation rises, particularly in the favored firms and industries. Some of the gains to owners of the favored enterprises will be consumed by the efforts to secure or maintain the political favors. The employees of some of these firms also may be able to share in the gains. Nonetheless, in at least some countries, the owners of capital and technical expertise, who were probably well rewarded because of their scarcity in the first place, now get even higher rates of return. Since it was the wealthier individuals and larger firms that initially were able to organize fastest, and since the mobilization of large amounts of capital and the acquisition of rare expertise requires wealth, the protection in most cases presumably favors the wealthy.

In addition, the protection makes the country's currency more valuable than it would otherwise be; less of the national currency is supplied to buy the foreign exchange needed for imports. The higher the price of the national currency, the more expensive the country's exports and the less of them foreigners will buy. The exports are in general the goods that the country has a comparative advantage in producing. Poor developing nations naturally have a lot of poor people and thus cheap labor, and some natural resources, so they tend to have a comparative advantage in producing goods that are intensive in labor and natural resources. The owners of labor and of natural resources, and the peasantry in particular, are the victims of the loss in exports. In some African countries, especially, the rural exporters are further exploited by government marketing monopolies that give the farmers only a portion of the price at which the government sells their commodities. The plentiful factors of production earn relatively little to begin with and the loss of export earnings reduces their incomes still further. The owners of the plentiful factors—which include in every developing nation the working poor—not only are denied access to cheaper imports by the protection, but also get lower prices for the labor and the products they have to sell.

There are a host of qualifications and technical niceties that it would be interesting to explore at this point. It is also important to point out that situations are somewhat different in each country. Nonetheless, the general nature of the process is clear. The most substantial and wealthy interests are relatively better organized in the unstable society, but they often own an unrepresentative mix of the country's productive factors. They obtain policies that favor themselves and work in different ways against the interests of the larger unorganized groups in the society, thereby making the distribution of income far more unequal.

The available statistics are poor and incomplete, but it is clear that many of the unstable countries have unusually unequal distributions of income, with giant fortunes juxtaposed with mass poverty. In some of these countries it is obvious even from casual observation that, as the foregoing argument would lead us to expect, the unskilled workers are trying desperately to get out, and (when they think the chances of being nationalized are not great) the multinationals are trying to get in. A research assistant and I have compared some (very shaky) data on income distribution across countries with some (even shakier) data on the degree of instability. The weakness of the data and the multiplicity of alternative explanations of the results have forced me to conclude that the tests are not worth relating here. But for whatever little they are worth, they are consistent with the theory.

All the arguments and evidence in the preceding chapter about the losses from protection also apply to the unstable developing countries, especially the smaller ones. Thus the perverse policy syndrome described above promotes inefficiency and stagnation as well as inequality.

When the import-substituting industries in the capital and other metropolitan areas are protected and cartelized, they can survive even if they pay wages far above the competitive level. This allows greater gains from the monopolization of the labor force and promotes unions, although episodic repression and the difficulties of organizing large-scale collective action may prevent unionization. Whether unions emerge or not, the population of the capital city—even the poor—will tend to have more influence on public policy than their rural and provincial cousins because of the inadequacies of the transportation system. Popular demonstrations, strikes, and riots in the capital are a special threat to governments.

The civil and military bureaucracies, which are well placed to influence any government, will be disproportionately in the capital city.

University students, with their untypically intense interest in politics and flexible schedules, are usually important in politics and are often in the large cities. The unions, the bureaucracy, and the students frequently will have different ideological colorations than the owners of large firms, but they may be equally disposed to economic nationalism and may not in practice be much in conflict over the detailed and inconspicuous policies the separate small groups normally seek. In any case, the bureaucracy, and often also the unions and the students, will support the subsidization of life in the capital and perhaps other large cities.

The provision of extra facilities and other forms of subsidization to urban areas encourages more migration to the capital and to other cities, beyond that already spurred by the import-substitution policies. So another aspect of the perverse policy syndrome is inefficiently large capital cities and major metropolitan areas. The capital cities of most of the poorer nations today are vastly larger in relation to the population of these nations than were the capital cities in the developed nations when those nations had the levels of per capita income the poorer countries have.

The unstable countries are so diverse, and their policies influenced by so many factors, that the preceding argument should be regarded as a "researchers' parable" rather than an analysis; it should be read as a story meant to have heuristic value. Researchers and others with a specialized knowledge of particular unstable countries will, it is hoped, be stimulated to analyze the situation in a particular country, or some small set of countries, in a systematic way.

One type of inquiry that is needed is historical. Some of the countries that now have the perverse policy syndrome, or something rather like it, were probably once in a different situation. For some Latin American countries in the nineteenth century, for example, it is worth asking whether the group that could best organize to influence the government would have been a small group of landed families of great wealth. The difficulties of transportation would have made their collusion more difficult, and sometimes their power may have been exercised only locally, in a feudal fashion. If these families could collude on national policy, however, they would have had interests different from those who profit from the perverse policy syndrome. As owners of land and sometimes of labor in peonage, they would have held a mix of factors representative of the economies of which they were a part. As such they would have gained from liberal trade policies. To the extent that their poorer compatriots also owned some land and labor, they too would have profited. With revolutions and the gradual growth of cities, landed magnates lost influence or disappeared. Liberal and socialist writers in the capital cities pressed for egalitarian policies that did not appeal to the great landowners. There is a need for research to determine whether the changes have, in fact, reduced inequality. In some countries we may find that the small groups in urban areas that have influenced policy more recently have a vested interest in less efficient policies, and ones that have more inegalitarian consequences as well.

XI

Now that we have considered the unique inequality of the caste system, the racial discrimination in South Africa, and the inegalitarian policies of the top-heavy societies with the perverse policy syndrome, we can examine a modern myth that has in my judgment forced needless poverty and humiliation on millions of people. Among economists, who are about the only people who have given the matter specialized study, there is a consensus that competitive markets are efficient. Indeed, in economic theory the definition of a perfectly competitive market entails that it is perfectly efficient, with the only possible improvement being in the distribution of income that results. Even among those who are in other vocations, there is, at least in the developed countries, a fairly widespread understanding that competition encourages efficiency.

There is at the same time the standard assumption, among economists as well as the laity, that competitive markets generate a considerable degree of inequality. A soft-hearted majority holds the further view that government action—or in some versions the operation of unions, professional ethics, and so forth—is needed to reduce the inequalities generated by the market. A hard-boiled minority willingly accepts or even rejoices in the inequality or believes that governmental efforts to reduce inequality are harmful. Most of the soft-hearted and most of the hard-boiled agree in taking it for granted that markets generate considerable inequality and differ about whether this inequality is unjust. The economist often speaks of the trade-off between efficiency, obtained through competitive markets, and equity, obtained at some social cost by other means.

Perhaps the most intelligent and humane expression of the view that competitive markets are a source of considerable inequality that government and other nonmarket institutions then reduce at some social cost is Arthur Okun's widely respected book, *Equality and Efficiency: The Big Trade-Off.*[23] In this book it is taken for granted that governments are an egalitarian force that evens out the inequality resulting from the operation of markets, and that some price must be paid for this reduction in inequality because it interferes with the operation of generally efficient markets. Some other writers suppose that unions and other special-interest groups reduce the inequalities that result from competitive markets.

I submit that the orthodox assumption of both Left and Right that the market generates more inequality than the government and the other institutions that "mitigate" its effects is the opposite of the truth for many societies, and only a half-truth for the rest. In South Africa there are black workers who are paid *one-eleventh* as much as white workers doing slightly different jobs that require about the same degree of skill. In a truly competitive economy, as the textbooks lucidly explain, it is difficult indeed to see how people with the same skills and effectiveness could earn very different rates of pay in the long run. Employers could profit by hiring the low-wage victims of discrimination, and firms that refused to do so would eventually be driven out of business by their lower-cost competitors. As we should expect, employers in South Africa argue that they should be allowed to use the African workers for jobs that are now restricted to whites. If this is allowed, both efficiency and equity will improve. In India many tens of millions of people historically have been condemned, and their children after them, to lives of special poverty and humiliation by caste rules that prevent the free operation of markets; and these rules have led to inefficiency and stagnation as well as inequality. Most of the countries of this world are unstable developing nations, and in most of them the policies on international trade, foreign investment, and many other matters make these societies generate colossal inequalities as well as inefficiency. This is evidence that, as I argued in justification of Implication 9, the gang fight is no gentler than the individual duel.

Now let us turn to the developed democracies with their welfare states. Those of us who believe that we ought to make a decent provision for the least fortunate in our societies, even though it will require that we make some sacrifices ourselves, have to face up to the logic of collective action. We can help our friends, relatives, or neighbors and can see the benefits that result from our generosity, so we may make significant sacrifices on their behalf. But if we strive as individuals to reduce the poverty in the country in which we live, we find that even if we gave up all of our wealth it would not be enough to make a noticeable difference in the amount of poverty in the society. The alleviation of poverty in a society is, in other words, a public good to all those who would like to see it eliminated, and voluntary contributions will not obtain public goods for large groups. If everyone who is concerned about poverty made a contribution to its alleviation, in the aggregate that would, however, make a difference. So a majority of us in each of the developed democracies votes for raising some money by imposing compulsory taxes on ourselves, or more precisely on the whole society, and devoting these monies to the needy. Since the alleviation of poverty on a society-wide basis is a public good, efforts to redistribute income to the poor as a group require governmental action. In this respect, it is true that governments in some societies do mitigate inequalities. Since both the taxes and the transfers have adverse effects on incentives, it is also true that there are trade-offs between equality and efficiency.

The trouble is that the current orthodoxies of both Left and Right assume that almost all the redistribution of income that occurs is the redistribution inspired by egalitarian motives, and that goes from the nonpoor to the poor. In reality many, if not most, of the redistributions are inspired by entirely different motives, and most of them have arbitrary rather than egalitarian impacts on the distribution of income—more than a few redistribute income from lower to higher income people. A very large part of the activities of governments, even in the developed democracies, is of no special help to the poor and many of these activities actually harm them. In the United States there are subsidies to the owners of private airplanes and yachts, most of whom are not poor. The intervention of the professions and the government in the medical care system, as I have shown elsewhere,[24] mainly helps physicians and other providers, most of whom are well-heeled. There are innumerable tax loopholes that help the rich but are without relevance for the poor and bail-outs for corporations and protection for industries when the workers' wages are far above the average for American industry. There are minimum-wage laws and union-wage scales that keep employers and workers from making employment contracts at lower wages, with the result that progressively larger proportions of the American population are not employed. The situation in many European countries is much the same and in some cases a little worse.

The reason that government and other institutions that intervene in markets are not in general any less inegalitarian than competitive markets is evident from the discussion in chapter 3 of Implications 3 and 9. There is greater inequality, I hypothesize, in the opportunity to create distributional coalitions than there is in the inherent productive abilities of people. The recipients of welfare in the United States are not organized, nor are the poor in other societies. But in the United States, as elsewhere, almost all the major firms are represented by trade associations and the professions by professional associations. There are admittedly differences in the productive abilities of individuals, just as there are differences in height. But such measurement as we are now capable of suggests that the individual differences are normally distributed—the vast majority at least fairly close to the middle. There are a few dwarfs and a few giants, but not many. Larger differences are apparent, it is true, in the holdings of capital and some huge fortunes. Yet, if the accumulation of capital is unobstructed and policies such as those in the perverse policy syndrome are avoided, the return to capital will fall as more capital is accumulated[25] and the wages of the labor with which the capital is combined will rise; it is no accident that wages are highest in the countries that have enjoyed the greatest accumulation of capital. If economic nationalism does not keep the capital from crossing national borders, more will have an incentive to migrate to areas with the lowest wages and thus significantly raise the wages of the poorest. As the history of India tells us, even in the longest run there is no comparable tendency for inequalities to diminish over time through distributional coalitions.

XII

Another myth that generates a lot of poverty and suffering is that the economic development of the poor countries is, for fundamental economic or extra-institutional reasons, extremely difficult, and requires special promotion, planning, and effort. It is sometimes even argued that a tough dictator or totalitarian repression is required to force the sacrifices needed to bring about economic development. As I see it, in these days it takes an enormous amount of stupid policies or bad or unstable institutions to *prevent* economic development. Unfortunately, growth-retarding regimes, policies, and institutions are the rule rather than the exception, and the majority of the world's population lives in poverty.

The examples of successful growth that have been referred to in this study did not occur because of any special promotion or plans. Neither did that of Korea, Taiwan, Hong Kong, or Singapore. The former two received some aid from the United States, but they also felt compelled to spend unusually large amounts on military purposes. If the analysis in this book is right, the growth in Germany and the United States before World War I was more the result of a widening of product and factor markets than of any special promotion or plan. So it was with the growth in early modern Europe. Britain did not seek or plan to have an industrial revolution; it grew for other reasons such as those explained earlier in this book. In the many countries that have failed to grow or failed to grow as fast or as far as the leaders, there are quite enough stupidities, rigidities, and instabilities to explain the lack of success.

Some people suppose that it is more difficult for poor nations to grow now than it was in the eighteenth or nineteenth centuries, and that the explanation for this is in some sense also economic rather than institutional. This overlooks the fact that the poor nations now can borrow the technologies of more developed nations, some of which will be readily adaptable to their own environments, and improve their techniques of production very rapidly. Great Britain in the Industrial Revolution could improve its technology only through the inventions that occurred in that period. Similarly, most highly developed nations today can improve their technology only by taking advantage of current advances. The poorest of the developing nations can telescope the cumulative technological progress of centuries into a few decades. This is not only an obvious possibility but has actually occurred in places like Korea, Taiwan, Hong Kong, and Singapore. The nations of continental Europe and Japan were far behind the United States technologically at the end of World War II, but they borrowed American technology, grew far faster than the United States, and very nearly caught up with the United States in both technology and per capita income in less than twenty-five years.

In claiming that international product and factor markets unobstructed by either cartelization or governmental intervention will bring irrepressible and rapid growth to any poor country, I am *not* arguing that laissez-faire leads to perfect efficiency. As I pointed out in chapter 3, I do not assume perfect competition anywhere in this book. As it happens, most of my own writing in economics is about externalities and public goods, which normally keep a laissez-faire economy from achieving Pareto-optimality and which I believe are quite important.[26] An economy can be dynamic and rapidly growing without at the same time being optimal or perfectly efficient. An economy with free markets and no government or cartel intervention is like a teen-aged youth; it makes a lot of mistakes but nonetheless grows rapidly without special effort or encouragement.

If poor institutions that prevent or repress growth are the norm in much of the world, it may not help to say that "only" institutional problems stand in the way of rapid growth in poor countries. If poor institutions are so common, it presumably is not always easy to obtain good institutional arrangements and the rapid growth that they permit. Still, the problems are more likely to be solved if they are understood than if they are not.[27]

XIII

As might be expected from my concern about ideological preconceptions, and from the methodological discussion in chapter 1 on the standards a satisfactory answer must meet, I do not believe any of the ideological approaches are sufficient to meet our needs. In keeping with that belief, I want to underline the contrast between the argument here and the classical liberal or laissez-faire ideology. The present argument and the classical liberal ideology do share an appreciation of the value of markets. An appreciation of markets is common to nearly everyone, Right or Left, who has given the matter a decade or more of specialized study. If you stand on the shoulders of the giants, it is virtually impossible to see it any other way.

But there the similarity between the present argument and classical liberal laissez-faire ideology stops. As I read it, the ark and covenant of the laissez-faire ideology is that the government that governs least governs best; markets will solve the problem if the government only leaves them alone. There is in the most popular presentations of this ideology a monodiabolism, and the government is the devil. If this devil is kept in chains, there is an almost utopian lack of concern about other problems.

If the less optimistic theory in this book is right, there often will *not* be competitive markets even if the government does not intervene. The government is by no means the only source of coercion or social pressure in society. There will be cartelization of many markets even if the government does not help. Eliminating certain types of government intervention and freeing trade and factor mobility will weaken cartels but will not eliminate many of them. Moreover, the absence of government intervention (even if it were invariably desirable) may not be possible anyway, because of the lobbying of special-interest groups, unless we fly to the still greater evil of continuous instability.

The questions of whether laissez-faire alone is sufficient to prevent or eliminate cartelization, and whether laissez-faire is in the long run not viable because special-interest groups will accumulate and lobby it out of existence can be settled only by an appeal to the facts. Thanks to British imperialism, history has given us one experiment of remarkable aptness. Milton and Rose Friedman, in *Free to Choose*,[28] made much of a comparison between Japan after the Meiji restoration in the late 1860s and India since World War II. The point of comparison was, of course, that the Japanese after the Meiji restoration had relatively free enterprise, along with very low tariffs, whereas independent India has had dramatically interventionist and protectionist policies. As the Friedmans correctly point out, the policies the Japanese chose produced great growth, but those India chose failed. There is a great deal to be said for this comparison and for the policy lesson the Friedmans draw from it. I should also point out that, like most other economists of my generation, I have learned a lot from Milton Friedman's exceptionally lucid, fresh, and penetrating technical writings.[29] And I greatly respect the depth of the Friedmans' convictions.

Withal, there is an ideological—as opposed to a scientific—element in the comparison, and an instructive one at that. Of their comparison, the Friedmans write, "Economists and social scientists in general can seldom conduct controlled experiments of the kind that are so important in the physical sciences. However, experience here has produced something very close to a controlled experiment to test the importance of the difference in methods of economic organization. There is a lapse of eight decades in time. In all other respects the two countries were in very similar circumstances."[30]

An even closer approximation to the controlled experiment of the physical sciences is possible—the same one, without the "lapse of eight decades in time." It is all too often forgotten that one of the finest examples of laissez-faire policy was British rule in India. India had one of the most thoroughgoing laissez-faire policies the world has seen, and it was administered with considerable economy and efficiency in the best British civil service tradition.[31] Entrepreneurs and capitalists from all over the world were free to sell or buy in India or to set up businesses there, as were Indians themselves. No doubt there must have been favoritism to British firms, but where and when in human history was there much more laissez-faire impartiality? There was less government intervention than in Japan after the Meiji restoration. Tariffs were used only to raise revenue and part of the time there were not even revenue tariffs. Those who incorrectly ascribe most economic development to state intervention might claim that India failed to grow because it did not have an independent government that could engage in economic planning and promote development. This argument is not, however, open to the advocate of laissez-faire ideology, for that ideology does not require an active independent government, and in any case the experience of Hong Kong argues that colonies can grow with extraordinary rapidity.[32]

A half-century or more of laissez-faire did generate some growth in India, but nothing comparable to what occurred in Japan. Laissez-faire led to some change and loosening of India's caste system, and some new special-interest organizations emerged. My guess is that if India after World War II had followed the policies the British once required, it would have done better than it has. Nonetheless, the fact remains that more than a half-century of laissez-faire did not bring about the development of India or even get it off to a good start. The laissez-faire ideology in its focus on the evils of government alone clearly leaves something out. I submit that it is the distributional coalitions, which over millennia of history in India had hardened into castes.

Another great experiment in laissez-faire was conducted in Great Britain itself. Britain generally followed laissez-faire policies at home as well as abroad from about the middle of the nineteenth century until the interwar period. (The United States in the same period had highly protectionist policies and in this and some other respects, such as the subsidies to railroads, fell considerably short of laissez-faire.) In this book I have argued, as would the ideological enthusiasts for laissez-faire, that the free trade policy Britain followed has limited the extent of distributional coalitions there. Things could be worse in Britain, and would have been had Britain had the highly protectionist policies of Australia and New Zealand. Nonetheless, as the theory here argues, laissez-faire did not prove to be dynamically stable—Britain abandoned it. Neither was it sufficient to prevent cartelization in many sectors.

During the nineteenth and early twentieth centuries, precisely when and where laissez-faire policy was at its peak, Great Britain acquired a large proportion of its dense network of narrow distributional coalitions. It was in this same period, too, that the British disease emerged and British growth rates and income levels began to lag.

Stagflation, Unemployment, and Business Cycles: An Evolutionary Approach to Macroeconomics

7

Throughout this book I have emphasized the contributions of my predecessors and contemporaries, the parts of the present theory that are drawn from prior work, and the cumulative character of research in any science, be it physical or social. In part, perhaps, this emphasis rests on my observation that those writers who are most assertive about the novelty of their work and the failings of their predecessors are frequently the least original; if this observation is general, there is something to be said for the opposite strategy. I would prefer to construct a tower, an arch, or even a gargoyle on a great cathedral that will last for ages than to take credit for singlehandedly constructing a shack that will be blown away by the next change in the winds of intellectual fashion. Therefore, in this chapter I will continue to admire and to build upon prior contributions, but the strategy at this point raises two difficulties.

The first is that, because of the aspects of prior contributions that I shall need to discuss and the inherent difficulty of the subject, the account in this chapter cannot be quite so simple and sparing in its use of technical concepts as the previous chapters have been. Those who have never before studied any economics may have to read more slowly. I dearly hope that this admission will not stop anyone from pressing on. Naturally, I have saved the best till the last: this chapter contains some of the strongest evidence in support of the present theory and perhaps the most important application of it to current problems of public policy. Moreover, I would like to think that the noneconomist who has persevered through the book thus far is so intelligent that he or she will enjoy mastering this one climactic chapter. I realize that in saying this I flatter some readers, and perhaps indirectly and inappropriately the book as well. But I sincerely believe that it is important, for both intellectual and political reasons, to bring the laymen who have followed the argument thus far through the analysis of this last chapter. I have accordingly devoted many hours to making the argument as transparent to all intelligent readers as it is within my powers to make it. These matters are not, I like to think, explained more simply elsewhere.

The second difficulty is that the distinguished economists that I shall admire and exploit in this chapter have often disagreed, even vituperatively, with one another. This has not been a serious problem in earlier chapters. Although laymen think economists disagree about everything, there is a considerable degree of consensus about the microeconomic theory, or theory of individual firms and markets, that has helped to inspire what I have done so far. The great majority of serious, skilled economists, be they of the Right or of the Left, of this school or of that, accept basically the same microeconomic theory. They often have remarkably similar views on many practical microeconomic policies, such as the tariffs and trade restrictions discussed in the last two chapters. Unfortunately, many of the economists who use and respect the same microeconomic theory strenuously disagree about macroeconomic theory, or the study of inflation, unemployment, and the fluctuations of the economy as a whole.

This disagreement may suggest that my strategy of building upon prior work now must be abandoned. Who will agree with my praise and use of prior contributions when the authors of those contributions have spoken so disparagingly of each other's work? Nonetheless, I have learned a good deal from each of the factions. And the centuries of work on the great cathedral must continue. The quarreling masons have not been working on this part of the cathedral from an agreed design, but I believe that they have hewed out of the granite most of the building blocks that are needed.

II

Why is there exceptional disagreement about macroeconomic theory and policy? Some economists suppose that one side or another is logically in error. Although there are plenty of logical errors, they can be demonstrated to be errors by rules of logic accepted by all sides. This, and the high professional rewards for such demonstrations, pretty well ensure that a school of macroeconomic or monetary thought cannot thrive for long on logical mistakes. The degree of cunning exhibited in debate by some leading protagonists of each persuasion and their skill in the use of microeconomic theory also argue that logical errors would not be the basic source of disagreement. Admittedly, there is bias and even fanaticism in some partisans that might impair their reasoning, but if so, we still need to explain why the fanatic temperament leads to more error and disagreement in one area of economics than in another.

The matter is not so clear-cut when empirical inferences are at issue. Sometimes different schools of thought emerge principally be-cause of different judgments about inconclusive empirical evidence. When so much depends on the empirical evidence, the rewards to the empirical researcher who can show which side is most likely right are very great. If an investigation possibly could settle the dispute, it will almost certainly be undertaken. However, as I have argued elsewhere,[1] macroeconomic and monetary policies are like public goods in that they have indivisible consequences for whole nations at the least. The cause-and-effect relationships or ''social production functions'' for collective goods of vast domain are especially difficult to estimate, because ex-periments with the large units are so costly and the small number of these large units means that historical experience provides few natural experiments. Thus the empirical effects of various combinations of monetary, fiscal, and wage-price policy in different conditions some-times cannot be determined until additional evidence becomes avail-able. This is probably partly responsible for the special disagreement about macroeconomics.

Another source of the disagreement is that each of the competing theories, though containing valid and even precious insights, is a special theory that properly can be applied only in particular circumstances. The circumstances in which each of the competing theories is valid are different. Unfortunately, even those who respect the economics profes-sion as much as I must admit that *some* of the proponents of each of these theories tend, alas, to be doctrinaire. The doctrinaire exponents of these special theories, evidently overwhelmed by the valuable insights in their preferred theory and outraged that the familiar competing theo-ries are erroneous in the particular conditions in which the preferred theory is valid, claim that their favored theory is essentially true, where-as the competing theories are essentially false. These doctrinaire econo-mists are guilty of unconscious synecdoche—implicitly taking the part for the whole. Of course, special or incomplete theories can be extraordinarily valuable; indeed, no theory can be useful unless it abstracts from the unmanageable complexity of reality, so any useful theory must in some sense be incomplete.[2] Even the doctrinaire exponents of each of the theories recognize that their theory is simpler than the reality it is supposed to describe, but the matters from which the cherished theory abstracts are taken to be random, unimportant, exceptional, or outside economics.

Some theories can be *fatally* incomplete for some purposes—such as choosing macroeconomic and monetary policies for the United States and a number of other countries at the present time. A theory that abstracts from the very essence of a problem it is intended to solve is fatally incomplete. This chapter will endeavor to show that all the familiar macroeconomic theories, although full of profound and indispensable insights, are in this sense fatally incomplete—each theory has a hole at its very center.

A final source of the special disagreement in macroeconomics, then, is the inadequacy for present purposes of each of the familiar macroeconomic theories: if any one of them had the robust and compelling character of Darwin's theory of evolution or Ricardo's theory of comparative advantage, it might still be dismissed by some people. But it would not be dismissed, as is each of the familiar macroeconomic theories, by many of the leading scientists in the field. When scientific consensus is lacking, it is usually because the right path has not yet been found. There have been few times and places in the history of economics when an economist had a better warrant for trying an eccentric line of inquiry than in macroeconomics today.

III

The contending theories that will be considered here are the Keynesian, the monetarist, the ''disequilibrium,'' and the rational-expectations ''equilibrium'' models. Often, monetarist and rational-expectations or equilibrium approaches are thought to be the same, or perhaps different parts of the same theory; most advocates of the one also believe in the other. Similarly, disequilibrium theory is often considered a more modern form of Keynesian economics. For some purposes, however, it is essential to make distinctions among, and untypical combinations of, these models, which will be the case here. There are various other labels or approaches to the economy as a whole that receive attention in newspapers and political debates from time to time without generating serious attention in the technical journals. We shall not consider any of these approaches here, since they are too vague and superficial to be of any help.

Much of the debate between the Keynesians and the monetarists centers on what determines the level of spending, or the demand in money or nominal (that is, not corrected for inflation) terms, for the output of the economy as a whole. Monetarists argue that changes in the quantity of money are the only systematic and important sources of changes in the level of nominal income, whereas Keynes's theory also attributes a large role to budget deficits and surpluses and fiscal policy in general in determining the level of demand in the economy as a whole.

Even though Keynes's theory, like the monetarist model, focuses mainly on what determines the level of aggregate demand, it is absolutely essential to remember that Keynes *began* his dazzling, world-changing book with (and built his theory in substantial part upon) the idea that one very large and quite crucial set of prices was influenced by *something* beyond changes in demand, and indeed beyond supply and demand.

Keynes began his argument by attacking the classical or orthodox postulate that "the utility of the wage when a given volume of labour is employed is equal to the marginal disutility of that amount of employment." Pre-Keynesian economists had argued that if groups of workers through unions agreed not to work unless they received a stipulated wage, and that wage resulted in unemployment, this unemployment was not involuntary unemployment, but rather was due to collective choices of workers themselves. Keynes then assumed just such a situation:

> A reduction in the existing level of money wages would lead, through strikes or otherwise, to a withdrawal of labour which is now employed. Does it follow from this that the existing level of real wages accurately measures the marginal disutility of labour? Not necessarily. For, although a reduction in the existing money-wage would lead to a withdrawal of labour, it does not follow that a fall in the value of the existing money-wage in terms of wage-goods would do so, if it were due to a rise in the price of the latter [i.e., a rise in the cost of living]. In other words, it may be the case that within a certain range the demand of labour is for a minimum

money-wage and not for a minimum real wage. . . . Now ordinary experience tells us, beyond doubt, that a situation where labour stipulates (within limits) for a money-wage rather than a real wage, so far from being a mere possibility, is the normal case. . . .

But in the case of changes in the general level of wages it will be found, I think, that the change in real wages associated with a change in money-wages, so far from being usually in the same direction, is almost always in the opposite direction. When money-wages are rising, that is to say, it will be found that real wages are falling; and when money-wages are falling, real wages are rising. . . .

The struggle about money-wages primarily affects the *distribution* of the aggregate real wage between different labour-groups, and not its average amount per unit of employment. . . . The effect of combinations on the part of a group of workers is to protect their *relative* real wage.[3]

The central role of "sticky" (slow to change) wages in Keynes's theory, and one of the institutions that can cause this stickiness, are also emphasized in Keynes's chapter on "Changes in Money Wages":

Since there is, as a rule, no means of securing a simultaneous and equal reduction of money-wages in all industries, it is in the interest of all workers to resist a reduction in their own particular case. . . .

If, indeed, labour were always in a position to take action (and were to do so), whenever there was less than full employment, to reduce its money demands by concerted action to whatever point was required to make money so abundant relatively to the wage-unit that the rate of interest would fall to a level compatible with full employment, we should, in effect, have monetary management by the Trade Unions, aimed at full employment, instead of by the banking system.[4]

To be sure, Keynes's explanation of underemployment equilibrium did not consist merely of the assumption of sticky wages; pre-Keynesian theory already ascribed unemployment to unrealistically high wage levels, and Keynes was anxious to differentiate his theory from the theory that preceded it. Indeed, Keynes argued that reductions of money wages need not bring full employment, and that if they did it involved, in essence, "monetary management by the Trade Unions." As we know, Keynes also had new ideas about the demand for money as an asset and other matters that played significant roles in his theory. Still, the fact remains that although Keynes's theory argued for changing aggregate effective demand, especially through budget deficits and surpluses, and claimed to explain depression and inflation solely from the demand side, it nonetheless began and in substantial part rested upon the assumption that there were forces that influenced wages and that, within limits and at least for a time, did so in ways that could not be explained in terms of increases or decreases in the demand for labor or individual decisions to trade off more or less labor for leisure.

Unfortunately, Keynes never provided any real explanation of why wages were sticky, or what determined why they stuck at one level rather than another, or for how long. This is all the more troublesome because, on first examination, this stickiness is not consistent with the optimizing or purposeful behavior that economists usually observe when they study individual behavior. This incompleteness of Keynesian theory—the reliance on an ad hoc premise that has not been reconciled with the rest of economic theory—has troubled the leading Keynesian economists (and, of course, anti-Keynesian economists) for some time.[5] It also has been, in my judgment, a source of some of the failures of macroeconomic policies in the 1970s.

A similar uneasiness about an unexplained stickiness of certain wages or prices has pervaded the writings on disequilibrium theory, or the theory of macroeconomics that is based on the observation that some markets do not clear (that is, do not reach a situation where everyone who wants to make a transaction at the going price can do so, so that shortages or surpluses persist). In the seminal book in this tradition, Robert Barro and Herschel Grossman emphasized this uneasiness with exemplary scientific candor:

> One other omission from our discussion is especially embarrassing and should be explicitly noted. Although the discussion stresses the implications of exchange at prices which are inconsistent with general market clearing, we provide no choice-theoretic analysis of the market-clearing process itself. In other words, we do not analyze the adjustment of wages and prices as part of the maximizing behavior of firms and households. Consequently, we do not really explain the failure of markets to clear, and our analyses of wage and price dynamics are based on ad hoc adjustment equations.[6]

Perhaps this admirable uneasiness about a theory built on an unexplained ad hoc premise explains why the authors, heralded as leaders of the Keynesian-disequilibrium counterrevolution, by the evidence of subsequent works have joined the flight from Keynesian economics.

IV

Monetarist models and rational-expectations equilibrium theory have the supremely important virtue of avoiding any appeal to sticky or downwardly-rigid wages that are themselves unexplained. Monetarist and equilibrium theorists assume that changes in the quantity of money tend to bring about proportional changes in nominal income because the price level readily adjusts, and that real output is determined by resource availability, technology, and other factors outside the scope of monetary and fiscal policy.

The monetarist and equilibrium theories usually are not guilty of assuming arbitrary wage or price levels, but they fail to provide any explanation of involuntary unemployment or of massive and prolonged unemployment of any sort. In more recent years, it is true, some enlightening arguments that can explain *some* variations in the level of employment have been introduced by monetarists and others. "Search" models, for example, have been developed, which explain some unemployment on the ground that occasionally it will be in a worker's interest to spend full time searching for the best available job. Then there are the "accelerationist" (or "decelerationist") monetarist arguments, which are offered as accounts of brief periods of unemployment and recession; if there is a lower rate of inflation (or a higher rate of deflation) than expected, various decisions that were made on the basis of the false expectations could, because of various lags (that are not well specified or explained), bring about temporary unemployment and reductions in real output.

The rational-expectations equilibrium theorists proceed to a conclusion that may lead newcomers to macroeconomics to think that I am describing the work of theoreticians who have lost absolutely all touch with reality. The conclusion is that involuntary unemployment and depressions due to inadequate demand simply do not occur! Although I am not in sympathy with this conclusion, I plead with readers to be patient, for the equilibrium theorists have put forth intellectually useful models of extraordinary subtlety (see, for example, the impressive work of Robert Lucas, Thomas Sargent, and Neil Wallace). Moreover, as I will demonstrate later in this chapter, it is possible to draw insights out of this quite fundamental theorizing and use them in another theory that might appeal also to those who believe that equilibrium theory as it stands is bizarre. One such insight is the equilibrium theorists' favorite concept of *rational expectations.* Not all the definitions of rational expectations are exactly the same, but for present purposes it is best interpreted as the notion that people making decisions take into account all available information that is worth taking into account; economically rational expectations in this sense has all along been the usual implicit assumption in microeconomic theorizing.

Equilibrium theorists explain obvious variations in the rate of unemployment over the business cycle primarily in terms of voluntary choices concerning when appears to be the most advantageous time to take leisure or education or to forgo gainful employment in order to spend full time seeking a better job. Their arguments are too complicated to summarize without violating the general constraints that govern the exposition in this volume. The key to the equilibrium theory is nonetheless clear: it is the supposition that different groups in the economy have different information or expectations of the future, and that individual workers, despite rational expectations, temporarily misperceive real wages or real interest rates. Suppose that workers expect a higher rate of inflation than actually occurs. They may then conclude that a given money-wage that is offered promises a lower real wage than they eventually can obtain. Since the worker values leisure as well as money income, he may choose to remain unemployed until he is offered a job at the real wage he ultimately can command. If the worker is mistaken about the course of the price level, he may, according to this theory, remain unemployed until he discovers that his estimate of the change in the price level was wrong. Another possibility is that the misjudgment of the prospective change in the price level leads the worker to underestimate the real interest rate, so that he overinvests for a time in education and other forms of human capital. These arguments require that the employers and those workers who choose to remain employed have different information or judgments about the future course of the price level than do the unemployed workers. If the arguments are to explain the high and prolonged levels of unemployment that sometimes occur, they also require enormous changes in the supply of labor from relatively modest changes in perceived real wages.

Tne models of the kind I have just described fail to persuade even many monetarist economists, and of course they do not convince Keynesians. Robert Solow, for example, finds "these propositions very hard to believe, and I am not sure why anyone should believe them in the absence of any evidence."[7] But they have attracted a huge amount of attention among macroeconomists; my hunch is that there is an intuitive perception that the models eventually could help economists to work out something better.

Although the search, accelerationist/decelerationist, and equilibrium theories, which in most formulations attribute any macroeconomic problems to mistaken expectations, can explain *some* variations in the level of employment and the rate of utilization of other resources, they are not nearly sufficient to explain the depth and duration of the unemployment in the interwar period. If the economy is always at a full employment level of output, except when and only for as long as the rate of inflation that was anticipated exceeds that which occurs, why did the depression that began in the United States in 1929 and ended only with World War II involve such an enormous and prolonged reduction in employment and real output? Consider also the case of Great Britain in the interwar period. Britain then as now used a system for measuring unemployment that by comparison with current U.S. practice understates the degree of unemployment; yet, from shortly after World War I until World War II, Great Britain almost never recorded less than 10 percent unemployment.

This interwar experience could be explained on an expectations hypothesis only if people, in the midst of the greatest depression ever, expected an inflation so dramatic that it made sense to refuse to accept any wage or price unless it was significantly above the current levels, or far above the level that would clear current markets. This is—to put it mildly—doubtful, and it is even more doubtful that most people would have persisted in such wildly erroneous expectations for a dozen years in the case of the United States or for twenty years in that of Great Britain. Neither is it credible that, when unemployment and welfare arrangements were so much less generous than today and when most workers were the only source of support for their families, the natural rate of unemployment could leave a tenth to a fourth of the work force unemployed.

The inability of the search, monetarist, and equilibrium theories to explain the magnitude and tenacity of unemployment in the interwar period suggests that they are seriously incomplete. Some of the leading advocates of the expectations-oriented theories concede this and also agree that they are not nearly sufficient to explain the great depression.

Perhaps there are analogies to monetarist and equilibrium theories in the histories of other sciences. The avoidance of ad hoc assumptions is commendable and the effort to explain unemployment and business cycles with complete fidelity to well-tested theory is similar to what I advocated in chapter 1 and have tried to do in this book. But the unwillingness in most monetarist and equilibrium theorizing to go beyond the conventionally defined borders of economics or to take a completely different perspective on the problem needs rethinking. So does the attachment to "equilibrium," even in the wake of the colossal unemployment and reduction in real output in the interwar period. Equilibrium is a useful concept only if there is disequilibrium too. If the disequilibrium approach is ruled out and the economy is deemed to be in or near equilibrium even in major depressions and recessions, what observation or set of observations possibly could tend to call the theory into question? Equilibrium theory may have something in common with the attachment of nineteenth-century physicists to the concept of an "ether" that was supposed to fill all space and suffuse itself even into material and living bodies. The work of Einstein and others has led to the total abandonment of the unnecessary concept of ether. With a similarly excessive attachment to established theory, the Ptolomaic astronomers constructed "epicycles" to reconcile their observations of the planets' orbits with their assumption that the earth was the center of the system. Even given these epicycles, additional observations often required new estimates of cycles or epicycles of particular planets, with the result that new anomalies would crop up in other parts of the system. The Copernican heliocentric astronomy as developed by Kepler and Newton offers a far simpler and more persuasive conception.[8] Probably the intertemporal elasticities of supply of labor required to explain the unemployment in Britain and the United States in the interwar period as the result of voluntary choices of workers who thought they were well advised to hold out for higher expected real wages would introduce new anomalies into our econometric studies of labor supply. These studies have not revealed any great sensitivity of the amount of labor offered to small changes in the real wage.

V

The shortcomings of monetarism and equilibrium theory probably persuaded some economists to remain a while longer with Keynesian theory, notwithstanding its utter dependence on the unexplained assumption of sticky wages. But the Keynesian model (like some of the other macroeconomic models) has lately been contradicted by stagflation, or simultaneous inflation and unemployment. A Keynesian model cannot explain how high inflation and high rates of unemployment can occur together, as they did in the 1970s, and this is a problem for some of the other macroeconomic models also. Some Keynesian economists have tried to explain recent macroeconomic experience in Britain, the United States, and some other countries in terms of negatively sloped Phillips curves (observed tendencies for wage and price increases to vary inversely with the level of unemployment). There is no need to invoke the monetarist criticisms of the Phillips-curve concept to show that it is inadequate, for it is only a statistical finding (or a statistical finding for a certain period) in search of a theory. An explanation of stagflation is not an explanation at all unless it includes a general explanation of *why* a Phillips curve should have this or that slope, and *why* the curve shifts if it is alleged to shift. Any Phillips-curve relationship must be derived from the interests and constraints faced by individual decision-makers. The lack of an adequate explanation in Keynes of stagflation or Phillips curves—especially the tendency for short-run Phillips curves to move upward and become steeper over long periods of inflation—must have a lot to do with the apparent growth in skepticism about Keynesian economics in recent years. (Although he certainly exaggerated, Lord Balogh did not miss the direction of change when he lamented that "anti-Keynesianism was the world's fastest-growth industry.")[9]

"Implicit contracts" have also been brought to bear in efforts to explain the recent stagflation in ways that can be reconciled with Keynes. Implicit contracts have been used to explain such phenomena as very long-term employment relationships and temporal variability in levels of effort asked of employees, combined with stable wage levels, and for purposes such as these they are a most illuminating concept. They are not sufficient to explain any significant amount of unemployment, much less simultaneous inflation and unemployment. Indeed, insofar as implicit contracts bear on stagflation and unemployment, they are more likely to *reduce* than increase the extent of it. Essentially, workers and employers will enter into implicit contracts, like explicit ones, only if they feel that will be advantageous. People are risk averse, as implicit contract theory rightly assumes,[10] so that, other things being equal, they will prefer to enter into contracts that *reduce* the probability of layoffs. They could even gain from slightly lower wages if this were combined with an implicit or explicit agreement that the employer would make every possible effort to keep them employed. The employers would not gain from contracts with individual workers stipulating rigid wages or other conditions that would increase the probability of layoffs; rigid wages constrain employers and deny them potential gains. The most profitable implicit contract between employers and employees would enable them to let the wage, in effect, fluctuate in such a way that employers and employees jointly maximized the difference between the value of leisure and alternative work to the employee and the marginal revenue product of labor for the employer. These functions shift, sometimes frequently, so only a flexible wage would be consistent with the employment of the mutually optimal amount of labor. Of course, wages most often are not very flexible, but the main reason for this, as we shall see later, is not implicit contracts.

It can be difficult to work out a long-term contract that is completely successful in maximizing the joint gain of the worker and the employer, since only the worker may know the value to him of his leisure time and only the employer may know how much a given amount of labor will add to his revenue. In practice the employers and employee may not succeed in finding exactly that wage and quantity of employment that will give them the maximum joint gain over an extended period. One of the possibilities is that they will make an arrangement that ends up with the worker working less than he would have worked had there been perfect information on all sides. But it is preposterous to attribute any substantial amount of unemployment to this possibility, since if the losses of this nature are large, the two parties would not have any incentive to make a long-term contract in any case and would rely instead on a series of "spot market" deals. Thus implicit contracts cannot explain any substantial amount of unemployment, and on balance almost certainly reduce unemployment. The common arrangement whereby firms strive to keep workers on the payroll even during slack times and workers in turn do extra work at rush periods without demanding an increased wage is probably the most common type of implicit contract, and it reduces unemployment.

There are also "cost-push" explanations of inflation and stagflation, which attribute the inflation or stagflation to price and wage increases by firms and unions with monopoly power. As others have shown before, the typical cost-push arguments are manifestly unsatisfactory. They offer no explanation of why there should be continuing inflation or why there should be more inflation in one period than in another. They do not explain why an organization with monopoly power would not choose whatever price or wage it found most advantageous as soon as it obtained the monopoly power, after which point it would have no more reason to increase prices or wages than a pure competitor. In the absence of some adequate explanation of why organizations with monopoly power do not take advantage of that power when they first acquire it, or some explanation of why monopoly power should increase over time in a way consistent with the history of inflation or stagflation, the cost-push arguments are unsatisfactory. They must also be accompanied by some account of why governments or central banks would provide increased demand after the alleged cost-push had increased wages and prices, so that the cost-push would culminate in inflation rather than in unemployed resources. (With the theory offered in this book and some other ideas, one could construct a valid theory of inflation that would have a faint resemblance to the familiar cost-push arguments, but these arguments have been the source of so much confusion that there is probably more loss than gain from doing so.)

VI

What must we demand of a macroeconomic theory before we can find it even provisionally adequate? First, the theory should be deduced entirely from reasonable and testable assumptions about the behavior of individuals: it must at no point violate any valid microeconomic theory. This means, in turn, that it must not contain ad hoc, unexplained assumptions about anything, including sticky or downwardly rigid wages or prices; such rigidities may be introduced only if they are in turn explained in terms of rational individual behavior or rational behavior of firms, organizations, governments, or other institutions (and the presence of such institutions must again be explained in terms of rational individual behavior). I think the vast majority of economists, whatever existing macroeconomic theory they might prefer, agree that a macroeconomic theory should make sense at a microeconomic level as well. This is evident from the support for the work on the microeconomic foundations of macroeconomic theory going on in all camps (consider, for example, the wide influence of Edmund Phelps's volumes on the microeconomic foundations of macroeconomics).[11]

Second, an adequate macroeconomic theory must explain *involuntary* as well as voluntary unemployment and major depressions as well as minor recessions. There are, of course, large numbers of people who voluntarily choose not to work for pay (such as the voluntarily retired, the idle rich, those who prefer handouts to working at jobs, those who stay at home full time to care for children, and so on) and, given the way unemployment statistics are gathered in the United States and other countries, no doubt some of these show up in the unemployment statistics. Yet common sense and the observations and experiences of literally hundreds of millions of people testify that there is also involuntary unemployment and that it is by no means an isolated or rare phenomenon. Depressions in the level of real output as deep as those observed in the Great Depression in the interwar period surely cannot be adequately explained without involuntary unemployment of labor and of other resources. The Great Depression was an event so conspicuous that the whole world observed it, and the political and intellectual life in most countries was revolutionized by it. Only a madman—or an economist with both "trained incapacity" and doctrinal passion—could deny the reality of involuntary unemployment. The first condition set out above entails that the involuntary unemployment is not adequately explained unless it can be shown to be possible even when every individual and firm or other organization involved is rationally acting in its own interest; the *motive* generating the involuntary unemployment, that is, the interests that are directly or indirectly served by it, must be elucidated.

Third, the theory must explain why the unemployment is more common among groups of lower skill and productivity, such as teenagers, disadvantaged racial minorities, and so on. This outcome may seem only natural to the laity, but many of the prevailing theories about variations in employment and unemployment do not predict the pattern that is observed. The search-theory approach (like the notion of "frictional unemployment") predicts the most unemployment in "thin" markets where buyers and sellers are less numerous; an individual must search longer to find a counterpart for his employment contract. Generally, professional and other highly skilled workers are the most specialized and operate in the thinnest markets, and they should by the search theory have the highest unemployment rates. The largest single labor market is that for unskilled labor, where search unemployment should be lowest.

Fourth, the theory must be able to accommodate both equilibrium and disequilibrium, among other reasons because neither concept is empirically operational without the other.

Fifth, an adequate macroeconomic theory must be consistent with booms as well as with busts—with periods of unusual prosperity and with periods of underutilized productive capacity. It must be consistent with what we loosely call the "business cycle," although the absence of strong regularities in the length and extent of periods of prosperity and recession suggests that "business fluctuations" would perhaps be a better term. In other words, as Kenneth Arrow points out,[12] the theory must be consistent with the observation that neither depressions nor full-employment levels of production appear to sustain themselves indefinitely.

Sixth, the theory should be able to explain, without ad hockery, the really dramatic differences across societies and historical periods in the nature of the macroeconomic problem. If economic history were more widely taught in economics departments, the need for this requirement would long ago have been obvious, but modern trends in economics and econometrics have meant that economic history has, alas, been crowded out and even belittled.

Seventh, since the greater the explanatory power of a theory, other things being equal, the greater the likelihood that it is true, the theory ideally should be able, at least in its full or complete form, to explain some other, extra-macroeconomic phenomena. This is not an absolute requirement, but we should be uneasy if it is not met and reassured if it is. I must repeat again that the theory need not be monocausal, so that any number of factors that are exogenous to it may be terribly important, for macroeconomic problems as well as for other matters.

Eighth, as we already know from chapter 1, the theory should be relatively simple and parsimonious.

I submit that the following theory, when combined with familiar and straightforward elements from the four macroeconomic theories set out earlier in this chapter and with what has been presented in earlier chapters of this book, meets all eight of the above conditions. Partly to underline the simplicity of the argument, especially in contrast to many of the recent contributions to macroeconomics, and partly to reach students and policy-makers, the discussion will use only the most basic and simple theoretical tools.

VII

I shall first explain, subject to the constraints entailed in the first of the above conditions, one source of the involuntary unemployment of labor. Even though it is natural to begin with the simplest and most straightforward source and type of unemployment, it is vitally important *not* to use this first explanation in isolation from the rest of the argument. There is also unemployment or underutilization of machinery and other forms of capital in a depression or a recession, and although this usually does not conjure up such painful visions as does involuntary unemployment of labor, it also involves waste of productive capacity and in addition often contributes to the losses workers suffer in such times, since the idle capital means that less capital is combined with labor, and the demand for labor and wages can then tend to be lower than they might otherwise be. The demand for labor obviously depends on what is happening in the product markets in which the firms that employ labor sell their output, so the *amount* of involuntary unemployment of labor most definitely cannot be determined without looking at conditions in product as well as labor markets.

It would be easy but unhelpful to explain involuntary unemployment in terms of some allegedly persistent tendency of those involved to choose outcomes that are inconsistent with their interests. So I shall assume rational expectations, in the sense that individuals take into account all the information that it pays them to take into account—all available information that they expect will be worth more to them than it costs.

We also must define *involuntary* unemployment *very* strictly. If we let a wide variety of situations count as involuntary unemployment, it would again be easy to explain its existence, but nothing much would be gained. In particular, we must be certain that we do not include in our definition any voluntary unemployment, which is easily explicable as a preference for leisure or home-produced output over the earnings from work. I do this by reference to figure 1. This depicts, in the *MC* (marginal cost) or supply curve, the value of the time of workers in the form of leisure, home-produced goods, and any other opportunities. The demand for labor, or *MRP* (marginal revenue product) curve, consists of *points* on the separate marginal revenue product of labor curves of firms in diverse industries that have a demand for whatever type of labor is at issue.[13] In the interest of saving a few moments of time for those intellectually versatile noneconomists who have persevered through this chapter, I point out that *MC* or the marginal cost curve for labor is assumed to rise because as more labor is taken, workers with a lesser attraction to the labor force must be persuaded to take paid employment, and because each worker must be paid more to forgo leisure

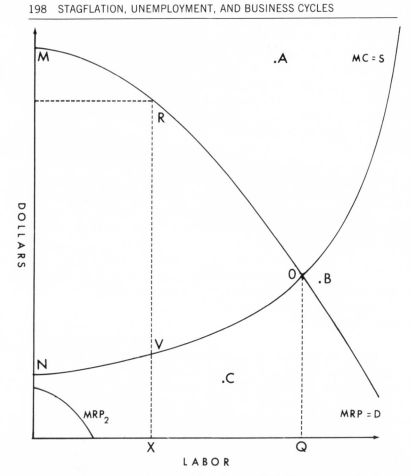

the more hours of work he has already supplied. The *D* curve declines because, among other reasons, the law of diminishing returns entails that additional labor of a given type will eventually add smaller increments to output.

At points to the right of the intersection of the two curves, such as point *B*, there can be no involuntary unemployment; the value of leisure or alternative opportunities is above point *B*, so no one will accept a job at that wage level, and when the amount of labor given by point *B* is already employed the employers would find that wage level *B* would cost more than the additional labor was worth to them anyway. In terms of the first quote from Keynes earlier in this chapter, we would have to move leftward to the intersection of the two curves to find the point where "the utility of the wage . . . is equal to the disutility of that amount of employment." Similarly, if anyone demanded a wage level such as that at point *A* there would also not be involuntary unemployment, because *A* is higher than the marginal revenue product of labor; the worker would be asking for a gift more than a job, for any employer will lose money from employing him at that wage. At a point such as *C* there is similarly no involuntary unemployment; this is below the value of time in alternative uses and the worker does not accept any job that pays only a wage of *C*.

We could also postulate a different type of labor with so little value to employers that the *MRP* curve was for all or almost all of its length *below* the *MC* curve, as MRP_2 is. In this depressing case, the worth of that type of labor is so low that no employer would gain from taking it, even if the wage were so low that even a normally industrious worker would not take it. A case such as this may be more tragic than involuntary unemployment, but we must not confuse it with involuntary unemployment. We know that patients in a hospital are not working, but we do not count them as or usually describe them as unemployed; the problem of people who cannot be productive, or whose productivity is so low that no one could gain from hiring them even if they put a negligible value on their time, is a problem of unproductive resources, not a problem of unemployment of resources—it does not imply any unutilized productive capacity.

There can be involuntary unemployment only in the roughly triangular area *MNO*. There is involuntary unemployment in our strict sense *only* if a worker's employment would add an amount to an employer's revenue that is greater than the value that the worker puts on his time, taking the value of leisure and all other opportunities for the worker into account.

Similarly, if a worker is unemployed because he believes that it is in his best interest to spend more time searching for work and therefore declines inferior employment opportunities while searching, this again is not involuntary unemployment. Personal observation may tell the reader that it is easier to get a job if one already has one, and that this type of search unemployment is rather rare. Whether this is true or not, if this type of unemployment occurs we must not call it involuntary; the worker is simply investing his time in the way that he believes will maximize lifetime income and satisfaction. If this type of unemployment were somehow prohibited, the national output and welfare would decline in the long run, since the worker in question presumably knows his interests and situation better than anyone else. On the other hand, if there is a social institution or public policy that inefficiently increases search costs or time spent in job queues, the extra searching is then required by the institution or policy, and this extra searching is no longer an investment that generates a social gain: any *extra* search unemployment due to such arrangements is defined to be involuntary.

Suppose, arbitrarily, that only *OX* workers are employed; there is then strictly involuntary unemployment of *XQ* workers, as that many have a marginal revenue product in excess of the marginal cost of their time. Note now the triangular area *RVO,* giving the area that is both above the marginal cost of the relevant labor and below the marginal revenue product of labor curve. This area represents a social loss, for the time of the workers would be worth more to employers than it is worth to themselves. Above all, *note that mutually advantageous bargains can be worked out between the unemployed workers and the employers;* they both will be better off by agreeing to an employment contract at a wage level between the two curves. *This will always be true if there is involuntary unemployment in the strict sense.*

In a Keynesian ''unemployment equilibrium'' these same gains would accrue to both employers and employees from making an employment contract; as time goes on, more such contracts will be made, so the ''unemployment equilibrium'' is not an equilibrium at all. Keynes was also talking about genuinely involuntary unemployment. The difficulty now being described is in fact a staff stuck right through the heart of Keynes's explanation of unemployment. I hasten to add that several others, such as Don Patinkin, have found this difficulty in Keynes earlier, usually by somewhat different paths, and that this is one of the reasons so many good economists have been searching for a solid microeconomic foundation for Keynesian economics, or else for an alternative to it. The fact remains that we do not have a satisfactory explanation of involuntary unemployment in Keynes, or for that matter in disequilibrium theory.

The involuntarily unemployed workers and employers in the real world do not have perfect knowledge, of course, and they may not know for a time of the gains they would acquire if they made a deal. Thus some of the workers might not become employed for a time. They would have to search, as would the employers, to obtain the mutual gains. Still, there need be no involuntary unemployment, because the workers would either continue at other jobs while they looked for better work, or else they would decide that the best way they could use their time was to invest it in searching; and as we indicated that sort of investment is not involuntary unemployment any more than investment in education is. One could appeal, as some equilibrium theorists do, to asymmetries in information that would make employers and employees estimate the *MRP* or *MC* curves differently, but this is an arbitrary and empirically implausible solution. Such misperceptions presumably could not last for twenty-year periods, such as the unemployment in Britain between the wars, or could not confuse such a large proportion of the work force as was unemployed in the United States from 1929 until World War II. We must seek some stronger and more durable influence preventing the mutually advantageous transactions between the involuntarily unemployed and present or prospective employers.

VIII

For the economist, it is natural to ask who in the government or elsewhere might have an interest in blocking the mutually advantageous transactions with the involuntarily unemployed. The president and governing political parties would not have any direct interest in blocking such transactions; they would risk losing the votes of both the prospective employee and the prospective employer. Everyday observation tells us that incumbents wish to run for re-election on "peace and prosperity" or "you never had it so good" platforms. The population at large would not want to block the transaction out of general human sympathy, and the business community as a whole would want the extra employment because of the extra demand it would bring to business in general.

The main group that can have an interest in preventing the mutually profitable transactions between the involuntarily unemployed and employers is the workers with the same or competitive skills. They have a substantial interest in preventing such transactions, for their own wages must be lowered as extra labor pushes the marginal revenue product of labor down. The only way that the existing workers can prevent the mutually advantageous transactions is if they are organized as a cartel or lobby or (as is very often the case) are in one way or another informally able to exert collusive pressure. The only *other group that could have such an interest would be a monopsonistic (or buyers') cartel or lobby of employers; it would need to block mutually advantageous transactions between individual employers and workers to keep wages below competitive levels.* No model of involuntary unemployment or theory of macroeconomics that ignores the motive that makes unemployment occur can be satisfactory.

The foregoing account has for expository reasons focused only on the labor market and *temporarily* assumed no cartelization or governmental intervention in the rest of the economy, where prices are perfectly flexible. This ensures that employers always will be able to sell their outputs. Of course, the same argument applies to the market for other factors of production and to product markets, where these applications are often much more important. The downward sloping curve in the figure could just as well have been a demand curve for a product and the upward sloping curve the supply curve or marginal cost of producing it. If something, such as a price that was too high, created underutilization of productive capacity, there would be the possibility of mutually advantageous gains in the triangle. Again, the only party that could have an interest in blocking these mutually advantageous transactions between buyers and actual or potential sellers would be the firms that profited from a noncompetitive price. They could prevent the mutually advantageous transactions only if they were organized as a lobby or cartel or could collude informally or tacitly.

As disequilibrium theorists such as Edmond Malinvaud have shown,[14] the price that does not clear the market (that is, consummate all mutually advantageous transactions) in a product market can also contribute to unemployment of labor or excess capacity in other product markets. Later in this chapter I shall consider the combined effects of distributional coalitions in both factor and product markets at the same time. Because of the findings of the disequilibrium theorists and of what I will present later, the above analyses of the labor market cannot be used in isolation and must be applied together with similar analyses of other factor markets and product markets.

The more extensive the special-interest groups and the non-market-clearing prices lobbying and cartelization bring about, the greater the variations in the rates of return for similar workers and for capital. The greater these variations, the more it pays to search for the higher returns. This extra search, however, is not a socially efficient expenditure on the gathering of information, and it is required only because of the special-interest groups, so it also generates involuntary unemployment. Some time is spent in job queues because of the non-market-clearing prices and wages, which further increases involuntary unemployment.

IX

We shall soon see that the above approach has some surprising and testable implications when placed in a general equilibrium context, but it will first be necessary to refer back to Implication 6 in chapter 3. That implication was that distributional coalitions generate slow decision-making, crowded agendas, and cluttered bargaining tables. In many cases, we found, it was also advantageous for these coalitions to be quantity-adjusters rather than price-adjusters.

The implication explains why many prices and wages in some societies are sticky. It takes a special-interest organization or collusion some time to go through the unanimous-consent bargaining or constitutional procedures by which it must make its decisions. Since all the most important decisions of the organization or collusion must be made in this way, it has a crowded agenda. Since the distributional coalition often has to lobby or bargain with others, it may face other organizations or institutions with crowded agendas, so bargaining tables may be cluttered, too. Thus it can be a slow process for a price or wage that is influenced or set by lobbies or cartels to be determined. Once the price or wage is determined, it is not likely to change quickly even if conditions change in such a way that a different price or wage would be optimal for the coalition. So special-interest groups bring about sticky wages and prices.

It is widely observed that prices and wages are less flexible downward than upward. Malinvaud, for example, speaks of the "commonly believed property according to which prices are more sticky downward than upward,"[15] and my colleague Charles Schultze's influential early work on stagflation builds partly upon that premise.[16] This observation is puzzling; any decision-makers, however much monopoly power they have, should choose the price or wage that is optimal for them and should on average lose just as much from a price that is too high as from one that is too low. It might seem, then, that if prices are sticky for any reason they should be equally sluggish going in each direction. There is observed stickiness going each way but many observations that this stickiness is more extreme or systematic on the down side. A cartel or lobby with slow decision-making will take time deciding either to raise or to lower prices and presumably its collective decision-making procedures are equally slow in each direction.

We can see from the analysis that led to Implication 6 that there is nonetheless an asymmetry. If one member of a cartel charges a lower price than the agreed-upon price, that hurts the others—they get fewer sales and lower prices. If a cartel member charges a higher price than the agreed-upon price, on the other hand, there is no harm to the others in the cartel. If there is a reduction in demand a cartel may wish that it had chosen a lower price, but because of the conditions adduced in the discussion of Implication 6 the decision to lower the cartel price will come only after some delay. If, from a position of equilibrium, there is a sufficiently small increase in demand facing the firms in the cartel, each firm can sell a little more at the old cartel price and enjoy increased profits, although not as much of an increase as if the cartel price had been adjusted promptly. Now consider an unexpected increase in demand so large that each firm can get *more* than the cartel price. No firm could have an objection if any other firm charged more than the cartel price, so for a time there will be upward flexibility in prices. The argument requires that monopolistic cartels are more common than buyers' cartels, and this appears to be the case.[17] A testable implication of the theory is that the converse phenomenon would be evident in monopsonistic cartels.

The location of price and wage stickiness across industries is also consistent with the theory. The theory implies that in sectors where there is special-interest organization there will be more stickiness, and (because of Implication 3) in industries where there is a fairly small number of firms that can collude more easily, there will on average be less price flexibility than in industries with so many firms that they cannot collude without selective incentives. Those large groups that are organized because of selective incentives may have even slower decision-making.

The sluggish movement of wages that are set by collective bargaining is well known. Wage flexibility appears to be particularly great in temporary markets where organization is pretty much ruled out, as in the markets for seasonal workers, consultants, and so on. There also appears to be less flexibility in manufacturing prices than in farm prices (except when farm prices are determined by governments under the influence of lobbies). This has been noted by observant monetarists as well as by Keynesians. Phillip Cagan, a leading monetarist, summarizes the evidence clearly and fairly:

> While manufacturing prices have at times fallen precipitously, as in the business contractions of 1920–21 and 1929–33, usually they

do not. To be sure, the available data do not record the secret discounting and shading of prices in slack markets, and actual transaction prices undoubtedly undergo larger fluctuations than the reported quotations suggest. The difference between reported and actual prices [will be] discussed further. It is not important enough, however, to invalidate the observed insensitivity of most prices to shifts in demand.[18]

F. M. Scherer and many others also present data indicating that there are greater fluctuations in farm and commodity prices than in prices in concentrated manufacturing industries.[19]

The present theory also predicts that there will be more unemployment among groups in the work force that have relatively low skills and productivity, as our list of conditions for a suitable macroeconomic theory suggested it should. As Implication 6 explained, distributional coalitions will more often than not bargain for a wage or price and permit employers or customers to make some of the decisions about who gets the resulting gains, so that the coalition will be able to minimize divisive conflict over the sharing of the gains of its collective action. When wages and salaries are set above market-clearing levels, the employer will choose and attract more qualified employees than with competitive wages, and the less productive may find that at the wage levels that have been established it is not in an employer's interest to hire them. If the less-qualified and the employers were free to negotiate any employment contracts they wished, the wages would vary with productivity, and workers with positive but relatively low productivity would find it easier to obtain jobs. The worker who is trained for a high-skill occupation but does not get a job because he or she has below-average skills for that occupation will oftentimes be able to get a job in a lower-paying occupation with lower average qualifications; but the unskilled worker is less likely to have any such inferior alternative employment to turn to. Of course, other factors are also important. For example, some of the construction and manufacturing activities that have strong unions and high wages are also sensitive to the business cycle and accordingly have unstable employment patterns.

X

Implication 6 also tells us something about how those prices and wages influenced by special-interest groups will react to unexpected inflation or deflation. A cartel or lobby will seek whatever price it believes best, but for the reasons explained in chapter 3 it will seek agreements or arrangements that last for some length of time. Collective bargaining agreements in the United States offer a clear, though perhaps extreme, example of this; they customarily last for three years.

Now suppose that there is unexpected inflation or deflation. With unexpected inflation the price the special-interest group obtained will become lower in relation to other prices than the group wanted or expected it to be, but the group will not quickly be able to change the relevant agreement or legislation. Since the cartel or lobby could only have gained from setting a supracompetitive or monopoly price, unexpected inflation will make the relative price it receives less monopolistic than intended. The price will also be closer to market-clearing levels than expected. An unexpected inflation therefore reduces the losses from monopoly due to cartelization and lobbying and the degree of involuntary unemployment. In a period of unexpected inflation an economy with a high level of special-interest organization and collusion will be more productive than it normally is.

In a period of unexpected deflation, by contrast, the price or wage set by a distributional coalition will for a time be even higher than the coalition expected or (if it had gotten its way completely) even higher than it desired. This will mean that the losses from monopoly are greater than normal and that the relative prices are even farther above market-clearing levels than normal, so involuntary unemployment will be unusually high.

We now have a better explanation than has previously been available for the familiar observation that in most economies *unexpected* inflation means reduced unemployment and a boom in real output, whereas *unexpected* deflation (or disinflation) means more unemployment and a reduction in real output. Although it has been shown in formal general-equilibrium models (in which special-interest groups were not taken into account) that "money is neutral," that inflation has no effect on relative prices and no impact on real output, we now see why this conclusion does not hold for most economies in the real world.

Naturally, if inflation rises to triple-digit levels (as it has in several countries) and there is great uncertainty about the future rate of inflation, special-interest groups will then seek to lobby or to bargain for prices or wages that are indexed to the rate of inflation. I have not examined the process when inflation rates are that high, but I would hypothesize that the economic results in real terms of higher-than-expected inflation or unexpected disinflation in such circumstances would be sensitive to the imperfections of the available price indexes. And these imperfections are substantial even in the best of circumstances. Strictly speaking, each consumer needs a separate price index if he or she is going to be perfectly indexed against inflation, because each consumer tends to buy a different bundle of goods and the price of each good tends to change by a different amount. But this proof that no special-interest organization could find an ideal price index for all its members is of minor importance when compared to the great shortcomings of the existing price indexes, even in the countries with the best statistics. The very substantial mismeasurement of the rate of inflation in the United States by the Consumer Price Index is well known. Some of the defects of this index could be corrected readily were there no lobbies resisting such correction, but other difficulties cannot in practice be solved. There is no way adequately to measure the changes in the quality of products, for example, and no way to adjust appropriately for the fact that consumers will take relatively less of whatever products rise most in price, so these goods will be overweighted in the price index. These and other problems are so difficult in practice that in the United States in the 1950s and early 1960s, when measured rates of inflation were already significant, skilled economists were seriously debating whether there was in fact any inflation at all.[20] Thus the impact of unexpected inflation or unexpected deflation is usually mitigated by indexing only in those cases where inflation has proceeded for some time at high levels.

XI

It is now time to extend the argument by recognizing that there are many different industries or sectors in the economy and that what happens in each sector affects and is affected by what happens in other sectors: that is, the argument must be put in a general equilibrium context.

To understand the present theory fully in a general equilibrium context, we must draw upon an important but inadequately appreciated insight of Robert Clower's.[21] The essence of Clower's insight can be seen by returning to figure 1. As we remember, there were unexploited gains unless mutually advantageous trades had entirely eliminated the triangular area. All the gains can be captured only if the price for at least the last unit of labor sold is the one given by the intersection of *MRP* and *MC* (demand and supply curves). If that price is not achieved, or if for any reason not all of the mutually beneficial trades are completed, the incomes of both the unemployed workers and the employers will be smaller. When we shifted to cartels in product markets it was obvious that the same point held: all the mutually advantageous transactions will not be consummated unless the price is right, at least for the last unit, and if all the gains from trade are not achieved, incomes on both demand and supply sides will be lower. If we now think of a complete general equilibrium system, as Clower did, we see that if there is not exactly the right price in *every* market, there will be unexploited gains from trade. If the general equilibrium system does not come up with an ideal vector of prices, then, there will be lower incomes throughout the economy. These losses—that is, the absence of the gains from many mutually advantageous but unconsummated transactions throughout the economy—will mean that aggregate demand for the economy's output is less than it would have been had the perfect vector of prices existed, and it could be very much less. Thus Clower discerned a factor that in principle could make the output of the economy as a whole fluctuate.

For some time, Clower's fundamental insight did not receive much attention. Later it was exploited by the disequilibrium theorists, but with the demoralization of some of these theorists by the lack of any explanation of why markets did not clear and the exodus from Keynesian types of thinking, its use seems to have diminished. I have been told by a deservedly eminent macroeconomist that if a general equilibrium system does generate a mistaken vector of prices, people can immediately gain from making the trades that will correct that vector of prices, and the system therefore quickly converges on the full employment level of output, so Clower's point is insignificant. I suppose that Clower's insight has not received more attention because most economists believed that there was nothing to stop the mutually advantageous trades; they would take place, if not promptly, then after only a modest lag, so Clower's point was of only transitory significance.

If my argument is right, there are those who do have an interest in blocking the mutually advantageous trades, and in some societies they are organized to block them, sometimes indefinitely. In stable societies these interests become *better* organized over time, so the problem, far from being a mere lag, can increase with time. The inefficiencies that result from special-interest groups, which my analysis in previous chapters indicates can be very large indeed, in turn affect the level of demand. Of course, if the accumulation is gradual, as I claim it is, no large macroeconomic fluctuations need emerge from this accumulation alone.

Now suppose that there is unexpected deflation or disinflation, or a sudden rise in the price of oil, or any other major change that entails that the economy can reach its full potential, or even return to its normal level of real output, only if it has new prices throughout the economy. As we know from the preceding account of unexpected deflation and disinflation, in an economy with a dense network of distributional coalitions the terms of trade will shift in favor of the organized sector. The slow decision-making explained by Implication 6 will keep the sector with organized special-interest groups from adjusting for a time, whereas what Sir John Hicks has aptly called the "flexprice" sector will adjust immediately. Accordingly, the degree of monopoly in the society and the number who are searching, queueing, or unemployed in non-market-clearing sectors increases. With an increase in the degree of monopoly and an increase in the amount of time spent in searching, queueing, and unemployment, there is less income in the society, and demand in real terms falls off. In other words, because of slow decision-making, crowded agendas, and cluttered bargaining tables, it can take a considerable time in some societies for a vector of prices as good as the pre-deflation or pre-shock vector to emerge. The result is a reduction in the demand for goods and for labor and other productive factors throughout the economy: there is a recession or depression.

Those prices set by distributional coalitions at monopolistic and above-market-clearing levels before the unexpected deflation or unexpected shock will now tend to be even higher than before, not only because of the direct effects of the deflation or the shock, but also because of the reduction of demand in real terms due to the general equilibrium effects that Clower and the disequilibrium theorists have pointed out. This in turn makes long-term investment risky, so investment spending can also fall off fast. Each of these developments will exacerbate the others, so there can be a vicious downward spiral, although the tendency of special-interest organizations and collusions to readjust their prices to the new situation will eventually offset the forces that reduce real output.

Though Malinvaud and the other disequilibrium theorists simply assumed some non-market-clearing prices and wages, their analyses of the process now being described is quite similar. Malinvaud most usefully has pointed out that in such circumstances there is "Keynesian" involuntary unemployment as well as "classical" involuntary unemployment.[22] The former, very loosely speaking, is the additional unemployment brought about because the quantity of goods purchased in the product market has fallen off due to non-market-clearing prices in those markets, which in turn reduces firms' demands for labor and multiplies the loss in employment due to wages that are above market-clearing levels. When wages are above market-clearing levels but the prices of goods are not, the involuntary unemployment that results is defined as "classical." Malinvaud judges that Keynesian unemployment is more common than classical unemployment.

According to my argument, we would need to look at the pattern of special-interest organization by sector to determine this, and the answer would vary from place to place and time to time. But whether Malinvaud is right or not, it is absolutely certain that the extent of involuntary employment cannot be understood, even to a first approximation, by looking at the coalitions in the labor market alone. I began with involuntary unemployment due to cartelization in the labor market because that is the simplest case to understand, but it need not be the most important source of involuntary unemployment; all types of cartels and lobbies need to be taken into account together for a satisfactory analysis of the involuntary unemployment of labor or the underutilization of any other resource.

As the earlier account of unexpected inflation should make clear, the opposite process tends to occur when unexpected inflation or major favorable exogenous events (such as major technological innovations or resource discoveries) happen. An economy can enjoy a boom in which the loss from its distributional coalitions is less than normal, and this can bring about a similar spiral of favorable effects until the special-interest groups have adjusted to the new situation, the promising investment opportunities have all been exploited, and so on.

Thus we have an explanation of frequent fluctuations in the level of real output or business cycles in societies with a significant degree of institutional sclerosis. This approach—the Clower-Olson approach, if I may call it that—is at no point inconsistent with any valid microeconomic theory.

XII

Now that I have put the argument in a general equilibrium context, we must examine the fact that some prices are not determined or directly influenced by distributional coalitions, even in a relatively sclerotic economy; there is in most economies not only a sector in which disequilibria persist for long periods but also a sector where prices can never be more than momentarily out of equilibrium. If a market is not cartelized or politically controlled, workers who cannot get employment because wages or prices are too high to clear markets in the sectors under the thrall of special interests are free if they choose to move into the flexprice sector.

If they do not reflect on the matter, some economists might argue at this point that this freedom of movement will ensure that there is full employment. The hurried economist might suppose that, even in the most highly cartelized and lobby-ridden economy, so long as any sectors remain open to all entrants, there will be no involuntary unemployment.

One of the lesser problems with this argument is that it ignores the time it would take for resources to shift sectors. The sticky character of the prices and wages in the organized sector implies that the flexible prices will initially absorb the whole of any unexpected deflation or disinflation, thereby making the relative prices in the cartelized or controlled sector even higher than before. The decrease in aggregate demand and higher relative prices together imply a substantial reduction in the quantity of goods and labor demanded in the organized sector. Thus full employment could require a substantial migration to the flexprice sector. Some of the owners of unemployed resources may suppose that because of either government action or equilibrating forces any recession or depression will be temporary and then it may not pay to move to the flexprice sector. Such a move will sometimes involve considerable monetary and psychic costs; consider, for example, the uprooting of families in major cities in order that they might seek employment in the rural areas where many of the goods with flexible prices are produced. Moreover, many of the resources used in the fixed-price or disequilibrium sector will not have more than a fraction of their normal value if shifted to the other sector; factories and machines are often constructed to serve only specialized needs, and workers with considerable industry-specific or firm-specific human capital may be able to do only

212 STAGFLATION, UNEMPLOYMENT, AND BUSINESS CYCLES

unskilled work for a time in other industries or firms. Some people describe themselves as unemployed if the only available work involves not only a change of occupation but a great change of status as well. And at the same time they might be too old to invest in a new skill requiring as much education, training, or service with a single firm as their prior skill. Unwillingness to invest in a second profession may be due to a deplorable conservatism in many individuals of middle age or older, but it surely often exists, and when it does, a full employment equilibrium literally could arrive only after most of those in the category at issue have retired. As Keynes wisely said, in the long run we are all dead.

Even if we take a timeless view of macroeconomic fluctuations and we unrealistically ignore the costs of the resource reallocation to the flexprice or equilibrium sector whenever aggregate demand is substantially less than expected, the fact that there are always some flexible prices need not ever insure full employment. A second problem with the hurried economist's general-equilibrium argument is that it overlooks what can best be described as the "selling apples on street corners" syndrome.

Though we are all distressed at the thought of unemployed workers who are reduced to selling apples, the economist who knows that the economy is a general equilibrium system will realize, if he does not let his emotions overcome his powers of analysis, that an increase in the number of those selling apples on street corners represents a helpful and equilibrating response to the situation. If there is a great increase in the number of people selling apples, we may reasonably infer that that sector is not organized and accordingly has flexible prices. Thus the move of unemployed resources into selling apples is a helpful shift of resources into the flexprice sector and is symbolic of the many other such shifts that take place. This "selling apples" argument is not, I insist, a parody, but rather a correct statement of *one* aspect of the matter; that this is so becomes evident when we consider the loss of welfare that would occur, for consumers as well as for workers, if streetcorner vending were prohibited during a depression.

What needs to be added is that *if distributional coalitions are ubiquitous and the unexpected deflation is considerable,* and the great obstacles to resource reallocation described above are overcome, the amount of resources that must transfer into the flexprice sector will be so great in relation to the size of the sector that prices in that sector, which already has borne the brunt of the reduction of the fall in aggregate demand, will fall *much* further. The ratio of prices in the flexprice sector to prices in the fixprice sector will be abnormal and the returns to resources employed in the flexprice sector will become very low indeed. In prosperous times, selling apples on street corners should bring the normal rate of return for industries with free entry, but with a large unexpected deflation it will become so low that this occupation is considered synonymous with abject unemployment. Herbert Hoover was accused of terrible insensitivity and political ineptness when he spoke of people who made great profits during the Great Depression selling apples on street corners; we can now see that his analysis was theoretically implausible as well.

The main point is this: what happens to the streetcorner vending of apples in a depression is what happens to *all* industries with free entry. In the United States in the 1930s, for example, the historic migration from farm to city was reversed. This reallocation of resources served a purpose, but the farm prices that were associated with this shift and the drop in aggregate demand were so abnormally low in relation to industrial prices and wages that there was widespread and effective political support for programs to raise farm prices. These prices were to some extent stabilized, and this was done *by requiring that some land and other resources by law remain unemployed* until a price ratio more nearly resembling the historic "parity" was established. It may be supposed that this action was a historical aberration. I offer the further hypothesis that it was not (similar things happened in many other countries) and that generally when a similar derangement of relative price levels occurs, government intervention to limit this abnormal fall in prices in flexible markets will occur.

When the proportion of cartelized and lobby-influenced prices becomes sufficiently great, any substantial reduction in aggregate demand will lead to underutilization of resources. This is partly because of the difficulties of resource reallocation in the short run. But it is partly because the shift of resources to the flexprice sector will eventually be so large in relation to the size of that sector that it will result in factor rewards so low that they are not distinguished from unemployment, or to additional government restriction of output or factor use to protect returns in the flexprice sector. (One result of the contribution that flexible prices make to regaining employment during a depression is that the flexprice sector diminishes further.) Although the abjectly low levels of return during a depression in the selling-apples or equilibrium sector in an economy with exceptional numbers of special-interest groups do not strictly qualify as involuntary unemployment by the very severe definition set out earlier in this chapter, it is surely not an abuse of language to describe them as "involuntary *under*employment." There is also in such times a notable increase in the incentive to search for openings in the disequilibrium or fixprice sector; queueing and search unemployment (which now is involuntary because of the institutionally determined disparities in prices and wages for resources of the same intrinsic value) rises dramatically.

XIII

The macroeconomic argument offered in this chapter has not touched on the relative significance of changes in quantity of money as compared with fiscal policy in influencing the level of spending or nominal demand. Nothing said so far precludes either the contention that the quantity of money is the only significant determinant of the level of nominal income or the contention that fiscal policy is also an important determinant. What determines the level of nominal spending is for the most part a separate matter that need not be discussed here, and this book has perhaps endeavored to cover too much territory as it is. I will accordingly leave any effort to explain the determinants of spending, or to deal with other respects in which the above argument is incomplete, to a future publication, in which I would not feel inhibitions about dealing with technical matters. In the meantime, my hope is that other economists, particularly those who (unlike myself) have specialized in monetary or macroeconomics, will find what has been said here worthy of extension and formalization; the progress will be incomparably greater if more than one person is involved. Until an analysis of the determinants of aggregate spending has been incorporated into the theory, we must be careful not to suppose that the theory here is sufficient to specify *all* of the macroeconomic characteristics of a period. It is not. One must recognize, for example, that there were extremely unstable and mainly deflationary monetary and fiscal policies in the early 1930s, and less unstable but mainly inflationary policies in the late 1960s and 1970s, in any comparison of those two periods.

What has been said above is sufficient, however, to show that this argument explains involuntary unemployment without at any point contradicting anything we know about microeconomics and the effects of the incentives facing individual decision-makers. No other macroeconomic or monetary theory succeeds in doing this. Still, it would be nice to see if the present theory has further testable implications that are different from those of other macroeconomic theories. If the further testable implications of the present theory should be confirmed, whereas those of competing macroeconomic theories should not, that would be important evidence to strengthen the macroeconomic argument here and the theory presented in the book as a whole.

Happily, there is a marvelously apt empirical test that bears on the validity of the present argument and also on that of all the alternatives that have been discussed. Keynes's *General Theory,* monetarism, disequilibrium theory, and equilibrium theory are all alike in claiming generality for all types of monetized economies, or at the least in failing to set out any conditions that tell the economist what special set of economies the theory is intended to explain. Keynes emphasized the generality of his theory even in his title and showed no hesitancy in using it to offer a new interpretation of mercantilistic economies and policies, although the underdeveloped mercantilistic economies were much different from the Western economies in Keynes's time. Similarly, many monetarists are ready to pass strong judgments on monetary and macroeconomic policies in economies of the most diverse kinds and levels of development and often make sweeping assertions; Milton Friedman's argument that inflation is "always and everywhere a monetary phenomenon" is one example of this monetarist claim to generality. If anyone should think that I have overstated the claims to generality of the established theories, he or she surely would concede that none of the existing theories spells out any ways in which macroeconomic or monetary problems will be vastly different in different types of societies or different historical periods. The generality and lack of distinctions among societies of various types no doubt reflects the depressingly unhistorical, unevolutionary, comparative-static, and institution-free character of much of modern economics.

By contrast, the present theory predicts that macroeconomic problems will be different in different societies. The above analysis makes it clear that if special-interest groups (or anything else) create only a *small* number of nonclearing markets in an economy, the problems due to these distortions will appear as sectoral, microeconomic, or local problems. An unexpected deflation or disinflation might make these problems worse, but because the problems are confined to a relatively small number of sectors, there would be no general depression or *macroeconomic* malady. An unexpected deflation or disinflation will not be terribly serious, because the harm it does will be confined mainly to a few sectors and the spillover of resources into the huge flexprice sector will be small in relation to the size of that sector, and thus fairly innocuous. Deflation or disinflation will influence the price level and nominal income but need not create much involuntary unemployment or have any substantial or sustained impact on the level of real output. In other words, the economy free of special-interest groups and the processes and legislation they bring about would behave much the way the less cautious monetarists and equilibrium theorists say that all economies do.

On the other hand, when an economy reaches the point where distributional coalitions are ubiquitous and the fixprice sector is large in relation to the flexprice sector, the theory offered here predicts that the macroeconomic situation will be different. An unexpected deflation or disinflation will then bring widespread losses and suffering from forced movement from the fixprice to the flexprice sector, from falling prices in the flexprice sector, from unemployment of those who could not or would not move, from increases in queueing and searching costs, and at the same time substantial losses of real demand that further aggravate problems because the vector of relative prices diverges far from the pre-deflation vector for that society and even farther from the ideal vector. The economy that has a dense network of narrow special-interest organizations will be susceptible during periods of deflation or disinflation to depression or stagflation. The present theory implies that some societies or periods of history will not suffer much involuntary unemployment or large losses of real output even from unexpected deflation or disinflation, whereas other societies will suffer significant involuntary unemployment and losses of real output. In addition, it predicts that any society with unchanged borders that enjoys continued stability will over time gradually shift from the former state to the latter.

XIV

Unfortunately, my knowledge of recent comparative macroeconomic experience across the world is not yet great enough to permit me to do the cross-sectional part of this empirical test as well as I would like. I shall be forced to consider only the largest countries and one prototypical smaller country. There is also the problem that different countries (or historical periods) may have had different monetary and fiscal policies partly or even largely because of political accidents or other causes exogenous to my theory. The degree of fluctuation in the level of real output and the extent of involuntary unemployment in my model depend not only on the length of time societies have had to accumulate special-interest groups, but also on the predictability and stability of monetary and fiscal policies and on the extent of any exogenous shocks an economy has faced. Thus one society (or historical period) could have had relatively minor business cycles and little involuntary unemployment, even though it had had a high level of special-interest organization, whereas another society with less institutional sclerosis may have had extraordinary monetary and fiscal instability. At least partly for these reasons, this cross-section or international comparison portion of the empirical test that has just been set out will not be at all compelling.

Yet it appears that Japan and, to a lesser extent, Germany have been able to keep unemployment of labor at lower levels during the stagflation that set in during the 1970s than have the United States and, especially, Britain. Unemployment statistics are gathered on different bases in different countries and are not comparable, with statistics in many other countries understating the degree of unemployment in relation to U.S. measures. However, the U.S. Bureau of Labor Statistics has converted the unemployment rates for the major foreign countries into figures comparable with those of the United States. These figures show that in 1975–76 Great Britain had an unemployment rate of about 5 percent and the United States about 8 percent, whereas Germany had an unemployment rate of about 4½ percent and Japan only 2 percent.[23] I do not have up-to-date comparable figures, but more recently the situation has become more striking, with U.S. unemployment rising above 9 percent in 1982 and British unemployment rates rising well over 12 percent even without adjustment.

Of course, any number of factors may be involved. But a glance at the inflation rates of these countries does not seem to support either the notion that expansive (that is, inflationary) monetary and fiscal policies will rule out unemployment or the argument of some monetarists that "inflation causes recession" or higher unemployment. From 1972 to 1979 the annual average rate of inflation was highest in Great Britain, at 15 percent, and fairly high in the United States, at 9.1 percent. Contrary to Keynesian demand-management notions both countries had high unemployment. Germany's inflation record, 5.5 percent, like its unemployment record, was better. Yet success at keeping down the inflation rate apparently is not essential to full employment, either; the Japanese rate of inflation was second highest, at 10.6 percent, whereas its unemployment rate was far and away the lowest.

Moreover, as my theory would lead the reader to expect, there has been more concern and difficulty in Britain than in any other country over "social contracts" and "incomes policies." Both the aspirations for such contracts and the failure of such policies is not, by my argument, surprising in a country with strong special-interest groups of a narrow kind. Germany has had not only fewer but also more encompassing special-interest organizations, and each of these features may very well have something to do with its better record on both inflation and unemployment.

There are all sorts of special circumstances in each of the four countries that help to account for the results, such as the special role in West Germany of guest workers, who may sometimes be sent home when unemployed. But we must also remember that West Germany and Japan have faced much larger shocks from the higher price of oil, since both are utterly reliant on oil imports. The United States, although a net importer, is one of the world's largest oil producers; and Britain, during this very period, has had the colossal good fortune to become an oil exporter. Still, only polar cases and large countries have been considered, so no conclusions are yet in order.

It is not possible to examine the experience of all countries, but there is one small country so prototypical that it is worth special attention. As I pointed out in chapter 6, Taiwan (like Korea, Hong Kong, and Singapore) has enjoyed fantastically high postwar growth rates. The Japanese occupation, we recall, had repressed special-interest organization in Taiwan, so the rapid growth is in accord with the theory offered in this book. If the argument in this chapter is right, countries with Taiwan's nearly complete absence of special-interest organization should be able to maintain something approximating full employment and full-capacity production even during an unexpected deflation or disinflation. By my reading of the statistics, Taiwan has in fact experienced dramatic disinflations with only relatively minor losses of real output. Those who have given the matter specialized attention also seem to have observed this. Erik Lundberg writes:

The postwar period began with the consumer price index rising about tenfold a year during 1946–49 and about 500 percent in 1949–50. By 1950–51 the rate of inflation was still out of control (80 to 100 percent a year). It is of great interest to determine how this very rapid inflation was dampened so quickly and brought down to manageable proportions by 1952 without a depression or a severe break in economic growth. . . .

Another central issue is Taiwan's success in bringing down the relatively high rate of inflation during 1952–60 (7 to 8 percent a year) to a remarkable stable value of money—the GNP deflator rising by 2 to 3 percent annually—and with a minimum of fluctuation. This achievement cannot be explained solely by monetary and fiscal policies.[24]

XV

Clearly the preceding examples do not provide any definitive empirical test.* But let us now look at changes in the United States over the relatively brief period since World War II. Since monetarists have in general been more resistant than Keynesians to suggestions that structural and institutional changes were among the causal factors in postwar inflationary experience, it may be expedient to take some of our facts once again from that careful monetarist writer, Phillip Cagan.

Cagan examined data on the changes in prices and in output for the United States since 1890. He found that the tendency for prices to fall during recessions has declined over time. He observes that

the change in rates of change [of prices] from each expansion to the ensuing recession became less negative and, in the last two cycles, the change became positive—that is, the rate of price increase in the recession exceeded that in the expansion, perverse cyclical behavior not exhibited before. The distinctive feature of the postwar inflations has not been that prices rose faster in periods of

*Another cross-sectional test was suggested when this book was in press: unemployment rates according to my theory ought to be higher in those states of the U.S. in which a larger proportion of the labor force is unionized. They are. Regressions on unemployment rates by state from 1957 to 1979 show that this relationship is statistically significant, and far stronger than the relationship between the percentage of the labor force in manufacturing and unemployment. The regressions neglect the important indirect effects of distributional coalitions other than labor unions, but these indirect effects are usually not confined to the state in which the coalition exists.

cyclical expansion—many previous expansions had much higher rates—but that they declined hardly at all, or even rose, in recessions. . . . The startling failure of the 1970 recession to curb the inflation was not a new phenomenon . . . but simply a further step in a *progressive* post-war development. . . . The phenomenon of rising prices in slack markets is quite common. . . .

Part of the smaller amplitude of cyclical fluctuations in prices reflects the reduced severity of business recessions since World War II, for which some credit goes to the contribution of economic research to improved stabilization techniques. Nonetheless, in addition to the smaller cyclical contractions in aggregate expenditures, the response of prices to a given amplitude of contraction has declined, so that now proportionately more of the contraction in expenditure falls on output.[25]

Jeffrey Sachs has also in a recent article corroborated Cagan's finding with somewhat different methods.[26]

Although the finding that what is loosely called *stagflation* has emerged recently is commonplace, there are two features of Cagan's observations that deserve to be emphasized. The first is his insistence that there has been a *progressive* or *gradual* emergence of this problem. This is certainly correct—the puzzling experience of the 1970s was foreshadowed, for example, in the 1950s, when the cost-push arguments first appeared. Yet nothing like this was evident early in the century or in previous centuries.

A second important feature of Cagan's observations is the point that, because of the changing behavior of prices, over time *an increasing proportion of the effect of any reduction in aggregate demand shows up as a reduction in real output.* Cagan does not discuss this, but straightforward observation suggests there has been a similar development in several other countries. This is exactly what the theory here would lead us to expect, but it is not implied by any of the nonevolutionary and institution-free macroeconomic theories.

XVI

The same tendency for unexpected deflation or disinflation to lead to more unemployment and larger losses of real output as time goes on appears in more dramatic form when we take a long-range historical perspective. Even though the reliable data needed to make definitive judgments about macroeconomic and monetary history in earlier centuries are lacking, the qualitative evidence and the scattered data that do exist are sufficient to have generated almost a consensus among economic historians about certain broad outlines of historical experience. These broad outlines, well-known as they are to economic historians, somehow have not been taken into account in either the Keynesian or the monetarist theories.

Perhaps the most prominent trend in all macroeconomic history has been the tendency in countries such as Britain and the United States for reductions in aggregate demand, whatever their causes, to have more and more impact on the level of real output as time progressed. This pattern is evident since at least the eighteenth century. There were great (and unpredicted) fluctuations in the price level, but these fluctuations did not, at the time of the Industrial Revolution and during most of the nineteenth century, bring about large-scale unemployment or substantial reductions in real output. In still earlier eras of history, economies were relatively parochial, with trade barriers of the kind described in chapter 5 around small communities, so it is difficult to speak of uniform national macroeconomic developments. But in the mercantilistic period Britain, particularly, had become a centralized state with few internal barriers to trade. This meant it could, and did, easily experience nationwide inflations and deflations. After this jurisdictional integration and the civil war and political instability of the seventeenth century, the inflations and deflations appear to have had only minor and transitory effects, if any, on the level of employment or real output. Similarly, the United States from the onset of its national history was a national economy that could, and did, experience inflations and deflations, but again these appear to have had only a small impact on the level of employment and real output.

While situations began to change somewhat in the latter part of the nineteenth century, the years from the peak of inflation of the Napoleonic Wars in 1812 to the low point in 1896 nonetheless will serve to illustrate the point. Over that period in Great Britain the price level fell by more than one-half. The price level in the United States fell even more. Yet during that period the Industrial Revolution continued in Britain and the United States also enjoyed remarkable growth and prosperity. Broadly speaking, the longest period of peaceful growth in per capita income that the world has ever seen took place in a period in which the price level was, more often than not, falling. As the nineteenth century wore on, the bottom years of the cycle probably brought increasing unemployment, but by comparison with twentieth-century experience the downswings in the cycle brought relatively small reductions in real output.

There were, of course, many "panics" and "crises" even in the early nineteenth century. It was naturally when the price level fell that those who had borrowed money tended to have the hardest time paying it back; they were paying a higher real interest rate than they would have paid had the price level not fallen. As the Populist movement in the nineteenth-century United States indicates, those who had borrowed money when prices were higher certainly did not like the deflation. When prices fell and some firms could not pay their debts, there could be a panic, especially in view of the unstable banking system (particularly in the United States), which often led to bank failures. These panics and crises depressed expectations and led to some reductions in employment and real output, but in terms of the experience of the 1930s, or our sense of what would result from comparable falls in the price level today, the effects were relatively minor and brief.

This can best be illustrated by comparing the depression of the interwar years with what was perhaps the greatest previous U.S. monetary contraction. Milton Friedman and Anna Schwartz say that "to find anything in our history remotely comparable to the monetary collapse from 1929 to 1933, one must go back nearly a century to the contraction of 1839 to 1843."[27] Indeed, as some detailed estimates by economic historian Peter Temin show, the contraction in the money supply was even greater in 1839–43 than in 1929–33. *The fall in the price level was substantially greater: −31 percent in 1929–33 and −42 percent in 1839–43.* But consumption in real terms, which decreased by 19 percent from 1929 to 1933, increased 21 percent from 1839 to 1843. More dramatically still, *the real gross national product, which decreased by no less than 30 percent from 1929 to 1933, increased by 16 percent from 1839 to 1843.* (See table 7.1 below, reproduced from Temin's *Jacksonian Democracy*.)[28] As Temin aptly points out in another book,[29] the unemployment of resources in the United States in the depression that started in 1929 had no precedent in any prior contraction:

> The economic contraction that started in 1929 was the worst in history. Historians have compared it with the downturns of the 1840's and the 1930's, but the comparison serves only to show the severity of the later movement. In the nineteenth-century depressions, there were banking panics, deflation, and bankruptcy, in various proportions. But there is no parallel to the underutilization

Table 7.1. Comparison of 1839–1843 with 1929–1933 (in percent)

	1839–43	*1929–33*
Change in money stock	−34	−27
Change in prices	−42	−32
Change in number of banks	−23	−42
Change in real gross investment	−23	−91
Change in real consumption	+21	−19
Change in real gross national product	+15	−30

NOTE: The 1839–43 data are taken from peak to trough of the respective series, and dates differ somewhat. Data on money and banks are from late 1838 to late 1842; data on prices, from calendar-year 1839 to calendar-year 1843; data on GNP, etc., from census-year 1839 (year ending May 31, 1839) to census-year 1843.

SOURCE: 1839–43—Tables 3.2, 3.3, 5.2 [in Peter Temin, *The Jacksonian Economy* (New York: W. W. Norton, 1969, 1975)]; Gallman, private correspondence; U.S. Historical Statistics, p. 624; 1929–33—Ibid., pp. 116, 143, 624, 646.

of economic resources—to the unemployment of labor and other resources—in the 1930's.

The value of goods and services in America fell by almost half in the early 1930's. Correcting for the fall in prices, the quantity of production fell by approximately one-third. Unemployment rose to include one-quarter of the labor force. And investment stopped almost completely. It was the most extensive breakdown of the economy in history.

The difference in the character of the macroeconomic experience between the nineteenth and twentieth centuries is evident even in the language of daily life. Although some writers have exaggerated the newness of the term, the fact remains that unemployment is a term that came into common use only late in the nineteenth century. The *Oxford English Dictionary* states that the word *unemployment* has been in common use since about 1895, but E. P. Thompson points out that the word can occasionally be found in Owenite and Radical writings as early as the 1820s and 1830s.[30] Early observers of unemployment tended to use such circumlocutions as ''want of employment'' or ''involuntary idleness.'' The usual German word for unemployment, *arbeitslosigkeit,* was also rarely used before the 1890s. The usage of the French word *chomage* goes back to the Middle Ages, but this word also has connotations of leisure, as in the expression *un jour de chome* for a day or holiday on which no work is normally done.[31] If the falling price level in the early nineteenth century had led to widespread and continuing unemployment of labor or other resources, some word to describe such an important, if not tragic, state of affairs would surely have come quickly into common usage in the languages of all the relevant countries.

The extent to which a reduction in aggregate demand is reflected in unemployment of resources and reductions in real output must be distinguished from the magnitude of fluctuations in aggregate demand. The years since World War II, as Cagan pointed out, have by historical standards been relatively stable, in part because of what economists and governments have learned about stabilization policy. But the evidence cited shows that because of increasing inflexibility of prices, as time goes on, a stable society suffers more unemployment and a greater loss of output for any given reduction in aggregate demand.

This historical evidence, like the international comparisons cited earlier, is not explained by any of the conventional macroeconomic theories. They say nothing at all about what historical periods or societies would suffer the most unemployment and loss of real output when there is unexpected deflation or disinflation. Their emphasis on generality leaves the impression that the consequences of bad fiscal or monetary policies would be much the same in all monetized economies. The theory offered here, by contrast, does predict the international differences and the gradual changes over time in stable societies that we have observed.

XVII

The time and the place where Keynes developed his brilliant theory, the parts of the world where it became the orthodoxy, and the character of the Great Depression also fit with the argument. Keynes was, of course, working out his dazzling ideas in Great Britain in the 1920s and 1930s. The society in which he wrote had accumulated far more special-interest organizations and collusions than any other society at that time. The pattern of demand for exports and other goods that the British economy faced was far different from that before the war, and the industries in which Britain had comparative advantage had changed, too. Britain thus needed a new structure of relative wages and prices and a considerable reallocation of resources. In the absence of price and wage flexibility and in the presence of entry barriers, the reallocation of resources proceeded slowly; there was a great deal of unemployment of resources. For a time this problem was exacerbated by Churchill's overvaluation of the pound in the mid-1920s. Still, if the relevant wages and prices had fallen enough, British resources would nonetheless have been fully employed. But the British institutional structure had been developing for a long time, and the relevant wages and prices did not fall in the short run, and some not even in the medium. In a sufficiently long run, these wages and prices would have adjusted, but by then, as Keynes well knew, a good proportion of the population at issue would be dead. Thus Keynes's *General Theory* is, in fact, an ingenious and enlightening but by no means truly "general" theory. Had Britain emerged from World War I with the clean institutional slate that Germany had after World War II, Keynes would probably not have written the book.

The problems that Britain faced and the diverse difficulties of other countries at the time Keynes worked out the ideas in the *General Theory* (and the *Treatise on Money*) were made very much more serious by the reverse jurisdictional integration and rampant economic nationalism in the world economy after World War I. The Austro-Hungarian empire was divided at Versailles into many smaller states. In general these new nations were economically nationalistic and protectionist. The Soviet Union had relatively little trade with the outside world. Protection increased dramatically elsewhere as well; even Britain and the British Empire abandoned free trade policies. On top of this, the world economy was further deranged by extravagant demands by the European allies for reparations from the defeated nations, unrealistic demands by the United States for repayment of the debts its allies had contracted during the war, and beggar-thy-neighbor and other foolish exchange-rate policies in many countries. The loss of potential gains and even past gains from trade in the world economy must have been very large indeed. By the logic described earlier this loss would have reduced the real demand for output everywhere, especially the demand for exports.

The huge and prosperous United States might have survived these international difficulties without calamity had it chosen the right policies. In addition to making other mistakes, the United States joined in the restrictionist and protectionist binge; it slapped unprecedented quotas on immigration and passed the Fordney-Macomber and then the still higher Smoot-Hawley tariffs. Although labor unions favored and were implicated in the immigration restriction legislation, for example, it is important to emphasize that by modern American standards only a very modest proportion of the labor force was unionized. The efforts of employers to keep out unions by following union wage scales and the concentration of unions in conspicuous and important labor markets gave them an influence far beyond their membership, but this membership in the 1920s was decreasing.

As Implication 3 predicts, small groups organize first, and small groups of business firms appear to have been far and away the largest source of the problem. There was, as Lester V. Chandler aptly described it, "the trade association movement of the 1920s. Strongly approved by Herbert Hoover as Secretary of Commerce, trade associations were established in virtually every major industry and in many minor ones. . . . Many, probably most, of the trade associations restrained competition."[32] The success they met in initiating an orgy of tariff-raising in a country and a period with a relatively strong support of free-market ideology suggests how strong they must have been; this suggestion is confirmed in several studies by leading political scientists.[33] The tariff is the mother of all manner of combinations and collusions, and further business cartelization and oligopolistic collusion were greatly facilitated. This in turn must have encouraged slow consensual and constitutional decision-making about prices, especially in the industrial sector.

The extremely unstable American banking system of the time, the satiation of the opportunities for investment in certain sectors, the limitation on the demand for American exports due to foreign tariffs, the adverse impact on investor confidence of the stock-market crash, and perhaps still other factors brought about a reduction in spending. When this happened, many prices, especially in the manufacturing sector, naturally did not fall promptly or in proportion to the reduction in demand. And indeed the statistics that have already been discussed show that, whereas agricultural prices and other flexible prices fell dramatically, a host of other prices, particularly in concentrated and organized industrial sectors, fell slowly and by relatively little. With these inefficient prices the gains from trade were much less than before and real incomes and demands for output lower, and this, in combination with the deflation and the volatility of investment spending that Keynes emphasized, meant that the demand for labor and other factors of production fell dramatically, and by so much that rigidities in the labor market that would not have been nearly so serious by themselves had substantial quantitative effects.

Even then, the unemployment problem would not have been so serious or so prolonged but for what followed. There were intense complaints in the apple-selling or flexprice markets about the disproportionate drops in prices and low returns. In addition, the laissez-faire doctrine that all would be well if the government left the economy alone (except, in some versions, for providing protection against foreign competition) was largely discredited in the minds of most Americans by the manifest failure of capitalism and the conservative administrations of Coolidge and Hoover to prevent the depression. There followed an avalanche of measures designed to intervene in markets by fixing prices and wages at "fair," "reasonable," or "full cost" levels—that is, at levels that would be profitable for the firms and workers who were already securely established in the market, but that would make it unprofitable to hire the additional workers or sell the extra goods that would have brought the economy back to prosperity. These efforts began in the Hoover administration. The Davis-Bacon Act of 1931, for example, made it illegal for contractors or subcontractors on federal construction projects to pay less than what the secretary of labor deemed to be the prevailing wage rate in that locality, which was typically the union wage rate in the fairly heavily unionized construction industry. The Norris-LaGuardia Act of 1932 ended the use of the powers of courts to limit combination in the labor market.

Then came the National Recovery Administration (NRA) created in 1933. It not only allowed but enthusiastically encouraged each industry to set up a "code of fair competition" and a "code authority." The codes of fair competition typically required "fair" behavior with respect to output, prices, and various trade prices, and also "fair" wages, hours of work, collective bargaining, and so forth. It is estimated that 95 percent of industrial employees came to be covered by these codes.[34] Although the NRA also stipulated minimum wages and rules against wage-cutting, the interests of the trade associations of business firms seemed more significant. As Franklin Roosevelt later described it, the "codes were developed, as a matter of Administration policy, from proposals initiated from within the industries themselves. All but a few of them were sponsored and initially proposed by at least one trade association. [The NRA gave] industry the opportunity for self-government, many trade associations which had been inactive for years came to life again and many industries which did not have trade associations hastened to organize them."[35] In 1935 the Supreme Court declared the NRA unconstitutional. Some of its activities were transferred to other agencies and diverse acts (such as the National Labor Relations Act of 1935 and the Wagner Act of 1937) were passed to maintain wages and promote unionization. Unionization meanwhile had increased significantly and no doubt greatly influenced the wage policies of many firms who feared independent or "outside" unionization; by the spring of 1934, one-fourth of all industrial workers were employed in plants with company unions, which were usually organized after strikes or organizing efforts by independent unions.[36] Membership in independent unions rose from somewhat more than three million in 1932 to eight million in 1938.

In short, the onset of the depression led to the official promotion of business and labor combinations and to legislation and regulation that prohibited ever more unemployed labor and other resources from making mutually advantageous contracts: more and more workers, consumers, and firms were prohibited from making the deals that would have filled up the triangular areas like those depicted in figure 1. In addition, the Agricultural Adjustment Act and other legislation fixed some farm prices and mandated the nonuse or unemployment of acres of land and of other agricultural resources because farm prices were fantastically low, among other reasons because of a migration of unemployed resources into agriculture.

In these circumstances policies to increase aggregate demand, such as those advocated by Keynes, made a lot of sense. To the extent that deflation could be stopped and prices increased, the prices set in nominal terms by the slow-moving combinations and regulatory processes were made lower in relative terms and thus less harmful. Since interest rates were already low and some people apparently were hoarding money, it is also not astonishing that Keynes would feel that increasing the money supply might not be sufficient and would advocate deficit spending by government. I do not know just what contribution each policy or development made to the increasing aggregate demand during the New Deal years. There was an inflow of gold and some monetary expansion, but most famously there was Franklin Roosevelt's controversial budget deficits. The combined effect of Roosevelt's expansionary demand policies, confidence in the banking system due to federal deposit insurance, some monetary expansion, and slow downward adjustment of some cartelistic prices and wages was evidently greater than all the increases in unemployment of resources brought about by the new cartelization and governmentally set minimum prices and wages. Unemployment was somewhat lower and real output somewhat higher in 1940 than it had been when Roosevelt took office in 1933.

Thus it is hardly surprising that Keynes had a profound impact upon the United States, and indeed upon the whole English-speaking world, most of which has enjoyed unusual political stability and accumulated dense networks of special-interest groups. From this perspective it is no accident that postwar German opinion, for example, has not been nearly as susceptible to Keynes. As always, many factors were involved; the number of technically trained economists has been many times larger in the English-speaking world than elsewhere, and thus there were more who were enthralled with the subtlety and sophistication of Keynes's book.

We are now in a position to see that, although an expansion of aggregate demand such as Keynes advocated in a depression can sometimes offset the effects of special-interest groups and unwise macroeconomic policies, the level of aggregate demand is at best a secondary and temporary influence on the level of involuntary unemployment. Involuntary unemployment can only be explained in terms of the interests and policies that rule out mutually advantageous bargains between those who have their own labor or other goods to sell and those who would gain from buying what is offered. A low level of or even a drop in aggregate demand is neither a sufficient nor a necessary condition for involuntary unemployment. That a declining or low level of aggregate demand need not cause a depression or involuntary unemployment is evident not only on theoretical grounds but also from the historical experience cited earlier in this chapter.

That involuntary unemployment can result with a high and increasing level of aggregate demand is evident from the fact that, whatever level of inflation is anticipated, a distributional coalition still has an incentive to set real prices or wages at levels that will block mutually advantageous trades outside the coalition and thus keep the market from clearing; if unemployed resources eventually could get employment in the flexprice sector, there would still be some involuntary unemployment due to the excessive queueing and searching brought about by the gratuitous disparity in returns to homogeneous resources. That involuntary unemployment can occur with a high and increasing level of aggregate demand is also demonstrated by the recent stagflation; in some years in which GNP in money terms has increased, there has also been high unemployment. There must have been an increase in aggregate spending or the higher nominal GNP could not have been purchased, yet unemployment remained and sometimes increased.

Since inadequate aggregate demand is not the main or ultimate source of involuntary unemployment, continuous, fast-changing demand management with fine tuning does not make sense. This is not only because, as others have pointed out, our knowledge is not good enough for fine adjustments, but also because demand management is not the main dial in any case. It was a great idea in the depths of the U.S. depression in 1933—when no one had a reason to fear any harmful inflation and when many special-interest organizations were in the process of trying to lower their prices from 1929 levels and did not expect price increases—to try to offset the mischievously high prices in the fixprice sector by using every method to augment aggregate demand. The extra spending could offset the drop in demand caused by the unemployment and the monopolistic pricing and might also help by raising the price level and thus changing the relative prices in the fixprice sector. But such an expansion may do little but bring about more inflation if the organizations are accustomed to demand management and will offset any expected expansionary fiscal or monetary policy by setting still higher prices. Sometimes, as I have shown elsewhere,[37] monetary and possibly fiscal policy can be changed faster than the distributional coalitions can alter their prices, and this opens up the possibility that demand management can achieve some gains in real output by changing policies after most of the distributional coalitions have chosen their prices. But changeable and unpredictable policies can have costs of their own, so this does not appear to be a permanent solution.

The ultimate source of the problem is that Keynes did not explain the inflexibility of many wages and prices or point out that such an explanation should be the very *core* of *any* macroeconomic theory, so some of his followers assumed they were more or less arbitrarily determined. Keynesians talked a lot about the ''core'' rate of inflation—that is, the rate of increase of those prices and wages that change relatively slowly—but what determined which prices and wages were the core ones, and what made them change, was not in their theory. If these core prices and wages were arbitrarily determined or the resultant of exhortatory ''incomes policies,'' there was no reason to suppose they would be greatly affected by increases in aggregate demand, so some Keynesians in the 1970s recommended even more expansive policies to cure the unemployment, thereby generating pointless inflation.

There are similar holes, just where the core ought to be, in the monetarist and equilibrium theories. These theories contain little or no theory of what makes some prices change only rarely and slowly; this is one of the reasons they offer no explanation of involuntary unemployment. Many economists in both Keynesian and monetarist camps have often referred to minimum-wage laws, labor unions, and the like as sources of sticky wages and unemployment, but passing references are not nearly enough. They do not explain what interests these sticky prices serve or how they emerged. If the most important phenomena in macroeconomics—the ones that give rise to unemployment and fluctuations in the level of real output—are not integrated into a macroeconomic theory, then that theory is like Hamlet without the Prince of Denmark.

XVIII

To say that Keynes's theory is crucially incomplete, and incomplete in a way that has been profoundly misleading, does not deny the magnitude of his contribution to macroeconomic theory. In a sense, he created the field. Keynes's emphasis on the demand for money as an asset, on the special volatility of investment as compared to consumption expenditure, and on expectations have enormously enriched our understanding of macroeconomic and monetary problems. Most of the monetary and business cycle theory that appeared before his *General Theory* now seems terribly primitive. Keynes, with the help of Hicks, also provided the intellectual framework needed to consider the supply and demand for money simultaneously with the intentions to save and invest. Having done all this and more, Keynes hardly can be blamed for failing to provide a theory of supply-price, such as has been offered here. But he should have pointed out the risks and limitations inherent in this omission and should not have claimed a specious generality. His reputation in the very long run might have been greater had he been more attentive to the cumulative nature of any science and less emphatic about the extent to which he differed from his predecessors.

One of the reasons I think it is important to emphasize Keynes's contribution to macroeconomic analysis and debate is that some of the monetarist and equilibrium-theory writing, for all its value to me and to the profession, has almost seemed to be inspired by a desire to demonstrate that the exact opposite of what Keynes concluded or recommended was right. Sometimes polemical victory has seemed to be more important than creativity. My impression may be wrong and unfair and, if so, I apologize. But why, then, have so many brilliant and valuable criticisms of Keynesian economics said little or nothing about involuntary unemployment, or about the manifest failure of the American economy and some others automatically to sustain full-employment levels of output? Above all, when millions of people are alive and ready to testify to the massive suffering and terrifying unemployment of the interwar period, why build a macroeconomic theory on the assumption that the economy is at or near an ether-like equilibrium and that neither involuntary unemployment nor deep and prolonged depressions can occur? And why complain vociferously about the rapidly increasing and harmful influence of government and the perniciousness of labor unions, but then build macro models on the assumption that the economy is essentially free of governmentally or cartelistically set prices, or is even perfectly competitive?

My hope is that the debate over Keynes soon can be left to the historians of economic thought, freeing the colossal talents in all the schools to focus on macro models that follow the monetarists and equilibrium theorists in their insistence that the macro theory must rest on valid microeconomic theory, and that follow Keynes in recognizing that involuntary unemployment is possible and that a laissez-faire economy in a stable society will not permanently and automatically sustain a full-employment level of output. It may be that I emphasize these conditions simply because they are conditions satisfied by my own theory, but I would be interested to see what arguments any skilled economist would propose for why a macroeconomic theory should not meet both of these conditions (or, for that matter, all the conditions for an adequate macro theory in the list set out earlier in this chapter).

XIX

For the most part, I am leaving the policy implications of the theory offered in this book aside for now. It would require another book to explore all the implications of the present theory in combination with familiar microeconomic theory and other considerations. Besides, it is best to focus first on getting the theory right, leaving the policy implications until later (among other reasons, because it is less likely that preconceptions about the "right" policy will distort the theory). It may be useful, nonetheless, to say a few tentative words.

The most important macroeconomic policy implication is that the best macroeconomic policy is a good microeconomic policy. There is no substitute for a more open and competitive environment. If combinations dominate markets throughout the economy and the government is always intervening on behalf of special interests, there is no macroeconomic policy that can put things right. In the invaluable but perhaps misleading language of Milton Friedman and Edmund Phelps, the "natural rate of unemployment"—essentially, the rate of unemployment when the price level or inflation rate generally expected is the one that actually occurs—will be very high. The need for better microeconomic policies and institutions has been most eloquently stated by the British economist James Meade, who said that "the natural rate of unemployment is unnaturally high." This statement is true not only for his own country, but to an extent for many others as well, not least the United States.

A second policy implication, also unoriginal, is that the disinflationary policies needed in so many countries at the present time should, in most cases, be steady and gradual policies, as well as resolute and believable ones. It has sometimes been suggested by economists who place almost exclusive emphasis on "expectations" that if the public actually could be made to believe that the government or central bank would institute a truly anti-inflationary policy and adhere to that policy for a long period, then a short and sharp contraction would solve the problem. Such a policy can work in a society with few distributional coalitions but not in one with many. The slow decision-making of such coalitions entails that they will not be able to adjust quickly, however certain they may be about the government resolve and however deep the short slump will be. Although it is an extreme case, consider again the Danish cartel referred to in chapter 3, which took ten years to adjust its policy despite disappearing profits. There is at the same time considerable evidence that special-interest groups do eventually adjust to the reality in which they find themselves. One example is the wage cuts sometimes accepted by unions when the firms that employ them are about to go broke.

The third and last macroeconomic policy implication to be considered at the moment is that tax and subsidy schemes designed to lower the natural rate of unemployment can in some societies make an important, if probably only temporary, contribution, when—and only when—they are combined with good monetary and fiscal policies. When the natural rate of unemployment is unnaturally high, it can be lowered somewhat by special taxes on firms that raise wages by a greater percentage than, say, the expected increase in productivity in the economy at large. Alternatively, if it is politically more feasible, firms can be given a subsidy that diminishes when they grant such an increase. This will give the firm an incentive to bargain for a lower wage increase and, on getting it, the firm will have an incentive to hire more workers than otherwise, thereby reducing unemployment. A disadvantage of such a policy is that it will discourage firms for which it is optimal to upgrade the skill mix from doing so, with some loss of economic efficiency. That is one reason policies of this kind presumably should be temporary and should not be offered (as they sometimes are) as panaceas or ideal solutions. I have been advocating such policies for a decade,[38] and Henry Wallich and Sidney Weintraub (the first to propose such schemes) have been advocating them far longer. A great many eminent economists have in recent years joined the chorus, but still without the least political success. I nonetheless maintain that such policies are politically achievable. They could be palatable when combined with policies favorable to the groups that would lose something from them (for example, senior workers with good job security). Such a tax usefully could be applied as well to price increases of large firms, although it would raise difficulties of administration and enforcement. Another policy in the same spirit advocates wage subsidies to firms that enlarge their work force by taking on workers from categories in which there is high unemployment. It cannot be stressed too strongly, though, that all such policies are definitely not cure-alls and are no substitutes for good monetary and fiscal policies and sound microeconomic policies and institutions.

XX

As I mentioned at the beginning of this chapter, a macroeconomist should be slightly uneasy if a theory explains nothing besides macroeconomic phenomena and should be somewhat reassured if a theory not only meets the specified macroeconomic conditions but explains other phenomena as well. Of course, this condition echoes the argument in chapter 1 about the need for theories with broad explanatory power, consilience to explain phenomena of very different kinds, and parsimonious simplicity as well. We are back to "the standards a satisfactory answer should meet."

I hope those who remain advocates of alternative macroeconomic conceptions, and advocates of alternative explanations of the growth rate or social structure of this or that country, will ask themselves how wide a variety of phenomena their theory can explain while retaining its simplicity. The theory offered here is certainly a simple one, at least by the standards of my discipline.

The theory here is consistent with the rapid postwar growth of West Germany and Japan, with the slow growth and ungovernability of Britain in recent times, and at the same time with Britain's record as the most rapidly growing country in an earlier time. It is consistent with the slower growth of the northeastern and older midwestern regions of the United States and with the faster growth of the South and the West—and offers a statistically significant explanation of the growth of the forty-eight states as a whole.

The theory also is consistent with the rapid growth of the six nations that founded the Common Market, the rapid growth of the United States throughout the nineteenth century, and the rapid growth of Germany and Japan in the later part of the nineteenth and early twentieth centuries. The theory fits the growth of Britain and of Holland and (less clearly) of France in the early modern period and their roles in the rise of the once-backward civilization of Western Christendom. It explains the decline of old cities in the midst of these expanding countries and the scattered, transactions-intensive putting-out system. The theory is consistent with the phenomenal postwar growth of Korea, Taiwan, Hong Kong, and Singapore and with the guild-ridden stagnation of the China that was first exposed to European pressure, not to mention the similar stagnation in India. Finally, the theory fits the pattern of inequalities and the trade policies of many of the unstable developing countries, and a number of other facts as well.

The evidence is perhaps not sufficient for us to say to what extent the theory succeeds in explaining the British class structure, the Indian caste system, and the timing and character of the stronger forms of racial discrimination in South Africa. It is best to be cautious when there is not enough sound quantitative or historical information. Yet the theory certainly explains each of these phenomena far better than any other theories do.

The *same* theory that parsimoniously explained the foregoing was the one that I used with very little addition to explain involuntary unemployment, depressions and stagflation, and other macroeconomic phenomena as well, without at any point making ad hoc or unreasonable assumptions about individual behavior. And it is powerful evidence for the present theory that, unlike any other theory, it explains the pattern of the development of the macroeconomic problem over time. When we take all these explanations together, we see that the theory is powerful and consilient as well as parsimonious. It is hard to see how it could explain so many diverse phenomena so simply if it were wholly or mainly false.

But even if the theory here should to my surprise be *entirely* correct, it still considers only one among the many factors affecting the phenomena I have endeavored to explain. The overwhelming significance that other factors will sometimes have can perhaps best be illustrated by considering what would happen if the findings of future research should resonate with what I have said here, and all the pertinent specialists should in time be persuaded by my argument. Suppose further that the message of this book was then passed on to the public through the educational system and the mass media, and that most people came to believe that the argument in this book was true. There would then be irresistible political support for policies to solve the problem that this book explains.

A society with the consensus that has just been described might choose the most obvious and far-reaching remedy: it might simply repeal all special-interest legislation or regulation and at the same time apply rigorous anti-trust laws to every type of cartel or collusion that used its power to obtain prices or wages above competitive levels. A society could in this way keep distributional coalitions from doing any substantial damage. This remedy does not require any major expenditure of resources: intelligent and resolute public policies would by themselves bring great increases in prosperity and social performance. So sweeping a change in ideas and policies is extraordinarily unlikely. But this scenario is nonetheless sufficient to show that if the argument in this book or other arguments of similar import should be unexpectedly influential, then the predictions derived from this book will be falsified.

Obviously, distributional coalitions will oppose the repeal of special-interest legislation and the imposition of anti-trust policies that deny them the monopoly gains that their capacity for collective action could otherwise obtain. The limited impact of economic education in the past, even on matters on which there has been professional consensus, suggests that the coalitions will often be successful. Keynes went much too far when he wrote that the world is ruled by ideas and little else. Yet the great influence of his writings on public policy, and the more recent impact of his critics, shows that ideas certainly do make a difference.

May we not then reasonably expect, if special interests are (as I have claimed) harmful to economic growth, full employment, coherent government, equal opportunity, and social mobility, that students of the matter will become increasingly aware of this as time goes on? And that the awareness eventually will spread to larger and larger proportions of the population? And that this wider awareness will greatly limit the losses from the special interests? That is what I expect, at least when I am searching for a happy ending.

Acknowledgments

My strategy in research is to attempt to say or write something audacious enough to elicit intelligent criticism, to reflect at length on that criticism, and then to maintain the self-confidence needed unreservedly to make every amendment, abandonment, or extension that could be appropriate. Even if I believe a criticism is mistaken, I strive (sometimes unsuccessfully) to take that as evidence that I need to improve my exposition. While working on this book I have accordingly obtained criticisms from hundreds of people—experts in almost every pertinent specialization, in most parts of the world, and from almost every ideological shading. As a result, a large part of any merit this book may have is due to my critics.

I am indebted to each and every critic, but the number is so very great that it is not feasible to list them all. This is not only because of the excessive number of pages such a listing would require. I was using the criticism-seeking strategy even before I knew I would be writing a book along these lines, and I have been using it for so many years on this book alone that I have undoubtedly forgotten some of those who helped. In some cases the critics were questioners in large audiences, whose names I never knew. In selecting for special mention some critics whose help is recent or for other reasons especially memorable, I am no doubt doing an unjustice to others, and even to some whose help was quite valuable. I am deeply sorry for this and hope that those I have accidentally slighted will forgive me.

Those who provided crucial help and encouragement in the earlier and more primitive stages of this effort needed special patience, and I am especially thankful for that. John Flemming, coeditor of the *Eco-*

nomic Journal, was an extraordinarily generous and penetrating early critic, and I am sorry that I have never sent him the ready-to-publish article that I led him to expect. Robert Solow was another invaluable source of early encouragement and help, as were Moses Abramovitz, Samuel Brittan, Sir Alec Cairncross, Walter Eltis, Daniel Patrick Moynihan, Daniel Newlon, and Thomas Wilson. Those who have done or are doing complementary or collaborative work have also been particularly helpful, most notably Kwang Choi, Jean-François Hennart, Gudmund Hernes, Dennis Mueller, and Peter Murrell.

In 1978 Robin Marris proposed and chaired a conference to assess and criticize a paper I had written on the matters discussed particularly in chapter 4 of this book. He invited experts from various countries and specialties to this conference, some of whom wrote extended comments that are published in Dennis Mueller's *Political Economy of Growth.* I am deeply thankful to Robin Marris for promoting this conference, to Dennis Mueller for editing and contributing to the book that grew out of it, to the National Science Foundation for providing the principal funding for it, and to the Deutsche Forschungsgemeinschaft, the Centre National de la Recherche Scientifique, and the Ministry of Education of Japan for financing some of the travel to it. Finally, each of those who attended the conference or contributed papers has helped me more than he or she probably realizes. The mere listing of names and affiliations that follows does not do them justice:

Moses Abramovitz (Stanford U.), J. C. Asselain (U. de Bordeaux I), Ragnar Bentzel (Uppsala U.), James Blackman (National Science Foundation), Samuel Bowles (U. of Massachusetts), Myles G. Boylan (National Science Foundation), Camilo Dagum (Ottawa U.), James Dean (Simon Fraser U. and Columbia U.), Stephen J. DeCanio (U. of California, Santa Barbara), Edward Denison (U.S. Dept. of Commerce), Raymond Courbis (U. of Paris), John Eatwell (Trinity, Cambridge), Walter Eltis (Exeter, Oxford), Francesco Forte (U. of Torino), Raymond Goldsmith (Yale U.), Jean-François Hennart (Florida International U.), Gudmund Hernes (U. of Bergen), Sir John Hicks (All Souls, Oxford), Ursula (Lady) Hicks (Linacre, Oxford), Helen Hughes (World Bank), Charles Hulton (Urban Institute), Serge-Christophe Kolm (CEPREMAP, Paris), Hans-Juergen Krupp (U. of Frankfurt), Franz Lehner (Ruhr U. Bochum), Harvey Leibenstein (Harvard U.), Edward J. Lincoln (Johns Hopkins U.), Edmond Malinvaud (Inst. National de la Statistique, Paris), R. C. O. Matthews (Clare,

Cambridge), Christian Morrisson (Ecole Normale Superieure), Daniel H. Newlon (National Science Foundation), Yusuke Onitsuka (Osaka U.), Sam Peltzman (U. of Chicago), Richard Portes (Birkbeck, London), Frederic L. Pryor (Swarthmore College), Walter Salant (Brookings Institution), Hans Soderstrom (U. of Stockholm), Ingemar Stahl (U. of Lund), Carl Christian von Weizsacker (U. of Bonn), Hans Willgerodt (U. of Cologne), Wolfgang Zapf (U. of Mannheim).

I am similarly indebted to Roger Benjamin for bringing early drafts of part of this work to the attention of critics in political science, to Marian Ash, Myles Boylan, Jan de Vries, Stanley Engerman, I. M. D. Little, R. C. O. Matthews, and Edmund Phelps for exceptionally generous help, to Nuffield College, Oxford, and especially to Brian Barry for hospitality and comment when I had some of my early thoughts on this, to the staff of Resources for the Future and especially Emery Castle and Joy Dunkerley for patient encouragement, and to the participants in the pleasant seminars organized by the Lehrman Institute around early drafts of this book, including particularly Donald Dewey and Kelvin Lancaster. My wife, Alison G. Olson, has as a professional historian a special appreciation of the importance of prose that is whenever humanly possible free of specialized technical language, and I am indebted to her for invaluable instruction in the art of writing clearly, as well as for many other things. My brothers, Allan and Gaylord, have also helped in many ways.

My colleagues at the Department of Economics at the University of Maryland have been exceptionally generous and stimulating. I must emphasize Martin J. Bailey's patience with the delays in our collaborative work occasioned by my preoccupation with this book, Christopher Clague's years of helpful and penetrating comments on this and my other writing, and Charles Brown's and Paul Meyer's criticisms of many early drafts. Adele Krokes's help also deserves special emphasis, not only because of her incredibly patient typing and word processing, but even more because of the efficient way she helps to organize my hectic professional life. I am also thankful to those who have provided research assistance over the years I have worked on this book, especially Terence Alexander, Kwang Choi, Brian Cushing, Cyril Kearl, Douglas Kinney, Natalie McPherson, James Stafford, Fran Sussman, and Howell Zee.

Finally, there are the many kind people who have read and criticized the last two drafts. I am grateful not only to many of those named earlier, but also to Alan Blinder, Roger Boner, Barry Bosworth, Shannon Brown, Bruce Bueno de Mesquita, Martha Derthick, Dudley Dillard, Bruce Dunson, James Galbraith, John Goldethorpe, Donald Gordon, Daniel Hausman, Russell Hardin, Michael Hechter, Gail Huh, Peter Katzenstein, Donald Keesing, Robert Knight, Robert Mackay, Cynthia Taft Morris, Douglas North, Joe Oppenheimer, Clarence Stone, Maura Shaw Tantillo, Charles Taquey, Neil Wallace, Oliver Williamson, and Horst Zimmermann.

Unfortunately, there has not been time enough to do justice to many of the more recent comments. I fear I have perhaps also failed to comprehend fully some of the criticisms, and despite my general strategy I have stubbornly resisted a few, including one or two that were most severe. Thus the faults that remain in this study—and I fear, partly because of its scope, that there may be a great many—are entirely my responsibility.

Notes

CHAPTER 1

1. From "The First Book, Entitled Clio," *The History of Herodotus,* trans. George Hawlinson (New York: D. Appleton and Company, 1882), 1:121, 122.

2. Irving B. Kravis et al., *A System of International Comparisons of Gross Product and Purchasing Power* (Baltimore and London: Johns Hopkir.. University Press for the World Bank, 1975), especially p. 8.

3. New York: Collier, 1962, p. 476 (6th ed., London: J. Murray, 1872). For an analysis of the power of theories, see Anatol Rapoport, "Explanatory Power and Explanatory Appeal of Theories," *Synthese* 24 (1972):321–42. I am thankful to Russell Hardin for advice on the power of theories.

4. *The Philosophy of Inductive Sciences* (New York: Johnson Reprint, 1967), 2:65 (3rd ed., London: Parker, 1858); see also Paul R. Thagard, "The Best Explanation: Criteria for Theory Choice," *Journal of Philosophy* 75 (February 1978):76–92. I am thankful to Daniel Hausman for calling the concept of consilience to my attention and for his penetrating criticisms of an earlier draft of this book, and to Stephen Brush for providing helpful references on this subject.

CHAPTER 2

1. Cambridge: Harvard University Press, 1965, 1971. The 1971 version differs from the first 1965 printing only in the addition of an appendix. Some readers may have access to the first paperback edition published by Schocken Books (New York: 1968), which is identical to the 1965 Harvard version. Readers whose first language is not English may prefer *Die Logik des Kollektiven Handelns* (Tübingen: J. C. B. Mohr [Paul Siebeck], 1968), or *Logique de*

l'Action Collective (Paris: Presses Universitaires de France, 1978). Translations in Japanese (from Minerva Shobo) and in Italian (from Feltrinelli) are forthcoming.

2. There is a logically possible exception to this assertion, although not of wide practical importance, that is explained in footnote 68 of chapter 1 of *The Logic,* pp. 48–49.

3. David J. McDonald, *Union Man* (New York: Dutton, 1969), p. 121, quoted in William A. Gamson, *The Strategy of Social Protest* (Homewood, Ill.: Dorsey Press, 1975), p. 68.

4. *The Logic,* p. 85.

5. This means in turn that sometimes individual corporations of substantial size can be political combinations with significant lobbying power. On less than voluntary corporate contributions, see J. Patrick Wright, *On a Clear Day You Can See General Motors* (Grosse Pointe, Mich.: Wright Enterprises, 1979), pp. 69–70.

6. *The Logic,* pp. 132–67.

7. Erik Lindahl, "Just Taxation—A Positive Solution," in Richard Musgrave and Alan T. Peacock, eds., *Classics in the Theory of Public Finance* (London: Macmillan, 1958), pp. 168–77 and 214–33. In a Lindahl equilibrium, the parties at issue are each charged a tax-price for marginal units of the public good that is equal to the value each places on a marginal unit of the good. When this condition holds, even parties that have vastly different evaluations of the collective good will want the same amount. It would take us far afield to discuss the huge literature on this matter now, but it may be helpful to nonspecialists to point out that in most circumstances in which the parties at issue expect Lindahl-type taxation, they would have an incentive to understate their true valuations of the collective good, since they would get whatever amount was provided however low their tax-price. There is an interesting literature on relatively subtle schemes that could give individuals an incentive to reveal their true valuations for public goods, thereby making Lindahl-equilibria attainable, but most of these schemes are a very long way indeed from practical application.

8. See my primitive, early article, "The Principle of 'Fiscal Equivalence,'" *American Economic Review, Papers and Proceedings* 59 (May 1969):479–87.

9. See, for a leading example, Martin C. McGuire, "Group Segregation and Optimal Jurisdictions," *Journal of Political Economy* 82 (1974):112–32.

10. See most notably Wallace Oates, *Fiscal Federalism* (New York: Harcourt Brace Jovanovich, Inc., 1972).

11. For very early work on the limited information voters may be expected to have, see Anthony Downs's classic *Economic Theory of Democracy* (New York: Harper, 1957).

12. I am indebted to Russell Hardin for calling this point to my attention.

For a superb and rigorous analysis of the whole issue of collective action, see Hardin's *Collective Action* (Baltimore: The Johns Hopkins University Press for Resources for the Future, forthcoming).

13. There is another consideration that works in the same direction. Consider individuals who get pleasure from participating in efforts to obtain a collective good just as they would from ordinary consumption, and so are participation altruists (described in the first footnote in this chapter). If the costs of collective action to the individual are slight, the costs of consuming the participation pleasure or satisfying the moral impulse to be a participant are unlikely to prevent collective action. With the diminishing marginal rates of substitution that are described in the footnote, however, the extent of collective action out of these motives will decrease as its price rises.

14. *The Logic,* pp. 5–65.

15. The assumption that there are two firms that place an equal value on the collective good is expositionally useful but will not often be descriptively realistic. In the much more common case, where the parties place different valuations on the public good, the party that places the larger absolute valuation on the public good is at an immense disadvantage. When it provides the amount of the collective good that would be optimal for it alone, then the others have an incentive to enjoy this amount and provide none at all. But the reverse is not true. So the larger party bears the whole burden of the collective good. (The party that places the larger value on the collective good has the option of trying to force the others to share the cost by withholding provision, but it is also at a disadvantage in the bargaining because it will lose more from this action than those with whom it is bargaining.) Thus a complete analysis of the likelihood of collective action must consider the relative sizes or valuations of the collective good of the parties involved as well as the size of the group; see the references in the next note on "the exploitation of the great by the small" and other consequences of intragroup variations in valuations of collective goods.

If the corner solution with the larger party bearing all the burden does not occur, and both firms provide some amount of the collective good under Cournot assumptions, then the two firms will tend to be of exactly the same size, as in the example chosen for expositional convenience in the text. Assume that each firm has to pay the same price for each unit of the collective good and that they have identical production functions for whatever private good they produce. Since they must, by the definition of a pure collective good, both receive the same amount of it, they can both be in equilibrium under Cournot assumptions only if their isoquants have the same slope at the relevant point. That is, the isoquants describing the output that results from each combination of the private good and public good inputs for each of the firms must have the same slope if the two firms enjoying the same amount of the collective good are each purchasing some of it at the same time. Under my identical production function and factor price assumptions, the two firms must then have exactly the same output or size.

Similarly remarkable results hold for consumers who share a collective good. Either the consumer that places the higher absolute valuation on the public good will bear the entire cost or else they will end up with equal incomes! When both consumers get the same amount of a collective good, they both can be continuing to purchase some under Cournot behavior only if they both have the same marginal rate of substitution between the public good and the private good, and thus (with identical utility functions and prices) identical incomes. Unless the two consumers have identical incomes *in the beginning,* there is inevitably exploitation of the great by the small. One possibility is that the richer consumer will bear the whole cost of the collective good. The only other possibility with independent adjustment is that the public good is so valuable that the richer consumer's initial purchases of it have such a large income effect on the poorer consumer that this poorer consumer ends up just as well off as the initially richer consumer, so both buy some amount of the collective good in equilibrium. I have profited from discussions of this point with my colleague Martin C. McGuire. For a stimulating and valuable, if partially incorrect, argument along related lines, see Ronald Jeremias and Asghar Zardkoohi, "Distributional Implications of Independent Adjustment in an Economy with Public Goods," *Economic Inquiry* 14 (June 1976):305–08.

16. *The Logic,* pp. 29–31, and Mancur Olson and Richard Zeckhauser, "An Economic Theory of Alliances," *Review of Economics and Statistics* 47 (August 1966):266–79, and my introduction to Todd Sandler, ed., *The Theory and Structure of International Political Economy* (Boulder, Colo.: Westview Press, 1980), pp. 3–16.

17. No strategic interaction is observed among firms in perfectly competitive industries or among buyers of automobiles, for example. In such situations no one finds that his own interests or choices depend on the choices of any other individual in the group or industry, so they have no incentive to bargain with one another. A sufficiently large subset, if it could obtain the collective good of a bargaining organization for the subset, would have an incentive to bargain with others in the group. But when genuinely large groups are at issue, the size of the subset that is large enough to have an incentive to bargain is itself so large that the collective good of the bargaining organization for the subset cannot be obtained without selective incentives. Another way of stating the point is to say that the bargaining costs of getting the bargaining organization for the subset are themselves prohibitive, so that any further bargaining costs are irrelevant when group size increases still further, i.e., to the point that a still bigger subset would be needed. This indicates that approaches to genuinely large or "latent" groups that focus on bargaining costs and strategic interaction are not getting at the essence of the matter.

CHAPTER 3

1. Niccolò Machiavelli, *The Prince*, trans. George Bull (Baltimore: Penguin Books, 1961), p. 51.

2. Edward Shorter and Charles Tilly, *Strikes in France, 1830–1968* (London and New York: Cambridge University Press, 1974), pp. 154–55.

3. Max Weber, *Theory of Social and Economic Organization*, trans. Talcott Parsons and A. M. Henderson, ed. Talcott Parsons (New York: Oxford University Press, 1947), p. 318.

4. I am thankful to Peter Murrell for help on this point.

5. Gordon Tullock and Anne Krueger are to the best of my knowledge the pioneers in this literature. For reprints of their initial articles and especially pertinent articles by Keith Cowling and Dennis Mueller, Richard Posner, and Barry Baysinger, Robert B. Ekelund, Jr., and Robert D. Tollison, plus other useful papers, see James M. Buchanan, Robert D. Tollison, and Gordon Tullock, eds., *Toward a Theory of the Rent-Seeking Society* (College Station, Tex.: Texas A. & M. University Press, 1980).

6. A measure that would reduce economic efficiency if introduced in a Pareto-efficient society could conceivably increase efficiency in a society with prior distortions. See R. G. Lipsey and R. K. Lancaster, ''The General Theory of the Second Best,'' *Review of Economic Studies* 24, no. 63:11–32.

7. One of the questions left aside was raised by the concept of ''mass movements'' fashionable among sociologists in the 1950s and 1960s. This concept emphasizes that membership in organizations that are smaller than the state (and presumably small or subdivided enough so that there is social interaction among members) can reduce alienation and increase social stability. In my judgment there is an important element of truth in this concept, and I have found it useful in some of my own writings, particularly those cited in note 21 below. But this element of truth is more than offset in many societies by the contribution these organizations make to divisiveness and ungovernability, as is explained in the remainder of the discussion leading to Implication 4. The prospective publications that will relate the point from the literature on mass movements to the argument in this book, and the reasons that integration is omitted from this book, are set out in note 21.

8. Again, this qualification is introduced because of the possibility of ''second-best'' problems. It is, for example, possible that the monopolization of a previously competitive but highly polluting industry could increase economic efficiency if there were no effluent fee on the pollution. In this example, the logic is quite simple: the industry when competitive had an output that was inefficiently large because the social cost of its pollution is neglected by the competitive firms. Since monopolists have an incentive to restrict output, the loss from pollution would be reduced by monopolization, and if the pollution

were serious enough this could be of greater value than the market output forgone.

9. Arnold Harberger, "Monopoly and Resource Allocation," *American Economic Review* 44 (May 1954):77–87. See also Harvey Leibenstein on X-efficiency, *Inflation, Income Distribution and X-Efficiency Theory* (London: Croom Helm; New York: Harper and Row, Barnes and Noble, 1980).

10. To the best of my recollection, in a guest lecture at Princeton University in the 1960s.

11. See Dennis C. Mueller's concluding essay in the book he edited on *The Political Economy of Growth* (New Haven: Yale University Press, 1983).

12. Kenneth Arrow, *Social Choice and Individual Values,* 2d ed. (New Haven: Yale University Press, 1963). For a more accessible proof of Arrow's theorem and a survey of related issues, see Dennis Mueller, *Public Choice* (Cambridge: At the University Press, 1979).

13. See, for example, Morris Fiorina, "The Decline of Collective Responsibility in American Politics," *Daedalus* 109 (Summer 1980):25–46; this issue has the title *The End of Consensus.* See also the writings of E. E. Schattschneider, *Party Government* (New York: Farrar and Rinehart, 1942), *Politics, Pressures, and the Tariff: A Study of Free Private Enterprise in Pressure Politics, As Shown in the 1929–1930 Revision of the Tariff* (Hamden, Conn.: Archon Books, 1963), *The Semisovereign People: A Realistic's View of Democracy in America* (New York: Holt, Rinehart, and Winston, 1960), and *The Struggle for Party Government* (College Park, Md.: University of Maryland, 1948).

14. See note 12 above.

15. "How Are Cartel Prices Determined?" *Journal of Industrial Economics* 5 (November 1956):16–23.

16. *Industrial Market Structure and Economic Performance* (Chicago: Rand McNally, 1970), p. 161. I am thankful to Jean-François Hennart for calling this and the previous reference to my attention.

17. M. A. Adelman of M.I.T. made this type of argument in a seminar a few years ago at Resources for the Future in Washington. Of course, Adelman recognized that some nations with their own nationalized oil companies were not covered by the argument.

18. William Baumol, John C. Panzar, and Robert Willig, *Contestable Markets and the Theory of Industry Structure* (San Diego: Harcourt Brace Jovanovich, 1982); see also Baumol's "Contestable Markets: An Uprising in the Theory of Industry Structure," *American Economic Review* 72 (March 1982):1–15.

19. See Avinash Dixit, "A Model of Duopoly Suggesting a Theory of Entry Barriers," *Bell Journal of Economics* 10 (Spring 1979):20–32, and "The Role of Investment in Entry-Deterrence," *Economic Journal* 90 (March 1980):95–106.

20. See Richard Schmalensee, ''Economies of Scale and Barriers to Entry,'' *Journal of Political Economy* 89 (December 1981):1228–38.

21. ''Rapid Growth as a Destabilizing Force,'' *Journal of Economic History* 23 (December 1963):529–52; ''Agriculture and the Depressed Areas,'' *Journal of Farm Economics* 46 (December 1964):984–88; ''Economics, Sociology, and the Best of All Possible Worlds,'' *The Public Interest* 12 (Summer 1968):96–118; and the introduction and epilogue (coauthored) to *The No Growth Society,* edited with Hans Landsberg (New York: W. W. Norton, 1974).

One reason that I have not in this book gone into the social costs that unprecedented rapid growth can sometimes have is that it would make the present theory much more difficult to refute. The theory here makes predictions about economic growth as it is conventionally defined and (for recent periods) measured in the national income statistics issued by the governments of most developed countries. I argue in ''The Treatment of Externalities in National Income Statistics'' (in Lowdon Wingo and Alan Evans, eds., *Public Economics and the Quality of Life* [Johns Hopkins University Press for Resources for the Future and Centre for Environmental Studies, 1977], pp. 219–49) that the national income statistics often do not properly take account of various environmental and social side effects. These statistics nonetheless offer an objective and generally unbiased test of the present theory and in addition provide far better insight into the progress of societies and the well-being of people in them than many people realize.

Another reason why I have omitted the social disruptions that rapid economic growth can occasionally cause, and the contributions (discussed in note 7 above) that some special-interest groups can sometimes make to social stability, is that the accumulation of these groups in the long-stable societies that are a principal focus here creates the ungovernability discussed in connection with Implication 4 and also decidedly destabilizing frustrations, as more and more people come to realize that their societies are very far from being as productive (or as fair) as they could be. Thus the inclusion of the matters I have omitted does not lead to any major change in any of the conclusions here.

A final reason for excluding these matters is that I have discussed most of them elsewhere, in the publications so tediously cited above, and I will relate these and other issues to the present argument in forthcoming books. The sometimes disruptive effects of rapid growth and the relation of the economy and economic theory generally to social, political, and environmental issues will be discussed in ''Beyond the Measuring Rod of Money''; this is a book that I very nearly decided to publish in the 1970s, but I decided this subject was so vast that it needed years of additional thought—I hope to finish revising it soon after this book is published. The relationship between the development of special-interest groups and other institutions and the development of stability in less developed countries will, if all goes well, be the subject of still another book. This last will be an expansion of an unpublished paper I wrote and circulated in the early 1960s under the title "Economic Growth and Structural Change" (and more recently in a revised form under the title "Diseconomies of Scale in Development"). It will emphasize the special problems of instability and inefficiency of large-scale organizations in poor societies, both now and before the Industrial Revolution.

I apologize for leaving out certain considerations that some readers may feel would affect their assessment of the importance of the theory in the present book, but surely this book is sweeping enough as it is.

22. Even if the innovation in this firm is a labor-saving innovation, a sufficiently powerful union could in principle take advantage of it to make all workers better off; it could appropriate a portion of the savings from the innovation for the workers and offer as much of this portion as was needed as an inducement to the number of workers who were no longer needed to seek employment elsewhere. The workers might do still better if the innovation in the firm were a capital-saving innovation, like the less expensive but superior computers that have been developed recently. Workers as a whole could lose from an economy-wide labor-saving innovation. The fact remains that a sufficiently powerful union could, if bargaining costs and delays are ignored, serve its members' interests by encouraging the firm with which it bargains to adopt any innovations that increased the total surplus available for profits and wages in the aggregate.

23. This special case occurs when there is such an underutilization of labor in relation to the amount of other factors that the average product of labor would increase if another laborer were added. But the profit-maximizing firm could never be in this range.

24. Sir John Hicks, "Structural Unemployment and Economic Growth: A 'Labor Theory of Value' Model," in Mueller, *The Political Economy of Growth*.

25. Strictly speaking, Hicks's proof applies only to a two-sector economy with labor as the only factor of production. The essence of this argument is, however, applicable to economies with any number of industries and factors of production.

26. To avoid complications with income effects that are of no importance here, I assume that we are speaking of an income-compensated demand curve.

27. They would not, however, necessarily want the number of workers or other sellers to fall below the point where the average product of the factor was at a maximum.

28. I am thankful to Christopher Clague for emphasizing the magnitude of the other factors involved here. These are illustrated by the endogamous rules of some groups that have average or below-average levels of wealth, power, and prestige.

29. Charles Schultze, *The Public Use of Private Interest* (Washington, D.C.: The Brookings Institution, 1977).

30. Morris Fiorina and Roger Noll, ''Voters, Legislators and Bureau-cracy—Institutional Design in the Public Sector,'' *American Economic Review, Papers and Proceedings* 68 (May 1978):256–60.

CHAPTER 4

1. Gustav Stolper et al., *The German Economy, 1870 to the Present* (New York: Harcourt Brace and World, 1967), pp. 258–61.

2. Richard E. Caves and Masu Uekusa, *Industrial Organization in Japan* (Washington, D.C.: The Brookings Institution, 1976).

3. I am grateful to Gudmund Hernes for educating me on the substantial significance of the encompassing of special-interest organizations in postwar Germany.

4. For a good description and analysis of French growth from a more orthodox perspective, see J.-J. Carré, P. Dubois, and E. Malinvaud, *La Crois-sance Française,* which is also available in English translation as *French Eco-nomic Growth,* trans. John P. Hatfield (Stanford: Stanford University Press, 1975). I am grateful to Edmond Malinvaud for taking an early, primitive ver-sion of the present argument quite seriously and offering a severe criticism of it. I do not think Malinvaud's criticisms apply to the present book.

5. The need to draw also upon another part of the present theory to explain French experience is evident from the useful criticism of an early version of the present argument written by J.-C. Asselain and C. Morrisson, ''Economic Growth and Interest Groups: The French Experience,'' in Dennis C. Mueller, ed., *The Political Economy of Growth* (New Haven: Yale Univer-sity Press, 1983). Asselain and Morrisson show that instability and invasion by themselves are not nearly sufficient to explain the whole story of the evolution of special-interest groups and growth rates in France. Valuable as Asselain's and Morrisson's criticism is, I do not think it does full justice to the extent to which instability, invasion, and ideological division have slowed the develop-ment of French labor unions, and since the largest part of the national income is paid in wages to labor, this is quantitatively very important. There is much to be said for Asselain's and Morrisson's emphasis on how economic adversity can facilitate special-interest organization; but recessions also can weaken special-interest organizations, as the recent experience of American and British labor unions shows, and boom conditions are often periods of exceptional growth of such organizations (e.g., the growth of American labor unions in both world wars). In view of the generally ambivalent relationship between economic progress or retrogression and special-interest organization, I would continue to attribute a significant role to instability and invasion—and the wide ideological

divisions that go with them—in retarding the development of special-interest organizations. It is difficult to see how any French economic organization with a massive clientele would not have been cowed by, say, the Nazi hegemony and occupation, or that any such organization would not have been handicapped at times by the intense ideological divisions in French society.

6. See, for example, M. W. Kirby, *The Decline of British Economic Power Since 1870* (London: George Allen and Unwin, 1981).

7. Relative rates of growth must be used in this argument because the rates of growth of the slowest growing and the fastest growing countries alike were faster in the 1950s and 1960s than in any previous period, and far higher than during the Industrial Revolution. One explanation of this is the apparently increasing pace of scientific progress in the modern world. This progress is essentially exogenous to a single national economy like the British economy; it depends on the advance of science over the world as a whole rather than in any single country. Many advances in basic science in any case may often be largely independent of current economic developments and of the institutions on which the present theory focuses. In view of the importance of developments like the world's rate of basic scientific advance that are exogenous to my theory, it does not predict absolute rates of growth. Since all countries have access to essentially the same basic scientific knowledge, the relative rates of growth of different countries in any one period can depend to a great degree on the institutions and policies of that country, so the present theory can therefore generate predictions about relative rates of growth.

8. Verlag Dokumentation (Pullach bei Munchen, 1973).

9. Peter Murrell, ''The Comparative Structure of the Growth of West German and British Manufacturing Industry,'' in Mueller, *The Political Economy of Growth.*

10. Some observers are taken by the idea that Germany and Japan have grown so rapidly since World War II because, it is supposed, they were fortunate to have their existing factories and machines destroyed by bombing and other combat, and therefore had no choice but to invest in the most modern plant and equipment. Britain, by contrast, is supposed to have been cursed with a large inheritance of capital that was not up-to-date. A moment's reflection will, however, make it clear that a profit-maximizing firm that owns plant and equipment that is not up-to-date will be either better off for owning the old capital or alternatively no worse off than if it had no capital left at all. If the use of the old capital will generate receipts in excess of average variable costs, the firm will profit from using the old capital and be better off than if it did not own this capital. Should the use of the capital not generate a return above average variable costs, the profit-maximizing firm will not use it, and will be in essentially the same position as it would have been had this old capital been destroyed. The most that bombing of old capital could do is to save a country some

wrecking costs of capital goods it needed to tear down, and this hardly could be quantitatively important. Everyday observation also confirms that it is not an advantage to be forced to start from scratch. The poorest developing countries certainly do not have a lot of old machinery and factories, yet most of them are not growing very rapidly. Germany and Japan invested so heavily in the 1950s and 1960s as compared with Britain that they must have more outdated capital goods than the British do, but yet they continue to grow faster than the British. Thus nations are not being irrational when they regard the bombing of their industry as a hostile act and try to defend themselves against such bombing.

11. If we assume that the percentage of income saved rises with income, and that there are no inflows or outflows of capital, a country with a hard-working population will save and invest more than a country that is identical to it in everything except industriousness. It will accordingly grow faster. I am thankful to Tatsuo Hatta and I. M. D. Little for calling this and other possible connections between industriousness and growth to my attention.

12. Samuel Brittan, "How British Is the British Sickness?" *Journal of Law and Economics* 21 (October 1978):245–68.

13. Ibid., table 9, p. 254.

14. David Smith, "Public Consumption and Economic Performance," *National Westminster Bank Quarterly Review*, November 1975, pp. 17–30.

15. David S. Landes, *The Unbound Prometheus* (Cambridge: At the University Press, 1969), pp. 39–122. These quotations are taken from widely scattered sections of chapters 2 and 3.

16. I am grateful to Daniel Patrick Moynihan for reminding me of the purpose Smith had when using this expression: "To found a great empire for the sole purpose of raising up a people of customers, may at first sight appear a project only for a nation of shopkeepers; but extremely fit for a nation whose government is influenced by shopkeepers" (*Wealth of Nations* [New York: Modern Library, 1937], p. 579).

17. Christopher Hill, *The Century of Revolution, 1603–1709* (New York: W. W. Norton, 1961), and J. H. Plumb, *The Growth of Political Stability in England, 1675–1725* (London: Macmillan, 1967).

18. See chapter 4, "Orthodox Theories of State and Class," in *The Logic*, pp. 98–110.

19. See, for example, Mancur Olson, "The Principle of Fiscal Equivalence," *American Economic Review, Papers and Proceedings* 59 (May 1969):479–87 and Martin C. McGuire, "Group Segregation and Optimal Jurisdictions," *Journal of Political Economy* 82 (January/February 1974):112–32.

20. Cambridge: At the University Press, 1981.

21. One need not agree with George Bernard Shaw "that all professions are conspiracies against the laity" (*The Doctor's Dilemma*, 1906), for one to believe that the honored place held by the professions in modern society, and

the fact that most intellectuals are in the professions, lead many to neglect their cartelistic aspects.

22. The ruptures of medieval class patterns and barriers that apparently have been due to the sweeping changes in technology and modes of life since the onset of the Industrial Revolution suggest an intriguing extension of the present theory. If there are sufficiently drastic and rapid changes in an economy, so that utterly new industries, occupations, and modes of living rapidly arise, the existing distributional coalitions (which make decisions in the relatively slow fashion described in Implication 6) may find the new activities beyond their scope and control. Peter Murrell's finding that new industries are less likely to be controlled by distributional coalitions than old ones also calls attention to this possibility. Thus when economic growth is not only rapid but also characterized by large discontinuities, it could tend to bypass existing special-interest groups and leave them relatively less important in the society than previously. This could in the extreme even offset the accumulation of the distributional societies described in Implication 2; drastic economic instability as well as political instability can at times weaken special-interest organizations. Although extremely rapid and discontinuous growth introduces some of the social costs discussed in notes 7 and 21 in chapter 3, it is nonetheless worth looking into the possibility that public policies occasionally could be designed to promote exceptionally discontinuous and rapid growth partly because this would reduce the significance of distributional coalitions and the social rigidities they help to engender. Such policies would most often be feasible for poor developing societies that can transform their technologies by borrowing those already developed in more prosperous societies. Eventually, if time permits, I hope to examine this possible extension of the theory in a detailed way, or alternatively to provoke others to do so. The importance of this extension is due partly to the possibility that it could illuminate a way of introducing an economic and possibly quite desirable form of instability that could delay or prevent the development of institutional rheumatism.

23. The evidence that there is greater sensitivity to certain class or group distinctions and barriers in Britain than in various comparable societies is unfortunately mainly informal and anecdotal rather than quantitative. But there are mountains of casual evidence on this point, and the evidence and perceptions of British observers appear to be in close accord with those of foreign visitors to Britain. One interesting example of this is the distinctive response of British commentators on the earliest versions of the present argument, written before the implications of the theory for class and group barriers were apparent to me. Most British commentators, however generous they might be, were quick to point out that my argument did not take account of the special characteristics of one or another of the British social classes, such as the alleged bloody-mindedness of the British working class or the allegedly aloof and anticommercial

attitudes of the British upper classes, or of the British class system as a whole. At first I resisted these criticisms as only ad hoc arguments; I foolishly over-looked the fact that not a single commentator from anywhere made any similar comments about any other country, and even somehow neglected memories from my own time as an American undergraduate at Oxford—which memories strongly supported my British critics' contentions that the British class system was distinctive and harmful to British economic growth. Finally I realized that, if my argument was right, the British critics who pointed out that one had to take account of the class system also had to be right, and I then generalized my theory. Once the theory was generalized to cover social rigidities, it was almost inevitable that the additional application of it that is set out in chapter 6 would come to mind. If my theory as generalized has any value, much of the credit is due to my many British friends and critics.

Massive and consistent as the casual evidence that there is a distinctive class system in Britain seems to me to be, it is nonetheless useful to seek quantitative and systematic evidence as well. A consensus among observers obviously has meaning, but the perceptions of casual observers do not have the precision and ready comparability that is desirable. On the other hand, quantita-tive evidence of an incomplete or inadequate kind should not necessarily be given more weight than a vast amount of casual evidence.

Unfortunately, the types of quantitative studies that are now available do not provide appropriate tests of the hypothesis about social exclusion that my theory generates. One reason is that this hypothesis relates to social exclusion or discrimination but does not claim to explain any correlation between the status of parents and children that is due to different-sized legacies of human and other capital. As the application of the theory in chapter 6 should make clear, my theory, if correct, explains any systematic tendency to exclude, or to discrimi-nate against the actual capabilities of any group or class of adults in a society; it does not, however, explain any differences in capabilities that are due to dif-ferences in upbringing and educational opportunities, except to the extent that these differences in turn are explained by the impact of the distributional coali-tions in the parents' generation on the distribution of income. The quantitative studies of social mobility that exist now relate the social prestige of the occupa-tions of fathers to the social prestige of the occupations of their sons. To the extent that the social prestige of the occupations that sons practice is due to the amount and kind of human capital they acquired, it is generally not explained by my theory.

A second reason why the existing quantitative studies do not provide a good test of my argument about social involution is that these studies consider social mobility from one generation to another, and the majority of the distribu-tional coalitions in Britain and other Western countries are not strictly multi-generational. That is, most of them do not restrict membership in the coalition to their own offspring. The Indian and South African distributional coalitions considered in chapter 6 do this; so do some European coalitions such as the nobility and certain labor unions, but so far they appear to be less common in the West than single-generation coalitions. To the extent that membership in distributional coalitions is not passed from one generation to another, the exclusion and discrimination inherent in these coalitions will not be captured by studies of the degree of association between the occupational prestige of fathers and sons.

A third reason why the studies of the association between the occupational prestige of fathers and sons do not offer a sufficient test of the present theory is that they leave out so much: differences in accent, dress, or style across different social groups; the role of inherited fortunes and titled aristocracies; the degree of resentment faced by uninvited entrants to established occupations or industries; the extent to which people are conscious of or sensitive about their social or class position; attitudes toward business; and attitudes toward entrepreneurship (which probably leads to the most dramatic changes in socioeconomic position). One measure of the significance of some of these variables that the existing quantitative studies leave out is the degree to which class and social position are correlated with allegiance to political party. Here it is significant that the association between socioeconomic status and adherence to the Labour and Conservative parties in Great Britain has been very much stronger than the corresponding association between socioeconomic position and affiliation with the Democratic and Republican parties in the United States (see Reeve D. Vanneman, ''U.S. and British Perceptions of Class,'' *American Journal of Sociology* 85:769–90). It might be objected that this British-American difference is due to the different nature of the political parties in the two countries rather than to any differences in the social structure, but since the political parties are in turn partly a reflection of the socioeconomic situation, and have the policies they do partly because of their desire to attract support, this objection is not convincing.

Although the existing types of quantitative studies of social mobility are by no means sufficient to test the present theory, they are nonetheless extremely useful for a variety of purposes. They also seem to show faint traces of the involutional process that my theory describes. Donald J. Treiman and Kermit Terrill, in ''The Process of Status Attainment in the United States and Great Britain'' (*American Journal of Sociology* 81 [November 1975]:563–83), find the rate of social mobility marginally lower in Britain than in the United States. Similarly, the data in papers by Robert Erikson, John Goldethorpe, and Luciene Portocarero (''International Class Mobility in Three Western European Societies,'' *British Journal of Sociology* 30 [December 1979]:415–41; ''Social Fluidity in Industrial Nations: England, France, and Sweden'' [mimeo]) suggest that Sweden (whose more encompassing coalitions have a smaller incentive to exclude than their narrower counterparts in Britain) has somewhat more social mobility than England.

I am grateful to Otis Dudley Duncan, John Goldethorpe, Robert Hauser, Keith Hope, Donald Treiman, and Reeve Vanneman for helpful conversations or correspondence about social mobility, but it should not be assumed that they are in agreement with what I have said.

24. In Mueller, *The Political Economy of Growth.*

25. On Swedish economic history and policy, see Assar Lindbeck, *Swedish Economic Policy* (Berkeley and Los Angeles: University of California Press, 1974); for a discussion of the advocacy or adoption of policies consistent with growth, see especially pp. 24, 229–30, and 246.

26. I am thankful to Sten Nilson of the University of Oslo for this suggestion, and for letting me see his draft on "Organizations in Norway after 1955"; see also Lindbeck, *Swedish Economic Policy,* especially p. 6.

27. This paper on the Scandinavian experience is being prepared in collaboration with Gudmund Hernes of the University of Bergen.

28. *The Logic,* chapter 3.

29. On emulation and the desire for large scale in relatively undeveloped countries, see Alexander Gerschenkron, *Economic Backwardness in Historical Perspective* (Cambridge: Harvard University Press, 1962), pp. 5–30.

30. See Jeffrey G. Williamson and Peter H. Lindert, *American Inequality* (New York: Academic Press, 1980) and Allen Kulikoff, "The Progress of Inequality in Revolutionary Boston," *William and Mary Quarterly* 28 (July 1971):375–412.

31. Williamson and Lindert, *American Inequality.*

32. See Richard Nisbett and Lee Ross, *Human Inference: Strategies and Shortcomings of Social Judgment* (Englewood Cliffs, N.J.: Prentice-Hall, 1980), especially chapter 3.

33. Kwang Choi, "A Study of Comparative Rates of Economic Growth" (forthcoming, Iowa State University Press) and Kwang Choi, "A Statistical Test of the Political Economy of Comparative Growth Rates Model," in Mueller, *The Political Economy of Growth.*

34. Spearman rank correlation coefficients between years since statehood and *LPI, PN,* and per capita *LPI, PN* were respectively $-.52$, $-.67$, $-.52$, and $-.52$, and the correlation coefficients were in every case significant.

35. Farm organization membership need not be correlated with union membership, but farm groups focus almost exclusively on the farm policies of the federal government, and any losses in output due to them must fall mainly on consumers throughout the United States, rather than in the state in which the farmers are organized, so farm organization membership probably should not be included in tests on the forty-eight contiguous states. By contrast, the victims of any barriers to entry or restrictive practices by unions or professional organiza-

tions are likely to be disproportionately from the area in which the special-interest organization operates.

36. Choi, ''A Study of Comparative Rates of Economic Growth.''

37. C. Vann Woodward, *The Strange Career of Jim Crow*, 3rd rev. ed. (New York: Oxford University Press, 1974).

38. If all goes well (it rarely does), I shall devote my presidential address to the Southern Economic Association to this question; it will be published in the *Southern Economic Journal* in early 1983.

39. I am thankful to Ed Kearl for help on this point.

40. I am grateful to Moses Abramovitz, Geoffrey Brennan, and Simon Kuznets for giving me a fuller appreciation of the salience of this distinction.

41. ''Thoughts on Catch-Up,'' October 1978, manuscript distributed to the conference on ''The Political Economy of Comparative Growth Rates,'' University of Maryland, December 1978.

42. See Moses Abramovitz, ''Notes on International Differences in Productivity Rates'' in Mueller, *The Political Economy of Growth*.

43. As I argued earlier, differences in per capita income induce migration that tends to eliminate the differentials. Thus within any country with freedom of movement the model here should be tested on changes in total rather than per capita income. The significance of migration is shown by the fact that the catch-up hypothesis performs much better with per capita than with total income as the dependent variable; indeed, it then decisively outperforms the independent variables suggested by our model.

44. *America's Third Century* (New York: Harcourt Brace, 1976), pp. 72–74.

45. Choi, ''A Study of Comparative Rates of Economic Growth,'' and ''A Study of Comparative Rates of Economic Growth among Large Standard Metropolitan Statistical Areas'' (unpublished manuscript, 1979).

46. Peter Murrell, ''Comparative Growth and Comparative Advantage: Tests of the Effects of Interest Group Behavior on Foreign Trade Patterns,'' *Public Choice* 38 (1982):35–53, and ''The Comparative Structure of Growth in the Major Developed Capitalist Nations,'' *Southern Economic Journal* 48 (April 1982):985–95.

CHAPTER 5

1. Edwin M. Truman, ''The European Economic Community: Trade Creation and Trade Diversion,'' *Yale Economic Essays* 9 (Spring 1969):201–51; Mordechai Kreinen, *Trade Relations of the EEC: An Empirical Investigation* (New York: Praeger, 1974), pp. 25–55. See also John Williamson and Anthony Battrill, ''The Impact of Customs Unions on Trade in Manufactures,'' in Melvyn G. Krauss, ed., *The Economics of Integration* (London: George Allen & Unwin, 1973).

2. Bela Balassa, "Trade Creation and Trade Diversion in the European Common Market," *Economic Journal* 77 (March 1967):17.

3. Fernand Braudel, *Capitalism and Material Life,* trans. Miriam Kohan (New York: Harper and Row; London: George Weidenfeld and Nicolson, 1973), pp. 439–40.

4. M. J. Daunton, "Towns and Economic Growth in Eighteenth-Century England," in Philip Abrams and F. A. Wrigley, eds., *Towns in Societies* (Cambridge and New York: Cambridge University Press, 1978), p. 247.

5. Charles Pythian-Adams, "Urban Decay in Late Medieval England," in Abrams and Wrigley, *Towns in Societies,* pp. 159–85.

6. Domenico Sella, *Crisis and Continuity, The Economy of Spanish Lombardy in the Seventeenth Century* (Cambridge: Harvard University Press, 1979), p. 136. On these matters see, for example, Jan De Vries, *The Economy of Europe in an Age of Crises* (Cambridge: At the University Press, 1976); Dudley Dillard, *Economic Development of the North Atlantic Community* (Englewood Cliffs, N.J.: Prentice Hall, 1967); Henri Pirenne, *Economic and Social History of Medieval Europe* (London: Routledge and Kegan Paul, 1936); and Douglass C. North, *Structure and Change in Economic History* (New York and London: W. W. Norton, 1981).

7. Braudel, *Capitalism and Material Life,* pp. 404–05.

8. Herbert Kisch, "Growth Deterrents of a Medieval Heritage: The Aachen Area Woolen Trades before 1790," *Journal of Economic History* 24 (December 1964):517–37.

9. Adam Smith, *An Inquiry Into the Nature and Causes of the Wealth of Nations,* ed. R. H. Campbell, A. S. Skinner, and W. B. Todd (Oxford: Clarendon Press, 1976), p. 146.

10. See, for example, Christopher Hill, *The Century of Revolution, 1603–1709* (New York: W. W. Norton, 1961), and J. H. Plumb, *The Origins of Political Stability in England, 1675–1725* (Boston: Houghton Mifflin, 1967).

11. I am grateful to Jan De Vries for helpful conversations about the Dutch Republic as well as other matters. See, for example, William Doyle, *The Old European Order, 1660–1800* (Oxford: Oxford University Press, 1978), p. 31; Richard W. Unger, *Dutch Shipbuilding before 1800* (Amsterdam: Van Gorcom, 1978); and Robert DuPlessis and Martha C. Howell, "Reconsidering the Early Modern Urban Economy: The Cases of Leiden and Lille," *Past and Present* 94 (February 1982), pp. 49–84.

12. See, for example, Charles Cole, *Colbert and a Century of French Mercantilism* (New York: Columbia University Press, 1939), especially volume 1, chapter 7, and volume 2, chapter 12; Doyle, *The Old European Order,* map 7, p. 401; Pierre Goubert, *Cent Mille Provinciaux Au XVIIe Siecle: Beauvais et le Beauvaises de 1600 à 1730* (Paris: Flammarion, 1968).

13. I am grateful to Wolfgang F. Stolper for calling this expression to my attention.

14. In Dennis C. Mueller, ed., *The Political Economy of Growth* (New Haven: Yale University Press, 1983).

15. White Plains, N.Y.: International Arts and Sciences Press, 1973. On similar findings on growth and protection in developing countries see Ian Little, Tibor Scitovsky, and Maurice Scott, *Industry and Trade in Developing Countries, A Comparative Study* published for the Organization for Economic Cooperation and Development by Oxford University Press, 1970.

16. See Dumas Malone, ed., *Jefferson and His Times,* 2:166; see also Thomas Jefferson's letter to James Madison in which he says, ''I hold it that a little rebellion now and then is a good thing, and as necessary in the political world as storms in the physical,'' quoted in Merrill Peterson, ed., *The Portable Thomas Jefferson* (New York: Viking, 1975), p. 417. I am thankful to Connie Schulz for help at this point.

17. Charles P. Kindleberger, *Europe's Postwar Growth* (Cambridge: Harvard University Press, 1967).

18. For a related argument about ''contradictions,'' see Samuel Brittan, ''The Economic Contradictions of Democracy,'' *British Journal of Political Science* 5:129–59, reprinted as chapter 23 of Brittan's *Economic Consequences of Democracy* (London: Temple Smith, 1977).

CHAPTER 6

1. Max Weber, *The City,* trans. and ed. Don Martindale and Gertrud Neuwirth (New York: Collier Books, 1962), pp. 95–96.

2. David B. Weisberg, *Guild Structure and Political Allegiance in Early Achaemenid Mesopotamia* (New Haven: Yale University Press, 1967); Isaac Mendelsohn, ''Guilds in Babylonia and Assyria,'' *Journal of the American Oriental Society* 60 (1940):68–72, and ''Guilds in Ancient Palestine,'' *Bulletin of the American Schools of Oriental Research* 85 (1942):14–17.

3. See, for example, Theodore W. Schultz, *Transforming Traditional Agriculture* (New Haven: Yale University Press, 1964).

4. London: Longmans, Green, 1909; reprint ed., Taipei: Ch'eng-wen, 1966, p. 24. See also John Stewart Burgess, *The Guilds of Peking* (New York: Columbia University Press, 1928; reprint ed., Taipei: Ch'eng-wen, 1966); Peter J. Goles, ''Early Ching Guilds,'' and Sybille Van Der Sprenkel, ''Urban Social Control,'' in G. William Skinner, ed., *The City in Late Imperial China* (Stanford: Stanford University Press, 1977), pp. 555–80 and 609–32, respectively.

5. Morse, *The Guilds of China,* p. 21.

6. Ibid., pp. 21, 27, and 11.

7. ''Chinese Guilds or Chambers of Commerce and Trades Unions,'' *Journal of the [North] China Branch of the Royal Asiatic Society* 21 (1886):141.

8. Ibid., pp. 182–83.

9. Shannon R. Brown, "The Partially Opened Door: Limitations on Economic Change in China in the 1860's," *Modern Asian Studies* 12 (1978):187.

10. Ibid., and Shannon Brown, "The Ewo Filature: A Study in the Transfer of Technology to China in the 19th Century," *Technology and Culture* 20 (July 1979):550–68; "Modernization and the Chinese Soybean Trade, 1860–1895," *Comparative Studies in Society and History* 23 (July 1981):426–42; "The Transfer of Technology to China in the Nineteenth Century: The Role of Direct Foreign Investment," *Journal of Economic History* 39 (March 1979):181–97; and Shannon R. Brown and Tim Wright, "Technology, Economics, and Politics in the Modernization of China's Coal Mining Industry, 1850–1895," *Explorations in Economic History* 18 (January 1981):60–83.

11. "More than any other mature non-Western state, China has seemed inadaptable to the conditions of modern life," in John K. Fairbank, *Trade and Diplomacy on the China Coast* (2 vols., Cambridge: Harvard University Press, 1953; reprint ed. in one vol., Stanford: Stanford University Press, 1969), p. 4.

12. Alvin Rabushka, *Hong Kong: A Study in Economic Freedom* (Chicago: University of Chicago Press, 1979).

13. See, for example, Susan B. Hanley and Kozo Yamamura, *Economic and Demographic Change in Preindustrial Japan, 1600–1868* (Princeton: Princeton University Press, 1977).

14. Milton Friedman and Rose Friedman, *Free to Choose* (New York: Avon Books, 1981).

15. In this account of Japan, I have drawn particularly on conversations with my friend Yasukichi Yasuba of Osaka University, who may not, however, necessarily agree with my argument. I have also been particularly helped by William Lockwood's *The Economic Development of Japan* (Princeton: Princeton University Press, 1968); Johannes Hirschmeier, *The Origins of Entrepreneurship in Meiji Japan* (Cambridge: Harvard University Press, 1964); W. G. Beasley, *The Meiji Restoration* (Stanford: Stanford University Press, 1972); and John W. Hall and Marius B. Jansen, eds., *Studies in the Institutional History of Early Modern Japan* (Princeton: Princeton University Press, 1968).

16. Angus Maddison, *Class Structure and Economic Growth* (New York: W. W. Norton, 1971), p. 43.

17. Ibid., pp. 22–23.

18. Jewaharlal Nehru, *The Discovery of India,* ed. Robert I. Crane (New York: Anchor Books, Doubleday and Company 1946, 1960). The quotes are from widely scattered sections of the book, and presented in a different order here than they are in the book. I believe that they nonetheless fairly represent Nehru's views on these matters.

19. W. H. Hutt, *The Economics of the Colour Bar* (London: Merritt and

Hatcher Ltd. for The Institute of Economic Affairs Ltd. by Andre Deutsch Ltd., 1964).

20. Ibid., p. 62.

21. Ibid., p. 69.

22. There is the possibility, mentioned in the last chapter, that exporters would want a tariff in order to engage in price discrimination. On the politics of the discrimination against rural export industries in many developing countries, see the works of Robert H. Bates, especially *Markets and States in Tropical Africa* (Berkeley: University of California Press, 1981). I am grateful to Barry Weingast for calling Bates's work to my attention.

23. Washington, D.C.: The Brookings Institution, 1975.

24. Introduction, Mancur Olson, ed., *A New Approach to the Economics of Health Care* (Washington, D.C.: American Enterprise Institute, 1982).

25. Actually, as the ''Cambridge controversy'' shows, there is the possibility of paradoxical results when dealing with capital in the aggregate. Strictly speaking, I should have said, ''the price of each type of machine or other capital good will tend to fall as more of each is accumulated.''

26. Mancur Olson and Richard Zeckhauser, ''The Efficient Production of External Economics,'' *American Economic Review* 60 (June 1970):512–17; Mancur Olson, ''The Priority of Public Problems,'' in Robin Marris, ed., *The Corporate Society* (London: Macmillan, 1974), pp. 294–336; ''The Principle of Fiscal Equivalence,'' *American Economic Review: Papers and Proceedings* 59 (May 1969):479–87; ''The Treatment of Externalities in National Income Statistics,'' in Lowdon Wingo and Alan Evans, eds., *Public Economics and the Quality of Life* (Baltimore: Johns Hopkins University Press for Resources for the Future and the Centre for Environmental Studies, 1977), pp. 219–49; and U.S. Department of Health, Education and Welfare, *Toward A Social Report* (Washington, D.C.: U.S. Government Printing Office, 1969), written with others.

27. I have been working off and on since the early 1960s on ''Diseconomies of Scale and Development''—that is, on the special problems the less developed countries have in creating stable and effective large-scale institutions, and on similar problems that the European societies also faced in preindustrial times. My hope is that eventually that argument, in combination with the present theory, would help us understand this problem.

28. Friedman, *Free to Choose,* pp. 49–55.

29. See, for example, the next chapter of this book, and also my article with Martin J. Bailey and Paul Wonnacott, ''The Marginal Utility of Income Does Not Increase: Borrowing, Lending, and Friedman-Savage Gambles,'' *American Economic Review* 70 (June 1980):372–79. See also Mancur Olson and Martin J. Bailey, ''Positive Time Preference,'' *Journal of Political Economy* 89 (February 1981):1–25.

30. Friedman, *Free to Choose,* p. 49.

31. See, for example, Vera Anstey, *The Economic Development of India,* 4th ed. (London: Longmans, Green, 1952), pp. 107–14 and 345–63. The extreme laissez-faire character of British policy in India is evident even in articles concerned with the exceptions and inconsistencies in it; Sabyasachi Bhattacharya quotes British officials ruling out progressive taxation for India on the noninterventionist principle that it was "no part of the functions of fiscal arrangements to equalize the affairs of men." (See his "Laissez Faire in India," *Indian Economic and Social History Review* 2 [January 1965]:1–22.)

32. Alvin Rabushka, *Hong Kong: A Study in Economic Freedom* (Chicago: University of Chicago Press, 1979).

CHAPTER 7

1. In "Beyond the Measuring Rod of Money," (book, forthcoming), and in "Environmental Indivisibilities and Information Costs: Fanaticism, Agnosticism, and Intellectual Progress," *American Economic Review, Papers and Proceedings* 72 (May 1982):262–66, and (quite unsatisfactorily) in "Evaluating Performance in the Public Sector," in Milton Moss, ed., *The Measurement of Economic and Social Performance: Studies in Income and Wealth,* vol. 38, National Bureau of Economic Research (New York: Columbia University Press, 1973), pp. 355–84.

2. That is one reason why I believe there can be no satisfactory monocausal theory.

3. *The General Theory* (London: Macmillan and Co., 1945), scattered quotations from pp. 5–15.

4. Ibid., pp. 262–67.

5. See, for example, Edmund S. Phelps, ed., *Microeconomic Foundations of Employment and Inflation Theory* (New York: W. W. Norton, 1969).

6. *Money, Employment, and Inflation* (Cambridge: At the University Press, 1976), p. 6.

7. In "Alternative Approaches to Macroeconomic Theory: A Partial View," *Canadian Journal of Economics* 12, no. 3 (August 1979):342.

8. See Owen Gingerich, "Crisis versus Aesthetic in the Copernican Revolution," in Arthur Beer and K. A. Strand, eds., *Vistas in Astronomy,* vol. 17 (Oxford: Pergamon Press, 1975), pp. 85–95; Thomas S. Kuhn, *The Copernican Revolution* (Cambridge: Harvard University Press, 1957); Kenneth F. Schaffner, *Nineteenth-Century Aether Theories* (Oxford: Pergamon Press, 1972); Lloyd S. Swenson, Jr., *The Ethereal Aether* (Austin: University of Texas Press, 1972).

9. *Challenge Magazine* 22 (1979):67.

10. Martin J. Bailey, Mancur Olson, and Paul Wonnacott, "The Marginal Utility of Income Does Not Increase: Borrowing, Lending, and Friedman-Savage Gambles," *American Economic Review* 70 (June 1980):372–79.

11. See the anthology cited in note 5 above and Edmund S. Phelps, *Inflation Policy and Unemployment Theory* (New York: W. W. Norton, 1972).

12. In "What Macroeconomic Theory Is Best," a paper read at a session I organized at the Southern Economic Association meetings in New Orleans, November 1981.

13. Note that the argument speaks of "points on the marginal revenue curves" rather than of such curves or aggregations of such curves. The *MRP* curve of a firm is not the demand curve for a factor when there is more than one variable factor. A change in the price of a factor affects the demand for it not only through substitution and output effects, but in other ways as well. For an analysis of some of the complexities of this relationship, see Charles Ferguson, "Production, Price, and the Theory of Jointly Derived Input Demand Functions," *Economica* 33 (November 1966); "'Inferior Factors' and the Theories of Production and Input Demand," *Economica* 35 (May 1968); and *The Neoclassical Theory of Production and Distribution* (London: Cambridge University Press, 1969), chapters 6 and 9.

14. Edmond Malinvaud, *The Theory of Unemployment Reconsidered* (Oxford: Basil Blackwell, 1977).

15. Ibid., p. 102.

16. *Recent Inflation in the United States,* Study Paper no. 1, Joint Economic Committee of the U.S. Congress (Washington, D.C., 1959).

17. I am thankful to Peter Murrell for calling this point to my attention.

18. Phillip Cagan, *The Hydra-Headed Monster: The Problem of Inflation in the United States* (Washington, D.C.: American Enterprise Institute, 1974). Also in Cagan's *Persistent Inflation* (New York: Columbia University Press, 1979).

19. F. M. Scherer, *Industrial Market Structure and Economic Performance* (Chicago: Rand McNally, 1970), p. 291.

20. I am thankful to Michael Parkin and Robert Barro for impressing me with the importance of the point that coalitions would in many circumstances have an incentive to index agreements, and to Stanley Engerman for reminding me of the debate about whether there was really inflation in the 1950s and early 1960s.

21. Robert W. Clower, "The Keynesian Counterrevolution: A Theoretical Appraisal," in F. H. Hahn and F. P. R. Brechling, eds., *The Theory of Interest Rates* (London: Macmillan; New York: St. Martin's, 1965).

22. Malinvaud, *The Theory of Unemployment Reconsidered,* p. 31.

23. *Monthly Labor Review,* April 1977. The inflation rates cited in the next paragraph are from Arnold Harberger and Sebastian Edwards, "International Evidence on the Sources of Inflation," unpublished manuscript.

24. See, for example, Erik Lundberg, "Fiscal and Monetary Policies," in Walter Galenson, ed., *Economic Growth and Structural Change in Taiwan*

(Ithaca: Cornell University Press, 1979), pp. 263–307. I am especially thankful to Howell Zee for help on this issue.

25. Cagan, *Persistent Inflation*. The quotation is from scattered sections of Cagan's essay.

26. Jeffrey Sachs, "The Changing Cyclical Behavior of Wages and Prices: 1890–1976," *American Economic Review* 70:78–90.

27. *A Monetary History of the United States, 1867–1960* (Princeton: Princeton University Press, 1963), p. 299.

28. Peter Temin, *The Jacksonian Economy* (New York: W. W. Norton, 1969), table 5.1, p. 157.

29. *Did Monetary Forces Cause the Great Depression?* (New York: W. W. Norton, 1976), p. xi.

30. E. P. Thompson, *The Making of the English Working Class* (New York: Pantheon, 1964), p. 776, n. 2. I am grateful to Peter Murrell for this reference. The word *unemployed* goes much further back, and was used, for example, to describe fallow land; note this passage from *Paradise Lost:* "Other creatures all day long rove idle unimploid, and need less rest" (iv, 617).

31. See John A. Garraty, *Unemployment in History* (New York: Harper and Row, 1979), p. 4.

32. *America's Greatest Depression, 1929–1941* (New York: Harper and Row, 1970), p. 226.

33. See E. E. Schattschneider, *Politics, Pressures, and the Tariff* (New York: Prentice-Hall, 1935) and E. Pendleton Herring, *Group Representation Before Congress* (Washington, D.C.: Brookings Institution, 1929), especially p. 78.

34. Chandler, *America's Greatest Depression*, p. 230. I have also been greatly helped on the NRA and the history of the Great Depression by reading an unpublished paper by Martin N. Baily and chapter 9 of Friedman and Schwartz, *A Monetary History of the United States, 1867–1960*.

35. As quoted in Chandler, *America's Greatest Depression*, p. 231.

36. Ibid., p. 232.

37. "An Evolutionary Approach to Inflation and Stagflation," in James H. Gapinski and Charles E. Rockwood, eds., *Essays in Post-Keynesian Inflation* (Cambridge, Mass.: Ballinger Publishing Company, 1979), pp. 137–59.

38. "On Getting Really Full Employment without Inflation," in David C. Colander, ed., *Solutions to Inflation* (New York: Harcourt Brace Jovanovich, 1979), pp. 183–87; and "'Incentives-Based' Stabilization Policies and the Evolution of the Macroeconomic Problem" in Michael P. Claudon and Richard R. Cornwall, eds., *An Incomes Policy for the United States: New Approaches* (Boston, The Hague, and London: Martinus Nijhoff, 1981), pp. 37–77. The latter paper is in large part the same as the one cited in n. 37.

Index